THE ANSCHLUSS MOVEMENT
1918-1919

Memoirs of the
AMERICAN PHILOSOPHICAL SOCIETY
Held at Philadelphia
For Promoting Useful Knowledge
Volume 103

THE

ANSCHLUSS MOVEMENT

1918-1919

AND THE

PARIS PEACE CONFERENCE

ALFRED D. LOW

Professor of History, Marquette University

(Joint translation of German and French quotations
by Rose S. Low and the author)

AMERICAN PHILOSOPHICAL SOCIETY
Independence Square • Philadelphia
1974

*To the victims of the annexation
of Austria of 1938*

"Among all the formidable events which characterize our era, the link-up of the German Austrians with the Germans of the *Reich* is the most significant, the one of broadest world-historic consequence." Werner Sombart (November, 1918)

"The total loss of the German *Reich* in Europe would have been more than balanced if the German demand for the *Anschluss* of German Austria had met with the approval of the Allies . . . Could one seriously expect that the Allies, after defeating Germany by an exertion of their last ounce of strength, would stand by to watch the vanquished emerge even stronger and mightier than before?" Erich Eyck (*Geschichte der Weimarer Republik*, 1954)

Acknowledgments

The author is grateful to the American Philosophical Society and to Marquette University for a grant which enabled him to engage in research in several European archives and libraries. Marquette University and the Department of History also gave generous assistance for the typing of the manuscript.

Among the archives and libraries consulted were the British Public Record Office (especially materials of the British Foreign Office), and the British Museum, London; the French Foreign Ministry Archives and the Library of the French Foreign Ministry, Quai d'Orsay, and the Bibliothèque Nationale, Paris; the German Foreign Ministry Archives and the Library of the German Foreign Ministry, Bonn, the German Federal Archives, Koblenz, the Allgemeines Archiv and the Geheimes Staatsarchiv, Munich; the University Libraries of Bonn and of Florence, Italy, and the League of Nations Library, Geneva, Switzerland. The author has also consulted the Österreichisches Staatsarchiv, and the resources of the Nationalbibliothek and the library of the University of Vienna. He has likewise utilized the microfilm copies of the German Foreign Ministry Archives 1918-1920, most of which are located in the National Archives, Washington, D.C. He owes thanks to all those who gave permission to make use of these materials.

The author wishes to express his gratitude to Archivrat Nemeth of the Österreichisches Staatsarchiv, Vienna, and to the staff of the many foreign and domestic archives and libraries listed in the foregoing. He has been given generous assistance by the library staff of Marquette University, particularly in connection with the interlibrary service, and has also received most welcome aid from the staff of the libraries of the University of Wisconsin-Milwaukee and the Public Library of Milwaukee.

Acknowledgment is due to Dr. R. J. Rath, editor of the *Austrian History Yearbook 1968-1969* (1970), for permitting the use of several paragraphs from my article "Austria between East and West, Budapest and Berlin, 1918-1919," and to the Bildarchiv of the Österreichische Nationalbibliothek, Vienna, for permitting the reproduction of four illustrations picturing Otto Bauer, Karl Renner, Ludo Hartmann, and Ulrich von Brockdorff-Rantzau. Similarly, Praeger Publications Inc., New York, has given kindly permission for the reproduction of two maps from the work by K. R. Stadler, *Austria* (1968). Dr. Zbynek Zeman, author of *The Break-up of the Habsburg Empire 1914-1918*, has allowed the use of one map from this work which appeared in the Oxford University Press, London. Holt, Rinehart, Winston has granted permission for the reproduction of one map from the work by C. G. Haines and W. Walsh, *The Development of Western Civilization*, 1941.

As indicated on the title page, the numérous German and French sources upon which this study rests have been jointly translated by my wife, Dr. Rose S. Low, and myself. For translations from all other languages I alone bear responsibility. My daughter Suzanne deserves thanks for having excerpted a source in the National Archives, Washington, D.C. and having typed part of the manuscript; and my daughter Ruth for having typed the other part.

Alfred D. Low

Milwaukee, Wisconsin
August 1972

viii

Abbreviations

A.A.	— Politisches Archiv, Auswärtiges Amt, Bonn
A.E.	— Affaires Étrangères, French Foreign Ministry, Quai d'Orsay, Paris
B.A.	— Bundesarchiv, Koblenz, Germany
F.O.	— Foreign Office, either Berlin, Vienna, London, or Paris, depending on context
F.R.U.S.	— Foreign Relations of the United States
F.R.U.S., P.P.C.	— Foreign Relations of the United States, Paris Peace Conference
G.A.	— Geheimes Staatsarchiv, Munich
O.S.	— Österreichisches Staatsarchiv, Neues Politisches Archiv, Vienna
N.A.	— National Archives, Washington, D.C.
N.A.,T 120-3270	— Microfilm of captured German documents, deposited in National Archives, Washington, D.C.
P.R.	— Public Record, London

CONTENTS

ILLUSTRATIONS

Page

THE ANSCHLUSS MOVEMENT
1918-1919

Introduction

A FTER the breakup of the Habsburg monarchy, Austrians of diverse political persuasions turned quickly toward Anschluss with the new German Republic. The movement for union with the Reich, which aimed at the solution of Austria's staggering economic, political, and national problems, was at first only moderately supported by Germany, though that support soon grew stronger. In the peace treaties of 1919 the victorious Allies prohibited German Austria's union with Germany and even insisted that German Austria (Deutsch-Österreich) change its name to the Austrian Republic (Österreichische Republik). Between the two wars the Anschluss movement figured large on the horizon of European history. Its "fulfillment" in 1938, when Hitler incorporated Austria into Germany, immediately undermined the stability and peace of Europe and the world. A year and a half after Austria's absorption into the Greater Reich Europe was aflame. Austria's significant role in the balance of power in Europe, always apparent, was thus dramatically and, in view of the tremendous sacrifices and losses of World War II, most painfully brought home to Austrians and the world at large.

It was thus hardly surprising that on November 1, 1943, the allies, in their Declaration of Moscow, loudly proclaimed their intention to restore Austria's independence. After a ten-year occupation of the country they signed the Austrian State Treaty in 1955, which recognized Austria's independence, integrity, and permanent neutrality, and prohibited the Anschluss in less uncertain terms than had been the case in 1919.

The early postwar Anschluss movement of 1918-1919, which is the subject of this study, was led by Austria's Socialists and was supported by numerous other *grossdeutsch* oriented groups — altogether a majority of the Austrian people — and welcomed by many circles in Germany. But Germany, fearing retaliatory Allied strikes, did not dare to

1

press vigorously forward as the Austrian leadership had hoped. The Germans were held back especially by the fear of having to pay an exorbitant price for the union in the impending peace treaty.

The pro-Anschluss wave of 1918-1919 was followed in the twenties by acquiescence to, though not reconciliation with, the status of independence, by polarization, under the impact of the growing Nazi threat to Austria from without and within, of Austrian public opinion in the thirties, and by the seeming enthusiasm of many, the accommodation of numerous others to the *fait accompli* of the enforced annexation of 1938. But in 1945 when the Austrian Nazis were utterly discredited and powerful new forces were emerging, a great majority of the Austrians wanted separation from Germany and restoration of Austria's independence. The consummation of the Anschluss had produced no love but had aroused repulsion. After seven years of Nazi domination and Nazi-imposed hardships during a war of conquest, there followed a decade of occupation by the Great Powers. By 1955, the formerly widely spurned sovereignty had acquired a new value throughout the country and became the object of deep appreciation and a new dedication.

With Austria's separation from Germany and restoration of her independence, history has taken its full circle. It has left many Austrians in a bewildered state of mind. The frequent changes of Austrian opinion on the Anschluss issue have played havoc with political continuity and frequently have caused embarrassment. The teaching of Austrian history and patriotism in the country's schools in particular has been made a difficult task.

The *grossdeutsch* concept prior to 1918 and the Anschluss movement in the immediate postwar period were closely linked with liberalism and democracy and Social Democracy respectively. But its "fulfillment," its victory in 1938, was reached under the sign of the swastika. The idea of the Anschluss has thus been tainted for all times to come with the "philosophy" of National Socialism, with extreme German nationalism, militarism, imperialism, and extermination. This association is likely to doom it not only in the eyes of democratic Germany and Austria, but also in the eyes of the Great Powers and the neighboring European peoples. In the mind of Europe the Anschluss is indissolubly bound up with German domination of the continent. On all these grounds German hegemony and the Anschluss concept belong to the irretrievable past.

Nothing would be more unjust and would more surely defeat genuine historic perception than to judge the events of 1918-1919 with the yardstick gained from the annexation of 1938. In his book, *Anschluss an die Zukunft*, 1963, the Austrian Socialist Günther Nenning, while criticizing his own party—he held that the Social Democrats should have relinquished the pro-Anschluss position in the early thirties, instead of clinging to it in spite of the mounting Nazi threat—rejected, correctly, the identification of a pro-Anschluss position in 1918-1919 with that of extreme German nationalism: "He who then favored the Anschluss of Austria with Germany was neither mad nor mistaken." Yet he is on less firm ground when he disputes that in 1918-1919 a link-up of Germany and Austria would have created an imbalance in Europe and when he doubts that it would have disturbed European unity.

The most persuasive Allied argument against the Anschluss in 1918-1919 was the assertion that it posed a long-range, if not immediate, threat to Europe's equilibrium, a threat, irrespective of the pacific and democratic professions and pledges of the then dominant German and Austrian political groups, to Germany's and Austria's neighbors. The new German Republic, which gave moderate support to the Anschluss movement, increasingly at times under pressure of public opinion, was little concerned with a European balance of power. It wished to retain as much as possible of Germany's patrimony and even hoped for the inclusion of German Austria, though it was unable to press vigorously toward it. The leaders of both Austrian and German Socialism were convinced that the Anschluss was a necessary fulfillment of the German national revolution and also imperative for the fulfillment of Socialism.

There is probably no need to justify the present publication. Of the scholarly studies on the Anschluss movement which have appeared in English, German, or French, most have concentrated on the thirties and the spectacular and dramatic, though hopeless, struggle which

Austria waged against the National Socialist Reich which was set to crush Austrian independence, while claiming to "liberate" the Austrian people. The focus of their work was on the tug-of-war over Austria and on the complex and confused Austrian scene. They centered their study on the tactics and strategy of National Socialist foreign policy and on the steadily weakening resistance of the Western Powers which followed a policy of appeasement, and of Italy which increasingly shifted her interests from Central Europe to Africa and the Mediterranean World.

None of the published studies, however, focuses exclusively on the Anschluss in the immediate postwar period when, after the breakdown of the Habsburg monarchy, union with Germany became technically feasible. The present study concentrates on the Anschluss movement in 1918 and 1919 in both Austria and Germany. It also attempts to analyze the policies of the Great Powers toward Austria and the Anschluss and to trace the significant interaction between Vienna, Berlin, and the Paris Peace Conference on the one hand, and public opinion in the countries of the Entente and their emerging policies on the other.

At the end of the war German Austria faced the world in desperate loneliness and in economic misery. Threatened by new neighbors which only yesterday had been her subject peoples, she was lamenting her present, questioning her past, and doubtful of her future. Union with Germany seemed thus to many Austrians the only solution of her staggering problems. To Germans and Germany, on the other hand, the Anschluss movement appeared like an historic windfall, an unexpected boon and consolation in the midst of national catastrophe, a compensation for anticipated heavy territorial losses, and a hope to pull themselves the more quickly out of the morass of defeat.

The right of German Austria to link up with Germany and the latter's right to receive her Austrian brethren was eagerly embraced and propagated by many circles in both countries, both by national-minded and Socialist groups. Virtually all German political parties favored the link-up with Austria. In their view, the Anschluss would fulfill the old *grossdeutsch* dream and accelerate Germany's resurgence. According to Austrian Social Democrats, the union would solve Austria's otherwise insoluble economic, social, and political problems and pave the way toward bold Socialist experimentation. Social Democrats in both countries sincerely believed that the epitaph of imperialism could be safely written, though nationalists, militarists, and rightists were already preparing for a build-up of Germany's military might and were beginning to display their true anti-democratic and anti-Weimar colors. In the view of German Social Democrats and bourgeois democrats, the Anschluss would strengthen the democratic and republican foundation of the new Reich and inject a spirit of national enthusiasm and general hopefulness into German life at a moment of national despair. According to many German chauvinists, however, Germany, through union with Austria, would be back on the road to recovery, power, and greatness, and would soon be ready to strike out in new directions.

Yet neither in Austria nor in Germany was there anything approaching unanimity on the problem of the Anschluss. Serious doubts, not always openly expressed, held many Austrians and Germans back; the latter, on the whole, never grew as enthusiastic as many of the Austrians, and never displayed the same exuberance and driving power. It was Austria's very weakness, at the root of the country's pathetic dependency on the West, which spurred its at times seemingly reckless drive toward union. Austria seemed to have little to lose by the Anschluss and much to gain. On the other hand, Germany's great stakes at the Paris Peace Conference which would decide about disputed regions along her extended borders made her wary and cautious.

The history of the Anschluss movement in 1918-1919 is the history of a failure. It is probably on account of this failure that it has not attracted sufficient interest. However, its examination is instructive in several respects. The issues and problems centering around the Anschluss, the arguments and counter-arguments which were to keep the issue boiling between two world wars, were heard on the historic stage in 1918-1919 as never before. And to the student of the Anschluss movement in the thirties and that of Europe between the two world wars it ought to give perspective and greater perception. Many of the reasons for the failure of the 1918-1919 movement—the hostility of the Entente, in combination with strong though partly suppressed opposition in Austria, and the lukewarmness and vacillation of Germany at a decisive moment—account, partly at least, also for the reversal of the Anschluss at the end of World War II.

The author's opinion on the Anschluss movement in 1918-1919 is embedded in the account and analysis of this study. Yet the reader is perhaps entitled to a brief statement of his views on the Anschluss question in general and on some of its implications. A native Viennese, the author studied at the University of Vienna in the thirties when Austria became the open target of virulent National Socialist aggression. Increasingly beleaguered from without, the Austrian republic was undermined from within by its own formidable fifth column. Traditionally strong German national impulses and drives were then on the increase in Austria, and the University of Vienna in particular, faculty and students, became one of the very citadels of extreme German nationalist and National Socialist strength. The political forces which were in control of Austria and operated in her defense were generally of little appeal to democrats and progressives; semi-fascist, they leaned on Mussolini's Italy for external support. There was never any doubt in the author's mind as to the existence of a distinct Austrian outlook and mentality. But though he shared the sentiments of opposition to the Anschluss with a totalitarian, aggressive and warlike Germany with about two-thirds of the Austrian population, he then and later remained unconvinced as to the existence of a distinct Austrian nationality. This concept seemed so patently designed to offer theoretical prop to Austria's independence.

A case for Austria's independence could and can well be made without the assumption of a separate Austrian nationality. The days of the national state which must comprise all members of the same nationality who live on contiguous territory belongs to the past. That the growth of such a state is inevitable, irrepressible, and progressive is a myth, a questionable historic legacy of nineteenth-century national and democratic growth, repudiated by its terrible abuse in the twentieth century. It is also belied by its cancerous growth the

very moment the German national state reached its "fulfillment" with the annexation of Austria, a growth beyond this
still limited frame to the most grotesque and pretentious imperial dimensions.

The historic events described in this study are not based
upon personal memory, since they fall into the earliest
childhood of the author. The writer has therefore been able
to approach the study of the Anschluss movement in
1918-1919 *sine ira et studio.* He has not hesitated to draw the
conclusions which historic evidence seemed to demand;
however, it will remain for others to render judgment.

It is the author's view that after the First World War the victorious Allies had no realistic alternative but to insist on
Austria's independence. The formation of the much discussed Danubian Confederation was bound to fail in view of
the deep-rooted opposition of the liberated nationalities to
recreate under a new form a state structure which was bound
to be reminiscent of the old repressive Habsburg monarchy.
It can hardly be seriously maintained that for the sake of the
principle of national self-determination the victorious Allies
should have permitted vanquished Germany to annex
Austria, irrespective of an actual change of the German mind
on the role of the Reich in Europe, and in complete disregard
of new political realities, the basic interests of its many
nationalities, and of the need for European security and a
reasonable balance of power. Nevertheless, this point was
made, frequently by German nationalists who only a year
earlier had jubilantly approved of Germany's exceptionally
harsh peace treaties of Brest Litovsk and Bucharest, and by
German Social Democrats who had then seen fit merely to
abstain from voting. The German demand for national self-
determination in Austria in 1918-1919 was bound to raise the
question of what Germany would have asked in victory if she
asked for so much in defeat and was thus likely to deepen the
doubts and fears of the Allies in regard to the Reich. To
demand of the victor the fruits of victory was surely
unrealistic and had elements of demagogy.

The fear of Germany's staging a quick comeback was
widespread, as was the not unfounded conviction that the
German revolution had failed to overthrow or even weaken

the old social strata and Germany's military clique, that it had missed giving the Reich a truly democratic foundation and had left Germany as unrepentant as ever.

Yet to assert that the Allies could opt for nothing but Austria's independence is not equivalent to saying that subsequent Allied policy toward Austria and the extent of economic assistance offered was beyond reproach. The Austrian economy between the wars remained in poor condition; unemployment was exceptionally high and the Austrian living standard was definitely lower than in neighboring countries. Following World War II, the Allies have shown greater understanding for Austria's economic needs. No serious question has since been raised as to the economic viability of the small Austrian state, a matter frequently alluded to between the wars.

About half of Chapter One traces the historic background of the Anschluss concept in the Austrian empire, Germany and Europe at large before World War I and up to the autumn of 1918. The account of events in the years 1918-1919 is in the main chronologically organized, centering as it must on Austria and Germany and shifting from Vienna and Berlin to the capitals of the Great Powers and especially to Paris, the seat of the Peace Conference. Soviet Russia has been relatively briefly dealt with owing to her immersion then in her own problems and the relatively limited extent of her interest in the Anschluss question in particular, her relative impotence at the time, and her absence of course from the Paris Peace Conference.

The article by Duane Meyers, "Berlin versus Vienna," *Central European History* **5**: pp. 130-175, and *The Anschluss Question in the Weimar Era. A Study of Nationalism in Germany and Austria, 1918-1932* by Stanley Suval, Baltimore, (1974), have appeared too late for inclusion in the Bibliography; the latter study, however, devotes only eighteen pages to the Anschluss question in 1918-1919.

The numerous German quotations in my study will appear in the original in a German version in Vienna in 1975.

I. Toward the Breakup of the Habsburg Empire and the Dream of a Greater Germany

1. THE HABSBURG MONARCHY, IMPERIAL GERMANY, AND THE GERMAN AUSTRIAN PROBLEM

"We need neither all nor part of German Austria. . . . A fusion of German Austria with Prussia would not materialize, and in any case to govern Vienna as an annex of Berlin would be impossible." Otto von Bismarck

"The question of a very close union [of Germany] with Austria-Hungary is preoccupying a surprisingly large number of people in both countries at this time and is already being studied by our appropriate departments." Bethmann-Hollweg, September 1915

T HE major theme of German history of the nineteenth century was that of the unification of the German nation. The revolution of 1848-1849 had failed to bring about political unity, but Prussia's wars under Bismarck's leadership against Denmark, Austria, and France and her military victories paved the way for German unification under Prussian aegis. They led to the exclusion of Austria from German affairs and to the solution of the age-old German question on the basis of the *kleindeutsch* program. The adherents of the *grossdeutsch* program which had focused upon a Greater Germany were vanquished and their concept was pushed into the background of the historical stage. In 1871 and for years to come Bismarck's accomplishment was applauded by most Germans, but it fell short of uniting all the Germans of Central Europe: those inhabiting the Austrian monarchy were left outside the Reich.

The internal politics of German Austria in the late nineteenth and early twentieth century were decisively affected by these developments. There emerged in the German-inhabited portions of the Habsburg monarchy three large distinct ideological and political camps, the Christian

13

Social conservative, the socialist, and the national camp. All three originated in the eighteen eighties when their "founding fathers" were temporarily linked in a circle around a controversial political personality of some historical significance, the young Georg von Schönerer.[1] Both the German national and the socialist movement were *grossdeutsch* oriented.

Passionate and militant, Georg von Schönerer became the founder of the German national party with its twin ideas of radical nationalism and virulent anti-Semitism; he was a genuine forerunner of Adolf Hitler who paid an appropriate tribute to him in *Mein Kampf*. When he in 1873 took his place in the Austrian Reichsrat at the extreme left, he first seemed to act as a spokesman for the lower classes. His Pan-German group adopted an increasingly anti-Austrian, anti-Habsburg, anti-Semitic, and anti-Catholic attitude, which made it difficult for the emerging Christian Social movement to cooperate with it.[2]

But the Christian Socials were even more opposed to Austrian liberalism with its anticlerical, *kulturkämpferisch*, and individualistic bent. The liberals represented the upper bourgeoisie in which Jews played an important role. In their struggle with their political rivals in the national and Social Democratic camps, the Christian Socials were also hard pressed on the issues of German nationalism and the cultivation of the German language and culture and had to strike a strong national pose.

In view of the importance of the *grossdeutsch* orientation in the German national and Socialist camps, it will be necessary to examine briefly these movements in pre-war Austria and in the Reich.

In their concern for the threatened national interests around a wide circle of disputed linguistic boundaries in North Bohemia, Southern Tyrol, Southern Styria, and Southern Carinthia, the German nationalists in the Habsburg monarchy claimed to be fighting a desperate rearguard bat-

---

[1] A. Wandruszka, "Österreich's politische Struktur," Benedikt, 1954: pp. 289-485, especially pp. 291-293.

[2] Professor Foerster, 1916: p. 25, Bavarian ambassador in Berne during the year 1918-1919, considered it, rather prophetically, "extraordinarily disastrous that wide circles of German Austria lacked a firm religious counterweight against nationalist passions."

tle. They accused the Vienna government of pursuing a deliberate policy of Slavicization in the Austrian empire, distorting every minor concession to the Slavs into a surrender of German Austrian interests. In 1910 the Austrian Pan-Germans founded the *All-deutsche Vereinigung*, based on the program proposed by Schönerer himself. This platform was considered by some of the party leaders as a "a declaration of war against dynasty, government, Judaism, and Rome."[3]Article I of the program demanded the Anschluss in a somewhat disguised manner: "We strive for a relationship of the former German Länder of Austria with the German Reich which will permanently guarantee the preservation of our *Volkstum*."

Schönerer himself aimed at the Anschluss of German Austria and the creation of a Greater Germany.[4] On December 18, 1878, in the Austrian House of Deputies, he openly expressed his wish that German Austria should belong to the German Reich. Another time he voiced the hope that the day would come when a German army would march into Austria and write "finis" to Austrian history.[5] It was thus hardly surprising that the Austrian government looked upon Schönerer, his extremist followers, and their various front organizations as enemies of the state.

At its climax Schönerer's Pan-German party had only as many as twenty-one deputies in the Reichsrat. After the introduction of the universal suffrage in 1907 the party's strength dwindled down to three deputies. In 1911, when the last elections were held before the fall of the monarchy, the Pan-Germans gained only four seats out of 232 occupied by deputies of all German parties.

It was the radicalism and the excesses of Schönerer's Pan-German group which repelled many German Austrians. Most of them felt themselves culturally a part of the German nation; they were concerned with its welfare and favored close diplomatic ties with the Reich. But they were loyal to the Austrian empire and the Habsburgs and felt that it was that dynasty which served their own best interests. The poet Robert Hamerling gave expression to the dual loyalty of the

---

[3]Pichl, 1909: **1:** p. 85.
[4]*Ibid.*, p. 70.
[5]*Ibid.*

Germans of Austria in his poem "Vaterland und Mut-
terland," calling Germany the fatherland and Austria the
motherland. Most German Austrians, filled with great
historic traditions, still felt that they were playing the leading
role in the Habsburg monarchy and rejected Schönerer's
negative attitude toward the Austrian empire. They refused
to leave center stage and commit political suicide. Oscar Jászi
in his penetrating work *The Dissolution of the Habsburg
Monarchy* distinguished between true irredentas in the Dual
Monarchy (the Italian, Rumanian, and Yugoslav irredentas)
and pseudo-irredentas among which he listed the German one.
As Professor Herkner, a protagonist of the Anschluss
movement in 1918-1919, succinctly put it: "They [the German
Austrians] believed it was better to lead seven nations than to
become a hinterland of the Hohenzollern."[6]

Both in 1866 and after the German unification of 1871
Bismarck rejected the inclusion of German Austria into the
Reich.[7] He felt that the preservation of the Austrian empire—and with it the perpetuation of German Austrian and
Magyar hegemony—would best further Germany's vital interests: "The balance of power in Europe makes it mandatory
for Germany to preserve the Austro-Hungarian monarchy as
a strong and independent power; in this cause we may pledge
the peace of the country with good conscience if the need
arises."

When some of the Pan-German leaders in Austria raised
the specter of a German irredenta, German official foreign
policy lent them no encouragement, neither under Bismarck
nor under his successors. The predominance—economic and
social, if not always political—of the German Austrian
element in the Habsburg empire rendered real services to
Germany. While German youth "looked steadily," as one of
their songs had it, and "full of confidence" to the German
fatherland, Bismarck assigned the German Austrians not
only an eminent role in the Austrian empire but also looked
upon Austria as a stepping stone for Germany toward the
East: "The German Austrians are justified in aspiring to
political leadership and should safeguard the interests of
German *Kultur* in the East, serving as a buffer between Ger-

---

[6]Herkner, Triepel, 1919: p. 9f.
[7]Bismarck, 1913: **2:** p. 51.

mans and Slavs by preventing their collision." The German Austrians in turn had come to appreciate Bismarck's policy toward them, once German national unity was attained. In July, 1908, in an editorial, "In Bismarck's Gedächtnis," the Vienna *Reichspost* wrote as follows: "We Germans have suffered much on account of Bismarck, but we also have benefited greatly through him. This great man . . . was an opponent of the Pan-German program, since he gave recognition to the special tasks of the Germans of Austria in the multinational Habsburg empire."[8]

The preservation of the Habsburg monarchy had become a cornerstone of German policy. The writer Hermann Bahr, a noted Austrian patriot, who as a student had been expelled from the University of Vienna for participating in pro-German demonstrations, later told the story of how he had journeyed as a delegate of the Austrian Burschenschaften to the Reich; he was lectured to by von Rottenburg, Bismarck's assistant, about Austrian patriotism and the need for the preservation of a strong Austrian state and of the unique cosmopolitan Austrian culture.[9] And in the post-Bismarck era, in June, 1898, von Bülow wrote to Prince Lichnowsky as follows: "Our political interests, to which all Platonic sympathies should be subordinated . . . , like in the preservation of Austria-Hungary's present independence as a Great Power. These interests demand that we be on our guard to discourage disintegrating tendencies in Austria, whether they originate with the Czechs, the Poles, or the Germans." The German Austrians should not remain in doubt that the Reich could never support any attempt aiming at the separation of the German provinces from Austria.[10]

To Bismarck the new Reich was the culmination of a long development, triumphant victory after a hard-fought battle. To the still surviving adherents of Greater Germany the unification of 1870-1871 was a bitter disappointment of their hopes that Austria would be included in the new German state. And the to Pan-German extremists the Reich was at

---

[8]*Ibid.*, p. 291; *Reichspost*, Aug. 1, 1908, quoted by Brockdorff-Rantzau, *A.A.*, Akten betreffend Beziehungen zwischen Österreich und Deutschland, Öst. 95, v. 15-16, A 12242.

[9]Bahr, 1915, quoted in Andreas, 1927: pp. 32-33.

[10]Sosnosky, 1912: p. 207; Bülow to Lichnowsky, June, 1898.

best a springboard, German domination of the European continent and the world their goal.[11]

In general Pan-Germanism was irreconcilable with the territorial *status quo* and with maintaining peace in Europe, though in regard to territorial ambitions Pan-Germans sharply diverged from each other. Dr. Lothar Werner, writing in 1935 about *Der All-deutsche Verband 1890-1918*, remarked that only "a few foolish, radical-minded people on both sides of the border longed for" the reintegration of the German provinces of Austria into the German realm; such a course would become a problem for them only in the most serious emergency, "the annihilation of Germandom under Slavic domination."[12] Under the leadership of Professor Hasse the Pan-German League thought the continued existence of the Austro-Hungarian monarchy the best policy for Germandom and for the Reich. Many Pan-Germans in the Reich regarded Austria with disdain and judged the alliance with Germany to be basically in Austria's interest.[13] Reisman-Grone even declared in the book *Der Erdenkrieg und die Alldeutschen* (1913) that the Danubian monarchy "will ruin us, if we continue to be connected with this corpse."[14] Occasionally the Pan-German League tried to remind the Austrians that having a German ally was a stroke of good fortune for them, and spoke of the "still [!] existing alliance" between the two monarchies.[15] There were also clearly contradictory views within the Pan-German League in regard to the future of the Austrian empire and the question of German Austria's Anschluss with the Reich. But the main thrust of the ideology was unmistakable and its direction became increasingly apparent.

Before 1918 both German and Austrian *Staatsraison* militated against the Anschluss of German Austria with Imperial Germany. But at the war's end, when the great dangers of Weltpolitik and of the excessive burden of the far-flung colonial empire had become apparent to Berlin and all German sacrifices seemed to have been made in vain, many Germans condemned the false colonial and maritime orientation

[11]*A.E.*, Allemagne NS73, French Embassy, Berlin, to F.O., Aug. 29, 1898.
[12]Werner, **278**: p. 126.
[13]*Ibid.*, pp. 126-128.
[14]Reisman-Grone, 1919: p. 70.
[15]Class, 1910: p. 42.

of past German politics. Many others adopted the view that
Weltpolitik had not only done irreparable harm to Germany,
but had also caused the ruin of Grossdeutschland. In their
view, German policy should have been directed toward
Austria and Central Europe rather than overseas. In a speech
in Dresden in July, 1900, already the Social Democratic
leader Wilhelm Liebknecht had lamented that Austria, "the
outpost" of Germany, had been sacrificed by the Germans. In
a mistaken view of what constituted the greatness of Germany they had sought afar, "where there is nothing to seek,"
what actually was "in our front yard."[16] Similarly, the old untiring Austrian advocate of the Anschluss, F. G. Kleinwaechter, voiced later the view that imperial Germany should
have pursued the goal of regaining ten millions of her "expelled racial brethren," instead of acquiring colonies in Africa
and the South Pacific. "But the German Austrians were
forgotten."[17]

During the half-century between 1870 and 1914 the
Austrian empire had indeed been taken for granted by most
Germans. The specter of the breakdown of the Habsburg
empire and the probable impact of the new geopolitics of
Central Europe upon Germany had haunted many, but an
actual disintegration of the Austrian monarchy had seemed
remote and unreal. Beyond that, few Germans then thought
in concrete terms of the danger that Czechs might become
overlords of a German minority of three and a half million
people. It remains of course doubtful whether by exercising
proper "foresight" before 1914 Germany might have been
able to stem the political and national tides in the adjoining
Austro-Hungarian realm, and, by concentrating her energies
exclusively on the stabilization and strengthening of the
political *status quo* in Central Europe, might have been able to
avert disaster for herself and the Danubian monarchy.

During the war the Germans of Austria identified themselves with their state more closely than ever. It seemed that
at the moment of crisis they had come fully to appreciate how
great their stake in the Habsburg empire actually was. They
felt themselves masters in their half of the empire and were
unwilling to relinquish their preeminent position in the post-

---

[16]Grossmann, 1919: pp. 18-21.
[17]Kleinwaechter, 1964: p. 11.

war period. A clue to the political objectives of the German Austrians may be gained from the "Demands of the Germans of Austria for a Reorganization after the War," a manifesto made public in 1916.[18] "We Germans in Austria," the document read, "can best serve the interests of the German nation by supporting the creation and maintenance of a strong and mighty Danubian state which will remain in the closest alliance with the German Reich." In the future, Austria must be governed in a consciously German fashion. The German Austrians, the manifesto asserted, must insist on German as the language of administration.[19] The tenor and content of this program were unmistakable.

As early as September, 1914, Julius Sylvester, president of the Austrian Chamber of Deputies, had urged giving permanent expression to the wartime alliance between Germany and Austria by creating a firm political and economic postwar association. The Austrian deputy Franz Jesser predicted the rise, after a successful war, of a new mid-European community extending from the North Cape to the Dardanelles and from the Channel coast to the mouth of the Danube, a "preponderantly German *Mitteleuropa*" which would offer security to the German nation and Reich.[20] Walter Rathenau, then preoccupied with securing strategic war materials for Germany (after the war he was to become Germany's foreign secretary), similarly suggested, in a memorandum addressed to Chancellor Bethmann-Hollweg, the creation of a combined German-Austro-Hungarian and even Franco-German customs union. What was sketched here was the then widely appealing ideology of Mitteleuropa.

In the midst of the war the man who more than anyone else was responsible for making the word Mitteleuropa a household word in the German language and for giving it meaning and content was Friedrich Naumann. While appealing to all, including the German nation, for tolerance and cooperation for the sake of all nationalities and for a spirit of compromise and flexibility, the "supranational conception of Mitteleuropa" had, as Naumann admitted, "a Ger-

---

[18]"Demands of the Germans of Austria for a reorganization after the War," Nachlass Baernreither, quoted by Meyer, 1955: pp. 177-178.
[19]Kleinwaechter, 1964: p. 31.
[20]Quoted by Meyer, 1955: p. 138.

man nucleus." Mitteleuropa, "obviously," would use the German language, a recognized universal tongue. The
civilization to emerge in the area, he wrote, would be "rich
and varied" and "integrated with a German core."

Friedrich Naumann's Mitteleuropa with its imperial
dimensions opened up a new vision of Central Europe for
both Germans and Austrians. What he proposed was a combination of the German empire and the Habsburg monarchy
for the purpose of far-reaching economic and military integration. His Mitteleuropa, in spite of its name, did not
preclude the adhesion of Turkey, and some enthusiasts of
the new concept were even in favor of reaching out for Holland and Scandinavia.[21] A number of organizations both in
Austria and Germany began to do spadework toward the
creation of Mitteleuropa.

Actually Naumann's work was only one of a rich crop of
more than fifty specific projects altogether which appeared
during the war years and were aimed at the economic integration of Central Europe. Among numerous other books
on Mitteleuropa the following made a special impact: *Minister
Freiherr von Bruck: der Vorkämpfer Mitteleuropas* (1916) by
Richard Charmatz and *Das grössere Mitteleuropa* by Ernst
Jäckh (1916). According to Jäckh, the new Mitteleuropa was
by far a larger concept than the old Mitteleuropa. This view
was also shared by other writers on this increasingly popular
subject, the historian Hermann Oncken of Heidelberg and
the Berlin economist Max Sering, as was evident in the very
titles of their works, *Das Alte und das Neue Mitteleuropa* (Gotha,
1917) and *Westrussland in seiner Bedeutung für die Entwicklung
Mitteleuropas* (Leipzig, 1917), respectively.[22]

The Mitteleuropa projects found ardent proponents in
Germany extending from one end to the other of the political

[21]Heuss, 1959: p. 422.

[22]Some Western historians, Meyer, 1955, and May, 1966: **1:** pp. 153-154, have
tended to interpret the Mitteleuropa idea as "essentially a product of war" and
have rejected it as an explanation of why war erupted in the first place. F. Fischer,
Norton: p. 10, holds that Meyer in the foregoing study "seriously underestimates"
the strength of prewar movements which called for Mitteleuropa as "a federation
of Europe under German leadership as a basis for Germany's colonial empire." In
Fischer's view Mitteleuropa was not a war-child, but was born much earlier.
Besides, the concept of Mitteleuropa was sharply criticized by anti-imperialist and
socialist Austrian and German writers during the war. A major issue seems to be
whether a victorious Germany would have stopped short of the Mitteleuropa goal,

spectrum, from the Alldeutschen, whose goals went of course far beyond Mitteleuropa, to the right-wing Socialists, whose ambitions were likewise not confined to Central Europe proper. In German Austria, the German Nationals and the right-wing Socialist camp grew enthusiastic about the Mitteleuropa plans. Only the left-wing Socialists rejected them as imperialist projects, while many Christian Socials for different reasons remained cool toward them.

The arguments advanced in behalf of Mitteleuropa seemed persuasive. A large economic area in Central Europe would provide higher living standards and a better division of labor; it would lead to greater specialization and would bestow large benefits upon both consumer and producer. German capital investment would speed the industrialization of the region and lead to its integration and the further growth of all means of communication, and would result in more rapid progress in the field of social legislation. The book market was flooded by a great number of economic publications on Mitteleuropa developing these various prospects.[23]

The wartime project of Mitteleuropa and the postwar plan of the Anschluss were obviously different schemes and born of quite different circumstances. At the height of their vogue only a few years separated them. Both were movements aimed at rapprochement and possibly fusion, though the former would have brought a larger dowry to the marriage — the non-German peoples. The first-named project presupposed victory by the Central Powers, the last-named was contingent on Austria's defeat and disintegration and the resolve of a vanquished German Reich and of "left-over" German Austria to join forces. The peoples of both German states would have to overcome the psychological shock of the debacle and be unwilling to tolerate the military, political, and economic disadvantages of a reduced existence.

As much as the projects of Mitteleuropa and of the Anschluss differed from each other, the position taken toward them by various German and Austrian political groupings

---

respectively of the "Grösseres Mitteleuropa." An examination of the treaties of Brest Litovsk and Bucharest dictated by Berlin in 1918 would seem to answer this question rather negatively.

[23]Gratz and Schüller, 1925. See also Herkner, 1916: **2:** pp. 479-493; Sweet in Hantsch and Novotny, *Festschrift . . .* , 1957: pp. 180-212.

reveals certain similarities. Austrians seemed more enthusiastic in regard to both projects than Germans, though
numerous groups among the latter were ardent partisans of
both concepts.

The wartime ideology of Mitteleuropa aimed at the quick
implementation of integration, as the governments of the
two Central European empires well understood. First, Berlin
took the initiative. In November, 1915, Erich von
Falkenhayn, chief of the German General Staff, placed
before Chancellor Bethmann-Hollweg a project aimed at the
creation of a "Central European league of states" (Mit-
teleuropäischer Staatenbund) which was to be based upon a
military alliance between Germany, Austria-Hungary,
Bulgaria, and Turkey, and supplemented by economic and
cultural agreements. The most significant Austrian proposal
was the 100-page *Denkschrift aus Deutsch-Österreich*, whose
authors were the noted historian Heinrich Friedjung,
Michael Hainisch, later president of the Austrian Republic,
Professor Eugen von Philippovich, social scientist and member of the Austrian Upper House, and Professor Hans
Uebersberger, a specialist in East European history at the
University of Vienna.[24] These men, leaning toward reform in
domestic matters, shared the German national point of view.

The *Denkschrift* proposed that through establishment of a
common customs area the two Central Powers be closely
joined together on a permanent basis. This was to create a
power bloc which would radiate its influence into many areas,
especially the Balkans, Poland, and Belgium. The heart of
the plan was a twenty-five-year defensive alliance aimed at
the maximum integration of the armies of Germany and
Austria-Hungary without, however, destroying their identity.
The plan was based on the recognition of Germany's superior
military structure. As in Falkenhayn's proposal, the military
link-up was to be supplemented and bolstered by a customs
alliance. This time Bethman-Hollweg was much more
responsive than he had been to Falkenhayn's suggestions. He
proposed that in the event of victory German relations with
Austria-Hungary become more intimate politically and
economically, but "first of all in military respects."[25]

---

[24]Denkschrift aus Deutschösterreich, Nachlass Baernreither, quoted by Meyer,
1955: p. 145.
[25]Sweet, Hantsch and Novotny, *Festschrift* . . . , 1957; p. 190.

The Austrian government responded to German proposals for closer postwar union with great caution. While agreeing in principle to a strengthening of the bonds between the two realms, it clearly and resolutely rejected many a criticism of the Austrian empire's policy. It repudiated the charge that Austrian policy endangered the eminent position of the Germans in Austria.[26]

Emperor Charles, court cirlces, and Austrian patriots in general were especially fearful that Germany's plans for tightening economic ties and the military alliance both during and after the war would whittle down Austria's proud sovereignty. In May, 1917, the emperor revealed to Czernin that "a brilliant German victory would be our ruin." Peace on the basis of the *status quo* would be best for Austria, "for then Germany would not be too arrogant, and we should not have broken irreparably with the Western Powers who are not invariably our enemies." If the continued existence of the monarchy was at stake, peace should be sought even without the consent of Germany. Peace without annexation seemed to the emperor to be the best solution, and after the war, "as a counterweight," an alliance with France, in addition to one with Germany, would be in order.[27]

The alliance between Germany and Austria-Hungary linked two partners unequal in virtually every respect — industrial development and technological know-how, ethnic homogeneity, temperament and character, and the extent of their political ambitions in Europe and the world at large. German Austrians looked with ambivalent feelings upon the German ally, revelling in his military valor and taking pride in his economic and cultural accomplishments, but also frequently revealing bitterness and anger at Berlin's overbearing superiority and contemptuous behavior toward them as allegedly backward brothers. On October 23, 1907, the German ambassador in Vienna, Karl von Wedel, wrote to Chancellor Fürst von Bülow that, though Austria-Hungary was closely allied with the Reich, Germany had here "perhaps more foes than friends."[28] Closer acquaintance during the

---

[26]Werkmann, 1931: p. 56f.

[27]*Ibid.*, p. 59

[28]*A.A.*, Akten betr. Beziehungen Öst. zu Deutschland, 6. Aug. 1907-15. März, 1908; Öst. 95, v. 14-15, Oct. 23, 1907.

war with the rigid Prussian character did not endear it to
the easy-going, pleasure-loving Austrians. While the
comradeship-in-arms forged closer ties between Germans
and Austrians, at the same time the haughtiness of the German military commanders aggravated the differences between them. Yet the two empires needed each other in times
of war. *Nibelungentreue*, mutual fidelity, was hailed sometimes
as the key to victory and at other times as the key to survival.
And Germany responded to Austria's calls for military and
financial help and frequently sent food.

Yet there were patent differences in national interest between the Habsburg empire and imperial Germany. Time
and again the Vienna Foreign Office suggested to Berlin that
a pledge to restore Belgian independence after the war
would hasten the termination of hostilities. Berlin, however,
turned a deaf ear to the Vienna proposals for a compromise
peace and insisted not only on retaining Alsace-Lorraine at
all costs, but also on expansion in the East and West and on
excessive indemnites. And the Habsburg empire, facing irreconcilable Pan-German irredentists at home, feared a possible invasion by German troops bent on wresting control
from the allegedly weak and untrustworthy hands of their
ally. During the war years the Reich repeatedly demanded
German leadership in the Dual Monarchy as a guarantee of
the political and military stability and loyalty of the Habsburg
empire.[29]

A major wartime issue dividing the Allies was the future of
Poland. There were various German-sponsored schemes,
each of which would have turned Poland into a German satellite irrespective of her specific political status. According to
the "Austro-Polish solution," the Polish state, whose boundaries were not yet delineated, would be attached to the Habsburg empire. In the summer of 1915 Chancellor Bethmann-Hollweg consented with certain reservations to an
Austrian solution of the Polish problem, but Berlin, under
pressure from its military leaders, soon reversed its position
and the Polish question continued to divide the Central
Powers.

As the German historian Fritz Fischer sums it up, the
highest personages in Germany revealed the lowest opinion

[29]Fischer, Norton; p. 200.

of Austria-Hungary's military and economic strength and her political cohesion. "Germany was proposing to reorganize and penetrate Austria in order to keep in existence Germany's only partner in the world, to strengthen her and to bind her to Germany." Most of Germany's military and political leaders agreed with Falkenhayn in regarding Austria as "slack" and "slipshod," if not "a corpse," but like him considered it necessary to "chain" the Austrian monarchy to Germany, since after the war the Reich would be "bound more indissolubly than ever to our Austro-Hungarian allies." Germany also needed Austria as a bridge to the Balkans and Turkey.[30]

With the establishment of a virtual Hindenburg-Ludendorff wartime dictatorship in Germany, German Mitteleuropa projects took second place and East European schemes moved into the limelight. The eastward shift of Germany's war aims was brought about partly by opportunities presented by the debacle of Russian arms and the victory of the Russian Revolution and partly by the growing German doubts about the vitality of the Habsburg dynasty and the suspicion that the Dual Monarchy wanted to desert its German ally. After the peace of Brest-Litovsk, the plans embodied in Germany's great Easter Idea—which, according to Fritz Fischer, went far beyond Brest-Litovsk—torpedoed the Mitteleuropa concept. The latter, in his words, "was dropped by Germany in favor of absolute domination of the *Ostraum*—a goal as old as the Mitteleuropa idea itself."[31] It was the German military leadership which supported the *Ostraum* policy, while German political leaders such as Kühlmann and Hertling wanted Austria's active participation, on a more or less equal basis, in the implementation of plans relating to Mitteleuropa and Poland. At the meeting in Spa in May, 1918, however, the Kühlmann-Czernin agreement on Central Europe was replaced in favor of a project which bore Ludendorff's approval.

For Austria, and for her Foreign Minister Burián in particular, the abandonment of the Austro-Polish "solution" was a blow at the hope of saving the Habsburg monarchy. It also revealed the high-handed and arbitrary behavior of the Ger-

[30]*Ibid.*, pp. 204-207.
[31]*Ibid.*, p. 510.

man military toward the Austrian partner. Though there was no definite hint that the Austrian emperor was considering concluding a separate peace, there could be little doubt that, along with Austria's policy-makers in general, he was moved by the necessity of preserving the integrity of the Habsburg empire and the monarchy. In a confidential memorandum on April 12, 1917, he candidly warned Germany's political and military leaders that conditions in Austria's multi-nationality state were quite different from those in Germany, that Austria's military strength was nearing its end, and that the sufferings of the war must cease "at all costs . . . in late summer or autumn." The Austrian ambassador Hohenlohe in Berlin likewise reminded German officials that Austria's worsening situation made an early end of the war imperative.[32]

The Austrian emperor and Austrian officials also fretted under the increasing subordination of the empire to Germany and chafed at their government's having to take orders from Berlin. The American ambassador at Vienna, F. C. Penfield, reported to the secretary of state on March 13, 1917: "There are rumors of Austria-Hungary's tiring of the overlordship of Berlin, but fear alone is enough to stifle any governmental expression of this." Count Czernin bitterly complained to Conrad von Hötzendorff that Austria was the helpless vassal of Ludendorff and had to go on fighting as long as Berlin wished.[33] At the same time Hindenburg, anticipating a postwar "conflict" with Austria, postulated: "The alliance with Austria must continue."[34] The wartime relationship between the two allies was thus a tense and uneasy one, fraught with perils for both of them.

Mitteleuropa was the ideological quintessence of the wartime relationship between Germany and Austria. But neither in case of victory or defeat was a true Mitteleuropa, a genuine partnership between Germany and Austria, destined to survive.

The war economy in both Austria and Germany necessitated ersatz materials. It can be said that the sudden wartime enthusiasm for Mitteleuropa which swept through

---

[32]*Ibid.*, pp. 494-499.
[33]May, 1966: **2:** p. 500.
[34]Fischer, Norton: p. 437.

Austria and Germany was in a way itself only ersatz, a substitute for the idea of Grossdeutschland which the victories of Prussia in 1870-1871 had only shelved but not discarded. Still, the goal of Mitteleuropa lifted the eyes and hearts of many in Germany and Austria above the tribulations and sacrifices of the war and the wrangles within the alliance, and made them believe once more in a glorious future for both empires and for the German idea.

With the defeat of the Central Powers and the dissolution of the Habsburg empire the concept of Mitteleuropa was definitely destroyed. Yet out of the ashes of destruction rose, like a phoenix, the concept of the Anschluss, the idea of Grossdeutschland.

2. THE GREAT POWERS AND THE ANSCHLUSS THREAT. PREPARATION FOR THE PEACE CONFERENCE

> "It is necessary that an Austria, an independent Austria, exist, because it is indispensable for the European equilibrium and for the peace of the world." Georges Weil (*Le Pangermanisme en Autriche,* 1904)

I N order to understand the attitude and policies of the Great Powers on the Anschluss at the Paris Peace Conference in 1919 it will be necessary to examine Western public opinion on this issue before the outbreak of World War I, the slowly changing mood during the war, and the preparatory work of the foreign offices of the Great Powers on the union before the opening of the Peace Conference.

The question of the future of the Austro-Hungarian monarchy preoccupied before the war German Austrians, their kinsfolk in the Reich, the many non-German nationalities of the Habsburg Empire, and its immediate neighbors. This problem, as well as the possibility of the Anschluss and the impact of the dissolution of the Dual Monarchy upon the political equilibrium of the entire European continent, was, however, also discussed in a number of books which were published in France, the United Kingdom, and Italy around the turn of the century.[1]

An examination in the following of three of these books will cast light upon the prevailing fears in the West that the dissolution of the Austrian empire might seriously disturb the balance of power on the continent, create a vacuum in the

---

[1]R. W. Seton-Watson, *The Future of Austria and the Attitude of the Great Powers* (1907); Georges Weil, *Le Pangermanisme en Autriche* (Paris, 1904); André Chéradame, *L'Europe et la question d'Autriche au seuil du xxe siecle* (1906), and by the same author, *L'Allemagne, la France et la Question d'Autriche;* Réné Henry, *Questions d'Autriche-Hongrie et Question d'Orient* (Paris, 1903); Charles Loiseau, *l'Equilibre Adriatique* (Paris, 1901); and Luigi Chiala, *La Triplice e la Duplice Alleanza* (Turin, 1898).

29

heart of Europe, and move the Anschluss issue into the very center of the stage, opening up a Pandora box with all its disastrous consequences.

One of the most penetrating discussions of the problems that the Anschluss might create in Europe was offered by Georges Weil in *Le Pangermanisme en Autriche*, published in 1904. Its foreword was written by the noted French analyst of political and international affairs, Anatole Leroy-Beaulieu, former teacher of Weil at L'École des Sciences Politiques, who also wrote the preface of the book, *L'Allemagne, la France et la Question d'Autriche* (1903) by Rene Henry. According to Leroy-Beaulieu, in the event of German Austria's union with the Reich all of Europe was in peril: "All the small peoples of the continent, Denmark, the Netherlands, Belgium, Switzerland, Serbia, and Hungary would be reduced to the state of vassals of the new Holy German Empire [*sic*]." Facing such a colossus, even France and Italy would have difficulty in maintaining their independence. They would both be merely second-class states, "for France, so long the rival of Austria, can only remain a great power as long as a great Austrian state reigns along the Danube."

According to Leroy-Beaulieu, virtually all French students of the Danubian monarchy considered its existence essential for the peace of Europe. And he himself repeated the maxim proclaimed in 1848 by the Czech historian and political leader Palacký: "If Austria did not exist, one would have to invent her."[2] Although France was opposed to a rapidly growing Germany and at least indirectly opposed to her Austro-Hungarian ally, in the prewar days she was not in favor of that empire's disintegration; quite the contrary. She especially feared the permanent link of the German portions of that Danubian empire with imperial Germany.[3]

Even the expectation that Germany, in exchange for the gain in German Austria, might be prepared voluntarily to return Alsace-Lorraine — which Leroy-Beaulieu considered nothing but an "illusion"—"would not compensate for the perils of the obliteration of Austria."

According to Weil, the aims of Pan-Germanism in German Austria threatened to upset the European equilibrium. The

---

[2]Quoted by Weil, 1904: p. XV.
[3]Leroy-Beaulieu, preface to Henry, 1903: pp. VI-VII.

realization of the Pan-German idea would "reconstitute the most formidable, the most colossal empire." He considered the Pan-German temptations dangled in front of Germany to be very great.

> How indeed could Germany not wholeheartedly desire it [the Anschluss] as the event which would crown her triumph, as the success of a movement which would result in a formidable increase of her territories; a movement which would ultimately realize the old dreams of the Germanic race, the union of all of her children under a single crown, a movement which would send her triumphant armies down that majestic Danube, that marvelous, greatly coveted route toward the East. How could she not wish for the success of a movement . . . which would perhaps even give her that greatly desired exit on the Adriatic, the access to the Mediterranean . . . which would permit her to subject to her will the East, the South, or the West . . . which would make her the center of gravity of all of Europe, the mistress on land and at sea, the ruler of Europe, perhaps of the entire world.[4]

Weil admitted that the Bismarckian tradition was weighted against "seductions by the *grossdeutsch* ideal."[5] He also conceded that "the limitless dreams of German megalomania," the "false chimera of Great Germany [*la plus grande Allemagne*]," the restoration of a new Holy Roman Empire, were hardly in the true interest of the German nation. But he feared that the "splendid, marvelous, deceptive dream" would dazzle the Germans and win them over.

According to Weil, Italians had often given expression to the view that Italy should accept the annexation of German Austria by Germany in exchange for the return of "Italia irredenta," the eternal subject of Italian claims. But he warned that, in the event of the Anschluss, Italy would become the "vassal, the satellite, almost the slave of Germany which would surround her on all sides," turning her into a second-class state without a policy of her own. Great Britain, though incomparably more powerful than Italy, would also be affected by the Anschluss of German Austria to the Reich. At first glance though it would seem that Britain's sphere of in-

---

[4]Weil, 1904: pp. 246-247.
[5]*Ibid.,* p. 254.

fluence, quite distinct from that of Germany, would not suffer from this immense territorial accretion of the Hohenzollern empire. Yet this would not be the case. A Germany
which through the Anschluss had become "absolute mistress
of Central Europe, with one foot in Hamburg and the other
in Trieste, with her warships in full battle readiness at Kiel
and at Pola," would signify the end of the reign of Great
Britain in the Mediterranean.

Weil then turned to Russia and her possible interest in Germany's annexation of German Austria and Bohemia. As if
anticipating Russia's concern, Weil argued that a union of
German Austria with imperial Germany would force Russia
to declare war on Germany. Even a partition of the Austrian
empire could not produce a peaceful solution. Russia could
not permit Germany to annex Bohemia. The two giant empires, Germany and Russia, would face each other across an
excessively long common boundary. German naval control
could bar the Russian fleet from the Baltic and the Mediterranean. The triumph of Germany would signify the end of
Russia's influence in Europe; it would wipe out her colossal
efforts made over five centuries to set foot on the continent
and would throw her definitely back toward Asia, relegating
her to the rank of a non-European power.

"There remains France," continued the author.

> One may pretend that the question of the Anschluss does not
> affect us directly, that the expansion of Germany toward the
> East does not threaten us, that perhaps the deflection of
> Germany's ambitions and appetites from the West to the East
> might render her harmless to us. But let us remind ourselves
> first that *l'appétit vient en mangeant* and that having devoured
> Austria, Germany thereafter would turn against us . . . is it
> admissible even for one moment that this unheard-of
> extension of the victors of 1870, if it should come about, could
> leave us indifferent and insensitive?

Germany's thrust into the Adriatic would also mean the
ruin of French commerce. This danger aside, the alliance
with Russia, which would be so adversely affected by Germany's push into Austria, might drag France into war against
her will. Because of the many nationalities of Central Europe
which have a real sympathy for France, the latter could not

become a "mere on-looker at a cataclysm which would deprive peoples of their independence."

Weil solemnly warned against the Pan-German threat:

> For the triumph of this movement, the creation of this shapeless monster which Greater Germany would be, could break the European equilibrium and thereby lead us back to the most somber periods of history, to the sinister wars caused by conquering megalomania, to the formidable coalitions and to the dreams of universal domination which have never left behind them anything but rivers of blood and mountains of corpses.[6]

Georges Weil's views on the dangers of Austria's disintegration were, as Leroy-Beaulieu testified, widely shared in France in the prewar period. Yet Weil brought out with unusual clarity one particularly disastrous consequence of the breakup of the Dual Empire: the Anschluss of German Austria with imperial Germany and its likely devastating impact upon the position of the Great Powers in Europe. Weil's *Le Pangermanisme en Autriche* forecast the prohibitive policies which the Great Powers were to adopt *vis-à-vis* the Anschluss in 1918-1919.

Like the French writers Leroy-Beaulieu and Georges Weil, the noted English scholar and foremost expert on the Austrian empire, Robert W. Seton-Watson, writing under the pseudonym Scotus Viator, stressed in *The Future of Austria-Hungary and the Attitude of the Great Powers* (1907) the interest of both France and Great Britain in the preservation of Austria-Hungary as a Great Power. Such a policy aiming at preserving Austria's position would be "dictated solely by considerations of the balance of power in Europe."[7] As far as a possible union of German Austria with Germany was concerned, it would not be in the true interest of the Reich, though at first glance it might appear so:

> Such a policy offers many attractions to the political dreamer . . . a compact state would be formed in central Europe, far surpassing in strength the Medieval Empire in its most brilliant days. With a population of almost 80 million, its armed forces would be almost irresistible. . . . German com-

---

[6]*Ibid.*, pp. 259-271.
[7]Seton-Watson, 1907: p. VII.

merce would receive a powerful impetus from the extension of
the Zollverein to Austria, and would control an internal market
as large as that of the United States. The acquisition of Trieste
would ensure fresh triumphs to the German merchant
marine. . . . Germany would become beyond all question the
predominant power in the Balkan; and her hegemony from
Hamburg to Bassora on the Persian Gulf would soon enter the
range of practical possibilities.[8]

On the other hand, according to Seton-Watson, the difficulties created by a disruption of the Austro-Hungarian empire and a German intervention in behalf of the German
Austrian provinces (and possibly also of Bohemia and
Moravia) would be numerous and a "source of endless
dangers and confusion."[9] It was hardly an exaggeration to
say that Austria-Hungary, despite its domestic quarrels,
formed the pivot of European politics and that its disappearance would deal a fatal blow to the balance of power.
France's position as a great power would be at stake, a view
emphasized in the speeches of such well-known politicians as
Messrs. Deschanel and Pelletan. The probable result of German intervention in favor of the German Austrian
population would be war with France into which Italy and
Russia, taking the French side, and most likely Great Britain
too, would be drawn.[10]

Both the French and British historians, Weil and R. Seton-
Watson respectively, saw in the Anschluss the harbinger of a
European-wide war. A noted Italian historian, Gaetano
Salvemini, though especially hostile to the Habsburg empire,
similarly voiced concern over Greater Germany's threat to
Italia irredenta and of her immobilizing Italy on all sides.

From his wartime book with the ominous title *Delenda
Austria* (Paris, 1918, in French, translated from the Italian) it
emerges clearly that in the event of the dissolution of the
Austrian empire a position hostile to German Austria's Anschluss would also be taken by many Italians. In spite of his
doubts about the desirability of Germany's becoming Italy's
direct neighbor, Salvemini did not oppose the union
outright. He recommended a strongly nationalist, anti-

[8]*Ibid.*, p. VIII.
[9]*Ibid.*, p. V.
[10]*Ibid.*, pp. 3-5.

Habsburg as well as anti-German policy for Italy. He considered destruction of the Habsburg monarchy "the only guarantee" for effectively providing for Italian security.[11] Italy could not keep Trieste and Istria and maintain the military domination of the Adriatic without holding Austria, the vanguard of Germany, away from the entire length of the Adriatic coast.[12] And Austria could not be kept away unless she was destroyed. The German government was already in power in Austria-Hungary,[13] and after the war the Austrian empire, if not dissolved, would increasingly lean on Germany and would devote all its efforts against Italy and Italian liberty.[14] Not only the Austrian empire, but Germany too was Italy's enemy. Germanic attacks against the Italians of the Trentino were directed not from Vienna, but from Munich.[15] It was therefore imperative that after the war the Entente isolate Germany in Europe and surround her with a chain of force in such a manner that any possible revanche was hopeless from the start.[16]

Salvemini did not seem to object to a postwar incorporation of German Austria into the Reich; not because Italy's interest would not be adversely affected by it, but rather because the benefits to Italy of the destruction of the Austrian empire would be incomparably greater. The danger of Germany's thrust toward Italy would not be measurably enhanced by a direct postwar annexation of German Austria.

Professor Salvemini's booklet accurately reflected the deep hostility in Italy to the Habsburg empire, as well as a widespread fear of Germany. Italy's ambivalent attitude in the immediate postwar period in regard to the Anschluss — uneasiness over the proximity of the German colossus, but greater fear of the resurrection of the Austrian empire — was also clearly mirrored in Salvemini's analysis of Italy's foreign policy problems to the north.

---

[11]Salvemini, 1918: p. 20. Salvemini, born in 1873, was professor of history at the University of Florence between 1917 and 1925. He was co-director of the political journal *L'Unità* and served also as deputy in the Italian Chamber during the years 1919-1921.

[12]*Ibid.*, p. 26.

[13]*Ibid.*, p. 49.

[14]*Ibid.*, pp. 24-25.

[15]*Ibid.*, p. 11.

[16]*Ibid.*, p. 18.

With the outbreak of the Great War the Allied debate about the future of the Austrian empire and the fate of its German Austrian population intensified. Though at critical moments during the nineteenth century C. M. Talleyrand, Lord H. J. T. Palmerston, and Lord R. A. T. Salisbury had stressed the importance of preserving the Habsburg monarchy in the interests of Europe's equilibrium, after 1914 the climate of English and French public opinion in regard to the Habsburg monarchy soon began to change. This change foreshadowed ultimate British and Allied policy toward the Dual Empire, but it never muted the voices which spoke on behalf of maintaining the Danubian monarchy. The Oxford historian J. A. R. Marriott reminded his compatriots that the Habsburg monarchy had not outlived its usefulness, and the British historian J. Ellis Barker came out in favor of the reconstruction of the Habsburg monarchy and even of a link-up of the German inhabited areas of Catholic Austria with the Catholic South German states and possibly Prussian Silesia. In the opinion of A. J. May, "a good deal of support" continued to exist in Britain for the preservation of the Habsburg monarchy. But at the same time there continued among British intellectuals the heritage of anti-Habsburg sentiments which extended back to the days of Prince Clemens Metternich[17] and ultimately they prevailed.

As far as France was concerned, an important segment of public opinion remained likewise in favor of the preservation of the Habsburg monarchy, even after the outbreak of the great war. The French professor and economist Arthur Girault came out for the Austrian empire as a necessary counterpoise both to Russia and Germany.[18] In a variation of J. Ellis Barker's scheme he favored a union of that part of the Austrian empire which was inhabited by the German Austrians, Magyars, and Czechs with the South German states and Prussian Silesia. Conservative French newspapers like *l'Echo de Paris*, edited by the ultra-nationalist writer Maurice Barrés, and the royalist and Catholic organ *l'Action Française* likewise came out in support of the maintenance of the Austrian monarchy. Charles Maurras, writing in *l'Action*

---

[17]May, 1966: **1**: pp. 223-230. See the entire chapter "Entente Opinion and the Danube Monarchy," pp. 223-249. About British prewar views of the Habsburg monarchy, see Hanak, 1962, ch. 1.

[18]For this quote and the following, see May, 1966: **1**: pp. 244-248.

Française, warned that the disintegration of Austria-Hungary would signify retrogression in Europe. Jean Herbette, editor of the *Echo*, agreed with Girault in recommending that the South German states be united with Austria to form a great Catholic German state as a barrier to Protestant Prussia. These French voices in favor of the preservation of Austria, welcoming even an enlarged Austrian state, were not only influenced by traditional pro-Austrian views but also by anti-German opinions. The destruction of the Austrian empire would make it impossible for the small Central European nationalities to resist Germany's juggernaut. Only a strong Austrian empire would attain this objective.

Other Frenchmen, however, had become increasingly critical of the Habsburg empire during the war. Since 1916 *Le Temps* and *Le Matin* had unleashed a vitriolic campaign against the Habsburg monarchy. *Le Temps* proclaimed: "To reach Germany by destroying Austria—that is the proper way." And Auguste Gauvain, editor of *Le Journal des Débats*, which had considerable appeal to political, financial and educational circles, favored the breakup of the empire. After the outbreak of the war, the Slavophile scholar Ernest Denis, professor at the Sorbonne, editor of *La Nation Tchèque*, contemplated a restructured Habsburg Confederation of four component units, one of which would be German Austria. But in the end he too became a proponent of the *Austria delenda* doctrine. The influential writer Yves Guyot (*The Causes and Consequences of the War*, New York, 1916) considered the Habsburg empire a "polyglot polyarchy" and held its disintegration unavoidable. He wanted the German-inhabited areas of Austria proper either to form a separate state or to link up with Bavaria.

Among British opponents of the Habsburg monarchy during the war who had come to favor its breakup were the noted historians George M. Trevelyan, J. Ellis Barker, and to a lesser degree Lord James Bryce and the influential British publicist H. Wickham Steed of the London *Times*. The latter, author of the widely read book *The Habsburg Monarchy* which had appeared in 1913 and was promptly banned in Austria, continued his anti-Habsburg activities during the war.

Closely linked with Steed was the scholar Robert H. Seton-Watson, a crusader, as stated, for the cause of the national aspirations of the South Slavs, Czechoslovaks, and

Rumanians. Before the outbreak of the war Seton-Watson had supported a trialistic solution — which Steed rejected — of the problems of the Habsburg monarchy, but later he became convinced that the disintegration of the Dual Empire was historically inevitable and morally imperative, and reluctantly came out for its dissolution. His weapon in the fight for the realization of the objectives of Central and East Europe's oppressed nationalities against the Habsburg monarchy was the periodical *The New Europe* which began to appear in October, 1916. It gathered around itself the historians J. Holland Rose, Ramsey Muir, and George W. Prothero, and also enlisted the services of French contributors such as Professors Louis Eisenmann, Charles Seignobos, and Ernest Denis, the journalist André Chéradame, and André Tardieu. The periodical aimed the shafts of its criticism against the alliance of the Habsburg monarchy with the German Reich and against Mitteleuropa and Pan-Germanism.[19]

Although many of the aforementioned writers and newspapers envisaged or favored the breakup of the Habsburg monarchy, they seemed to shy away from contemplating as a likely or inevitable consequence the link-up of the German Austrian remnant of the Dual Monarchy with the Reich, either with or without the Sudeten Germans. It was as if they wished to repress such an unpleasant prospect. Some, however, in both the United Kingdom and France, were not averse to a territorial combination of German Austria proper with the Catholic South German states, in order to weaken postwar Germany and create a new balance in Central Europe. This would be accomplished through the creation of a second German state, a German Austria enlarged at the expense of the Reich. On the whole, however, the pro-Anschluss current in British public opinion weakened decisively as the war dragged on.

Public opinion in the Entente countries was ultimately to influence the policy-makers in the West. But for a long time the French and English wartime governments entertained friendly feelings with regard to the Habsburg monarchy. Interested in splitting the Dual Alliance during the war and isolating Germany, Britain and her allies encouraged the

---

[19]*Ibid.,* **1:** pp. 242-243.

Austrian monarchy to sign a separate armistice and held out to her the possibility of preserving her territorial integrity. In the discussions held in Geneva between December 15 and 20, 1917, between Field Marshall Smuts, Philip Kerr, secretary to Lloyd George, and Count Mensdorff, former Austrian ambassador at the Court of St. James, Smuts asserted that nobody in England desired the destruction of the Austro-Hungarian monarchy.[20] Lloyd George appeared thus to continue a time-honored British policy when on January 5, 1918, in a wide-ranging and authoritative speech about the war aims of the Entente, he denied that Great Britain was fighting to destroy the Austro-Hungarian empire, and solemnly pledged its basic integrity.[21] Such assurances, it was also hoped, would entice the government of the Austro-Hungarian monarchy and also that of Turkey to conclude a separate peace with the Western Powers.

At least until early 1918 this policy corresponded to that of Britain's allies, including the United States. But in the course of the summer and autumn of 1918 it became increasingly clear that the Habsburg monarchy was doomed and that Allied declarations were not designed to arrest the trend, but rather to acknowledge it and speed it up.

While official British declarations prior to the summer of 1918 had given no clue to British intentions of breaking up the Dual Monarchy, a secret memorandum drawn up in the Foreign Office in the fall of 1916 had recommended both the dissolution of the Habsburg multinational empire and the Anschluss of the "German provinces of Austria" with Germany. In his memoirs of the Peace Conference, David Lloyd George, who became prime minister in December, 1916, praised as "remarkable"[22] this British memorandum, which

---

[20]Dawson, 1917: p. 148.

[21]*Times*, Jan. 6, 1918. Actually, one hour after this speech, Lloyd George called upon Wickham Steed. According to the latter, in his book *Through Thirty Years* 2: p. 180, the prime minister assured him that his restraint in regard to Austria was caused by "a good deal of tactics" which had prevented him "to go as far as you would like about Austria."

[22]The authors of this memorandum were Paget and Tyrrell, according to May, 1966: 2: p. 541.-Lloyd George, 1939: 2: p. 23, apparently wished to place the blame for the Austrian settlement and in particular for the prohibition of the Anschluss on France's shoulders. The available evidence, however, clearly shows that in 1918-1919 England was not in favor of the Anschluss and fearful of strengthening Germany. Lloyd George himself seemed even prepared to "impose"

had been prepared and signed by two prominent officials of the Foreign Office. Circulated to the Cabinet without any comment from Sir Edward Grey, it was not considered until the War Cabinet and Imperial Cabinet were set up in 1917.

The future of Austria-Hungary, the memorandum asserted, would depend very largely upon the military situation existing at the end of the war.

> If the situation should be one which enables the Allies to dispose of its future, there seems very little doubt that, in accordance with the principle of giving free play to nationalities, the Dual Monarchy, which in its present composition is a direct negation of that principle, should be broken up, as there is no doubt that all the non-German parts of Austria-Hungary will secede. The only objection that might occur to this radical solution would be the large accession of strength to the German population and of wealth by the inclusion of the Austrian provinces.

However, at the peace table Germany would lose more people than it was likely to gain through the Anschluss. In any event, this increase will not add to Prussia's power, but rather enhance the importance of the non-Prussian German states and substantially enlarge Germany's Catholic elements. The weakening of Prussia will diminish Germany's threat to Europe. "We therefore think that the drifting of the Austrian provinces to Germany need not alarm the Allies who are not intent on crushing Germany."

Assuming the Allies for purely political reasons contemplated to keep alive an independent Dual Monarchy, Austria-Hungary would remain subservient to her German ally. And the memorandum ended with the recommendation: "Let the Slav provinces of Austria constitute themselves into a Southern Slav state . . . which in turn, it is suggested, would be linked with Bohemia; let the German

---

a permanent separation of a German border region if it was "indispensable" to the security of Europe (Mantoux, 1955: 1: pp. 461-462). On English policy on the Anschluss, see "Die Anschlussfrage auf d.Pariser Friedenskonferenz 1919," Kleinwaechter and Paller, 1930: pp. 45-61, especially pp. 51-52 and 55. But these are forced interpretations to make it appear that the English political leaders were either in favor of, or at least did not oppose, the union. In either case the evidence is lacking or quite inconclusive.

provinces of Austria be incorporated in the German empire."[23]

Though British policy in 1919 was to abandon this point of view, the wartime document is of considerable interest. The striking permissiveness on the part of some members of the Foreign Office toward the Anschluss of Austria was to reappear during the months of October and November of 1918. This position was supported by arguments in behalf of the Anschluss of Austria, which were also used repeatedly during the year 1918-1919 by German Austria and by many Germans, as well as foreign proponents of the union.

While recommending the Anschluss of German Austria with Germany, the authors of the Memorandum pointed to the desirability of a "large, wealthy and influential southern Federation" within Germany. This suggestion, of course, was not likely to gain favor with the Germans. It aimed at a decentralization of Germany, the establishment of a separate Catholic South German state, a federation within a federal Germany, and a definite weakening of Prussia. After the armistice of 1918, the concept of a South German state, which found favor with the French, also continued to influence a broad current of English thinking about postwar Germany. Though these latter recommendations could not but displease the Germans, the main suggestion on the Anschluss of the "German provinces of Austria," if known, would have been quite welcome.

While the foregoing British document originated in the Foreign Office, British preparations for the Peace Conference were not limited to it. British experts had begun their activities as early as the spring of 1917 under the chairmanship of Sir George W. Prothero and had produced a number of monographs on territorial and political questions which were likely to be discussed at the end of the war, before the opening of the Peace Conference. But none of the twenty-five volumes published in 1920 under the title "Peace Handbooks" dealt to any extensive degree with the problems of Austria and the Anschluss.

The same holds true of the French counterpart to these British endeavors. In preparation for the Peace Conference the French government during the war had created the

_____
[23]Lloyd George, 1936: pp. 17-19.

Comité d'Études, whose task was to write position papers on definite territorial problems which were expected to figure prominently at the Conference. The Comité d'Études consisted of twenty-seven regular and five corresponding members and was presided over by the noted French historian Ernest Lavisse. Reports of its sessions were published in 1919 and served to guide the French delegation in its recommendations at the Conference.

The French were agreed on some war goals, but differed on others. Virtually all civilian and military experts expressed themselves in favor of the return of Alsace-Lorraine, of wresting the Saar from Germany, and of weakening the German colossus and reducing the power which Bismarck had created. Yet aside from these major objectives, the advisers of the wartime French cabinets offered different recommendations for a desirable settlement of German frontiers in the East and West. Strangely enough, the Comité d'Études had virtually nothing to say about the union of Austria with Germany, neither pro nor con. Yet pro-Anschluss voices found expression in some memoranda and notes written during the war for the Quai d'Orsay.

An unsigned project drafted in the French Ministry of Foreign Affairs in the autumn of 1917 (October 27), "Note préliminaire sur la réorganization de l'Allemagne," recommended strong military links with Great Britain, close economic ties with Great Britain and the United States, the permanent demilitarization of the Rhineland, and the promotion of German political and cultural disunity. The Anschluss, however, was not outright to be prohibited. Economic inducements were to be offered to Bavaria, Württemberg, Saxony, and other German states previously annexed by Prussia, in order to create a federation similar to that of the United States. It would be of benefit to the Allies to offer even "greater economic advantages to the Germans of Austria as well as to other states formed on the ruins of Austria-Hungary. These advantages would be designed to prevent the Germans of Austria from linking up with the United States of Germany."[24] Similar economic benefits, in-

---

[24] "Note préliminaire sur la réorganization de l'Allemagne," Ministère des Aff./Étrang., Oct. 27, 1917 (Bibl. de Documentation Internat. Contemp.), Klotz Archives, Paris, Fol. 223, Res. 18/1.

cluding an especially favorable customs union regime, should also be offered to the Rhineland. Such policies would not be in violation of the right to self-determination.

Another French blueprint, also originating in the French Foreign Ministry and dated a year later (October 25, 1918), "L'Allemagne de demain et les Allemands d'Autriche," permitted the union of Austria with Germany. The unknown author was hostile to the old Austrian empire and to Bismarck's Germany but entertained hopes for a restructured democratic Germany, even one enlarged by German Austria. Bismarck had pushed Austria out of Germany, but had quickly comprehended the necessity of leading her back. Striking an alliance with her, he made the Austrian empire "the avant-garde of Germany" and utilized her to the profit of the German empire.

Those who had believed that Austria was the very pivot of equilibrium and a "factor of peace" in Europe were mistaken, as the events of 1914 had demonstrated. If the Habsburg monarchy should continue to exist, the Germans of Austria, "a vigorous element, violently chauvinistic and attracted to Germany, will lead the entire system back into Germany's orbit." And France's sons would then see that the Habsburgs and their successors have again become "satellites of Germany with or without the Hohenzollerns; the nationalities of Austria [will] again [become] an instrument of German ambition. . . . To have a durable peace, Austria must be destroyed."[25] By the time allied policy had finally veered round to the death sentence against the Habsburg monarchy, the writer of "L'Allemagne de demain" had also come adamantly to oppose the preservation of the Austrian empire.

But the author was hardly less opposed to the imperial German structure which Bismarck had fashioned. Bismarck's creation, "a bureaucratized, formidable military machine, operating mechanically and ruthlessly," had also to be destroyed and Germany territorially much reduced. Prussia would also lose her territorial, political, and "military supremacy" within Germany. In exchange for these losses, union with Austria, considered in any case inevitable, should

---

[25] "L'Allemagne de demain et les Allemands d'Autriche," Oct. 25, 1919, Klotz Archives, Fol. 223, Res. 18/2.

be allowed. It would offer the advantage of altering Germany's internal political, religious, and cultural balance of power in favor of Catholic Austria rather than Protestant Prussia. The author tried to persuade his readers that the dangerous effects of the Anschluss were either negligible or largely imaginary. Yet it was quite evident that, while recommending German Austria's union with Germany, he was gripped by fear of the German neighbor, as the concluding remarks of his paper reveal:

> We have the right to want to live. Let us take our safety measures and permit German Austria to join a Germany reduced to merely Germans, since she would return to her in any case and since it is better to let her freely link up with Germany. Thus, realizing the strength of our neighbor, we shall be incessantly reminded that a peaceful and free France owes it to humanity as well as to herself to guard her security.

If such was the inner strength of the pro-Anschluss thesis among French experts, it was hardly surprising that its proponents were bound to play a losing game against their compatriot experts who warned against the union.

A pro-Anschluss point of view was also advanced at about the same time by the likewise unnamed author of "La Physionomie de l'Allemagne de demain au point de vue de la configuration et de la superficie en cas de réincorporation des allemands d'Autriche." By having to cede Alsace-Lorraine to France, some eastern territories to Poland, and some lands to Denmark, Germany would probably lose about 80,000 square kilometers and between 6 and 7 million inhabitants. But by gaining German Austria she would increase her territory by 83,952 square kilometers and by about 6 million people. France, slightly larger in territory than postwar Germany, would remain very inferior to Germany in population, but would have a better strategic and economic position than in the prewar period. Prussia in turn would be weaker than before. In any case, the annexation of Austria was not only inevitable, but also would not constitute such a danger for France as to justify rendering "sacrifices at any price." Instead of opposing the Anschluss, the French government should seize the initiative to demand "compensations."[26] Recommending a policy reminiscent of the German policy of Napoleon III, the author urged France to approach Germany "immediately," otherwise she would be left in a disadvantageous position.

In a position paper dated November 11, 1918, "Après la signature de l'Armistice, — Du sort de l'Allemagne unifiée," the noted historian Gabriel Hanotaux displayed a more skeptical attitude toward old Prussia, the new Germany and the security of France, and took a less conciliatory position. Prussia ought to be reduced to its pre-1866 boundaries and Germany should be restored to her "natural confederative existence." He warned that Germany, though "completely defeated and in apparent disintegration," was still determined to annex the German population of Austria. He had the distinct impression that there was agreement between Wilhelm II, Max of Baden and Ebert and his consorts to save at all costs the German Reich which Bismarck created. The Germans wished to exploit certain antagonisms among the Allies in order to reenter the European family of nations, "to reconstitute a unified Germany under a more or less liberal mask and to reinforce her with Germans of Austria — which would be a huge compensation compared to the losses they would suffer in other respects."[27] A unified Germany would obstinately claim the unification of all the Germans of Central Europe. If the Allied Powers proved to be negligent or blind, a Greater Germany and Mitteleuropa would somehow emerge, and it would then be Germany which "would have won the war."

A peace which would make it impossible for Germany to "tyrannize her weaker neighbors" would be good, any contrary concept dangerous and ineffective. Among the "conditions for an anti-Bismarck peace" which Hanotaux recom-

---

[26]"La Physionomie de l'Allemagne de demain au point de vue de la configuration et de la superficie en cas de réincorporation des allemands d'Autriche," Min. des Aff. Étrang., Klotz Archives, Fol. 223, Res. 19a2.

[27]G. Hanotaux, "Après la signature de l'Armistice.-Du sort de l'Allemagne unifiée," Min. des Aff. Étrang., Klotz Archives, Fol. 223, Res. 19a3. Nelson, 1963 (to whose work the author is indebted for having drawn his attention to the foregoing sources in the Klotz Archives) errs when he writes that Hanotaux opposed the Anschluss by "implication." The complete document shows that Hanotaux criticized the union directly and in no haphazard manner.

mended was to negotiate peace with all German states, dealing individually with the Bavarians, the Hessians, the people of Württemberg, and surely the German Austrians, rather than with Germany as a whole. This procedure was likely to strengthen the particularist principle among them. "By consulting them we recognize their independent existence." Hanotaux thus pleaded for German Austria's independence and opposed her union with Germany.

The union was also openly rejected by the French Army General Staff. It felt that German Austria was needed as a buffer state between Germany and Italy. Italy, driven by hostility toward Yugoslavia and by differences with France in the Mediterranean and over colonial issues, would move into Germany's orbit. A common Italo-German frontier would facilitate and cement the alliance between Rome and Berlin. Therefore, in French military opinion, such a frontier had to be definitely "prevented."[28]

Toward the end of the war French experts and advisers to the Foreign and War Offices were not agreed on the Anschluss. Of the five memoranda and notes referred to above, the authors of two did not oppose the union, though partly on the ground that they considered it inevitable and partly because they hoped for compensations or thought they discerned other advantages in it, such as an alleged beneficial and moderating influence likely to be exercised by German Austria on the Reich. But the majority inclined to opposition toward the union and, ominously, the French military were among them.

United States policy toward the Habsburg empire paralleled in some respects that of her allies; at first it did not desire the destruction of the Dual Monarchy. But when in the course of time internal disaffection and disintegration spread, experts and political leaders in America, as in the United Kingdom and even in France, toyed temporarily with the thought of a link-up of the German residue of the Dual Monarchy, German Austria, with the Reich.

Like her allies, the United States had not wished to break up the Austro-Hungarian monarchy, but had merely aimed at the diplomatic separation of the Austro-Hungarian empire

---

[28]"Propositions de l'état major de l'Armée, q'ème Bureau A," Nov. 23, 1918, unobtainable, Klotz Archives, quoted by Nelson, 1963: p. 116.

from Germany and the conclusion of a separate peace with the Danubian monarchy. On the other side, there were forces at work in Austria which were opposed to the Pan-German policy of the overweening ally and concerned about the preservation of the empire and the Habsburg dynasty. They looked eagerly toward the West and were ready to conclude a separate peace. When the United States declared war against Germany in April of 1917, she refrained, therefore, from a declaration of war against the Dual Monarchy. As President Wilson put it in his address to Congress on April 2: "That government has not actually engaged in warfare against citizens of the United States."[29] For the rest of the year diplomatic relations between the United States and the Austro-Hungarian monarchy continued being "halfway between friendliness and unfriendliness." The *Ballhausplatz* was still assured through the American ambassador Penfield that, provided that the government at Vienna was willing to negotiate a separate armistice, "there was no intention by the Allies to dismember their empire";[30] only Polish-inhabited regions would be liberated.

Yet President Wilson's hope of separating the Austrian belligerent from Germany evaporated into thin air and the chorus demanding a declaration of war against Austria grew louder. Former President Theodore Roosevelt added his voice to it. On December 4, 1917, Congress finally declared war against the Habsburg monarchy. President Wilson pledged to the peoples of the Austro-Hungarian monarchy deliverance "from the impudent and alien domination of the Prussian military and commercial autocracy."[31] But he also stated that it was not the intention of the United States "to weaken or to overthrow the Austro-Hungarian empire . . . our sole wish is that the affairs of its peoples in great and small matters alike should rest in their own hands."[32] While the ratio in the House of Representatives for the declaration of war against Germany in April, 1917, had been about 8:1 in favor, the vote in December was 385:1! Still, the

---

[29]Wilson, 1927: **1:** pp. 14-15.
[30]Lansing, 1935: p. 247. See also Taylor and Pares, 1956, especially Taylor, "The War Aims of the Allies. . . ."
[31]Wilson, 1927: **1:** p. 132, Dec. 4, 1917.
[32]*Ibid.;* also pp. 11-12.

vote was indicative of the growing anti-German sentiments in the United States rather than of an anti-Austrian mood.

In President Wilson's Fourteen Points of January, 1918, there was likewise as yet no thought of Austria's dismemberment. But thereafter his thinking underwent a radical change. American war goals now demanded the breakup of the Habsburg monarchy.

After the entrance of the United States into the war in April, 1917, President Wilson had directed Colonel Edward M. House to set up a commission to study the territorial problems which were likely to play a key role at the future peace conference and to make recommendations concerning the solution of these questions. The Commission came to be called the Inquiry. Experts were drawn from many walks of life, but university professors and scholars formed the bulk of the personnel. The Austrian Division of the Inquiry established its first headquarters at Yale University. A very substantial portion of the work of the Inquiry which pertained to Europe focused on Germany and the Austro-Hungarian monarchy. Of a total of 263 reports on Europe, 47, or 17 per cent, related to Germany, 52, or 20 per cent, to Austria-Hungary.[33]

One of the most important documents furnished by the Inquiry was the Memorandum submitted December 27, 1917, and entitled "The Present Situation: the War Aims and Peace Terms it Suggests." The Inquiry at this stage did not yet recommend the dissolution of the Austro-Hungarian monarchy, but rather its transformation, its federalization, in the hope that this would produce a strengthening of the Slavic nationalities and chart an independent foreign policy for the Habsburg monarchy. A major purpose of the proposals was to break the military tie between Germany and the Habsburg empire.

This report of the American Inquiry was used by President Wilson in his notable speech on January 8, 1918. He still refrained from considering the destruction of the Dual Monarchy as a war goal. To the contrary, in the tenth of his Fourteen Points he stressed that the "peoples of Austria and Hungary should be accorded the freest opportunity of autonomous development." Yet, beginning with the late

---

[33]Gelfand, 1963: p. 185.

spring of 1918, American and Allied war goals focused increasingly on the dissolution of the Austro-Hungarian empire. After having stirred up the nationalist discontent of the peoples of the Dual Empire, it turned out to be impossible to call a halt to their increasingly forceful and determined demands for the destruction of the multinational empire and the establishment of their own independent national states.[34]

Two days after President Wilson's speech on the Fourteen Points, on January 10, 1918, Secretary Lansing in a memorandum on "The Nationalities of Austria-Hungary" raised the question of the independence of the peoples of the Austro-Hungarian monarchy, such as the Czechs, Ruthenians, and South Slavs, and whether it was wise to preserve the Dual Monarchy. "I think," he wrote, "that the President will have to abandon this idea and favor the erection of new states out of the imperial territory."[35] These independent states would present an insuperable barrier to German ambition. At the time of the declaration of war against Germany the United States had declared the Dual Monarchy simply the vassal of the German government; in accordance with this view, the United States secretary of state held that the destruction of that monarchy would be a blow to Germany's imperialist drive to the east.

In a later memorandum, written May 20, 1918, Secretary Lansing, pursuing this theme, stressed that the liberation of the various nationalities from Austro-Hungarian domination would also free them from their "serfdom" to Germans and Germany. Since any hope for a separate peace, he wrote, was vain, "Austria-Hungary must be practically blotted out as an Empire. It should be partitioned among the nationalities of which it is composed." The present policy "which will contribute nothing to the success of the war and which is unjust to the nationalities subject to the dual crown" should be abandoned, and this should be done immediately, unconditionally and without ambiguity.[36] A few days later, in a letter to Lansing, President Wilson gave the policy that the secretary had outlined his full approval.

---

[34]The report is printed in full by Stannard Baker, 1922: 3: p. 28, Doc. 2. It was written by Dr. G. E. Mezes, David Hunter Miller and Walter Lippman.

[35]Lansing, 1935; pp. 261-262.

[36]*Ibid.*, pp. 268-271.

In October, 1918, when the clouds were gathering menacingly over the Dual Monarchy, the Austro-Hungarian government harked back to President Wilson's Fourteen Points which had merely called for the reorganization of the Empire, not for its destruction. Yet in his reply to the note of the Austrian government of October 7, which expressed their desire to enter upon peace negotiations with the Western Powers, the secretary of state pointed out that the United States had meanwhile altered her policy.[37] This message turned out to be the death knell of the centuries-old multinational Habsburg monarchy. In its reply of October 27 the Austro-Hungarian government, completely resigned, accepted the views of President Wilson "regarding the rights of the people of Austria-Hungary, particularly those of the Czechoslovaks and Yugoslavs."[38]

Late in October, 1918, Secretary Lansing, long a convinced enemy of Prussia and Prussian militarism, suddenly saw a new and worse danger to European and American civilization arising. Europe, he explained, faced "two implacable enemies of the Individual and its guardians, Political Equality and Justice. These enemies are Absolutism and Bolshevism. The former is waning; the latter is increasing." Absolutism was "the evil genius which plunged the world into the present war. Its complete defeat is drawing very year." In the meantime, a new "monster," Bolshevism, had arisen.

> [Its emissaries are] well supplied with funds in Germany and Austria, preaching their abominable doctrine to the starving, desperate and ignorant people. . . . A Bolshevik Germany or Austria is too horrible to contemplate. It is worse, far worse, than a Prussianized Germany and would mean an even greater menace to human liberty. We must not go too far in making Germany and Austria impotent or we may give life to a being more atrocious than the malignant thing created by the science of Frankenstein.[39]

Yet while cautioning against too harsh a treatment of Germany and Austria, which might push these countries into communist arms, Secretary of State Lansing did not go so far

---

[37]Temperley, 1921: **1:** pp. 452-453, Wilson's note of Oct. 18, 1918; also p. 449.
[38]*Ibid.*, **1:** pp. 456-457.
[39]Lansing, MMS, Library of Congress, Memorandum on Absolutism and Bolshevism, Oct. 26, 1918.

as to suggest permitting the Anschluss; nor did he then recommend forbidding it. But about five weeks earlier, he had favored union for a short time.

In his account "The Peace Negotiations" Lansing wrote that he had prepared on September 21, 1918, a memorandum of his views as to the territorial settlements, which would form "not instructions, but a guide in drafting instructions for the American commissioners;" when he did so, he had received no intimation that the president himself would head the American delegation to Paris. In this memorandum, as the German and Austrian proponents of the Anschluss were quick to point out after the publication of Lansing's book in 1921, he had contemplated the Anschluss of Austria. Both Otto Bauer in *Die österreichische Revolution* (1923) and Dr. H. von Paller in *Der grossdeutsche Gedanke* (1928) made the most of Lansing's statement of September, 1918.[40]

It is correct that point eleven of Lansing's twenty-nine points had this to say: "Reduction of Austria to the ancient boundaries and title of the Archduchy of Austria. Incorporation of Archduchy in the Imperial German Confederation. Austrian outlet to the sea would be like that of Baden and Saxony through German ports on the North Sea and Baltic."[41] Austria would be a state like the latter states, a part of Germany.

This pro-Anschluss view was all the more striking since Lansing, as has been shown, was fully aware of the danger of Prussianism, Pan-Germanism, and of German expansionism in general. At the very beginning of the Memorandum he pointed at the danger that the Pan-Germans now had in vanquished and impotent Russia an opportunity to develop "an alternative or supplemental scheme to their 'Mittel-Europa' project." Lansing wanted to make sure that the peace treaty should not leave Germany in direct or indirect possession of any route to the East. He also wanted Danzig to be ceded to Poland, Alsace-Lorraine to France, Belgium and Luxembourg restored, and the colonies to be taken from Germany. One of the factors, Lansing insisted, to be kept constantly in mind in writing the peace treaty was the "imperative need of rendering Germany impotent as a military power." Yet in spite of all this, in September of 1918 he

---

[40]Bauer, 1923: 145-146 and Paller, 1928: pp. 115-116.
[41]Lansing, 1921: p. 195.

favored the Anschluss of a reduced Austria with Germany, even with imperial Germany! His suggestion regarding the Anschluss was certainly out of harmony with most of his other rather harsh recommendations on a treaty with Germany.

Did Lansing believe that a Greater Germany was likely to withstand Bolshevism better than two separate German states? Did he perhaps think that he could enlist the movement toward German unity and German nationalism against Bolshevism? And was he therefore prepared to deliver Austria to the former?

In any case, Lansing could not have been very determined on the Anschluss project; he apparently did not promote it at all. On March 1, 1919, long after the Peace Conference had begun its work and the American position had crystallized on a good number of key problems, Lansing, at a meeting of the Commissioners Plenipotentiary in Paris at which President Wilson was present, made the amazing admission that he did not know what the American position toward the Anschluss was![42] Since this was probably correct, he might have been expected still to break a lance for the union—if, of course, he had only cared sufficiently about it. Yet his view about the need for removing Germany's potential threat was seemingly a more permanent element of his thought than the fleeting recommendation for Austria's Anschluss with Germany, and promptly won out over it.

Since Lansing's opinion of Germany as a potentially menacing power was not far removed from that of France, he had no great difficulty in finally agreeing with the clearly emerging French point of view on the necessity of prohibiting the Anschluss, the increasingly similar British position, and the parallel views of numerous American experts.

For the moment, until the Peace Conference turned its full attention to Austria, the foci of the Anschluss movement were Vienna and Berlin.

---

[42]*F.R.U.S., P.P.C.,* **11:** pp. 87-88. Secretary Lansing became increasingly doubtful of the general validity and applicability of the principle of national self-determination and moved toward the French-Italian point of view of considering strategic frontiers a safer device for "preserving peace in the world" (Confidential Memoranda, Lansing Papers, June 21, 1919).

3. THE AUSTRIAN SOCIAL DEMOCRATIC PARTY AND THE GROSSDEUTSCH TRADITION

"The day on which Austria united with Germany would be one of the most beautiful moments of my life." August Bebel

DURING the year 1918-1919 it was Austrian Socialism which was to become the driving force in the Anschluss movement both in Austria and Germany. The national posture of Austrian and also of German Socialism was not a matter of mere political opportunism and tactics; it harked back to the revolutionary national legacy of 1848-1849.

In the prewar period German national feelings had run deep in German Austria. They had gripped not only the intelligentsia and the bourgeoisie but also the circles of the young German Austrian Social Democracy. They had found support in the *grossdeutsch* views of the leaders of German Social Democracy such as Karl Marx, Friedrich Engels, and Ferdinand Lassalle. Lassalle had pointed to the overthrow of the dynasties in both Vienna and Berlin as a prerequisite for the desired complete unification of the Germans of Central Europe. Similarly, Friedrich Engels insisted that the *grossdeutsch* solution might become a reality in the event of the breakup of the Austro-Hungarian monarchy: "The complete dissolution of Austria is the first prerequisite for the unity of Germany."[1]

The *grossdeutsch* tradition continued to be strong under the leadership of Wilhelm Liebknecht and August Bebel. On November 22, 1918, the leading Austrian socialist Friedrich Adler quoted Liebknecht who in 1871 during his trial for high treason had thus bared his soul: "Since my youth a twofold ideal gripped me: A free and unified Germany and the emancipation of the working class." For this "double

---

[1]Bauer, 1923: p. 51; see also Engels in *Commonwealth*, Aug. 31, 1866, reprinted *Archiv f. Geschichte d. Sozialismus*, xv p. 214.

goal" he had fought, pledging: "I shall fight as long as there is breath in me." Adler continued:

> During his entire life Liebknecht has remained an irreconcilable Grossdeutscher and has hated Bismarck not only because he furnished an imperial crown to the Hohenzollern instead of creating a German republic, but because, instead of establishing a state for the entire German nation, he threw a portion of this Germany to the Habsburgs.[2]

And according to Friedrich Adler, the same *grossdeutsch* point of view was shared by August Bebel.

> He too has remained a Grossdeutscher during his entire life. When Comrade Bebel was last in Vienna, on June 24, 1912, he spoke openly to an intimate circle on matters about which it was not advisable to talk frankly. A good archivist has discovered the stenographic record of that speech. August Bebel said then: "It was one of the saddest days of my life when it became known in the year 1866 that Austria was excluded from the Confederation; and *it would be one of the most beautiful moments of my life when the day came on which Austria would be united with Germany.* [My italics, A.D.L.] You Austrian party comrades are flesh of our flesh, bone of our bones. It has always been painful for me that we do not jointly consult and act. The German party has followed the activities of the Austrian party with interest.... We hope that the day will come when we shall be able to sit down and pursue our goals as we can pursue them only if a strong Social Democracy operates in the German Reich. This is the wish which I express today." Bebel, who had always stood for the class struggle and against German imperialism, was a convinced Grossdeutscher during his entire life, for he saw that through the Anschluss of German-Austria with Germany the conditions of the class struggle in Germany could be appreciably improved.[3]

The early period of Austrian Socialism began in the era of the *Vormärz*, comprised the stormy year 1848, and extended into the eighties when Austrian Socialism became a democratic mass movement. It was already marked by a

---

[2]*Arbeiter-Zeitung*, Nov. 22, 1918.
[3]*Ibid.*, Italics A.D.L. See also Hänisch, quoting Liebknecht's speech, Grossmann, 1919: pp. 18-21. Liebknecht criticized that Austria, "the Vorland of Germany" had been "sacrificed to an anti-German dynastic policy." See also F. Adler, ed. *Victor Adler. Briefwechsel . . .*, pp. 547-548 and 504-505.

dichotomy between a moderate and a radical wing. After the Hainfeld Party Congress in 1888 and 1889 began the work of unification under Victor Adler. For three decades Adler, a physician by profession and Jewish by descent, a great organizer (rather than theoretician), had by the sheer power of his personality become the undisputed leader of the united Austrian Social Democratic party. Not until November, 1918, was the rising party to share in the power of the state.

Through a compromise between the "moderates" and the "radicals" Victor Adler helped to create a party which, excepting minor losses to the extreme left during the war years and especially the critical year 1918-1919, was to maintain its organizational unity and strength, while the workers' movement of other European countries, challenged by Moscow, was to be split from top to bottom, with fateful consequences to itself and the future European democracy. In spite of its dedication to and faith in its own revolutionary Marxist theories, the Austrian Social Democratic party was permeated by the "revisionism" of the German socialist theoretician Eduard Bernstein, without, however, daring to acknowledge it. Under the leadership of Victor Adler, the "Hofrat [court councilor] of the Revolution," as he once called himself ironically, the revolutionary proletarian party had come to be transformed into an actual pillar of support for the integrity of the Habsburg monarchy; it was often jokingly referred to as the "K.K. [kaiserlich-königlich, imperial-royal] Sozial-Demokratie."

The Social Democratic party's nationality program was adopted at Brünn in 1900. Even though the endeavors of the leading young theoreticians of the party, such as Karl Renner and Otto Bauer, were doomed to failure, the conception of the Great Austrian state had drawn the Austrian Social Democratic party within its orbit. Karl Renner became a convinced partisan of the preservation of the Habsburg monarchy. In 1907 Otto Bauer, too, though representing the left wing of the party, voiced his opinion regarding the great internal strength of the monarchy and derided "the foolish views of ignorant men" who were already prepared to bury it. The Austrian working class must fight the class struggle on the basis of the existing state. It refused to carry on the "irresponsible policy of going to the brink," to set its hopes upon the "disintegration of the Austrian monarchy."[4] "The next goal of the proletariat of all nationalities of Austria cannot be the realization of the national state, but only the national autonomy within the existing political framework."

Before the outbreak of war in 1914, the growing nationalism in the empire had affected virtually everyone, including the German Austrian workers and their leaders, such as Victor Adler, Pernerstorfer, Renner, and Leuthner. It had led to a split between the German Austrians and the Czechs. Even the cherished organizational unity of the Austrian Social Democracy broke into pieces. The Czechs formed their own national-socialist parties and trade unions. The rise of a small German National-Socialist Workers party in the Sudeten German area was a clear indication of the spread of radical nationalism even among socialist workers. While earlier Victor Adler and Pernerstorfer, starting out in the German national-democratic camp, had become converts to socialism, now Riehl, a disciple of Pernerstorfer, turned to virulent nationalism.[5] In the election of 1911 the Deutscher Nationalverband scored heavily and moved as the strongest group into the Chamber of Deputies; its victory made a deep impression upon the Social Democratic leadership.[6]

When war broke out in August, 1914, Austrian Social Democrats, like their German comrades, adopted a patriotic line. But with the outbreak of the Russian Revolution and the entrance of the United States into the war, the intensification of Austria's internal problems, especially her national ones, and the growing disappointment over the continuation of the war, skepticism and a feeling of impending doom became widespread. The generation gap within the leadership of the party, between Victor Adler and Karl Renner on the one hand, and Friedrich Adler, Victor Adler's son, and Otto Bauer on the other, highlighted internal political divisions.

With the coming of the war, a wave of patriotism and German-Austrian nationalism swept through the empire with elemental power. The first emotion-filled weeks perplexed

[4]Bauer, 1924: p. 505 f.
[5]In the period between the World Wars the Austrian National Socialists frequently harked back to Pernerstorfer as the spiritual leader of National Socialism. Wandruszka, Benedikt, 1954: p. 435.
[6]*Ibid.,* p. 437.

and confused the leadership of the Social Democratic party. The war split the party into a right and left wing, the so-called "Social Patriots" and "Internationalists," who, as far as censorship permitted, fought a battle of their own in the organs of the party and the trade unions. The right wing was formed by the great majority of the political leaders of the party, the trade unions, Grossösterreicher like Renner, the "nationals" like Victor Adler, Pernerstorfer, and Leuthner, and the adherents of Naumann's concept of Mitteleuropa. The left comprised socialist academicians led by Danneberg and the younger generation of leaders, Bauer, Deutsch, and Friedrich Adler. After a while, Austerlitz and the editors of the party organ, the *Arbeiter-Zeitung,* moved into the camp of the "Left." The assassination of Prime Minister Count Stürkgh by Friedrich Adler gave the latter wing a powerful impetus as well as a hero.

Returning from a Russian prisoner-of-war camp to Austria in 1917, Otto Bauer steered the Social Democratic party to the left and, after Victor Adler's death on November 11, 1918, became his successor as leader of the party and foreign minister of the First Austrian republic. Karl Renner was to play an eminent role not only as chancellor of the First, but also as chancellor and first president of the Second Austrian republic. By 1918 both Bauer and Renner were known as writers and recognized as men of wide and deep knowledge. Bauer was a brilliant theoretician. While dedicated to revolutionary socialism, he was also keenly aware of the political limitations of revolutionary action in little Austria and always remained loyal to democratic principles. Renner was a more pliable and practical politician and of a more opportunist bent. Bauer came from a well-to-do Jewish family and had spent his youth in Bohemia; Renner was the son of a peasant family in southern Moravia. Both came from German borderlands where the nationality struggle had reached an acute stage, and it was hardly accidental that both turned their attention early in their lives to the nationality problem. Under the pseudonym Synopticus, Renner had published in 1901 the book *Zur österreichischen Nationalitätenfrage* and *Staat und Nation.* These writings were succeeded in 1902 by the work *Der Kampf der österreichischen Nationen um den Staat,* this time under the pseudonym Rudolf Springer. In 1907, at the age of twenty-five, Otto Bauer wrote a penetrating and original study *Die Nationalitätenfrage und Sozialdemokratie* in which he attempted to come theoretically and practically to grips with the nationality question in Austria. The Austrian historian A. Wandruszka wrote from the perspective of the Second Austrian republic:

> It will always be an honor for the Austrian Social Democrats that it was the first political group which sought theoretically and with acumen . . . the solution to a question that was not only the fateful problem of the Danubian monarchy, but, as is very clear to us today, the decisive problem of all Europe in the twentieth century.[7]

It was at the party congress in Brünn in 1899 that Austrian Social Democracy adopted its nationality program. When national passions reached menacing heights in Austria and threatened to paralyze Austrian parliamentarianism, the Austrian Social Democrats began to battle the state's centralism and its supporter, the German bourgeoisie. The party aimed at no lesser goal than the transformation of Austria into a federal state of autonomous nations.

When war broke out, the right wing was dominant within the Social Democratic party. After the return of Dr. Bauer from Russian captivity, the left wing of the party began to battle for self-determination of all nationalities in the Dual Monarchy, but gained ground only after the January strike of 1918. The nationality program which the Left then adopted was destined to become the political program of the Austrian Social Democratic party and played a key role during the death-struggle of the Habsburg monarchy in October and November of 1918. Beyond this, it made a considerable impact upon the Anschluss movement in 1918-1919. It asserted that "German Social Democracy, as a democratic, international, and revolutionary party," could not oppose the development of independent national states. "It must recognize the right to national self-determination" of Czechs, Slovenes, Croats, Serbs, and Poles.

But the nationality program of the Left also presented claims for the German Austrian population. "If German Austria is established, she will be able independently to deter-

---

[7]*Ibid.*, p. 434.

FIG. 1.   Dr. Otto Bauer, 1881-1938. Austria's foreign minister,
1918-1919.

mine her relations with the German Reich according to her
need and her will." While the nationality program of the Left
supported the endeavors of the non-German peoples for
liberation, it also endorsed the "union of all Germans in a
democratic German community." It asserted that it was the
duty of the Social Democracy of Slavic nationalities to battle
the attempt of their own bourgeoisie to enslave other nations.
The nationality program of the Left, developed in the days of
Brest Litovsk, was no doubt influenced by the far-reaching
nationality policy and propaganda of the Bolsheviks and
competed with it in seeming generosity,[8] but also insisted on
the rights of the German nation.

---

[8]Low, 1958, espec. Conclusion.

As Austria's foreign minister from early November, 1918, to July, 1919, and one of the prominent leaders of the Social Democratic party, Bauer at only thirty-seven years was the most important figure in the Austrian Anschluss movement of 1918-1919. In his book *The Austrian Revolution* (1923) Friedrich Adler was quoted as having given expression to the idea of a *grossdeutsch* union as against Pan-Germanism: "Pan-Germanism, that means as far as the German sabre reaches, but *grossdeutsch*, that is as far as the German tongue is heard." There could be little question that the program of the Left differed substantially from the extremist Pan-German war goals. Nor could there be any doubt that the addition of ten million German Austrians to the Reich would have made Germany the true winner of the war. Strangely enough, the Left was unwilling to face the geopolitical facts of life of Central Europe and admit that under the banner of self-determination a vanquished Germany would have been catapulted into a position of dominance in Europe. The Left preferred to look at the territorial problems from the angle of democracy and national "justice" and to ignore the reality of defeat, the concerns of the non-German nationalities about security and the problem of the balance of power in the new Europe.

In view of the military setbacks of the Central Powers during the summer of 1918 and the internal weakening of the Dual Monarchy, it was not surprising that the nationality program of the Left proved increasingly persuasive not only to the right wing of the party, but also to the German Austrian bourgeois parties. On October 4 the German Austrian national parties decided to accept the general principles of the resolution of the Social Democratic party as basis for further negotiations with its leaders.

By October, 1918, far-seeing German Austrians and particularly Austrian Socialists entertained little doubt that the days of the Habsburg empire were numbered. Victor Adler declared on October 4, in a session of the imperial Chamber of Deputies, the "bankruptcy of the old state" to be a fact: "The old Austria has disappeared."[9] The following day, in an editorial "The Right to National Self-determination," the

---

[9]*Arbeiter-Zeitung*, Oct. 5, 1918.

Arbeiter-Zeitung wrote: "Eight peoples live in Austria . . . But they repudiate the political order which is imposed on them . . . two-thirds of our population demand their right to self-determination against the forces of the established political structure."[10]

On October 13 the *Arbeiter-Zeitung* asserted that Czechs, Poles, and South Slavs wanted to establish their own national states. "We Germans in German Austria cannot prevent them from doing it; we are no longer strong enough," adding that the Austrian Social Democrats also would not wish to hinder them. Two days later the *Arbeiter-Zeitung* warned that the hour did not demand consolidating but rather dismembering the state structure which has become insupportable. "Political art cannot perform the impossible. The preservation of *this* Austria is simply impossible."[11] Thus, just before the Austrian emperor issued the October Manifesto attempting to save the fast-sinking Dual Monarchy, Austrian Social Democracy considered any attempt to salvage the empire beyond hope.

During the month of October the political future of German Austria became the subject of a thorough exposition in the pages of the *Arbeiter-Zeitung,* the major organ of Austrian socialism. On October 12 the *Arbeiter-Zeitung* published the article "Kleindeutsch und grossdeutsch" by Professor Ludo Hartmann, shortly to be appointed Austrian envoy in Berlin, in which the author contrasted the failure of the Frankfurt parliament of 1848-1849 to unify the people on a democratic and *grossdeutsch* basis with Bismarck's success, though the Iron Chancellor, satisfied with a *kleindeutsch* solution of the German problem, had left the German Austrians outside of the Reich. A few days later the *Arbeiter-Zeitung* published an unsigned article "Das neue Europa," which followed the same anti-Bismarck line, and recalled the *grossdeutsch* orientation of the German Social Democracy in juxtaposition to the anti-national, reactionary position both of tsarist Russia and of imperial Germany.[12] The article was designed to win reluctant workers over to the idea of union with Germany.

---

[10]*Ibid.*
[11]*Ibid.,* Oct. 15
[12]*Ibid.,* Oct. 17, "Das neue Europa."

In a series of further articles written in the *Arbeiter-Zeitung* in mid-October, Otto Bauer laid the theoretical foundations for the Anschluss movement and infused life into it by pointing to the economic, political, and national needs of German Austria, which were becoming especially acute during the last days of the Habsburg monarchy. On October 13, he urged the German Austrians to start thinking of "what was going to happen to us Germans in Austria" once Czechs, Poles, South Slavs, and other nationalities would separate from the monarchy. Aside from the small linguistic islands, the Germans in Austria lived concentrated in three regions which were geographically disconnected, Inner Austria, German Bohemia, and West Silesia with the adjoining areas of North Moravia and East Bohemia. The three regions were separated from each other by Czech-inhabited territory. "One cannot unite the three areas, which are territorially completely separated from each other, into one state. Therefore we cannot create one single German Austrian state; instead, we must set up three German Austrian states." The two last-named regions, the German Bohemian and the Silesian-North Moravian areas, were admittedly very small. Yet, according to Bauer, they could well exist as member states of a federation. In the German Reich and in the United States there were even much smaller member states.

The proposal to create three German Austrian states was meant to have only a transitory significance. Bauer continued that it was "quite clear" that none of the three states could remain completely independent. Even the largest among them, the Inner Austrian state, would be incapable of standing economically on its own feet. "They can either become member states within a federation of the Austrian peoples or they can join the German Reich in the same capacity." At the moment most German Austrians were thinking only of the first possibility.

It was by no means certain, however, that the other nations would approve the creation of an Austrian federal state. The Poles, aiming at complete independence, were opposed to it, and the South Slavs would wish only a "quite loose connection." "We cannot force them to enter this union," and German Austrian Social Democracy would not wish to do so even if it could. Therefore, there was only one possible program for the Germans of Austria. The three German areas would have to join the German Reich as a special member state. Within the Reich they would possess the same independence as Bavaria, Saxony, Baden, and others. "Such a move would not be altogether novel," since until 1866 German Austria, while belonging to the Austrian monarchy, belonged also to the German confederation. If the other nations did not wish any political link with German Austria, then "there remains for us no other exit" than Anschluss with Germany.

On October 15, Otto Bauer followed up his article of the thirteenth with one called "The right to self-determination and the economic regions." According to Bauer, the Germans were the "real industrial nation" in Austria-Hungary. Among the Czechs only two-fifths of the population were engaged in agriculture, while in all the other nations the overwhelming majority were so engaged. While the struggle of these nationalities for self-determination was not hampered by economic considerations, German Austria was deeply concerned about her economic future. She asked the question: "What will happen to our industry, if . . . the great economic region is broken up?

After the separation of the Ukrainians and the South Slavs, and assuming that the Czechs decided to stay with Austria, of the 51.4 million people who lived in Austria-Hungary in 1914 there would remain only 18.6 million. Once again Bauer reached the same conclusion: "There is only one way out: If the large economic region Austria-Hungary could not be preserved, we would have to seek the Anschluss with the large economic area of the German Reich!" [13]

While Bauer contrasted here the democratic movement for the Anschluss with the expansionist wartime project of Mitteleuropa, the following day he juxtaposed the new with the old Germany. In the article "Deutschland und wir" he compared the new emerging democratic, socialist, and pacific Germany with imperial Germany, long "the mightiest and most dangerous enemy of European democracy." Proud generals had dominated Germany and under the protection of their weapons *Junkertum* and big capital had dictated their policies to the nation. Imperial Germany had exploited the

---

[13]*Ibid.*, Oct. 15, Bauer, "Das Recht auf Selbstbestimmung und die ökon. Gebiete" see also his article in the Oct. 13 issue.

Russian empire's breakup by the most threatening endeavors. She had crushed the proletarian revolution in
Finland and the Ukraine.

> "She had wished to put Estonia, Livland, Kurland, Lithuania,
> and Poland in chains forever. She has dreamed of creating a
> powerful empire from the White Sea to the Black Sea and from
> the Bosporus to the Persian Gulf, based on subjects from two
> dozen nationalities: the border peoples joined to German
> Austria, where the Slavs, two-thirds of the population, were to
> be subjected to the *Deutsche Kurs*, to be permanently united
> with Germany for the *mitteleuropäisch* community. Turkey
> should also be organized by German officers and civil servants,
> German capitalists and engineers!" [14]

If this plan had succeeded, the march of democracy into
southern and southeastern Europe would have been
stopped! In addition, Germany had far-reaching imperialist
war goals in the West.

The Austrian Social Democracy, Bauer continued, had
always battled German imperialism, because its plans for
world domination prolonged the war and because Germany's
war against a powerful league of all free peoples of the earth
threatened the German nation itself, raising for it the "most
terrible danger." A German victory would have placed insuperable burdens on the march of freedom of the
non-German peoples, would have divided the world into
two enemy camps, and would have made a war of revenge
inevitable. Yet German imperialism was "no longer capable
of threatening the freedom of other peoples. Only the victorious imperialism is dangerous, not the vanquished one." It
was the Entente imperialism which could still imperil the
democratic order of the new Europe.

With the change in the fortunes of war the internal balance
of power within Germany had, according to Bauer, also been
substantially altered. Following the debacle of German imperialism, the domination by the former ruling classes and
the German military had vanished. The inner transformation
which had already transpired in Germany must surely not be
overestimated. The old forces had by no means been dis-

---

[14]*Ibid.*, Oct. 16, Bauer, "Deutschland und wir."

armed. In spite of the move toward parliamentarianism Germany was still far away from genuine democracy. "Also, a sliding back into the old course is still possible." Few such critical voices of yesterday's Germany and such critical assessments of contemporary German conditions were uttered at that time by German Majority Socialists in the neighboring Reich.

Yet Bauer was confident that the German people were going to take their fate into their own hands. The German Social Democracy, which before the war already had had the support of one-third of the German people, would no doubt obtain a majority in the Reich. While the forms of its struggle — whether the emphasis would be on revolutionary or peaceful change — could not be anticipated, victory for the forces of socialism and democracy in Germany was "certain." "[No] country in the world was as prepared for socialism as Germany." While the Russian proletariat represented only one-tenth of the population of that country, in Germany it constituted two-thirds of all people. Again, Bauer, taking apparent account of widespread anti-German feelings in German Austria, tried to distinguish between the Germany of tomorrow and that of yesterday. "It is important that we be aware of it so that the sentiments of yesterday do not lead to an error in our decisions of tomorrow."

If the other Austrian nationalities did not want a federation, German Austria would be compelled to seek union with Germany. The decision would certainly not be an easy one, since the Anschluss would "tear asunder old economic relations" and would bring Austria into new unaccustomed relationships. It would subject her to a new legal order which was unfamiliar to her, and "only through a difficult and painful process would our economy accommodate itself to new conditions." On the other hand, the Anschluss would bring Austria many a substantial gain.

In Austria, where national interests were opposed and the forces of the nationalities balanced each other, democracy would always remain limited by a power which rules above the peoples. Germany will be a nationally homogeneous state in which the sovereignty of the people can be completely realized. In Austria, class struggle will always be obstructed and remain confused because of national hostilities which divert the masses of the people from their social and political tasks. . . . In Germany, completely liberated from all difficulties of the national struggle, we would participate in the great decisive class struggles of the proletariat. In Austria we would remain in a federal union in which the majority of the population would be agrarian, since the economy would not yet have matured in the direction of socialism. The Anschluss with the German Reich would bring us into a community in which all objective preconditions of socialism were already provided.

The article showed Otto Bauer at his best. Though at the moment of this writing Germany had not yet become a republic, he seemed to be supremely confident that revolution was near. Bauer underlined the need for solving Austria's pressing economic problems within the framework of the German Reich, if a Danubian federation should prove unfeasible. He pictured the Anschluss as an economic, democratic, national, and socialist imperative.

Ideological clarification preceded and accompanied political action. On October 4, the German Austrian national parties had endorsed the Austrian Social Democratic party's nationality program based on national self-determination and democracy. And on October 21 the assembly of deputies of all the German electoral districts of the Reichsrat unanimously declared that the German people of Austria were resolved to form a separate German Austrian state and to regulate its relations with other nations in free agreement. The deputies proclaimed themselves the Provisional National Assembly of German Austria. Victor Adler as spokesman of the Social Democrats extended brotherly greetings to the Slavic and Latin comrades: "We congratulate them on finally being close to the realization of the right to self-determination which they have striven for so passionately, so heroically, so self-sacrificingly. We acknowledge this right to self-determination without qualification. We also demand it without qualification for our own German people."[15] Like Otto Bauer in the foregoing articles, Victor Adler also pointed out the possibility of a confederation of the nationalities of the Habsburg monarchy on the new basis of

---

[15]*Stenogr. Protokoll über die Sitzungen der Abgeordneten des österr. Reichsrates im Jahre 1918,* 1918, Oct. 21, 23, and 24. **4:** pp. 2773-3268.

complete equality, or, failing this, the likelihood of a union of German Austria with the German Reich.

During the month of October, 1918, Austrian Social Democratic leaders had placed the Anschluss on the agenda. But a majority of the workers, as Bauer himself later freely admitted, were still rather "coolly disposed" toward the concept of union with Germany.[16] As he had put it, "During the war they all had hated German imperialism too deeply to be enthusiastic about the Anschluss with that same Germany." But when revolution replaced the Hohenzollern dynasty and a socialist government assumed power in the Reich, the Austrian workers became more sympathetic to the union concept. The pathetic economic dependence of Austria on her neighbors, her military helplessness and painful isolation as well as the prospects of socialization and of a higher living standard prompted the mass of the Austrian workers to move quickly into the camp of the Anschluss friends. However, they never waxed quite as enthusiastic about the union as the socialist leadership.

[16]Bauer, 1923: p. 107.

4. THE DISSOLUTION OF THE HABSBURG MONARCHY AND GERMANY'S POLICY TOWARD THE ANSCHLUSS (JUNE-OCTOBER, 1918)

> "We must accept the fact that the Habsburg Monarchy will not survive the war in its present shape . . . But we may also cherish the hope that from the disintegration of that monarchy will arise the union of Germany with Austria, sought, but not secured, by our fathers in the period of the so-called wars of unification." Mathias Erzberger, July, 1918

THE louder the non-German and non-Magyar nationalities raised their voices in behalf of equality, autonomy, and the most thorough reconstruction of the Austrian empire, the more did the German Austrians of the Dual Monarchy look for a solution of most of their problems to their mighty neighbor, the German Reich. The fear of the disintegration of the monarchy and of being left face to face with a multitude of formerly repressed and hostile nationalities swelled the number of German Austrians who turned to Germany for help in their hour of need. In the event of the dissolution of the empire, many German Austrians appeared to favor the Anschluss with the Reich. In their view Germany seemed to offer the only hope for stability and salvation in the midst of a general breakdown.

Count Botho von Wedel, German ambassador in Vienna, had occupied his post since November, 1916; after the proclamation of a republic in both Berlin and Vienna in November, 1918, he continued to serve in Austria until July, 1919. On June 18, 1918, he reported to Germany's imperial chancellor that "we can count on the support of the German Austrians who hope that all salvation comes from Germany and from a close indissoluble union with us."[1] On June 29, 1918, he continued:

> During the last six weeks, since I returned from Spa, this state has rapidly slid downhill. Hunger, the failure of offensives, and domestic tribulations have led to a terrifying collapse of confidence. . . . If the breakdown has not yet occurred, it is only to be attributed to the law of inertia, the complete hopelessness which, from one revolution to the next, fears merely a growth of misery, and to our victories. If we are soon successful in France, I still believe that Austria will keep on an even keel for some time, but during the next winter disintegration is likely. Most responsible men, former ministers, generals, high administrative officers, top leaders of finance and industry—in short, the most talented and best men of the nation—say today quite openly: "Germany must intervene, otherwise Austria will go berserk" and warn us not to hesitate too long. Men who a few years ago would have been horrified by the thought now urge us to abandon our principle not to get mixed up in internal political matters here, and today place all their hopes on the moral or military intervention of Germany because they do not perceive of any other salvation.[2]

A German army entering Austria would not be rejected, the ambassador asserted confidently, on the contrary, "people would breathe freely and would be grateful to us." Yet "military intervention carries an odium, moral intervention is preferable."

Through "moral intervention" Germany would persuade Austria to remodel her internal structure, without having to use her power to attain these objectives. Wedel called upon the German press to urge the Austrian government to carry out far-reaching reforms. Perceiving the weakness of the Dual Monarchy in its present state, he questioned the value of an alliance with it: "With whom do we conclude an alliance? We cannot ally ourselves with a question mark." Hungary had 21 million people, Austria 31 million. Of the latter however, only 12 million were German. "We may con-

---

[1] *N.A.*, T 120-3270, Akten betr. Beziehungen Öst. zu Deutschland, 1918, 1919, Öst. 95, 6, Wedel to F. O., June 18, 1918.
[2] *Ibid.*, Wedel to Bergen, June 29, 1918.

sider at most 12 million as our allies." A strengthening of the
alliance was not possible as long as the other 19 million stood
aside and took no part in Austria's political life. Czechs and
Croats urgently desired to be Germany's allies, but the
Austrian government, Wedel commented bitterly, "does not
wish reconciliation, it wishes national strife in its own house."

In another letter to Berlin, dated August 30, Wedel considered it likely that a crumbling Austrian monarchy might
be forced by "our enemies" to forge a link in the economic
blockade against Germany or herself "continue to face the
blockade." In this case Germany would have to take "counter-measures." "I would assume, however, that we would find
German Austria on our side." In view of the "dangerous
maneuvres" of the Austrian Foreign Ministry, he raised the
question whether a démarche of Emperor William II with
Emperor Charles, perhaps during the next week, was not opportune. Then, however, he voiced the fear that "no time is
to be lost and that perhaps an immediate move against
Minister Burián is in order."[3]

On the very day Wedel wrote this letter, the Austrian
foreign minister Burián notified Berlin that a peace move
was "urgent and [could] no longer be delayed."[4] Burián
bluntly told the German government that, whatever course it
chose, Vienna would have to take matters into its own hands.
Germany was forewarned that the Habsburg monarchy, in
order to save herself, might have to enter into armistice
negotiations.

The warning from the *Ballhausplatz* reflected the rapidly
worsening situation. A few weeks later, on September 26,
1918, the German Embassy in Vienna reported: "The mood
toward us deteriorates from day to day. Where ten Austrians
gather there is perhaps one who defends Germany; the
others abuse us and seek to gather material which makes
defection appear justified."[5]

Though concerned about a separate armistice by Vienna,
Wedel, on the other hand, also discerned opportunities in the
breakup of the Austrian empire. On October 2nd he informed the German Foreign Office that there was

---

[3]*Ibid.*, Wedel to F. O., Aug. 30.
[4]*Ibid.*, Burián to F.O., Sept. 26.
[5]*Ibid.*, German Embassy, Vienna to F.O., Sept. 26.

developing in the disintegrating monarchy the "basis for a large-scale [German Austrian] irredenta."[6] Germany should beware lest she repulse the German Austrians. The Foreign Office in turn, while hinting at the ultimate goal of fusion of German Austria with Germany, made it clear that no stand could be taken at the moment. There can be no doubt "about the goal which is eventually to be sought. In the meantime, the scenes in Vienna are changing in so kaleidoscopic a manner that at present we must refrain from taking any position."[7]

But Wedel urged the Foreign Office to take a position, at least theoretically, "even if for the present it [was] not yet desirable to discuss this problem in public." The Foreign Office, as a Memorandum dated October 10 reveals, was careful, however, anticipating opposition by certain French and Italian political leaders to the demand for union of an emerging German Austria with the Reich.[8] The following day the German cabinet of Prince Max of Baden supported the Foreign Office opinion that Germany should not furnish strong support for the Anschluss if such policy would weaken German claims to disputed territories along her eastern and western frontiers.[9] On the same day Wedel recommended from Vienna the very same policy, stressing the importance of the threatened border regions, Alsace and Lorraine, the left bank of the Rhine, and the Saar.[10]

In a letter dated October 11 Wedel depicted the alternatives facing Austria on the eve of her disintegration; transformation of the Dual Monarchy into a state with Slavic hegemony, or disintegration of the Habsburg empire with German Austria moving toward "rapid" Anschluss with Germany. A transformation of the empire either into a multinational state, based on genuine national equality also for German Austria, or preservation of the national *status quo*, prolonging German and Magyar superiority, was no longer possible.

---

[6]*Ibid.*, Beziehungen Öst.z.D., 12. Sept. 1918-30. Nov. 1918, Wedel to F.O., Oct. 2, Tel. 682.

[7]*Ibid.*, F.O. to Wedel, Oct. 3, Tel. 1052.

[8]*Ibid.*, Memorandum "Österreich," Oct. 10.

[9]Mathias and Morsey, 1962: p. 212.

[10]*N.A.*, T 120-3270, Wedel to F.O., Oct. 11.

Following this analysis of the Austrian situation, Wedel, asked his superiors in Berlin for instructions regarding policy and methods.

> In view of the increasing gravity of the situation, a procrastinating answer appears no longer possible and a positive stand rather imperative. Therefore, directions are respectfully requested on how to reply if I should be asked the question. I suggest as a reply that we recognize the self-determination for Germans; and if, without our intervention, it should lead to a desire for the Anschluss, we should be receptive. The step would have to be undertaken by the German Austrians since every initiative on our part would be exploited by the Entente as manifestation of imperialist goals. A grand action, perhaps taking the form of the earlier Baltic desire for Anschluss, would not be suitable. In the framework of a general regulation of the nationality question at the peace conference, the Anschluss, which is embedded in the context of the Wilsonian points, could then without special fanfare *via facti* materialize.[11]

While the situation in German Austria, in the opinion of some people, pointed to union with Germany, that union was a solution by no means assured or clearly desired by all.

Faced with the Dual Monarchy's imminent breakup and the urgent demand for a clarification of Germany's policy toward the Anschluss, Germany's Foreign Secretary Solf on October 19 dispatched a letter to Ambassador Wedel in Vienna, by special courier. He wrote as follows:

> The questions raised in your telegram No. 730 of the eleventh of this month are so delicate and affect our alliance with Austria-Hungary so profoundly that for obvious reasons, I prefer to send you the requested reply through these channels which are closed to scrutiny by third persons. You will appreciate that it is only with a heavy heart that I approach the treatment of a problem which, in the last analysis, means the vivisection of our ally. I would have much preferred—if it had been possible—to continue along Bismarck's path and to pursue now and in the future a policy aimed at preserving and strengthening the Danubian Monarchy with which we had al-

---

11*Ibid.*, Tel. 730.

lied ourselves for defense against the dangers threatening from the East. A prerequisite for loyally carrying out this policy was the maintenance of the hegemony of the Germans in Austria and of the Magyars in Hungary.[12]

However, the Vienna government had failed to keep the German element, the strongest support of the Habsburg throne, satisfied. It had abused the loyalty and restraint of the Germans and "at their expense" had yielded to the ever increasing ambitions of the Slavic peoples. The Vienna government had taken "a completely negative attitude toward our admonitions." Such complaints about the alleged abandonment of the German Austrians by the Habsburg dynasty were a favorite theme among many contemporary Germans, including, as shall be seen, Kaiser William II and General Ludendorff.

The Germans in Austria, according to Solf, "closed in on all sides, united, and in self-defense sought Anschluss with Germany." The disintegration of the Dual Monarchy could apparently no longer be halted. While the Austrian events drove Germany "into an extremely unpleasant and undesirable dilemma," she faced duties of honor which could not be shirked.

The grave struggles of four years of war have raised and strengthened German national consciousness. No German, no party—I am including here the Socialist party—would now tolerate that our fellow-nationals [Stammesgenossen] across the border who have made the greatest sacrifices in blood for the defense and honor of the Danubian monarchy should be oppressed and Slavicized. . . . Thus, we must take care of the Germans and if necessary receive them hospitably.

The ambassador was urged to inform the Austrian representatives that Germany's aim was to strive for the preservation of the Danubian Monarchy as long as this was at all possible. "If, however, there should be a disastrous collapse in Austria, the Germans would, of course, find protection and support with us." But it was neither in the German nor German Austrian interest to "accelerate the present panic-like process

---

[12]*Ibid.*, Solf to Wedel, Oct. 19, 7479/H 18764-71.

of dissolution." A joint and united stand of the two empires at the peace congress would be "more advantageous for us."

> For your personal information I would like to remark in parenthesis that for tactical reasons it is advisable that all those territorial questions which will be discussed at the peace conference in accordance with the Wilsonian program, and which affect us directly — Alsace-Lorraine and Poland — should be settled and decided in our favor, as far as this is at all possible, before it becomes evident that the Anschluss of German Austria has to be reckoned with as a real factor. Otherwise, I am afraid that the increase in territory and power which obviously would fall to Germany by union with German Austria would provide the Entente with justification for demanding territorial compensations, for presenting claims to Alsace-Lorraine and to our areas with Polish population, and for extending those claims to include territories on the left bank of the Rhine, especially the Saar basin. On the other hand, making German Austria autonomous ought to be speeded up and carried through in such a way that this newly formed state could not be prevented at the peace conference from deciding its own destiny according to the recognized rights of self-determination.

In the event the Czechs should be represented at the Peace Conference by their own delegation, it would be advisable for the German Austrians to have also their own delegates and to "instruct them to maintain close confidential contact with us." In conclusion Secretary Solf invited Wedel to express his views on these matters and on the form in which, if the occasion should arise, "the Anschluss of German Austria with us could be brought about with the least difficulty and in the most expedient way."

Secretary of State Solf's letter to Count von Wedel clearly revealed imperial Germany's policy toward German Austria in the event of the expected breakup of the Habsburg monarchy. Solf declared himself in favor of the Anschluss of German Austria, but "for tactical reasons" strongly urged its postponement. Ironically enough, no shadow of doubt existed in his mind as to the ability of the Hohenzollern monarchy to ride out the military defeat which he anticipated.

Solf had also made it clear that after the disintegration of the Habsburg empire and the subsequent Anschluss of Austria the two independent states of "Bohemia" and Hungary should be drawn into Germany's orbit. The Anschluss would be followed by the establishment of a German "Mitteleuropa," of German hegemony over non-German peoples, such as Czechs, Slovaks, Magyars, and South Slavs. The link-up of German Austria proper was merely the stepping stone for German domination of non-German Central Europe. Anticipating the Austrian empire's early demise, Germany would have to become the heir of the Dual Monarchy and assume the leadership in Central Europe which in the past the German Austrian element and the Magyars had exercised.

The very reasons which the last imperial secretary for foreign affairs adduced against a premature proclamation of the Anschluss by German Austria and its implementation by Germany — fear that the Peace Conference would retaliate by imposing harsher territorial terms on Germany — were also to determine republican Germany's foreign policy after the November Revolution of 1918. From the last days of the Hohenzollern monarchy to the postwar republican period and the conclusion of the work of the Peace Conference in particular, Germany's foreign policy toward German Austria and the Anschluss was to maintain a striking continuity.

To the German Reich the progressing disintegration of the Dual Monarchy posed both military and political problems of the highest order, and of immediate urgency. They were taken up not only by Wedel, the German ambassador at Vienna, but also by Ludendorff, Germany's celebrated war lord, by Chancellor Prince Max of Baden, and by Kaiser William II himself.

On October 14 Erich Ludendorff, chief of staff, wrote to the Office of Foreign Affairs as follows:

The events of the last weeks focus special attention on Austria. If the Supreme Command of the army deals with this question, it does so because it is of decisive importance for our military future. Perhaps in the not too distant future we may be placed in the situation of having to give our military protection to Germandom in Austria. The German circles in Austria consider the growing appeasement by the government of the Slavic peoples striving for independence with mounting concern. One fears that the government, ready for far-reaching renunciation, will accept the demands of the Entente, which will condemn Germandom in Austria to annihilation, by dissolving the Danubian monarchy into individual states, such as Czechoslovakia and the South-Slavic realm.

Germany was no longer capable of halting the transformation of the Dual Monarchy.

It is not impossible that one day the non-German nationalities, with the knowledge of the Entente, will proclaim themselves independent and will thus confront us with a *fait accompli*. That in the future we can count on the friendship of a Czech and South-Slavic state as little as we now could upon the friendship of Poland needs no explanation.

The German Austrians had finally recognized this danger. In spite of party conflicts

one begins to feel as one people that claims for itself about the same rights which are to be conceded to the other nations. There is increasing discussion about whether it is not time to prepare the Anschluss with the German Reich. . . . For our further propaganda work in Austria it is necessary to make up our mind whether the German Reich is to look in a detached manner at this development or whether it should support it.

A German citizen in Vienna writes me: "A complete rejection is in general precluded, since Germany cannot wish to let slip the opportunity for territorial growth and more power. On the other hand, it is hardly possible that the German Reich already supports this development. At the moment, all that can be done would be to let the leading personalities in Austria who work toward the Anschluss secretly know that the Anschluss of German territories exactly corresponds to our wishes, but that it could in no circumstances be officially furthered by Germany!"

I fully agree with this view. That an Anschluss of territories of the German race will come sooner or later can hardly be doubted. Considering the disappointments which the war brings in other respects, this development would still be a valuable compensation which we must not disregard. I believe therefore that the moment has come to seek support by all

means, among the Germans of Austria as well as among the
Magyars.

I would be grateful to your Excellency for your comments so
that thereafter guidelines could be issued for military
propaganda in Austria-Hungary.[13]

Ludendorff had earlier abandoned all hopes for German
victory. Now he also freely conceded that Germany could no
longer undertake any salvaging operation in the Dual Monarchy. While pretending to deal primarily with the military
aspects of the problem of disintegration of the Dual Monarchy and its impact upon Germany and claiming interest
merely in "military propaganda," Ludendorff offered, of
course, political recommendations.

These recommendations were clearly contradictory. On
the one hand Ludendorff agreed with the view that the Anschluss could not officially be furthered by Germany. And
both he and Wedel, the German ambassador in Vienna, set
their hopes upon German Austria's taking the initiative and
carrying the brunt of the burden. On the other hand, Germany might be placed in a position where she would have to
give "military protection" to German Austria. Like Wedel five
days earlier, Ludendorff had asked Germany's foreign
minister Solf for his views on the Anschluss, so that the German army could undertake appropriate propagandistic
moves in Austria-Hungary. He had acted, however, on his
own authority when he sent "guidelines" to military representatives abroad.[14]

On October 29, imperial Germany's last chancellor, the
liberal Prince Max of Baden, took Ludendorff to task for his
propaganda activities. The latter had actually been dismissed
from his post of chief of staff of the army on October 24. The
chancellor criticized Ludendorff's instructions to German
military representatives abroad on two grounds: Apart from
the circumstance that through the publication of such a note
most serious political harm could be caused, it was "not the
duty of military representatives abroad to devote themselves
to political tasks."[15] Prince Max of Baden gave no indication
that he disapproved of the Anschluss policy as such or that he

---

[13]*Ibid.*, Öst. 95, v. 7, Ludendorff to Solf, Oct. 14.
[14]*Ibid.*
[15]*Ibid.*, Max of Baden, Oct. 29.

would discourage German Austria from pursuing it. He objected only to the apparently careless propagandistic manner of the army's chief of staff, which might prove damaging abroad and at home. In addition, at this very time when, under the impact of the impending military debacle and President Wilson's proddings, Germany was under new leadership and seemed to be moving toward democracy and to abandon its militaristic stance, the continued assertion of clearly political prerogatives by the military went directly against the new trend.

On the sixteenth of October, in a letter to the Reich's chancellor, Wedel described the "chaotic" political situation in Austria, but continued to utter a word of caution against intervention in Austria proper. He seemed quite willing, however, to move vigorously against North Bohemia whose Germans "we could not leave in the lurch," apparently expecting little or no resistance from the Entente in this case. Two days later, on October 18, Wedel reported that he had called a conference of German political and military representatives of the Dual Monarchy. Its participants, meeting in the German Embassy in Vienna, unanimously opposed the project of the Danubian confederation and underlined the danger of German Austria's joining a Slav-dominated political structure which was bound to be "hostile" to the Germans. Though the position of many German Austrians in regard to the Anschluss was still unclarified, the general consensus of the conference was that the Austrians "could not be abandoned." [16] This was also Ludendorff's and Emperor Wilhelm's view. Yet none of them was able to spell out concretely how Austria could be "protected."

The very day Ludendorff wrote to the German Foreign Office, October 14, 1918, Emperor Wilhelm himself penned a letter to the same address. In "Remarks about Austria" the Kaiser wrote thus:

The war broke out partly on account of Slavic hatred against culturally superior Germandom. The course of the war has disclosed a hatred of Germandom in all countries . . . which will result in a partial return to the fatherland of bordering

---

[16]*Ibid.*, Wedel to F.O., Oct. 16 and 18.

German territories. The result of the war will be an instinctive *concentration of Germans* around and close to *Germany* [italics in the text]. The unfortunate Austrian policy at the expense of and under steady disregard of the Germans has finally led to the present conditions. The independent Bohemian-Czech state must be regarded as our sworn enemy and Silesia must be protected against it.

Demonstrations in the Austrian Reichsrat offered to the Kaiser only new proof of the strength of the Anschluss movement and of the truth of his "thesis that the war is instinctively strengthening a feeling for racial kinship among all Germans, a feeling prompted by the necessity of self-defense, and thus preserving the life and future of their race." German Austria would act wisely to link up in some form with the German Reich, since her "battle for hegemony against autonomous Slav states . . . [was] hopeless." While writing these lines the emperor halted abruptly on seeing a dispatch from Vienna which stated that the German Austrians had agreed on Dr. Victor Adler's program to bring an autonomous German Austria as a *Land* into the German Reich — all of which confirmed his above conclusion.

While the Austro-Hungarian empire was in the process of dissolution and the threatening clouds moved closer to Germany, William II indulged in happy daydreams about imperial Germany's immediate future; these included the incorporation of German Austria into Germany but were by no means limited to it. It was important, he continued, that Austria retain Trieste, that the Baltic region be linked to Germany, and that Lithuania be supported against Poland.

What is right for the German Austrians and for German Bohemia, namely Anschluss to the German nucleus, is of course also fair for the "Baltic Germans." They too obey the law of German racial concentration for the protection of their way of life. . . . The Estonians have always been enemies of the Russians; their Anschluss will be easily [!] accomplished.[17]

For the Kaiser "Anschluss" was not a term limited to the German-Austrian racial brethren. It had a far wider ap-

---

[17]*Ibid.*, William II. to F.O., Oct. 14, "Bemerkungen über Österrreich."

plication—ironically enough, at the very moment when defeat stared Germany in the face.

Racial theories, including belief in German superiority and Slavic inferiority, dominated the thinking of Kaiser William II on the subject of Austria and the Anschluss even more than that of Ludendorff. The Kaiser, Ludendorff, and Wedel too were convinced of the permanent hostility between Germany and the Slavic world, did not wish to abandon German Austria to the Slavs, and were in favor of the Anschluss.

During the last days of the Austrian empire Prince Max of Baden and the imperial foreign minister Solf were also agreed that German Austria's proper place was with the German Reich. In October, German political leaders such as Gustav Stresemann, the right-wing chairman of the National Liberal parliamentary delegation, and the right-wing Social Democrat Gustav Noske voiced in the Reichstag their faith in Grossdeutschland. On October 22 Stresemann pointed out that the collapse of the Austrian empire need not usher in utter hopelessness. The German Austrians of all parties were at least nationally united. "When the world is reshaped in accordance with the concept of the right to national self-determination, then Germany will stand shoulder to shoulder with German Austria forever. During all these dark days we must not overlook this ray of light." And two days later Gustav Noske assured the Reichstag that many Germans followed the endeavors of the German Austrians "with the greatest sympathy." He voiced the hope that they would succeed "in shaping their future so that their Germandom will be wholly preserved."[18] In mid-July Mathias Erzberger of the Catholic Center party had already expressed the hope "that from the disintegration of the Habsburg monarchy would arise the union of Germany with Austria sought in the period of the so-called wars of unification."[19]

No one believed in the likelihood of obtaining, not to mention the propriety of claiming, new territories after a lost war. Wedel looked forward to the incorporation of German Bohemia as a "great gain for our fatherland," but thought it

---

[18]*Germany. Verhandlungen d. Reichstages;* dreizehnte Legislaturperiode 1914-1918, CXCIII, p. 6173, Oct. 22, 1918; *ibid.,* p. 6214, Oct. 24.

[19]Epstein, 1959: pp. 420-421, Appendix XI.

better not to talk about the Anschluss of German Austria proper, trusting that he would find her "on our side" in the end. Ludendorff was cheered by the outlook that German Austria would prove a "valuable compensation" for other "disappointments" which the end of the war was likely to bring. The Kaiser was prepared to add not only German Austria, but also other German-inhabited regions to Germany. Only those directly responsible for the conduct of foreign policy, such as Chancellor Prince Max of Baden and Foreign Secretary Solf, trod more carefully. But they did not raise any questions about the Anschluss either, merely about the particular timing, its "manner and form."

When the end of the war was clearly in sight, defeat, misery and Revolution threatened to cast a long shadow over German Central Europe. But official imperial Germany lived in a happy fantasy world of her own. Undeterred by all adversities, she was ready to play her favorite game of territorial aggrandizement and expansion into German-inhabited as well as non-German regions.

Inclusion of German Austria as a long-range, if not immediate, plan was by no means of interest only to the Kaiser and Germany's leading political and military figures, but even to the "radical" opposition, German Social Democracy. The Great German tradition was, as we have seen, deeply rooted not only in the Austrian, but also in the German Social Democratic Party. With the impending breakup of the Austrian empire, Germans of virtually all political persuasions, including the Left, showed keen interest in the possibility of linking German Austria to Germany. And German Socialists and Democrats in particular saw in the Anschluss movement a revival of the revolutionary and Great German concepts of 1848-1849, and welcomed the alliance between the proponents of democratic, socialist, and national ideas.

During the October days of 1918, the leading socialist organ, the *Vorwärts*, appeared definitely committed to the Anschluss in German Austria, which at that very moment was being strongly advocated by Austrian Social Democracy. Dr. Otto Bauer was given recognition by the right-wing German socialist paper in spite of his "radicalism" — his position was similar to that of the German Independents—because it always carried "a Great German connotation."

On October 24, the *Vorwärts* carried an article, "Deutsch-land's Grenznationalitäten,"which listed not only Alsatians, Poles, and Danes, but particularly German Austrians: "It remains the goal of German Social Democracy to provide all those who wish to remain with us or join us with a free comfortable home." In another article entitled "Deutschland und Österreich-Ungarn" *Vorwärts,* writing off Hungary as a future ally, addressed itself to the German Austrians who were threatened by "Slavic chauvinism" and to its own imperial government which it suspected of being over-cautious: "In this critical hour we expect that they will not be denied any possible help, if they turn toward us for support."[20] Apparently the socialist newspaper had some doubts about the warmth of hospitality and the depth of welcome which its own German government would extend to their Austrian brothers.

[20]*Vorwärts,* Oct. 22, 1918; *ibid.,* Oct. 24, "Deutschland's Grenznationalitäten."

5. EMERGING GERMAN AUSTRIA AND THE LAST DAYS OF IMPERIAL GERMANY (OCTOBER 21-NOVEMBER 9 AND 12, 1918)

> "It was self-evident that the German Austrians could not be abandoned. On the other hand, the Reich must in no case seize the initiative," Botho von Wedel, October, 1918

ON October 21 German Austria had moved a long way toward the establishment of a new independent state. On that day the deputies who had been elected to the Reichsrat from the German districts constituted themselves as the Provisional National Assembly of German Austria.[1] True, only a small minority of the deputies, members of the German-Austrian Independence party and of the National Socialist Workers' party, favored immediate Anschluss with the German Reich, while the majority were still in favor of the formation of a Danubian confederation. The bourgeois political parties still hoped to be able to preserve the unity and integrity of the Habsburg realm as well as the monarchic form of government. Thus the committee of the Provisional National Assembly, charged with preparing the agenda, hesitated to take another step toward union. The Assembly was further disheartened when it received a "hint" from Berlin "not to precipitate" matters.[2] But Victor Adler had already pointed out that the emerging German Austrian state would join the Reich if a new confederation failed to develop.

On October 21, the Provisional National Assembly had come rather close to adopting the Anschluss resolution. Had it been adopted in October, instead of on November 12, it

---

[1]*N.A.*, T 120-3270, Akten betr. Beziehungen Öst . . . , Wedel to Solf, Oct. 22. The day the German republic was proclaimed, Victor Adler sent congratulations to both socialist parties in Berlin expressing the hope that German Austria would participate in the elections for the joint National Assembly (Verein f. Gesch. d. Arbeiterbewegung, Vienna, Sitzungsprotokolle, Parteivorstand, July 27, 1916-Nov. 13, 1921, pp. 661-662).

[2]*N.A.*, T 120-3270, Wedel to Solf, Oct. 22.

would have amounted to a repudiation of the still-ruling Habsburg dynasty. And German Austria's Anschluss would have been a union with Hohenzollern Germany!

The Reich could not have ignored or rejected the Austrian resolution without admitting weakness and fear and committing an act of treason in the eyes of most Germans. Nor could it have implemented the resolution without stabbing her Habsburg ally in the back and confirming the Entente's worst suspicion about itself.

Referring to the first session of the Provisional National Assembly of German Austria, Wedel, in a letter to Secretary Solf, dated October 22, voiced his satisfaction that it was not moving too rashly toward the union and expressed his agreement with Solf's basic policy—approval of the Anschluss in principle, but using the utmost caution and delaying tactics. Yet he foresaw the day when the Germans of Bohemia would approach Germany and ask for assistance. In German Bohemia's case, Wedel favored a stronger course than was contemplated by the German government. He also recommended that Germany give support to the South Slavic unification movement and thus gain access to the Yugoslav Adriatic coast via German Austria. After the war Hungary would probably lean toward Germany, live in friendship with the Balkan states, and strive for reconciliation with the Slavs. He concluded: "In other words, I am hoping for a Mitteleuropa in a new and altered form."[3] So also did Secretary Solf, as his letter of October 19 revealed. And such caution as Wedel displayed in October, 1918, in regard to German Austria proper was partly motivated by his consideration that a direct Anschluss would run counter to the goals of Mitteleuropa. This concept might be of greater long-range interest to Germany than an immediate link-up with Austria.

In Wedel's view the Provisional Austrian National Assembly of October 21 had charted the right course. Following his advice, it had refrained from blurting out its desire to bring about immediate union with the Reich. No "premature" proclamation of the Anschluss had taken place. By maintaining its "loyalty" to the Austrian government, Germany had behaved correctly. Still, the idea of the future union with Germany had permeated the discussions.

---

[3]*Ibid.*

Wedel had imposed these cautious tactics on the Austrian leaders. He proudly reported that on the eve of the session of the Provisional Austrian National Assembly, on October 21, Austrian political leaders had greeted his warnings against undue haste "with great applause, openly recognizing its correctness and promising to act accordingly." He also impressed his own government with the need for restraint and was greatly pleased with the apparent identity of views on tactical problems.[4]

Wedel favored the Anschluss but was never impatient or overzealous and never prepared to grant extensive concessions to Austria, though in his view Austria was to play an important role in postwar Germany. There was no question in his mind about the need for preserving Prussia's supremacy in the German empire, though he did not fail to recognize "the defects of Prussianism."[5]

During the last days of the imperial Reich the German cabinet dealt also with another political question, the "particularist," if not secessionist, movement in the South which seemed to be linked with the Anschluss problem. In a session of the German war cabinet on October 31, 1918, Scheidemann spoke of the "particularist movement" which had sprung up everywhere in Germany, especially in the South, and disclosed that "in Bavaria the current slogan is: 'Away from Prussia. Let us link up with Austria. Away from the Reich.'" He warned, "This would be the worst thing which could happen to us."[6]

Fears of a separate Bavarian peace moved the German war cabinet to consider this threat in a session to which the Bavarian prime minister von Dandl was invited. At issue were statements made by several leaders of the Bavarian Center party, especially Dr. Heinrich Held.[7] According to von Dandl, Held had disavowed a statement allegedly favoring secession, but when questioned about it the Bavarian prime minister was evasive. He also admitted that a separate peace was much talked about among Bavarians, largely because of the immediate threats which had arisen on the Bavarian frontier. There seems to be little doubt that the following

---

[4]see 1) or *A.A.*, Öst. 103, v. 9, Wedel to Solf, Oct. 22.
[5]*Ibid.*
[6]Mathias and Morsey, 1962: p. 440.
[7]*Ibid.*, pp. 477-478.

statement ascribed to Dr. Held was actually made by him, as many witnesses testified to it. (Its contents are quite similar to those of an article published by Dr. Georg Heim, a fellow Bavarian, a few weeks later, on December 1, in the *Bayerischer Kurier.*) Dr. Held had been heard to assert that Bavaria would obtain better terms if she concluded a separate peace. According to this account, the Entente planned to set up a buffer state extending from Basel to Belgium and consisting of Alsace, the Palatinate, parts of Hessen on the left bank of the Rhine, the Rhineland, and Luxemburg. The coal of the Ruhr and Hanover would be added. Bavaria could not tie her fate indissolubly to a Prussia which was expected to be reduced to the possessions it had in 1814. "The question would arise whether the South German states should not link up with German Austria. Economic motives would probably lead to a rapprochement in the foreseeable future between this South German-Austrian confederation and Prussia."[8] It was quite clear that what Dr. Held recommended here was a breakup of Germany; thereafter South and West Germany would join arms with Austria. At the same time he held out only a vague promise of a rapprochement of the two halves of Germany, and only in an unspecified future.

Official Germany, of course, hoped to preserve Germany's integrity. More than that, it hoped to attract German Austria. Wedel himself counted heavily on Austria's future economic dependence on Germany as a factor likely to propel her toward union. "This Austria will need us as the baby needs the wetnurse."[9] On October 18 he expressed to Prince Max of Baden his conviction that "the cry for an economic Anschluss with the German empire will become more urgent from day to day."[10] Austria's economic weakness was an assurance that Germany's opportunities in neighboring Austria would wax rather than wane.

A few days later this weakness was bared when the emerging German Austrian state, pressed by food shortages, turned to the Reich. Von Waldow, the Reich's state secretary for Food, pointed out in the cabinet session of October 27 that Germany lacked surplus food and could not ship victuals

---

[8]*Ibid.*
[9]*A.A.,* Öst. 103, v. 9, Wedel to Solf, Oct. 22.
[10]*Ibid.,* Öst. 95, v. 7, Wedel to Max of Baden, Oct. 18, Report 276.

to German Austria for any extended period of time. He nevertheless admitted that such a decision was largely a political one. Whereupon Foreign Secretary Solf strongly urged the cabinet to assist Austria. Replying to Waldow, Philipp Scheidemann reminded him that the Social Democratic party had voted to aid the German Austrians and would defend this action to the workers. In the end the cabinet unanimously agreed to ship 10,000-12,000 tons of grain to Austria."[11] These supplies were expected to last only a few weeks.

Wedel was in close touch with the German Austrian political leaders during the days when the new German Austrian state was born. Three days before the meeting of the Provisional National Assembly on October 21, at a gathering in Vienna of the leading figures of the Christian Social and German National parties, he had pledged that Germany would not leave the "Austrian brethren in the lurch." In case of need "our door is open; they are heartily welcome." Yet he had also warned against "overhastiness," pointing out that the Entente might "turn the screws even tighter," and reminding them that their foremost task was to create a state with Vienna as capital.[12]

On October 23 Wedel reported that the presidium of the German Austrian National Assembly, Dr. Ringhofer, Dr. Seitz, and Fink and Sylvester had visited him in the Embassy to inform him and the imperial government of the establishment of the German Austrian state. Dr. Seitz in an official address had requested the support of the Reich for German Austria.[13] The German Austrian leaders did not conceal their eagerness for a union with what was still imperial Germany.

But at the moment Germany was more interested in preventing the rapidly falling Habsburg monarchy from signing the armistice which threatened to expose her flank. The German government had reacted with anger and bitterness to the note of the new Austro-Hungarian foreign secretary Count Julius Andrássy, succesor to Count Burián, when on October 27 he indicated the Dual Monarchy's

[11]Mathias and Morsey, 1962: p. 390.
[12]*A.A.*, Öst. 103, v. 9, Wedel to Solf, Oct. 22; also *ibid.*, Öst. 95, v. 25, Oct. 21, Nr. 806.
[13]*Ibid.*, v. 9, Wedel to F.O., Oct. 23.

preparedness for separate armistice negotiations. He recognized President Wilson's demands for the independence of the Slavic nations, Czechoslovakia and Yugoslavia, and at the same time broke the Dual Alliance of 1879, the bond which his father had helped to create. By going his own way he hoped to salvage the Habsburg monarchy and save the empire, particularly Hungary, from invasion. Simultaneously with the foregoing note, Emperor Charles sent a telegram to Emperor William II informing him that he had "made the irrevocable decision to ask within the next 24 hours for a separate peace and an immediate armistice."[14]

Foreign Secretary Solf then gave direct instructions to Wedel to mobilize German Austria's political parties and public opinion in the face of what he considered a deadly blow struck by the Habsburg monarchy against its German ally. He urged Wedel to protest to all German parties against the procedure of the Ballhausplatz which acted as representative of Magyar and Slavic special interests. German Austria should dispute that Count Andrássy had the right to negotiate in its name with the enemy and should disavow a separate peace with the Entente.

> "At the same time, will Your Excellency advise the Germans [German Austrians] to hasten the establishment of their state and its machinery, and point out to them the peril for Germany's territory which would arise if the Entente demanded to march through the [Dual] Monarchy. For your information: For obvious reasons the Anschluss of German Austria to Germany must absolutely not be officially announced at present. Besides, a move toward the Anschluss on our part could prompt the government there to demand the removal of our Embassy from Vienna which should be avoided at all costs, simply because of the development of the German situation there. In spite of all this, your Honor will be able to reply to possible questions by indicating that with all necessary caution we are prepared, at the conclusion of peace [!], to admit German Austria."[15]

The German foreign secretary was keenly aware of Germany's momentary impotence and preferred to

[14]*Amtliche Urkunden zur Vorgeschichte des Waffenstillstandes 1918*, (2nd ed., 1924), p. 205.
[15]*A.A.*, Öst. 95, v. 7, Solf to Wedel, Oct. 28, Tel. 1188.

procrastinate. By the time the peace treaty was concluded the Entente would have lost its leverage and would no longer be able to penalize Germany by wresting disputed border regions from her, in retaliation for the annexation of Austria.

With the Austrian empire in obvious disarray, Germany's interests were deeply involved in its fate. It is therefore hardly surprising that German propaganda resumed its course in Austria in an intensified manner. Early in October the German Foreign Office requested the Treasury to place "the sum of ten million marks at [its] disposition for secret political endeavors in Austria. In view of the urgent necessity for implementing the planned undertakings as soon as possible, I would be grateful to you for the most rapid acceleration of the matter." The request was approved on October 31, 1918.[16] German money thus began to pour into Austria to oppose, if feasible, a separate armistice and, while the Austrian monarchy was in the process of disintegration, to lay the groundwork for the later Anschluss. Financial support by the German government to the movement for union continued after the breakup of the Dual Monarchy when the German Austrian government began to move energetically toward the union. The proponents of Austria's independence or of her union with a Danubian confederation may have received similar support from abroad. The French especially were eager to purchase Austrian daily newspapers in order to influence Austrian public opinion.

While the Andrássy note of October 27 had had a demoralizing impact on Germany, it had a shattering effect on the crumbling Dual Monarchy. Count Andrássy was foreign secretary in the new government headed by Professor Lammasch. After accepting the resignation of the Hussarek Cabinet, Emperor Charles had invited Professor Heinrich Lammasch, an authority in international law and widely respected at home and abroad, to form the Cabinet. When invited to the same post earlier, in July, 1918, Lammasch had made his acceptance contingent on the fulfillment of several conditions—the federalization of the empire, abandonment of Germany in the war, and a rapprochement with the Western Powers with the object of a separate peace.[17] His ac-

---

[16]*Ibid.*, Solf to Treasury, Oct. 28; also Oct. 31.
[17]Strong, 1939: pp. 103-104.

ceptance of the post now, on October 24, signified the Dual Monarchy's resolve to conclude a separate peace and to cut ties with its wartime ally.

The government headed by Lammasch turned out to be a caretaker government which served only until November 11, 1918. Its real task was the liquidation of the empire. Even in the Austrian half of the monarchy to which its authority was confined it limited itself to arranging for the smooth and orderly transfer of authority to the new national states.

While new national governments assumed authority in the various parts of the former Habsburg monarchy, in German Austria herself the republican and revolutionary movement gained tremendous momentum. With the rapid growth of anti-Habsburg sentiments even among traditionally conservative German Austrians, the move toward Germany became irresistible. On October 30, the Provisional National Assembly of German Austria assumed legislative powers and elected the Staatsrat as an executive body. The latter appointed Victor Adler, leader of the Austrian Social Democratic party, as state secretary for foreign affairs. He was to function in this capacity until his sudden death on November 11.

On November 2 Adler made an official visit to the German Embassy and informed Wedel of the formation of the Austrian government, asking him also to request the Foreign Office to keep him as German representative to the new Austria. He also inquired whether Berlin wished to receive a German Austrian envoy in Berlin.

On November 3, the day the armistice was concluded at Padua, Victor Adler informed the German ambassador of the resolution on the armistice which had been passed by the Staatsrat and was to be published the following day. The German Austrian authorities notified therein the German government that a *force majeure* compelled them to accept the armistice terms. According to the resolution, the Staatsrat acknowledged the notification of Austria's High Command that it was compelled to submit to the conditions of the victor, since "German Austria no longer [had] an army of its own." Its units, composed of a Slavic and Magyar majority, "were no longer willing to fight." Therefore, German Austria was incapable of continuing the struggle alone.[18]

---

[18]*N.A.*, Akten betr. Beziehungen Öst . . . V. Adler to Wedel, Nov. 3, Nr. 929.

At the very moment the death-knell of the centuries-old Habsburg monarchy rang, the German Austrians once more proclaimed their past, present, and future loyalty to the German Reich and also asserted their claim to territory inhabited by Germans as far south as Southern Tyrol. As an immediate goal the Austrian resolution projected a "close and permanent association" between German Austria and the Reich. "We shall endeavor," replied the German foreign secretary on November 4, "in the event of the dissolution of Austria-Hungary, to obtain a friendly neighborly [!] relationship with its parts. Preparatory steps in this respect have already been taken. Will you please see to it that good relations are maintained between the Germans of the Reich and citizens of Austria-Hungary."[19] The German Austrians were not even singled out as a people in whom the Reich had a special interest! Warm words issuing from Austria met with a cold reception from Germany. However, these events took place on the eve of Germany's own surrender, against the background of widespread demoralization, and deep bitterness over Austria-Hungary's separate armistice. The desperate situation imposed utmost caution on Germany.[20]

During the days of October and early November, 1918, national and political revolution swept over Central Europe. While the German Austrian leadership displayed then eagerness for the Anschluss, Germany's leadership in turn concealed or suppressed its sympathy for the movement and proceeded cautiously, fearful lest it worsen its country's fate by a public profession of faith in the political unity of all Germans of Central Europe. It showed similar reluctance and moderation with regard to German Bohemia, its possible separation from the emerging Czechoslovakian state, and its Anschluss with the Reich. At the very end of a bitter war, it was neither materially nor psychologically prepared to challenge the victorious enemy. Diplomatic reserve was a matter of self-preservation.

When the Czechoslovakian republic was proclaimed in Prague on October 28, deputies from the German-speaking areas of Bohemia in the old Reichsrat constituted themselves as the Provisional Assembly of German-Bohemia and elected a government of their own. The same step was undertaken

[19]*Ibid.*, Solf to Wedel, Nov. 4.
[20]*Ibid.*, Embassy Berne to Chancellery, Nov. 7.

MAP 1.   The frontier with Czechoslovakia: the Sudeten problem.

by the deputies from the German districts of northern
Moravia and Silesia which likewise were not contiguous to
German Austria proper. They formed a new province, the
"Sudetenland," and likewise elected a provisional government.[21] The establishment of these two provinces was quickly
approved by the National Assembly of German Austria. A
clash of jurisdiction over these areas between the new
Czechoslovakian republic and German Austria was clearly in
the making.

Germany's dilemma in this situation was reflected in the
different positions taken by the German consul in Prague,
Freiherr von Gebsattel, and Ambassador von Wedel in
Vienna. The day after the proclamation of Czechoslovak independence, the former called on the new Czech government without having received proper instructions from

---

[21]Bauer, 1923: p. 105f.

Berlin.[22] Wedel, however, reflecting the strong position taken by the Austrian government in this matter, wanted Berlin to give German Bohemia at least diplomatic and moral support.[23] Gebsattel also came out strongly against any German military intervention either in Bohemia or in Vienna. Wedel contemplated intervention in Bohemia, while General von Cramon of the German military mission in Vienna, pointing to the danger of Bolshevism and the weakness of the new Austrian government, urged the German Supreme Command to prepare for an intervention not only in Bohemia but also in the rest of German Austria. Though he was uncertain whether Vienna would ask for help, he held that Germany could "legitimately" insist on the passage of German troops which were still on Austrian soil.[24]

The question of military intervention was also posed in regard to Tyrol. The Austrian empire's separate armistice at Padua on November 3, 1919, instilled fear throughout Germany and caused panic in Bavaria as well as in Tyrol which felt most threatened. The Tyrolese National Council, fearful of retreating marauders and of Italian invaders, turned then to Germany for help. However, when the German consul in Innsbruck, von Külmer, transmitted Tyrolese requests for assistance to the German Foreign Office, he was instructed to recommend to the National Council that it place German Austrian troops under the command of the German Austrian government. The Foreign Office also opposed any Bavarian military move into Tyrol for the defense of Germany's frontier.[25]

In the declining days of imperial Germany the Supreme Command was no longer in the position of making far-reaching decisions of its own. In the absence of clear policy directives from the German government, the Supreme Command urgently requested that the Foreign Office reach a decision on whether German troops were to cross into Austria or not.[26] Solf then advised Wedel to "extract" from

[22]A.A., Öst. 101, v. 43, Gebsattel to Max of Baden, Oct. 30, 1919, Report Nr. 237 and ibid., Nov. 2, Nr. 246.
[23]Ibid., undersecretary of state to Wedel, Nov. 2.
[24]Ibid., Öst. 95, v. 25, Hintze to F.O., Tel. 1233.
[25]Ibid., Öst. 103, v. 9, Külmer to F.O., Oct. 31, Tel. 12; ibid., F.O. to Külmer, Nov. 1, Tel. 9.
[26]Ibid., Hintze to F.O., Nov. 2, Tel. 2693.

the Staatsrat a plea for the occupation of Austria. On the same day, November 2, Wedel reported that Foreign Secretary Victor Adler had no serious objections to the occupation of German Austria, but that he considered it a "double-edged sword." It was obvious that Adler, while admitting the threat of Bolshevism in Austria, was opposed to a German take-over of the country. The German Austrian people would regard the entry of German troops as an "intervention" which would lead to the prolongation of the war. In conclusion Adler requested that he be informed at the earliest of any German decision to dispatch troops to Tyrol or Bohemia.[27]

The Austrian Staatsrat which met the same night raised no objections to the occupation of Tyrol, which on strategic grounds might be necessary for the security of the Reich. However, the Council postponed its decision about a possible German intervention in the rest of German Austria until the following morning.[28]

On November 3, one day after having raised the issue of Germany's military intervention in Tyrol and Inner German Austria, the German Foreign Office asked Wedel by telephone to ascertain whether the Staatsrat would object to the entry of German troops into Bohemia to restore order in Aussig. Though the Staatsrat first agreed to it, the Austrian foreign secretary Victor Adler seems to have changed his mind on the very same day. A telegram sent by Wedel informed the Foreign Office of Adler's belief that such intervention would be unnecessary, and conveyed his fear that it might lead to war between Germany and Czechoslovakia.[29] Thereupon Solf directed the Supreme Command immediately to stop the movement of German troops into Bohemia.[30]

In early November, 1919, General Gröner had stressed the need for the German army to enter Tyrol, since the loss of the Alpine passes would "imperil the defense of our frontier."[31] Though the German Foreign Office supported the ar-

[27]*Ibid.*, Solf to Wedel, Nov. 2, Tel. 1220; *ibid.*, Wedel to F.O., Nov. 2, Tel. 912.
[28]*Ibid.*, Wedel to F.O., Nov. 2, Tel. 920.
[29]*Ibid.*, Öst. 101, v. 43, Nov. 3, Memorandum; *ibid.*, Wedel to F.O., Tel. 928 and Nov. 3, Tel. 936.
[30]*Ibid.*, Schubert to F.O., Nov. 4, Tel. 2719.
[31]*Ibid.*, Grosses Hauptquartier 23c, v. 1, Gröner to F.O., Nov. 3, Tel. 118.

my's position, opposition was uttered in the cabinet itself. The occupation of Tyrol would make Austria a battleground and would be bitterly resented by her people. After another cabinet session, however, the Supreme Command won its point.[32] As Vice Chancellor von Payer put it, if the Supreme Command of the army declared that it was "necessary to defend Bavaria beyond the Bavarian frontier, we cannot refuse." The Bavarian government, fearful of the approach of enemy troops, panicked and pressed for the occupation of Tyrol. Berlin feared that further inaction on its part would only strengthen Bavarian separatism. Secretary Solf, who had pursued a policy of restraint during the month of October, changed his mind, now holding that "such scruples [by some members of the Cabinet regarding the occupation] would probably be overcome by the immediate Anschluss of Tyrol with the Reich or with Bavaria."[33]

The moment of crisis in the early days of November was to produce several striking turnabouts. The National Council of Tyrol which had just appealed for Germany's armed support, in a stunning reversal pleaded for occupation by Entente troops.[34] Tyrol thus revealed that it was more interested in order as such than in the Anschluss with Bavaria or the Reich. But the new Tyrolese request came too late to halt German implementation of Innsbruck's earlier call for help. German troops entered Tyrol. While the Austro-Hungarian Command protested against the entry of German troops into Tyrol, Under Secretary of State Otto Bauer was prepared to condone the German move as a "defense measure."[35] A few days later, however, Germany concluded an armistice and her troops withdrew from Tyrol.

The occupation of Tyrol by German troops was only partly prompted by German defense needs, and partly by the desire for an Anschluss of Tyrol, as Solf privately conceded.[36] Though he still clung thereafter to a cautious course in regard to the union of the rest of German Austria with the Reich, he may have felt that the occupation of Tyrol might

[32] Mathias and Morsey, 1962: p. 487f and pp. 504-506.
[33] A.A., Öst. 103, v. 7, Solf to Wedel, Nov. 4, Tel. 1238.
[34] Ibid.
[35] Ibid., Öst. 103, v. 9, Wedel to F.O., Nov. 6, Tel. 972.
[36] Ibid., Öst. 95, v. 25, Solf to Wedel, Nov. 8, Tel. 1290.

speed and strengthen the Anschluss movement in German Austria. As he made clear to Wedel on November 8, the Austrian court circles, the imperial Foreign Ministry, segments of the Austrian Civil Service and possibly the Catholic Church attempted to save the Habsburg dynasty "at our expense"! But Germany, he asserted now, had "a legitimate interest in seeing that these efforts do not impair the creation in one form or another of Grossdeutschland."[37] He especially recommended a stronger emphasis in Vienna on the Anschluss idea. Only the other day Berlin had restrained Vienna; now it prodded it! Similarly expressive of the new mood was an editorial of November 8 in the *Norddeutsche Allgemeine Zeitung* giving a boost to the Anschluss.[38]

Still the German government was careful to follow international proprieties. Though ready to take advantage of German Austria's permissiveness in regard to Tyrol, it was prepared to respect her prohibition concerning German Bohemia and Inner German Austria herself. On November 7, Wedel informed Victor Adler that German Austria herself would have to take the initiative in the matter of the union: "We for our part could not issue an invitation for reasons known to him."[39] But on the eve of his resignation Chancellor Max of Baden dispatched a telegram to Vienna, announcing the impending election of a constituent assembly which would determine the future form of government of the German state, "including those parts of it which might desire to enter the Reich." Thus it appeared as if in its last days the imperial German government was prepared to throw earlier caution to the winds.

Yet the German ambassador Wedel continued his careful course. He warned the German Austrian government to refrain from pushing the Anschluss resolution through the Provisional National Assembly on November 12. He suggested to the German Foreign Office that a decision on the Anschluss be reserved for the Constituent Assembly.[40] But the Austrian Social Democrats, as he put it, "could not be restrained," while the German Nationals "did not dare to cast

[37]*Ibid.*
[38]*Norddeutsche Allgemeine Zeitung,* Nov. 8, "Deutschösterreich," quoted *ibid.*
[39]*N.A.,* Öst. 103, v. 9, Tel. 981, Wedel to F.O.
[40]*Ibid.,* Öst. 95, v. 25, Nov. 7, Tel. 1028.

a vote in opposition." The hurried Anschluss resolution in German Austria on November 12 was passed against the advice and in spite of the warnings of the German ambassador!

The November Revolution of 1918 ushered in a new era. Central Europe, shaken to its foundation, was to give birth to new political, territorial and national entities whose populations were moved by new and radical social and political ideas. Yet the national drive toward the Anschluss between Germany and German Austria, which had made itself strongly felt in the last critical days of the declining Dual Monarchy and of imperial Germany, continued. During the November days, the Anschluss movement revealed itself as a vigorous force in German Austria; it produced a favorable echo even in defeated Germany, though registering only a reluctant and feeble response in the circles of the German government.

II. From the November Revolution to the German and Austrian Elections (January 19 and February 16, 1919)

1. THE NEW AUSTRIA, THE ANSCHLUSS RESOLUTION AND THE RESPONSE OF THE GERMAN REPUBLIC

"We request that you [Hugo Haase] and the German Government support these [Anschluss] endeavors of the German people in Austria and enter into direct negotiations with us about the union of German Austria with the German republic." Otto Bauer, November, 1918

O N November 9, 1918, the German republic was proclaimed; on November 12 German Austria followed suit. The centuries-old structures of the Hohenzollern and Habsburg dynasties had come crushing down. And the Austrian armistice was quickly followed by the armistice with Germany. At the same time the most radical party of the prewar period, the Social Democrats, gained sole power in Germany and began to dominate the coalition cabinet which had been set up in German Austria. The concept of Grossdeutschland, with a hallowed tradition going back to 1848, gripped people in both German-speaking states, as did the hope of linking forces and of marching forward together to the goal of socialism. Thus on November 12, the very day the new German Austrian republic was born, the Austrian Provisional National Assembly passed an Anschluss resolution and proclaimed German Austria a part of the German Republic.

The day the German republic emerged, the Vienna *Arbeiter-Zeitung* voiced its elation over what it considered an historic opportunity for all Germans to unite: "Only in [such a union] can the republic find protection against the overbearing imperialism of the Entente. And only in the republic can the German proletariat find all conditions for its liberation realized."[1] The following day the Socialist

---

[1]*Arbeiter-Zeitung*, Nov. 9, 1918, "Die deutsche Revolution."

101

newspaper saluted Germany. It admitted that "there was a time when we were ashamed to be Germans," namely when the German people "bore the chains of slavery and permitted their master to commit infamous crimes which filled the peoples of the earth with wild hate and with arrogant contempt for all Germandom." "Today, however, the proletariat of all countries will cheer the German people."[2] In the same issue, the *Arbeiter-Zeitung* raised the timely question of "German Austria's future." The article was signed "f.a.," signifying either Friedrich Adler or Friedrich Austerlitz. "What will be our fate?" he asked. "Can we continue in our loneliness and forsakenness, squeezed in by Slavic national states, and carry out the Sisyphus task of constructing an impossible state? . . . No, action is imperative and should be taken without delay." The writer asserted that "[it is] not merely passionate enthusiasm which draws us to Germany. . . ." An Austria on her own, unable to produce enough food for herself, would be condemned to "economic withering away." "How then shall we arrive at socialism?"[3]

Vanquished and in misery, the Austrian and German peoples, according to the writer, needed a "splendid political goal" which would touch both their socialist and national heartstrings and would serve as a consolation for their wartime sacrifices as well as a beacon of a glorious future.

An independent German Austria signified to its people a reduction in living standards, a general lowering of its prospects for the future, and a decrease in status.[4] The citizens of a great empire, its dominant race, would become the disinherited of a small, hardly viable state. No promise of radical social change, economic redistribution or egalitarianism was likely to absorb the shock of national and political humiliation. Thus the drive toward the Anschluss gained great momentum in German Austria.

The new Austria began her life under the most pressing economic conditions. The new state had lost the markets for its industrial goods as well as its sources of raw materials and foodstuffs. Cut off by high-tariff barriers from the other newly established and often hostile succession states, she was

---

[2]*Ibid.*, Nov. 10.
[3]*Ibid.*
[4]*Österreichischer Volkswirt,* Nov. 9.

MAP 2. The first Austrian republic—the heart of Europe.

beset by staggering economic problems. Her situation was further aggravated by the continuance of the Allied blockade even after the conclusion of the armistice.

The Cabinet which had been formed in November was a coalition comprising Social Democrats and Christian Socials. The former, though supported by no more than roughly two-fifths of the population, were the dominant partner. This was a period when propertied groups and the "bourgeois" parties had lost their traditional support in the army and police, and were still overawed by the revolution and on the defensive. The Austrian Social Democrats, unlike the German and Hungarian Socialists, had managed to maintain their organizational unity in the face of heavy pressure from the small but vociferous group of Austrian Communists and from large numbers of the working class which leaned toward radicalism.

The new German Austrian Cabinet had to cope with particularist and even separatist tendencies in its own country.

These tendencies deepened as a result of the differences be-
tween industrialized, cosmopolitan, secularist, and Socialist
Vienna and the agrarian, conservative, clerical, and Christian
Social provinces. Some of the provinces, such as Tyrol and
Vorarlberg, behaved as if they were sovereign units. The
new Austrian state was officially bound to recognize that the
provinces had free choice to join a federated German
Austrian state or to refuse to do so; Chancellor Renner him-
self admitted this the day the republic was born. The seven
Alpine provinces which declared their willingness to join with
Vienna proper in creating the new republic were Lower
Austria, Upper Austria, Salzburg, Tyrol, Vorarlberg, Styria,
and Carinthia.

In the last days of the imperial Reich, when Germany's interest in the Anschluss movement became clearly evident,
Prince Max of Baden had virtually invited German Austria
"to enter the Reich" and Vienna responded to it immediately.
On November 9, the day the republic was proclaimed in Germany, the Austrian Staatsrat dispatched a telegram, still addressed to Chancellor Max of Baden, in which it extended
fraternal greetings and most ardent good wishes for the
future of the German republic. The Staatsrat expressed the
hope that Austria would, "as soon as possible, participate in
the new construction and transformation of the German
Reich." Three days later, when the Austrian republic was
born, it immediately proclaimed its adherence to the new
Germany.[5] Article 2 of the proclamation stated that "German
Austria is an integral part of the German republic. Special
laws will be enacted to regulate the unification of the ad-
ministrative and legal systems." The noted jurist Hans Kelsen
later expressed his opinion that this article spoke primarily of
a hope rather than a *fait accompli*.[6] The declaration did not
exactly define Austria's legal position; it did not specify
whether she was a sister state, an autonomous province, or
any other distinct legal entity. In any case, in order to make
German Austria an integral part of the new German republic,
Germany would have to make a corresponding declaration.

One day after the proclamation of the Austrian republic
and the simultaneous passing of the Anschluss declaration,

[5]*Staatsgesetzblatt*, Nov. 15, pp. 482-483.
[6]Kelsen, 1923: pp. 35-36.

Botho von Wedel wrote to Berlin: "The die is cast; German Austria is united with Germany." Though the final decision, he continued, had originally been reserved for a constituent assembly, the Austrian people desired to follow the German example and join the German republic. The Socialist leaders, in his view, were compelled to follow the people's wishes in order not to lose touch with them. He now held that Berlin's objections to an immediate union seemed less convincing than previously. In view of the "social movement" sweeping westwards, the victors would not dare to impose an "imperialistic peace treaty" on Europe. Therefore the Anschluss would not bring any "harm to Germandom." Clearly, Wedel, breathing the intoxicating air of those days, was caught up by the general enthusiasm. A few days later, however, having had time to reflect, he complained bitterly that the Austrian Anschluss proclamation had been "premature."

Whatever the true significance of the Anschluss resolution by the Austrian National Assembly on November 12, 1918, its immediate effect was limited; it was largely declaratory in character. It met with icy silence from the German government. To official Germany the call for union from abroad came at a very inopportune moment, in the hour of defeat, hunger, and the breakdown of all hopes. At that time Germany was neither materially nor psychologically prepared for bold expansive thrusts into the neighboring German Austrian republic.

The German press, however, reacted more favorably. Even during the first weeks after the war's end, when the new German republic faced the rising threat of civil war, the German press, though cautious, made no attempt to hide its sympathy for the Austrian Anschluss movement. On the eleventh of November the *Vossische Zeitung* noted approvingly: "German Austria wants to belong to the Reich."[7] In the November 14 issue of the same newspaper Alexander Redlich, alluding in an editorial "Die gesamtdeutsche Republik" to the Anschluss resolution of the German Austrian National Assembly, declared himself more than gratified that Austria was "resolved not only to enjoy the fruits of future unity, but also to share in the burdens which precede it."[8]

---

[7] *Voss. Zeitung,* Nov. 11.
[8] *Ibid.,* Nov. 14, Redlich, "Die gesamtdeutsche Republik."

While the social democratic *Vorwärts* was alarmed at the "threatening disintegration" of the Reich and the separatist endeavors in the South and West of Germany, it felt encouraged by the German Austrian movement for union. On November 13 it saluted Austria and declared the Anschluss resolution of the Austrian National Assembly a "great success" for the German republic. "We greet the new Bundesrepublik with keen enthusiasm. Democracy has helped Great Germany into the saddle; she will certainly be able to ride." The *Vorwärts* criticized, however, bourgeois opposition "manoeuvres" in German Austria and also the particularist mood in Tyrol. The gist of the article was clear: The German working class was presented as being more loyal and national-minded than the German and German Austrian "bourgeoisie" and the Anschluss movement was given the seal of socialist approval, while its opponents were castigated. "Democracy" too was welcomed because of its contribution to the cause of German national unity.[9] Socialism and democracy were applauded for their beneficial side effects on German nationalism!

This was also the position taken by the noted scholar Max Weber in the November 6 issue of the *Frankfurter Zeitung*. Republicanism and constitutionalism were acceptable to Professor Weber if they furthered a nationally desirable goal. "The republic as a form of government appears at present the only way to bring to a solution the *grossdeutsch* problem we now face. We must support a form of government which permits the unification of the greatest possible number of Germans into a fatherland."

The acceptance of a democratic republic was "also dictated by the threat of alien domination."[10] There was little enthusiasm here for the new political order, the new democratic republic; the latter had to be made palatable to the German public by contrasting it with the terrible alternative, alien domination and continued national division! The republican and democratic convictions of many Germans, even of a scholar of Max Weber's standing, rested on rather narrow utilitarian and nationalist foundations.

---

[9]*Vorwärts*, Nov. 13.
[10]*Frankfurter Zeitung*, Nov. 6, M. Weber, "Die Regierungsform Deutschlands," also Nov. 22, first morning ed.

This was also true of Gustav Stresemann, leader of the German People's party. Still a monarchist and not yet reconciled with the Weimar republic, he moved to accept it in April, 1919, since it was only on a republican basis that a union with Austria, and hence Grossdeutschland, was possible.[11]

In the words of Henry Ashby Turner, *Stresemann and the Politics of the Weimar Republic* (1963), in the immediate postwar period Stresemann was "a fellow traveller on the Right." As late as February 14, 1919, he threatened the Frankfurt chapter of his party, the German People's party, that a commitment on its part to the republic would make him decide to leave public life altogether.[12] But two months later he completely reversed his position and persuaded his party to endorse the Weimar republic. It was the issue of Austria and the Anschluss which was responsible for this startling turnabout. On April 13 at the first congress of the German People's party he declared: "We must be clear about one thing, that Grossdeutschland can only be constructed on a republican basis." Only a republican Germany would be able to attract the Austrian republic. The link-up with Austria in turn would be the first step toward Germany's restoration to the position of a Great Power. In the words of Turner, Stresemann, "faced with an apparent choice between the old imperial ruling house and an enlarged and strengthened Reich, decided in favor of the latter."[13] With the adoption of the Versailles Treaty, however, Stresemann's brief flirtation with republicanism came to an abrupt end,[14] since that document prohibited the Anschluss. In the immediate postwar period Stresemann contemplated republicanism and democracy, just as long as they held out the promise of Germany's quick restoration to a position of greatness by way of the Anschluss.

While the concepts of German power and prestige still held many Germans enthralled, German spokesmen tried to persuade the West that the future of peace and democracy in Germany was tied to a "just" settlement, one which would not impose large territorial losses on Germany and would even

---

[11]G. Stresemann, *Reden und Schriften* 1: p. 263, quoted by Turner, 1963: p. 37.
[12]*Ibid.*
[13]*Ibid.*
[14]*Ibid.*, p. 40.

permit her to receive German Austria. Max Weber was prepared to renounce what he foresaw could not be saved, Alsace-Lorraine. But he warned the West not to deprive Germany of other territories "in the West, or even the East," and especially not to block the union of German Austria with Germany. Otherwise German pacifism, after the initial tiredness was overcome, would succumb to a German *irredenta.* "It does not depend on us alone whether pacifism can remain a permanent state of mind."[15] Weber considered the *Anschluss* a *sine qua non* of Germany's "pacific" growth.

On November 18 the journalist Alexander Redlich, in an editorial of the *Vossische Zeitung,* entitled "Demokratische Weltpolitik," continued in the same spirit by stressing that Germany "must comprise the entire area inhabited by German *Volksgenossen* [kinsfolk], as far as it does not already belong . . . to another state," as for instance German Switzerland.[16] "Democratic Weltpolitik" would thus have to insist on self-determination for German Austria. The same theme was developed simultaneously by other noted German writers and scholars, many of whom became political activists in behalf of the cause of the Anschluss.

On the eighteenth of November the *Vossische Zeitung* reported on German propagandistic activities in behalf of the Anschluss.[17] In the Hochschule für Musik in Berlin, a well-attended assembly demonstrated in behalf of the Great Germany concept.[18] Some of the speakers were Germans, others were German Austrians residing in Germany, such as Hermann Kienzl, Stefan Grossmann (who subsequently edited the speeches delivered at that time),[19] the German Bohemian writer Dr. H. Ulmann, who drew attention to the dire situation of the Germans in Bohemia, and Professor Alois Brandl, who spoke about the threat to German South Tyrol. There were also addresses by the Professors Heinrich Herkner[20] and Werner Sombart.

[15]*Frankfurter Zeitung,* Nov. 24, first morning ed., M. Weber.
[16]*Voss. Zeitung,* Nov. 18, Redlich, "Demokratische Weltpolitik."
[17]*Ibid.,* "Deutschland . . . und die Nationalversammlung."
[18]*Grossdeutsch oder Kleindeutsch.* Reden über den Anschluss . . . Nachwort von Dr. H. Triepel, 1919, Vorwort von St. Grossmann, pp. 5-8.
[19]*Ibid.,* Grossmann, pp. 14-17.
[20]*Ibid.,* Herkner, pp. 9-13.

The presence of Konrad Hänisch, Prussian minister of education, at the assembly was quite significant, though he disclaimed speaking officially for the German government. He voiced the hope that "for you [Austrians] over there, as well as for us over here, the old Schleswig Holstein slogan known to you all will now be valid for all time: 'Up ewig ungedeelt!' 'For ever undivided!' "[21]

The last speaker was the noted economic historian Werner Sombart. He expressed the opinion that of all the important events which characterized "our era," the union of the German Austrians with the Germans of the Reich was the most significant one. It was "meaningful" that the German people were attaining union, but especially so since it "comes about in the wake of a social revolution," and adopts truly popular forms, "without any undesirable admixture of too much capitalism and imperialism." Through the German Austrian movement "a patriotic tone," which would otherwise be lacking, "is carried into the social revolution." With the fusion of German Austria and Germany was "performed simultaneously a deed of highest social and utmost national consequence. . . . In this union of socialism with the idea of patriotism the German people manifests its individuality." The German people may draw from this union "courage and confidence" at a moment when "a revengeful, unchivalrous enemy is beating Germany to the ground and into the dust." Under these circumstances the prospect of fusion "gives us consolation and strength."[22]

Sombart's speech, while praising the union of socialism and nationalism, revealed the dominance of the latter. Nationalism took socialism in tow. In conclusion, the assembly finally adopted the resolution that a committee be established to propagandize the Great German concept.

The speeches delivered at the assembly in the Berliner Hochschule für Musik in the very aftermath of the Austrian Anschluss resolution were redolent of the heady atmosphere of national excitement and enthusiasm. They revealed the realization that a moment of great national opportunity had arrived. The perorations disclosed both fear that the Entente

[21]*Ibid.,* Hänisch, pp. 18-21.
[22]*Ibid.,* Sombart, pp. 29-31. Sombart's later endorsement of extreme German nationalism in its National Socialist variety was clearly foreshadowed in this speech.

might prevent Germany from reaping the national harvest and hope that Germany might, by acquiring Austria, balance the anticipated "terrible amputations." Thus, in spite of everything, war might still have brought significant gains.

German Austria's eagerness to unite with Germany the moment the war ended and republics were proclaimed in both countries found the German people on the whole receptive, though German authorities, in view of the shattering effect of war, defeat, and revolution, numb and devoid of initiative. An exception perhaps was the reaction of state governments such as those of Saxony and Bavaria which responded promptly to the Austrian Anschluss resolution of November 12 with a declaration of their own in favor of the union. But the revolutionary Bavarian government linked this proclamation with a strong dose of radical federalist thought, breaking a lance for a confederation of the "United States of Germany." Similarly, the program of the Bavarian People's party, rejecting the predominance of any single state in the Reich, asserted: "Berlin must not become Germany and Germany must not become Berlin." At the same time it proclaimed: "We welcome and further most warmly the Anschluss of all German brethren in Bohemia and the German Austrian *Länder* with the German Confederation." Bavaria's love for Austria revealed a distinct dislike and fear of Prussia. Munich clearly hoped that the Anschluss would restore a badly needed balance within Germany.

After the Anschluss resolution of November 12, 1918, the Austrian Cabinet, prepared to move full steam ahead, had lost no time in turning to the German government. On the thirteenth of November, Otto Bauer had sent a telegram to the people's commissar Hugo Haase congratulating him on his new post and notifying him that, in accordance with the wish of the Provisional National Assembly, German Austria "is and must remain a portion of the Great German Republic." He appealed to the German government to "enter into direct negotiations with us about the union of German Austria with the German republic and about participation in lawmaking and administration of the German Reich."[23] In

---

[23]Michaelis and Schrapler, *Ursachen und Folgen* . . . **3:** p. 286, Bauer to Haase, Nov. 13.

conclusion he urged Haase to assist Austria, economically cut off by the new national Slavic states, with coal and food. Austria was suffering "bitterly" from the scarcity of both. "I hope that the old friendly party-political relations which link us together will make it easier to establish a really close permanent union between Germany and German Austria."

In his letter of November 16, Haase replied that the Council of Commissars was prepared

> to talk with you in closest friendship about all questions relating to peace negotiations. We are therefore awaiting the arrival of representatives of German Austria in Berlin. We deeply regret the misery of our brethren in German Austria. We need not assure you that we have every intention of helping you. We shall try to establish immediately . . . whether and in what manner this is possible.[24]

Haase's reply completely avoided the Anschluss question and seemed evasive rather than promising on the subject of food.

Actually the German government had been more negative than Haase let Bauer know. On the previous day, November 15, Haase had confronted the German Cabinet—which was entirely socialist in its make-up—with the request of the German Austrians, "party comrades," for support not only for the delivery of food and coal, but also in the matter of the Anschluss. The minutes of the cabinet read as follows: "In replying, it has been decided to avoid the issue of the Anschluss in view of the general international situation. . . . Scarcity of food is also very pressing with us."[25]

---

[24]*Ibid.*, Haase to Bauer, Nov. 16.

[25]*B.A.*, Akten betr. d. Sitzungen d. Reichsministeriums, Protokolle, Alte Reichskanzlei, Nov. 15, 1918, E 626968. An unusually strong condemnation of the policies of Hugo Haase came from the pen of the historian Theodor Heuss, later president of the German Federal republic, in his biography on *Friedrich Naumann* (1937). This criticism is perhaps more revealing of Heuss' own strong *grossdeutsch* views, and also of the times when it was uttered, than it is a fair evaluation of the difficult position of Haase and, for that matter, of the German Social Democrats and the entire German government in the Anschluss question. Heuss wrote thus: "Hugo Haase, the people's deputy responsible for foreign affairs, was blind to the possibilities and obligations which arose, deaf in regard to the voice of the Austrians who now under socialist leadership demanded the *grossdeutsch* union" (p. 586). On several later occasions Haase spoke out on behalf of the Anschluss with unmistakable clarity.

The position of the German government had little of national heroics in it. It was hardly designed to stir the national emotions and was perhaps unmindful of the grand gesture. Yet given the hostility of the victorious Entente toward Germany and her past ambitions, the German government, still stunned by the avalanche from which the Reich had barely emerged, ignored the Austrian plea for the Anschluss and cold-heartedly declined even the request for food. As a compensation it was willing to reach an agreement with the Austrian government on tactical approaches during peace negotiations — which at that moment seemed still far away.

When von Wedel, officially still the imperial German ambassador in Vienna (a few days later he was appointed the German republic's ambassador to the new German Austrian republic), wrote to the German Foreign Office on November 17, he was probably not yet aware of the decision taken by the German Cabinet on November 15, but his recommendation on German Anschluss policy was equally cautious. Looking farther ahead — in the direction in which the German government was indeed to move during the following months — and convinced of Germany's stakes in the Austrian Anschluss movement, he recommended a modest amount of encouragement through private sources, if not by the government itself. In his opinion, the Austrian Anschluss declaration of November 12 had been "over-hasty."

> I had warned them in vain, suggesting that they leave the question of decision to the Constituent Assembly. . . . I consider a certain reluctance on our part the correct policy; I must, however, raise the question whether our press could not discuss the topic of the Anschluss in a friendly [!] way, which would not obligate us to anything, but would encourage our easily disheartened friends here and weaken the intrigues of the clerics.[26]

The pro-Anschluss movement in Austria should not be allowed to wither away because of German indifference. Wedel wanted Germany to keep the door open to Austria. At a later,

---

[26]*N.A.*, T 120-3270, Akten betr. Beziehungen . . . , Wedel to F.O., Nov. 17, Nr. 1028.

FIG. 2. Dr. Ludo M. Hartmann, 1865-1924. Historian. Austria's ambassador to Germany, 1918-1922.

more opportune moment, after having weathered the storm, the German government could speedily change its course and sail straight toward union.

After the Austrian Anschluss resolution of November 12 had been coldly received in Berlin, the German Austrian authorities had to accommodate themselves temporarily to the next best course, that of establishing a working diplomatic relationship with the Reich. While von Wedel remained as German ambassador in Vienna, the new German Austrian republic had to decide on appointing an envoy of the new state to Berlin. On November 18 the new German cabinet was officially asked whether Professor Ludo Hartmann would be *persona grata* as Austria's envoy. Hartmann, son of the noted German Bohemian poet Moritz Hartmann

—himself a champion of Grossdeutschtum in the Frankfurter Paulskirche of 1848-1849—was a distinguished historian
and known for his Great German orientation. The German
government replied promptly that it was "quite agreeable" to
the appointment.[27]

On November 22 Bauer made the additional request that
Hartmann be permitted to attend the conference of
representatives of the German states which was to open in
Berlin on November 25. This request was likewise granted
and the people's commissar Friedrich Ebert introduced Hartmann on his arrival as a "guest" of the Assembly. Hartmann
countered by remarking that he already felt "in every way a
member of the group." The exchange was revealing of the
different attitudes of Berlin and Vienna toward the union
and its implementation.

Actually, the new Austrian government had made a number of quick diplomatic moves toward Berlin before dispat-
ching Ludo Hartmann as its ambassador to the German
capital. It had first appealed, as mentioned, to the Council of
Commissars in the matter of food supply and support for the
Anschluss. Then on November 15, only three days after the
Anschluss resolution had been passed in Vienna, a member
of the Austrian Staatsrat, Dr. von Langenhahn, arrived in
Berlin. He was to negotiate, as the *Vossische Zeitung* reported,
with the government of the Reich about economic questions
and the inclusion of German Austria.[28] Dr. von Langenhahn
and the experts who accompanied him left Vienna probably

---

[27]*Voss. Zeitung*, Nov. 26, 1918. Ludo M. Hartmann (1865-1924) was both an
historian and educator of note. He was the son of Moritz Hartmann, widely known
revolutionary Austrian poet who had been also deputy to the Paulskirche in
1848-1849. Ludo Hartmann studied history in Vienna and Berlin and became
Privatdozent at the University of Vienna in 1889. A specialist in Italian history, he
also wrote the biography of his great teacher Theodor Mommsen and helped to
found the *Zeitschrift für Sozial-und Wirtschaftsgeschichte*. As an educator he gained
international reputation with the creation of the Vienna Volkschochschulen, called
also Volksheime. Since 1901 a member of the Social Democratic party, he was elected to
the Nationalrat in 1919, but lost his seat the following year. Serving in the crucial
postwar era as Austrian ambassador in Berlin, he resigned from his post after the
Austrian Social Democratic party left the coalition, since he did not want to act as
representative of a Christian Social government (Fuchs, 1949, and St. Bauer, 1926: 3;
pp. 197-208). Hartmann who listed himself as religiously not affiliated
("konfessionslos") was of Jewish background. His father was born a Jew, but in 1838,
when seventeen years old, he adopted Catholicism.

[28]*Voss. Zeitung*, Nov. 16.

either on November 13 or 14. The new republican Austrian government, proceeding with all deliberate speed, must have felt the most urgent need to enlist Germany's help in solving its problems.

A few days later Dr. Ludo Hartmann arrived in Berlin. In a brief address he lashed out at the Austrian opponents of the union with Germany, but assured Germans at the same time that the Anschluss was a "closed book" for German Austria.[29] On November 30 Ludo Hartmann appeared in the German Foreign Office and presented his credentials to the German secretary of state, Wilhelm Solf. Solf remarked on this occasion that the recent resolution of the German Austrian National Assembly had made "a deep impression" in Germany and had "aroused a happy enthusiasm." It represented "the fulfillment of long cherished, though not always loudly expressed wishes" — a reference to the widely noticed silence of the German Foreign Office and the German government in general. The German Austrians were of course "most welcome."[30]

Secretary of State Solf, contrary to the German Cabinet's decision of November 15, no longer avoided the issue of the Anschluss, but rather approved it. He did not refrain from making pledges. But he still expected two German states to be in existence when the peace conference opened its doors. Clearly, the union would have to be postponed until the victorious Western Powers had had full opportunity to examine the question and possibly veto it. Nevertheless, within a fortnight a perceptible shift had taken place in the German government's position.

The feeble response of the German government to the eager Austrian offer for union had caused bitter disappointment in German Austria as well as in Germany. Early in December Dr. Walter Schotte, editor of the journal *Mitteleuropa*, reported to Diego von Bergen, Austrian specialist in the Berlin Foreign Office, that on a recent visit to Vienna he was repeatedly asked why Germany did not want Austria's Anschluss. He had been challenged thus: "You are afraid of the Entente, aren't you? Our Anschluss movement could harm you, couldn't it?" Solf himself commented

[29]*Ibid.*, Nov. 25.
[30]*Ibid.*, Nov. 30.

privately on the "lukewarm" manner in which the Austrian proclamation on the union had been received and the need for making later "amends" for it. The Austrian government, though pretending to understand Germany's cautious and reluctant approach, felt rebuffed and was greatly disillusioned; so were many segments of the German population. The *Deutsche Allgemeine Zeitung* (previously the *Norddeutsche Allgemeine Zeitung*) promptly took notice of Austria's wounded feelings and her "chagrin."[31] Nevertheless, the *Deutsche Allgemeine Zeitung* defended German policy toward Austria: "At present [it] must pay special attention to all declarations of the Entente."

The Pan-German League, on the other hand, insisted on strong support of the Austrian movement for union. On December 7, through an article in the *All-Deutsche Blätter*, entitled "Die Bedrohung des Deutschtums in Österreich," it sharply criticized Haase and Ebert for their timid reaction to Vienna's offer to join the Reich and urged that Austria be welcomed "in word and deed." The more responsible *Vossische Zeitung* likewise rejected a policy based on extreme caution and castigated what it considered mere rationalizations for a timid German policy on the Anschluss. It remarked: "A government which has risen through revolution against the *Obrigkeitsstaat* can base its justification for existence only upon the concept of the people's state, that is, a state which consists of the community of the entire nation." In the view of the *Vossische Zeitung*, a democratic state had the solemn obligation of vigorously pursuing the realization of the Great German concept of the Anschluss.[32] Democracy and nationalism were to march hand in hand, just as in 1848-1849![33] While the Western world set great store by the democratization of Germany and hoped that a more peaceful attitude toward other European nations would automatically result from it, the interpretation of the new "democratic" state, as furnished by many German democrats and Socialists, bode ill for its hopes. It rather promised a more vigorous pursuit of nationally desirable and imperative foreign-policy objectives.

---

[31]*Deutsche Allgemeine Zeitung,* Nov. 18.
[32]*All-Deutsche Blätter,* Dec. 7; *Voss. Zeitung,* Nov. 19, also Nov. 30.
[33]*Ibid.,* Dec. 2, morning ed., Bernhard, "Deutsche Selbstbestimmung."

As far as German Austria was concerned, her very weakness, due to her economic and military vulnerability, in combination with the ideological drive of the ruling Social Democracy and its confidence in a socialist future, produced a certain dynamism, in the eyes of its opponents, recklessness. While the German government heeded the advice of Ambassador von Wedel to follow a policy of restraint in regard to the Anschluss, the Austrian government pursued a more resolute course. It was convinced that, if the movement for union was to get off the ground, both Austria and Germany would have to display bold initiative and unremitting drive. Austria for instance seemed prepared to arrange holding elections for the German Constituent Assembly. Berlin, however, urged Vienna to call off its preparations for the election. Though some members of the German Cabinet were in favor of Austria's participation in the Constituent Assembly, a majority opposed it. In his talk with Count von Wedel on December 1, the Austrian foreign secretary Dr. Bauer expressed his personal disappointment at the decision of the German government and the regret of his "political friends" that German Austria would not take part in the election to the German Assembly, which was set for January 19, 1919.[34] By the end of 1918, the German Cabinet was still divided on this issue, but the adverse majority decision was not challenged.[35]

The Austrians had participated in the Frankfurt Parliament of 1848-1849, though, as it turned out, with few favorable results. Was it likely that success would be theirs in 1919 when they were barred from participation?

The setting of 1918-1919 was of course very different from that of 1848-1849. The dispute between the *grossdeutsch* and *kleindeutsch* orientation, one of the main hindrances to successful unification in those mid-century days, had long vanished. With the dissolution of the Austrian monarchy, both Germans and German Austrians seemed to favor the *grossdeutsch* solution of the German question. In 1848-1849 the unification movement had failed largely because of internal German differences, the dispute between the Austrian Habsburg empire and the Prussian Hohenzollern state. In

---

[34]*N.A.*, T 120-3270, Akten betr. Beziehungen . . . , Wedel to F.O., Dec. 1.
[35]*B.A.*, Nov. 15, E 626968; also Cabinet session of Dec. 31, 1918.

1918-1919 it failed to achieve success because of resistance to the union by the Western Powers, opponents of Germany's aggrandizement, against which they had just finished fighting a long and bitterly contested war.

In view of the mounting Allied pressure against the Anschluss the opposing forces in the impending battle over the union entered the arena with unequal strength. Under these circumstances questions of tactics and strategy were bound to loom large on the side of the weaker party if it was to hope for any success. It was thus hardly surprising that the government of Austria, which was to carry the brunt of the diplomatic struggle during the coming months, gave its full and undivided attention to the problems of the most effective tactics and strategy with which to pursue its course toward union with Germany.

2. THE ANSCHLUSS AND THE DANUBIAN CONFEDERATION. AUSTRIAN TACTICS AND STRATEGY

"My policy is not to reject the idea of a Danubian confederation from the start, but to carry the negotiations
ad absurdum and thus to attain the only alternative still
possible, namely the Anschluss." Otto Bauer

THE basic alternatives for German Austria in 1918-1919
were Anschluss with Germany, union with neighboring
states in a Danubian confederation, or independence. The
latter was the first to be excluded as a genuine option by a
good number of Austrians who claimed that German Austria,
the pitiful remainder of the break-up of the Austro-
Hungarian monarchy, was not economically viable and had
no will for an independent existence.

The project of a Danubian confederation never did
develop beyond the drawing-board stage and actually included several versions with different political contexts.
Some people spoke of a union merely between German-
Austria, Hungary, and Czechoslovakia, which would have
placed the last-named in a hopeless minority position. Others
also included Yugoslavia, Rumania, and even Poland in such
a confederation, an arrangement which would have put the
former ruling peoples into a numerically inferior position.
None of the former oppressed nationalities of the Austro-
Hungarian monarchy was enthusiastic about a new political
structure which threatened to take away their newly won
sovereignty and virtually all were suspicious of the restoration
of the Habsburg empire under a new guise.

The French historian Louis Eisenmann, who had close
connections with the Quai d'Orsay, revealed to Ludo Hartmann, Austria's ambassador in Berlin, that the Danubian
project was by no means a precise and carefully thought-out

119

plan.[1] Nor were those Danubian confederation projects which had been hatched out in Central Europe clearly conceived; none had a sharply drawn political profile. A few spokesmen for the Slavic nations favored the Danubian project in the hope of controlling such an emerging confederation. Some people in Hungary and Austria propagated it for the opposite reason, confident that it might prove to be a device which would help them avoid paying the penalty of defeat, and a means to regain their formerly privileged position in the new political structure.

On December 5, 1918, the Austrian envoy in Budapest, Cnobloch, reported on interviews with Prime Minister Michael Károlyi of Hungary and Dr. Oscar Jászi, minister of nationalities. Károlyi had spoken with the greatest enthusiasm of a Danubian confederation which would consist of portions of the old monarchy, but which would also be joined by the neighboring states. He had raised the question whether German Austria's Anschluss endeavors were genuine or whether they were undertaken for "tactical reasons," to impress some of the new states. He had "expressed the point of view that German Austria's interests would indecate such a confederacy within the framework of which it would automatically obtain cultural and economic hegemony."[2]

Cnobloch had asked the foreign secretary Dr. Bauer for materials relating to the Austrian government's position on the federation project "about which everybody here wants to

---

[1] *A.A.*, Nachlass Brockdorff-Rantzau, 7/5, Anschlussfrage 1918-1919; Hartmann to Bauer on interview with Prof. E. L. Eisenmann, Jan. 21, 1919. Eisenmann, a noted authority on Austrian history, author of the classic *Le Compromis Austro-Hongrois de 1867*, Paris, 1904, served also as consultant and adviser to the Quai d'Orsay. — How great the resistance of the succession states to the Danubian federation project actually was, may be seen from an unprinted article of Professor Eisenmann which he wrote in the spring of 1919. He warned therein not to rush with this plan, since both Czechs and Southslavs might see in it a threat to their new independence. He rather recommended that trade agreements, judicial conventions and transport regulations be concluded between Austria and her Slavic neighbors. A political tie would automatically follow. Thus a notable adviser on Central Europe to the Quai d'Orsay wanted France and the Allies to follow in this matter a rather cautious course, in spite of the obvious need of countering the headlong rush of Austria toward the Anschluss ("Le problème de l'Autriche Allemande," Nachlass Professor Louis Eisenmann's, Paris, 16, 31. Général Délestraint).

[2] *O.S.*, K 913; Re: Ungarn und deutsch-ungarisches Gebiet, Cnobloch to Bauer, Dec. 5, 1918.

know." Dr. Bauer answered his letter, but not before December 23. The Austrian envoy was given to understand that, while the *Ballhausplatz* would not be unwilling to discuss the matter of a Danubian confederation, it did not think that would be a practical solution.[3]

The new democratic government in Budapest, headed by Michael Károlyi, aimed at preserving or restoring the historic integrity of Hungary and establishing the preeminent position of the Magyars in a Danubian confederation. Yet the Austrian socialist government was not receptive to the siren songs from Budapest. It hoped for and worked toward the Anschluss with a democratic and socialist German Reich, propelled toward it as much by German national as by socialist considerations.

Because of her dependence on the West for food, coal, and raw materials, and even for the defense of her threatened borders, German Austria was anxious to establish early diplomatic contact with the Entente. Still, by the end of 1918 no French envoy had yet arrived in Vienna, and none was to come until late March, 1919. Talks with the French, however, were carried on at that time on neutral ground in Switzerland. Both Paris and Vienna were interested in maintaining informal contact with each other, Paris to impress the Austrians with France's determined opposition to both Anschluss and Bolshevism, Austria to plead for food and raw materials from France and her East Central European allies. On December 24 Dr. Bauer, in a secret telegram to Baron Haupt who served as Austria's envoy in Berne, instructed him to continue his negotiations with representatives of the French government. Bauer's remarks paralleled those in his letter of the previous day to the Austrian envoy Cnobloch in Budapest. Haupt should make clear to his correspondents

> that German Austria was grateful for every concrete proposal relating to the formation of a federal state in the territories of the former monarchy and would examine each proposition in good faith, seriously and conscientiously. A mere customs union, however, could by no means be considered a solution likely to satisfy the interests of the participating states. As long as other national states reject the formation of a confederate

---

[3]*Ibid.*, Bauer to Cnobloch, Dec. 23, 1918.

structure, or concede it only under conditions incompatible with the existence of German Austria as a sovereign state, Austria must claim liberty for herself to seek the union which she needs to survive and cannot find anywhere else—the union with the German Reich.[4]

The line of policy which Dr. Bauer pursued toward the Entente, and the French in particular, was thus to stress Austria's absolute need for a union with a large state or combination of states, a Danubian confederation or, should that fail, with Germany. The possibility of the independent existence of Austria was definitely excluded.

It was only for tactical reasons, Bauer continued, that Berlin had shown reserve in this matter, to avoid the impression of being moved by expansionism and lust for conquest. The ruling circles in Berlin, however, were of the opinion that these considerations did not apply to German Austria:

> On our part the Anschluss must be rather resolutely demanded. The attitude of the Austrian envoy in Berlin is designed to persuade government circles in Berlin that too great a reserve on their part is likely to cool the ardor of the German-Austrian population, dampen its enthusiasm and defeat the Anschluss movement.

Writing a few days later, on December 31, 1918, Baron Haupt reported from Berne about the French Embassy's great interest in the Danubian federation project and also about a discussion on the Anschluss question which he had had with a confidant of the French government on December 29. He had pointed out that, without the guarantee of a Danubian confederation, German Austria would have no choice but the Anschluss with Germany.

> [His French informant] now suddenly made a surprising *volte face*. He asserted that France detested everything that strengthened Germany, but would make no objection to an Anschluss of German-Austria . . . *For every gain which Germany drew from it, she would lose out in other areas. Of course, German Austria, along with Germany, would have to bear the entire burden of the peace terms which would be imposed upon the latter. He was con-*

---

[4]*Ibid.*, K 109, Anschlussfrage, Bauer to Haupt, Dec. 24, 1918, pp. 33-34; also de Vaux to Bauer, Dec. 27, pp. 44-45; Bauer to Haupt, Dec. 29.

vinced that this would entail the economic ruin of German Austria and would therefore advise us not to pose any conditions for the entrance into the Danubian Confederation, since the Entente could not fulfill them, and to trust its word.[5] [Italics mine, A.D.L.]

Haupt had the impression that all this was "only designed to intimidate us and push us unconditionally into a confederation."

In spite of his perception, Haupt was seemingly puzzled by the rapidly shifting French line. He found it "impossible to discern a definite trend" in the Entente's policy toward Austria; he saw only "chaos and confusion" and "contrary tendencies" in the policy of the Western Powers. "In this state of affairs it would be premature to show one's cards." Though he considered the Entente's policy "bluff," he would nevertheless suggest proceeding in the matter of the Anschluss with Germany with "greatest restraint"; one should first resort to negotiations with Czechoslovakia about a guarantee of national equality for the German minorities and about the possible formation of an economic union in the Danubian area. This was the very view which had been expressed only a few days earlier, on December 28, by Baron de Vaux, also of the Austrian delegation in Berne, and it may have influenced Dr. Bauer. The Austrian delegation in Berne played an important role in shaping, if not Austrian policy, at least the Austrian government's tactical decisions on the Anschluss question.

Neither Baron de Vaux nor Haupt was suggesting that the Anschluss be permanently abandoned, but, considering the moment inopportune, they proposed that it temporarily be shelved. Their hope, however, that a renunciation of the Anschluss would bring in return, through intervention of the Entente, constitutional and national concessions for the German minorities of Czechoslovakia remained unfulfilled. German Austria, as events were to prove, was in no bargaining position. In the end she had no choice but to accept the prohibition of the Anschluss without obtaining any promises in return. Her attempt to pose as champion for the German minorities of Czechoslovakia was simply ignored by Prague as well as by the Peace Conference.

---

[5]*Ibid.*, Haupt to Bauer, Dec. 31, 216-220.

In 1918-1919 Dr. Bauer never ceased to ask for national self-determination for the Germans of Czechoslovakia, just as for the people of German Austria proper. But he did not propose the union of the German-inhabited regions of Czechoslovakia either with Germany or the German Austrian republic. In view of the Entente's position he considered the first-named "solution" academic; the latter was geographically impossible. But he hoped to see the over-throw of the bourgeois government in Prague or, failing this, to find in due time allies among the Czech Social Democrats and ethnic minority groups who would help form at least a confederate structure of the Czechoslovakian state.

The "posture of protest," however, which Bauer recom-mended to both German Austria and the Sudeten Germans was not to bring any positive results either. While the Austrian Embassy in Berne considered Dr. Bauer's tactics too rigid, Dr. Hartmann, Austria's envoy in Berlin, considered them too yielding. In early January, 1919, Bauer expressed to Hartmann—tongue in cheek, no doubt—the hope that he would take advantage of his visit to Switzerland (where he was meeting a French go-between) to contact the Austrian envoy in Berne, since the latter represented "a point of view which is contrary to yours." [6]

Bauer's own position on the Anschluss lay somewhere in between the course recommended by the Austrian delegation in Berne and that of Ludo Hartmann in Berlin—the former a cautious, if not defeatist policy, the latter an aggressive one. In the course of events Bauer was repeatedly called upon to restrain his ambassador to Germany, yet he himself was determined to bring about a union with Germany and con-sidered the admonitions from Berne to soft-pedal the An-schluss ill-advised. At the same time he considered the creation of a Danubian confederation not only less desirable, but utterly hopeless. In the prewar period he had supported the preservation of the Dual Monarchy; now he was opposed to its revival in any form—especially at the expense of sacrificing the Anschluss with Germany.

The early January correspondence between Otto Bauer and Ludo Hartmann revealed their sharp tactical differences.

---

[6]*Ibid.,* K 261, "Instruktionen," Jan. 1919; Hartmann to Bauer, Jan. 24, 1919, 245-247.

Hartmann, in an unusually frank and uninhibited manner, pounced on Bauer's recent article in the *Arbeiter-Zeitung* (December 25) on the Anschluss and the Danubian confederation:

> I can't resist observing that certain expressions in your article in the *Arbeiter-Zeitung* (which are identical with the views in the printed Memorandum which was kindly sent to me) mislead many into believing that you do not completely reject such a customs union [Danubian confederation] in spite of the strong arguments which you adduce against it. I suspect that these expressions purport to explain diplomatically Austria's love for peace and her willingness to discuss every possible suggestion.

Though Hartmann understood that Dr. Bauer's "softness" had only tactical motivation, he feared that the Austrian government's tactics might have undesirable—perhaps, in regard to the union, fatal—side-effects.

In reply, Dr. Bauer wrote Ludo Hartmann a letter dated January 3, 1919, which is one of the most concise summaries of the Austrian government's position on the Anschluss.[7] He admitted that the problem of the Anschluss had become the subject of a "very stormy discussion" in Austria. The only correct course was to assert that Austria was ready at any time to negotiate a Danubian confederation. "My policy therefore is not to reject from the start the idea of a Danubian confederation, but to carry the negotiations *ad absurdum*."

Dr. Bauer did never conceal his personal preference of the Anschluss over the confederation; he actually opposed confederation as much as many of the former Slavic inhabitants of the Dual Monarchy. Though convinced that the confederation would be a stillborn project, he feigned interest in it in order to strengthen Austria's bargaining position. He was willing to meet the Entente halfway and to enter into an academic discussion of a project cherished by many in the West. By making a display of being reasonable, he would disarm the Western Powers. Having accepted the concept of a federation and the need of the small states of Central

---

[7]*Ibid.*, K 261, I Deutschland (Anschluss), Bauer to Hartmann, Jan. 3, 1919, 102-105.

Europe, including the Austrian republic, to pool their resources for the purpose of economic survival and improvement, he was counting on the failure of this scheme and prepared the ground for the union of Austria with Germany. He was aware of the determined opposition to the Anschluss, especially in France and among many circles of the West, of the objections to it in Austria herself, and of the lukewarm attitude of many in Germany. But he perceived that in the midst of general uncertainty a resolute will and determined propaganda on the part of the Austrian government and of the Austrian and German friends of the union might have a decisive impact.

While these tactics were not likely to speed the union, an attempt to force a decision would probably mean risking the loss of German South Tyrol and German Bohemia. Bauer feared that the Entente would penalize Austria for the attempt to make the Anschluss a *fait accompli* by wresting these regions from her in the peace treaty. Acceptance in principle, of a Danubian confederation at least, would weaken the internal Austrian opposition as well as the opposition abroad. Time would work in favor of the Anschluss by bringing about favorable political changes in the succession states and the further disarmament of the Entente Powers. As he wrote to Hartmann, "I therefore request that in your activities in Berlin—which on the whole correspond to my intentions—you too show a little more restraint." Toward the German foreign secretary Count Brockdorff-Rantzau "one ought, of course, to cling steadfastly to the Anschluss as the ultimate Austrian objective. The German government should not be misled by Austria's tactical necessities, [that is, by our] considering other alternatives still open."

But Hartmann's reply of January 7 continued to criticize Bauer's tactical approach. Alluding to a contrary remark made by Bauer, Hartmann held that Brockdorff-Rantzau himself had no fear of a "connection" between the left bank of the Rhine and German Austria. Unlike Bauer, Hartmann also held that "[time] is not on our side." He did not know how he should "impose restraints" upon his activities in Berlin. Rebuffed and clearly offended, he hinted at his readiness to resign; he did not wish "to stand in the way," if

Dr. Bauer wished to "change the direction of the policy so far pursued by us."[8]

Bauer replied on January 13, claiming that Dr. Hartmann did not sufficiently differentiate between the official government attitude and public opinion as expressed by political parties and the press. "Your propagandistic activity in Berlin, which is primarily directed at influencing public opinion, has my full approval." But the Austrian government was in a different position, it could simply be compelled to carry on negotiations concerning the Danubian confederation if such negotiations were desired by the Entente.[9]

The internal dissension among the Entente Powers and the radical social movement in Europe were of the greatest significance for the entire continent, Bauer continued, and were likely to make radical changes in the future balance of power. This would make it possible for Austria to bring about the Anschluss "without having to pay an excessive price for it." Since, however, there were currently no such possibilities, he held the correct course to be strengthening the desire for the Anschluss on both sides of the border, "while officially procrastinating and awaiting the favorable moment." Only "tactical differences," Bauer claimed, lay between him and Dr. Hartmann.

The differences were substantial, nevertheless. Dr. Bauer, while working indefatigably toward the Anschluss, was intellectually resigned to the possibility of having to shelve it for a more "favorable moment." Hartmann, however, was too impatient to wait. Yet he could continue serving at the Berlin post, since he apparently hoped that a more auspicious moment might arise on the political horizon earlier than Dr. Bauer held possible.

From the dialogues between Dr. Bauer and Baron Haupt of the Embassy in Berne on one side, and Dr. Bauer and Dr. Hartmann, Austria's ambassador in Berlin, on the other, there emerged a clearer line of strategy and tactics on the Anschluss question which guided Austrian foreign policy until July, 1919, when Dr. Bauer resigned and the more flexible and pragmatic chancellor Dr. Karl Renner took charge also of the Austrian Foreign Ministry.

---

[8]*Ibid.*, Hartmann to Bauer, Jan. 7, pp. 102-109.
[9]*Ibid.*, Bauer to Hartmann, Jan. 13, pp. 111-114.

Tactical problems of the Anschluss policy figured large in Dr. Bauer's mind in regard not only to the Western Powers, but also to Germany. The Austrian foreign secretary was well aware of the force the Entente could bring to bear against both Germany and Austria. Yet he was bent on minimizing Germany's apparent fears of Entente policies. A stronger German initiative in the Anschluss question seemed to him imperative if the flame of Austrian desire for union was not to flicker out. "The opponents of the Anschluss in Austria were strengthened," he warned the German ambassador Wedel, because of the German government's cool and reluctant attitude toward the Anschluss. As the latter reported,

> he [Bauer] certainly understood why Germany was cautious and was leaving it to German Austria to bring about the Anschluss. He held, however, that we were entertaining illusions if we hoped thus to obtain more favorable peace terms. The Entente would force the worst possible peace terms upon us anyway, so that further escalation would no longer be possible. If we want to impose our will, we must resolutely put forth demands.[10]

Bauer's tactics toward Germany were clearly outlined. In his dealings with the German government and Wedel, he pressed for more initiative and a bolder course on the part of the German government.

While the Austrian government itself showed much greater determination, Bauer feared that any still more daring course would be merely self-defeating and harm rather than benefit the cause of the Anschluss. A few years later, writing on the events of these years, he attempted to justify his own resolute but still cautious policy against those critics who favored a policy of *fait accompli* in regard to the Anschluss. It appeared, Bauer wrote of the period immediately after November 12, "improbable" that the lost war would end with a significant increase of the population of the German Reich.[11] The Austrian government was also concerned about the territorial integrity of what remained of German Austria; it feared that the actual Anschluss would

---

[10]*N.A.*, T 120-3270, Wedel to Berlin, Dec. 5, 1918.
[11]Bauer, 1923: p. 141.

adversely influence the Peace Conference in regard to the fate of German South Tyrol, Carinthia, Lower Styria, and the districts of Znaim and the Bohemian Forest. Germany likewise was fearful that pressing for the Anschluss might entail territorial losses for the Reich, not to mention German Austria.

The Austrian government had even suspected that France would go further; that prior to the signing of the peace treaty, "at the moment we were actually attempting to effect the Anschluss, [France] would instigate the Czechs and Yugoslavs to occupy German Austrian territory and thus involve us in a war with our neighbors." Thus it appeared "much too risky to carry out the union with one stroke. We had to move step by step."

3. THE NEW GERMAN REPUBLIC AND THE UNION WITH AUSTRIA. WARNING VOICES

"Decisive factors favor at least a delay of such a solution [Anschluss] . . . . [The Entente's] suspicion in regard to the genuineness of the new [German] spirit has not yet been overcome." F. W. Foerster

AFTER the November Revolution swept Germany and Austria, the Socialists were in a dominant position in both republics. In Austria they also controlled the office of the foreign secretary. The conduct of the foreign policy of the new German Austrian republic lay until July 1919 in the hands of Dr. Otto Bauer, and thereafter in those of Dr. Karl Renner. In Germany, however, the new Social Democratic government entrusted the important Office of Foreign Affairs to a professional, thus emphasizing partly its own inexperience in foreign policy and partly its unwillingness to shoulder directly the major responsibility for liquidating the war and accepting the new peace treaty.

In Germany, Dr. Wilhelm Solf became foreign secretary in the last short-lived imperial Cabinet of the liberal chancellor Prince Max of Baden on October 4, 1918, when he was confronted with the thankless task of concluding the armistice negotiations. After the proclamation of the republic, he remained in this post at the wish of the Ebert-Scheidemann government,[1] in spite of his wartime pronouncements in support of the expansion of imperial Germany. In late December, 1918, however, he was replaced by Count Ulrich von Brockdorff-Rantzau. The latter was no less nationalist in outlook, though in the past he had been more critical of the Kaiser and imperial Germany's wartime policies. Though hardly a genuine democrat, he introduced himself to the

---

[1]*Frankfurter Zeitung*, Nov. 28, second morning ed., "Auswärtiges Amt. Konflikt zwischen Solf und den Unabhängigen."

German people as a "democratic" count.[2] Of the two German secretaries, Brockdorff-Rantzau was the stronger character and also the more imperious nature.

The same policy of trusting the expertise of the men who had served in the imperial Foreign Office also moved the Majority Socialists in their attitude to the leaders of the imperial German army. The new German cabinet failed from the very beginning to give the new political structure a solid democratic foundation and especially to create a loyal army, dedicated to the new republic and the democratic order. The Allies in turn suspected that the republic was built on quicksand and feared the expansion, under the guise of national self-determination, of a still militaristic Germany into adjoining territories and disputed regions.

In the cabinet session of November 18, Friedrich Ebert, soon to become the first president of the republic and the first Social Democrat to occupy so high a post, informed the other cabinet members that "Hindenburg has pledged his word of honor to support the new government. So has Groener. Therefore, there is no real reason to undermine Hindenburg's position."[3] The Council of Commissars accepted this view. Such confidence on the part of Germany's new republican and "revolutionary" leaders in the "loyalty" of the old reactionary, nationalistic and militaristic cliques which had served the Kaiser is virtually without parallel in the history of revolutions.

The imperial generals who remained in the saddle were not convinced republicans and democrats; nor were they willing to make peace with the new Europe. Only a few months later General Groener expressed his confidence in an early recovery of Alsace-Lorraine, banking heavily on American-French differences.

Dr. Wilhelm Solf, as mentioned, had been retained as foreign minister by the new republican and Socialist German Cabinet. But when during the month of November he dared to attack Bavarian separatism and Kurt Eisner's leadership in Munich and questioned the integrity of Hugo Haase, people's commissar and prominent leader of the Indepen-

---

[2] Holborn, Craig and Gilbert, eds., *Diplomats 1919-1939* 1: p. 133, also p. 132, judged Brockdorff-Rantzau correctly as having been "no genuine democrat."
[3] *B.A.,* Reichskanzlei, Cabinet session, Nov. 18, 1918, E 626985.

dents, he incurred the hostility of the Independents, coalition partners of the Majority Socialists.[4] Both the Bavarian prime minister Kurt Eisner[5] and the noted socialist theoretician Karl Kautsky, also an Independent and recently appointed undersecretary of the Foreign Office, came out in criticism of that department and demanded that the government rid itself of any man with a questionable record. The pacifist point of view could not be well advanced by "war agitators [Kriegshetzer]." [6] Nor did the Western Powers have much confidence in Solf. The Times of London spoke openly of "Allied distrust of Solf." [7] Past politics aside, there seemed to be increasing doubt that Solf was equal to his task.[8]

Yet not until December did the Cabinet extend feelers to Brockdorff-Rantzau, ambassador in Copenhagen, to ascertain whether he would be available as secretary of state. On December 13 it received his confidential reply, containing his acceptance and listing not only his program but also a number of "conditions" which they preferred to ignore. At the same time the Cabinet decided to accept Secretary of State Solf's letter of resignation.

Though Solf had served as minister of the republic for only five weeks, he represented the link between the empire and the republic, between the imperial and the republican

---

[4]Ibid. Hugo Haase had first been thought of as the leading candidate for the Foreign Office post. He in turn opposed Solf from the outset, as the Cabinet sessions reveal.

[5]Eisner considered Solf "the personification of prerevolutionary debits" (Scheidemann, 1921: p. 222).

[6]Shortly thereafter Karl Kautsky attacked Solf in the Freiheit, the main organ of the Independents (Nov. 28, 1918). For a view of Solf different from that of his contemporary opponents, see H. Holborn, Craig and Gilbert, Diplomats 1919-1939, pp. 130-131. Holborn considered Solf a liberal and a democrat and was rather critical of the Independents (p. 131). See also the laudatory biography by von Vietsch, 1961.

[7]Times, London, Nov. 22, 1918; also Dec. 16, "Through German Eyes." — In 1913, in an address in the Reichstag, which he partly repeated in an article on "German colonial policy," written in 1915 (Modern Germany in relation to the Great War, 1916), Solf spoke of "peoples in the German colonies as being in some cases far beneath us," as "ignorant" and "lazy"; "they must be tamed and enlightened." Even after it became obvious that the Council of Commissars, in view of Solf's differences with the Independents, would drop him from the post as foreign secretary, he wanted to remain as colonial secretary, apparently believing that the colonies would be returned to Germany (Cabinet session, Dec. 31).!

[8]Frankfurter Zeitung, first morning ed., Dec. 17, 1918, "Der Rücktritt Solfs."

foreign policy of the Reich. His policy concerning the Anschluss had been cautious rather than activist, as would probably have been the policy of any other German foreign secretary given those times and circumstances. His removal from the Cabinet came, as mentioned, as a result of strong pressure from the Independents whose break with the Majority Socialists was only a few weeks away. Yet the mistrust and hostility which Solf aroused among the Independents were caused more by his recent criticism of Bavarian socialist separatism and his past annexationist leanings than by a difference of opinion over the strategy and tactics posed by the problem of Austria's union with Germany. Many of the prominent leaders of the Independents supported the Anschluss, though in a lukewarm manner.

Ulrich von Brockdorff-Rantzau's career had included diplomatic service in St. Petersburg at the turn of the century. Later in Vienna he was first secretary, then consul of the German Legation (1901-1905). As consul general he served also in Budapest, only to return to the Embassy in Vienna. Such political views which he then expressed reveal him as a disciple of Bismarck in pleading for good relations with Russia. But privately he voiced the fear that an Austro-Russian rapprochement would lessen Austria's dependence on Germany, a dependence which he wished to preserve. Along with many other German and non-German contemporaries he feared Austria's impending disintegration; he admonished the German authorities not to accelerate Austria's decline, but rather to preserve the monarchy. Since 1912 he served as German ambassador in Copenhagen which proclaimed its neutrality when war broke out; in 1918 he was repeatedly mentioned as a possible candidate for the post of chancellor.

A believer in Germany's Weltpolitik and the power of her military might, he was as late as July, 1918, prepared to "annihilate" England and to "dictate" peace.[9] During the following year, as foreign minister of republican Germany, however, he was solemnly and with deep moral indignation to protest "dictation" by the West, the *Gewaltfrieden* which the Entente was going to impose on the German nation.

---

[9]*A.A.,* Nachlass Brockdorff-Rantzau's, 6/1, July 18, 1918, H 233269/270.

On March 27, 1918, Brockdorff-Rantzau suggested that Emperor William II head the movement toward democratization and found a "people's empire." [10] His criticism of the Kaiser's policy during the years of the war was interpreted by the German socialist leaders as an assurance of his "democratic" convictions.

Brockdorff-Rantzau entertained the highest conceptions both of his own and his nation's destinies. His lofty notion of a peace worthy of the German nation was indistinguishable from that of any nationalistic and imperialist-minded German politician of the Wilhelmian epoch, except perhaps that he wanted to exclude Army leaders from making foreign policy.[11] He considered General Groener's idea, expressed in 1919, that it might be possible to break up the wartime alliance of the Western Powers against Germany an illusion.[12] Since becoming foreign minister, he vigorously raised the Anschluss question.

German public opinion, though shocked by the outcome of the war, began gradually to recover and to become more assertive about the future peace treaty and the demand for the Anschluss. Still, there were individual Germans who opposed the union policy as hopeless and as one more likely to harm than to help the German people. Among them were a few socialist Independents, bent on avoiding a policy of nationalist aggrandizement, likely to alienate the Entente, and rather proposing to strengthen the foundations for a democratic and socialist transformation. Then there was the revolutionary communist Left, more interested in an all-German, even European-wide, social revolution than in the fulfillment of the goals of the German national revolution of 1848-1849, and, on the opposite pole, some East German Junkers, fearful that the threatening loss of German possessions in the East would outweigh any advantages to be accrued from the union with Austria.

---

[10]*Ibid.*

[11]*A.A.*, Nachlass Brockdorff-Rantzau's, Presseangelegenheiten 7/1, Rantzau Jan. 21, 1919; see also Nachl   Versailles I 8/7 H234094 f.: Stenogr. Aufzeichnung uber eine Unterredung mit General Groener. Differences between Brockdorff-Rantzau and Groener and later also General von Seeckt continued during the year 1919 and beyond; see especially the cabinet session of April 24, 1919 (Craig, 1964: pp. 365-366) which Groener attended.

[12]*A.A.*, Nachlass Brockdorff-Rantzau's, March 31, 1919.

Finally, some voices were raised against the Anschluss in Bavaria. Among those who foresaw the most adverse foreign reactions to the union with Austria and also opposed it on domestic grounds was Professor F. W. Foerster, Bavarian envoy in Switzerland. On the other hand, in Bavaria, where a separatist revolt was rampant against Germany's domination by Prussia which was held responsible for the defeat suffered by all of Germany, the concept of the Anschluss was curiously coupled with a proposal for the breakup of Germany. Some of the projects propagated in Catholic Bavaria supported the concept of union with a portion only of Germany, a largely Catholic Germany, which of course presupposed a split of the Reich. Its authors were Heinrich Held,[13] leader of the Bavarian People's party, and Dr. Georg Heim, a prominent figure in Bavaria's political and economic life. Professor Foerster's voice represented progressive forces anxious to realign Germany with the West on democratic and pacific lines rather than alienate it through the Anschluss. Held and Dr. Heim spoke for conservative Catholic-Bavarian groups some of which toyed with the idea of breaking up Germany, hoping to enlist the support of the Entente Powers for this scheme. Dr. Heim warned against the Anschluss of an undiminished Reich with German Austria. What he actually favored in December, 1918, was the union of German Austria with a German rump state.

After the proclamation of the German republic, the emergence of a Bavarian People's republic and the passing of the Austrian Anschluss resolution by the National Assembly only a few days elapsed before both the socialist Bavarian government and the Bavarian People's party, on November 15, demanded the incorporation of German Austria. The desire to link up with neighboring Austria, as well as the separatist mood in regard to Berlin, continued in Bavarian circles beyond the crisis days of late October and early November, being fed by national, socialist, and Catholic currents. On December 1, 1918, Dr. Heim published an article in the *Bayerischer Kurier*, offering a solution to the German Austrian problem which was quite at variance with the declared policy of the Bavarian government. Examining the

---

[13]Schwend, 1954: p. 60f.

urgent problem of German Austria's future relationship with the new Germany, he was convinced that "in no circumstances" would the Entente permit the union of ten million German Austrians with even a substantially reduced Germany. He envisioned and recommended a union between German Austria—or parts of it—with Bavaria, other South German states, and West Germany as far as the Elbe River. "Bavaria must either remain within the framework of the old Reich, renouncing this splendid prospect; or it must carry out this Anschluss. In my opinion, this solution is the only possible one." Such doubts as might arise that Austria-Bavaria would have no access to the sea and insufficient iron ore and coal could be resolved only "by including the old Rhenish confederacy, Hanover, West Germany as far as the Elbe and South Germany with Austria."[14] The prerequisite of such a "union" and "splendid prospect," as contemplated by Dr. Heim, was, of course, a split of the Reich from top to bottom.

Such a union between Bavaria and Austria, and possibly other German states, was anathema to most Germans, whether they were markedly national-minded or not. Dr. Heim's scheme itself, however, was expressive of strong anti-Prussian, even separatist tendencies, exacerbated by Germany's defeat. These trends found encouragement in some French and English circles which set their hopes upon some sort of Danubian confederation which would extend into Southern Germany.

Another German voice raised in warning against immediate Anschluss was as mentioned that of the noted liberal and pacifist Professor Friedrich Wilhelm Foerster, Bavarian ambassador in Berne, then the meeting ground of international diplomacy. He pointed out the determined opposition of the Entente to the union; German support for the Anschluss movement would only deepen the suspicion and fear of Germany in the West. In late 1918 and early 1919 Foerster repeatedly reminded the Bavarian premier Kurt Eisner of the importance of repudiating Germany's military past, openly admitting her war guilt and creating an atmosphere of confidence for dealing effectively with the Western Powers. On November 21 he wrote to Eisner from

---

[14]*Bayerischer Kurier*, Dec. 1, 1918.

Berne, mentioning the "confidence [placed] most especially upon Bavaria," and disclosing that his main activity in the Swiss capital consisted of dispelling the vast suspicion against the new Germany which continued to thrive.[15]

The crisis in 1918 and 1919 was to a large extent a crisis in confidence, the result of decades of hostility deepened during a long and bitter war. On January 23, after a talk with Hjalmar Branting, the leader of the Social Democrats of neutral Sweden, Eisner reported his impressions to a session of the Bavarian cabinet; "We Germans do not enjoy international confidence."[16] The Entente's skepticism that the German "revolution" had conclusively wrested power from the old ruling groups and militaristic circles was well warranted, as contemporary and later events were to prove. Upon Bavaria proper, however, the Western Powers looked with relative favor. Traditionally they had greater confidence in the particularist, more easy-going Catholic Germans of the South. They also seemed persuaded that the new Bavarian government was anti-militaristic and anti-Prussian. In France especially, hopes were entertained that a split of the South from the rest of Germany was not impossible and might prove beneficial.

In 1918, when Foerster spoke out on the Austrian question and the Anschluss, he was no newcomer to Austrian problems. He had taught at the University of Vienna before 1914 and had written a brochure, *Das Österreichische Problem*, which was published during the war, in 1916. He had criticized therein a Pan-German Austrian who desired the break-up of the Austrian empire. Foerster, a South German and critical of Bismarck and his work, nevertheless agreed with the great chancellor in believing that a "Slavic-Germanic Austria," a "reconciliation" of the Slavs with the Germans in Austria, was in Germany's interests. Such a reconciliation would be "a stronger protection against the Russian and Pan-Slavic danger than any military defense."[17] German Austrians would render Germandom a greater service if they "thoroughly divest themselves of German cultural arrogance and all German verbiage with its uncultivated . . . derogatory

[15]*G.A.*, Der Anschluss, MA 103022, Foerster to Eisner, Nov. 21, 1918.
[16]*Ibid.*, Eisner, Cabinet session, Jan. 23, 1919.
[17]Foerster, 1916; p. 7.

attitude toward the Slavic peoples." Though not uncritical of
the non-German peoples in the Austrian monarchy, Foerster
held that their national one-sidedness merely reflected undesirable German habits. He appealed to the German
Austrians to dedicate themselves unreservedly to the
"Austrian idea." [18] They should avoid improper identification with the Reich and desist from singing the *Wacht am
Rhein*. This made them suspect that in their heart they
belonged more to Germany than to Austria. . . . This injures
their political position in the Danubian realm." [19]

These prewar views make Foerster's main lines of thought
on the Austrian problem and its relation to Germany stand
out clearly. Though at the war's end the political situation in
Central Europe had radically changed, Foerster's opposition
to the Anschluss, his conviction of the continued importance
of the historic and cultural role of German Austrians, and his
fear of the excesses of German nationalism correspond fully
to his earlier views.

The new Bavarian government under Eisner's leadership
had promptly made an early public declaration in favor of a
federal union between German Austria and Germany. On
November 26, at the conference of the federal states, Eisner
had come out for the Anschluss of German Austria.[20] To
discount rumors of Bavarian separatism under his leadership, Eisner, after admitting that in Bavaria and elsewhere
there was "tremendous resentment against Berlin" for having
unleashed the world war, assured the assembly: "We want the
unity of the Reich, including German Austria."

It was the more startling that Professor Foerster dared
openly to raise serious questions about the Anschluss.

Not as ambassador, but as Professor Foerster who has seriously
studied the Austrian and Southeast European questions, do I
allow myself the following open discussion: as convincing as
such a union is from many points of view and as weighty as
may be the arguments advanced in its behalf, nevertheless,

---

[18]*Ibid.*, pp. 7, 34.
[19]*Ibid.*, p. 30.
[20]*Vorwärts*, Nov. 27, 1918.

very decisive factors still favor at least a delay of such a solution to this question, especially in view of the position which Entente circles take toward it.[21]

The hostility which has been aroused in the Entente against Germany has by no means yet been quenched, and suspicion in regard to the genuineness of the new German spirit has not yet been overcome. For this reason the Entente is emphatically opposed to an aggrandizement of Germany at this time, believing that it would strengthen the old spirit and result in a growth of the Pan-German outlook.

Should a union suddenly take place, the Entente would probably propose that Germany compensate for this aggrandizement by surrendering the left bank of the Rhine. In the Polish question too, [the Powers were prepared] to disadvantage Germany greatly. It would therefore be very dangerous to decide that question [Anschluss] positively at the very moment when the publication of the terms of the preliminary peace treaty is anxiously awaited.

The economic tradition of German Austria was oriented toward the Southeast; such a centuries-old past cannot be easily annulled.

The German-Slavic economic partnership which rests on this tradition also definitely requires a close political and cultural community.
    The same holds true of the Slavic partner. . . . I also believe that permanent separation of German Austria from its southeastern past does not lie in the true interest of German *Kultur*-work. The old purpose of the southeast German march was to further German cultural might through federation with the Slavic world. New forms must now be found for this federation; one must not accept the present separation as something irreversible. A German Austria dissolving in the German Reich, or even one linked only politically with Germany, could not by any means exercise the influence which would be possible within the framework of a southeastern

---

[21]*G.A.*, Akten d. Minister. d. Äusseren, Anschluss, Foerster MA 103022, "Zur Frage d. Vereinigung von Deutschösterreich mit d. deutschen Republik," p. 39.

federation. Finally, such a confederation would also be of decisive importance for the European peace. All the new Slavic states will perish because of their nouveauté, or will succumb to Bolshevism, or will set themselves mutually afire if they are not firmly tied to an older political culture. This is also the main reason why the Entente, especially England, following the tradition of Grey, favors that confederation. It would therefore be very important for our foreign policy not to run counter to the intentions of the Entente in this respect, at the very moment when we are facing famine and are entirely dependent on the good will of our enemies.

It is by no means certain that later on a federation of intimate nature could not develop between a new southeast Confederacy, including German Austria, and the German republic. German Austria would then serve as a connecting link for a future federation of the German world with the Slavic community.[22]

Professor Foerster's superior, however, Bavaria's prime minister Kurt Eisner, remained favorably disposed toward the Anschluss. On January 21, 1919, he sent the following telegram to Foerster: "I beg you occasionally to clarify publicly that your views on the Anschluss of Austria are your private views and are not identical with my views or those of the Bavarian government." Faced with mounting opposition at home, Eisner identified himself with the strong pro-Anschluss sentiments in Bavaria. Catholic circles in Bavaria welcomed a pro-Austrian and pro-Anschluss position and looked upon it with enthusiasm not only from the religious and national point of view, but also from the local Bavarian and anti-Berlin angle. Also, as a socialist Eisner was closer to the leftist Austrian Social Democrats than to the Majority Social Democrats in Berlin.

In the political atmosphere of the immediate postwar period it was an act of courage by Foerster to dissent publicly not only from the feverishly nationalistic public opinion in Germany, but also from the declared policy of the revolutionary and — where the Austrian question was concerned — national-minded government of Bavaria whose spokesman he was. Yet the arguments he advanced were not

---

[22]Ibid.

merely based upon consideration of the vital interests of the victorious Entente. He was convinced that it was in Germany's very own interests at the war's end not to make excessive and unreasonable claims.

Foerster's views were widely resented in Germany and he became the target of wide-ranging attacks. On January 24, 1919, the leading organ of the majority Socialists, the *Vorwärts*, took him to task for having said that the Anschluss was a "narrowly nationalist" concept, while the Austrian confederation corresponded to the idea of a league of nations. Numerous German and Austrian Socialists rejected the position that, as internationalists and friends of the new socialist world order, it was their duty to refrain from furthering national objectives.

But the most serious attack against Foerster was staged behind the scenes and originated with the German Foreign Office. It feared that his public statements would stiffen French resistance to the union, as "against [the position] of the United States, England, and Italy who will hardly prevent the Anschluss of German Austria with us," and would also arouse new opposition in German Austria. The German undersecretary of state let the Bavarian government know that Foerster's statements "threatened important German interests" and that it would be desirable if the Bavarian press made its opposition to Foerster clear. After vain efforts of the Foreign Office to enlist some noted Germans in a public debate with him, the *Deutsche Allgemeine Zeitung* of January 24, 1919, finally took Foerster to task in an article bearing the title "Deutschland und Österreich." It stated that Germany, while wishing to maintain peaceful relations in Europe, would not abandon German Austria to her ruin; any German diplomat who expressed a contrary view was not only "no diplomat," but "sinned against the nation in an inexcusable manner."

The newspaper called upon the Bavarian government to disavow its envoy in Berne. Kurt Eisner, however, informed the Berlin chargé d'affaires that, though the Munich government did not agree with Foerster, it was more tolerant than its predecessor under the old regime and permitted officials to voice their private opinions in newspapers. But on January 22 the *Neue Zeitung* published Eisner's official disavowal of

Professor Foerster's views on the Anschluss and gave the assurance that the Bavarian prime minister looked upon the union "as one of the most important duties" of his government.

Professor Foerster's warning against the Anschluss cause and ignoring the concerns of the victors and the rest of Europe was an altogether rare, though not unique, phenomenon in Germany. There were a few influential German Socialists, mostly Independents, who, differing from Eisner, also spoke out against what seemed to them a clear case of Germany's expansionism into Austria in disregard of Europe's fears, and at a most inopportune moment.

Baron Haupt, the Austrian envoy in Berne, reporting to Vienna about the Congress of the Second International on Swiss soil in early February, 1919, "regretted" that Professor Foerster's position was strengthened by two eminent leaders of German democratic socialism, the "orthodox" Marxist Karl Kautsky and the leader of "revisionism," Eduard Bernstein. In many respects, these men stood at opposite poles of German Socialism; but they agreed in their opposition to the war and now to the Anschluss. Eduard Bernstein in particular revealed in numerous talks a strong dislike of the Anschluss project. According to Haupt, "he justified this attitude to me by pointing out the psychological necessity of taking the French mentality into consideration. . . . Like Foerster, he advanced against the national point of view the French demands for compensation which had to be expected in this case." [23]

Eduard Bernstein was a courageous individualist who had frequently dared to swim against the stream, as in his early appeal for a revision of the Marxist doctrine and his pacifist challenge to the Social Democratic party which supported Germany's war effort. Once again, he challenged the great majority of his comrades and countrymen on the Anschluss. Bernstein was as opposed to German adventurism in the German Bohemian question as in the German Austrian question. "All violent attempts going beyond the emphasis of law would, in the present world situation, harm none more than us Germans, without benefiting the German Austrians and

---

[23]*O.S.*, K 109, Anschlussfrage, Haupt to Bauer, Feb. 21, pp. 327-330.

German Bohemians in the least." He would not wish to advise the latter in regard to their desires and how to manifest them. "But the German republic must not look toward conquest and aggrandizement and approach the table of the peace conference with that in mind. Our people do not wish to become embroiled in new international entanglements; it has had to suffer enough from those which have arisen so far. That may sound to some like cowardice, yet it is only a warning not to abandon ourselves to misleading expectations."[24] Yet, on the whole, only a handful of socialists and pacifists warned the nation against insisting on the immediate Anschluss. Though Ludo Hartmann, the Austrian ambassador in Berlin, privately berated German Social Democrats, especially the socialist Ebert-Haase government for being too "lukewarm and weakly" on the subject of the union,[25] the majority of Social Democrats and their leading newspaper, the *Vorwärts*, championed the cause of the Anschluss. True, German Austria's appeal to Germany for help right after the Armistice and revolution had hardly come at an opportune moment; it was virtually ignored. Yet the new German socialist government seemed quickly to regain its spirit and began to lay the groundwork for the incorporation of German Austria. The Reich was encouraged by the circumstance that the Western Powers, though apparently opposed to the Anschluss, never proclaimed prohibition of the union to be their irrevocable policy. Berlin therefore began to grope for indications of the limits set on its movements by the Entente.

In this search the German government turned to its ambassadors in the capitals of the neutral states with which it still entertained diplomatic relations, Berne, The Hague, Copenhagen, and Stockholm. As Scheidemann later explained it, the German government had "no direct relations" with the enemy countries; thus Copenhagen, where Brockdorff-Rantzau served as envoy, and Berne, where von Romberg was replaced by von Adolf Müller, were invaluable for establishing contact with the Allies. Both envoys, according to

---

[24]*Ibid.*
[25]*O.S.*, K 261, Hartmann to Bauer, Dec. 3, 1918, pp. 98-101; see also Hartmann regretting that Bernstein defended the cautious attitude of the German government, *ibid.*, K 109, Anschlussfrage, Dec. 31, pp. 209f.

Scheidemann, through their reports "decisively" contributed to the making of "our foreign policy at the time." [26] The purpose of the inquiry now made by Berlin was to ascertain the likely reaction of the Great Powers, and to a lesser degree also of their smaller allies and the neutral Powers, to the Anschluss movement. German policy-makers could then anticipate the moves of these Powers in the event that the question of the Anschluss was directly posed.

One of the most revealing replies was sent from Copenhagen by none other than the German ambassador Count Ulrich von Brockdorff-Rantzau who only a few weeks later was to become German foreign minister and to play a key role in the conduct of German postwar foreign policy in regard to Austria and the Anschluss. As far as the Danish press was concerned, it expressed fears that "Pan-German republican projects" were already being forged in Germany.

Brockdorff-Rantzau thought that Denmark, under the stewardship of her prime minister Eric Scavenius, would probably be favorably disposed to the Anschluss, but Scavenius felt that the Allies would try to prevent the union with Germany. According to Brockdorff-Rantzau, Scavenius was personally convinced that the Anschluss of German Austria with the Reich would take place "some day." It would be hard for the Entente, he asserted, to prevent it in the long run.[27]

Perhaps Brockdorff-Rantzau's reply offered a little more than his "impression" of the Danish prime minister's views on the Anschluss; it may well have contained some of his own. There is convincing evidence to show that Brockdorff-Rantzau, before and after assuming high office, himself anticipated a *Gewaltfrieden*. Such a peace would include the denial of the right to self-determination for Alsace-Lorraine and other threatened areas and the prohibition of the Anschluss. Any thoughtful contemporary of this period, witnessing Russia's humiliation and Germany's triumph at Brest-Litovsk and the subsequent turbulent course of events and Germany's debacle must have questioned the permanency of peace treaties and the lasting significance of their

[26]Scheidemann, 1921: p. 192.
[27]*N.A.*, T 120-3270, Akten betr. Beziehungen . . . , Brockdorff-Rantzau, Nov. 21, 1918.

stipulations. In any case, accident or not, the views on the Anschluss reported by Brockdorff-Rantzau in November of 1918 as those of the Danish prime minister Scavenius turned out surprisingly to be his own views once he assumed the Office of German foreign secretary.

The German ambassador to The Hague, Rosen, gave as his impression that the Netherlands would maintain great caution towards the Anschluss of German Austria, but were not "unfriendly" toward it. France would be "unconditionally" opposed to it and England, he feared, would be influenced by the French government, a prognosis which proved to be correct.[28]

From Stockholm, Ambassador Lucius reported that the Italian envoy Tomasini welcomed the Anschluss, since it would weaken Prussia's influence in the Reich, but Lucius wondered whether, if, and to what degree this view reflected that of the Italian government.[29] From Berne, Ambassador Romberg echoed Lucius in saying that France would oppose the Anschluss since it would strengthen Germany and would also likely raise the question of compensation, in particular the problem of the left bank of the Rhine. Though England had just indicated through Bonar Law her lack of opposition to the union, in view of France's attitude he warned against posing the question of the Anschluss, especially before the signing of the peace treaty. His views too turned out to be unusually perceptive.[30]

The replies Secretary Solf received accurately reflected France's determined opposition, England's early hesitancies — but also her desire to please the French ally — and Italy's, for the moment at least, favorable attitude to the Anschluss. The capitals of the neutral countries also registered opposition or caution in regard to the Anschluss. In general, the envoys recommended not to press the issue.

In view of the opposition of the Entente, the hesitation of the German government, and the division in Austrian and German public opinion, many proponents of the fusion, even the German ambassador von Wedel, were at times sufficiently discouraged to abandon all hopes for the short-

---

[28]*Ibid.*, Rosen to F.O., Nov. 22, Tel. 907.
[29]*Ibid.*, Lucius to F.O., Nov. 22, Tel. 1419.
[30]*Ibid.*, Romberg to F.O., Nov. 24, Tel. 2113.

range progress of the Anschluss movement. On December 10, Wedel reported that the Americans, the English, and even the Italians seemed to be turning toward the French point of view. He believed that the recent reverses of the movement for union could be attributed to Austria's having mistakenly proclaimed the Anschluss "too early." "The program was good, but the tempo too rapid."[31] What Wedel tended to overlook was that the Austrian government and Austria's Social Democratic party were, by necessity, faced with problems of foreign relations and foreign policy from the moment of the birth of the Austrian state. The German government on the other hand first faced the problem of coping with the revolutionary masses and of the radicalization of the revolution. Foreign policy had to take a backseat.

In mid-December the German Workers' and Soldiers' Council convened in Berlin. It was immersed in domestic problems and not weighted down by the Anschluss. But the traditional German primacy on foreign policy was soon reflected even in the pages of the *Vorwärts*. The socialist newspaper, after warning the Workers' and Soldiers' Council not to replace the parliamentary system with the Soviet system, turned to "serious matters," in other words, to German foreign policy and the likelihood of Germany suffering territorial losses in the peace treaty in the border regions, in Alsace-Lorraine and in areas along the Rhine. In this context it pointed to France's determined opposition to the Anschluss. The French press was castigated for "laughing at German Austria's intention of joining Germany," considering it a "utopia."[32]

In November the German Cabinet had advised the Austrian government against holding elections for the German Constituent Assembly, but in the weeks that followed at least some of the German Cabinet members developed second thoughts about it. In the Cabinet session of December 31, 1918, Hugo Preuss suggested in a debate on Alsace-Lorraine that Germany tell the Austrians "that they are welcome" too. In the afternoon of the same day Ebert also raised the question of the participation of German Austria in the work of the National Assembly. So far Germany had

[31]*Ibid.*, Wedel to F.O., Dec. 10.
[32]*Vorwärts*, Dec. 16, 1918.

exercised restraint toward German Austria to avoid giving the French an excuse.

> However, after we have been confronted with a *fait accompli* regarding Alsace-Lorraine, we should consider whether this is the time to take a decisive step toward asserting that the Germans in German Austria are entitled to vote and that deputies elected in Austria may appear in the National Assembly, so that we may have from the very beginning a National Assembly which includes German Austria.[33]

He admitted that no unity had yet been attained on the question of an election in Austria.

Ebert himself was one of the activists in the Anschluss question. But both the German Austrian and the German governments were to refrain from arranging an Austrian election for the German Constituent Assembly. At the year's end the German government had risen out of the despair and lethargy of the November days, but it was still rather unsure of itself in both domestic and foreign affairs, and was only groping toward a policy on the Anschluss.

On December 30 Brockdorff-Rantzau had assumed the post of German foreign secretary. Hartmann was the first envoy to call on him, thus losing no time in seizing the diplomatic initiative and impressing upon the new German minister the Austrian government's determination to speed the implementation of the Anschluss. Referring to the Anschluss proclamation of November 12, 1918, he assured the German foreign secretary that the Austrian government was prepared to offer "still more *faits accomplis.*" According to Hartmann, the new German foreign secretary had hastened to assure him that he was a "great friend" of German Austria and of the Anschluss movement. Thereupon Hartmann pointed out that the cool attitude of the German government had had "a chilling effect on the people of German Austria and would definitely obstruct the course of development. I also stressed that I held the argument which was advanced in justification for this attitude—namely fear of the Entente—to be invalid." [34]

---

[33]*B.A.*, Akten betr . . . Reichsministerium. Alte Kanzlei, Cabinet sess. Dec. 31, 1918.

[34]*O.S.*, K 109, Hartmann to Bauer, Dec. 31, 1918, pp. 209-213.

FIG. 3   Ulrich von Brockdorff-Rantzau, 1869-1928. Germany's foreign minister, 1918-1919.

Brockdorff-Rantzau must have been sufficiently impressed with the determined and hard-driving Austrian envoy. According to Hartmann,

he asked me directly what I thought should be done. I voiced the view that the assumption of office by a new government and his taking charge of the Office of Foreign Affairs offered an opportunity to make a more resolute declaration on the German Austrian question and he let me dictate the substance of such a declaration about which, of course, he would have to consult with his ministerial colleagues. I suggested that in this declaration he first state that . . . President Wilson's Fourteen Points and the right to self-determination of nations should also be applied to the German people; second, that, legally speaking, German Austria had already promulgated the Anschluss with Germany; third, that the German government had acknowledged with pleasure the Anschluss declaration of the German Austrian National Assembly of November 12, 1918; and fourth, that the German Constituent Assembly, which is to convene in the near future, would give its consent to the bilateral treaty and ratify it.

He had talked in the same vein, Hartmann continued, with Chancellor Scheidemann. He had proposed to Scheidemann, his secretary Heinrich Schulz, and to Ebert that an Austrian with a consultative voice might be officially included in the Council of Ministers. "This proposition appeared to both Scheidemann and Count Brockdorff-Rantzau rather bold, but quite deserving of consideration." Hartmann conveyed his impression that the new foreign secretary was "quite serious" about the Anschluss.

By the year's end the Anschluss movement was not yet in high gear; but with courage regained and self-confidence restored hopes were somewhat brighter on both sides of the border which separated Germany from Austria than they had been in the dark November days.

4. THE CHANGING FORTUNES OF THE ANSCHLUSS MOVEMENT

"I would generally recommend to you [Brockdorff-Rantzau] not to make yourself an exponent in the Anschluss question, but to further the cause as far as it is politically useful. . . ." Botho von Wedel, January, 1919

DURING the first weeks of its life the new government of the German republic was unresponsive to the overtures from Vienna. Germany as a whole still seemed paralyzed as a result of revolution and defeat. And in Austria wide segments of the population and even many national-minded intellectuals were cool toward the union. Fear of radicalism in Germany, the existence of anti-Catholic sentiments in the Reich dating back to the *Kulturkampf* if not to earlier times, the strong economic interests binding the Austrian economy to that of the succession states, the vast economic dislocations in Germany, and the opposition of the Entente to the union project — all this held many Austrians back. It was as if the Austrian movement, after its initial forward thrust on November 12, was sliding back.

On December 7, Count von Wedel reported thus on the situation in German Austria:

The Anschluss movement in Germany and Austria has recently lost considerable ground. Only the Socialists have remained loyal to the idea. The bourgeois parties are lukewarm. This stands out less in the Viennese press than in the provincial press, though Viennese papers too have produced headlines like "Against the Anschluss with Germany," which they would not have dared four weeks ago. Aside from utterances in the press, this change of public opinion is not tangible. Yet there are whisperings in the capital and in the crownlands: "After all, the Anschluss could not be carried through in Germany, the Entente would not tolerate it. . . ." The reasons for the change of attitude are numerous.

150

First, the well-oiled agitation of industrial circles is opposed to the Anschluss and has not been unsuccessful. . . . The news from the Reich has also had an alarming effect. The lack of unity among the ruling circles, the threat to the unity of the Reich, the Spartacus agitation, the economic policy of the Räte [Soviets], the strike movements, etc. . . . and finally the impotence, the loss of German territories, the economic misery, all these have produced a state of fatigue and apathy in which one longs only for quiet, peace, bread, and coal, and inclines to pacific submissiveness toward all stronger powers.[1]

During the course of the next few weeks the mood in Austria failed to improve.[2] The Austrian press and public opinion remained clearly divided. On January 1, the Catholic *Reichspost* spoke out with a vengeance against pursuing the Anschluss. To insist on union with Germany, when Austria was so dependent on the Allies for food, raw materials and coal, would mean to permit "stubborness and foolishness" to become a "national outrage." "We must renounce the desire for Anschluss with Germany." The following day the Socialist *Arbeiter-Zeitung* admitted, in spite of its pro-Anschluss sentiments, that the desire for union was by no means universal, and that in some circles plain fear prevailed. "There are so-called honest Viennese who are afraid of the merger with Germany."[3]

The plain truth was that the Anschluss movement registered a decline even among Austrian Social Democrats, its most resolute partisans, as the German ambassador in Vienna conceded. On January 5 Wedel wrote thus:

The agitation against the Anschluss has grown like an avalanche. The interpretation of the German government's attitude as cool and of North German public opinion as considering a Catholic increase undesirable, receives credence everywhere. The adherents of the Anschluss are discouraged and decline rapidly; even Socialist circles are growing weak. If we do not move soon, Anschluss will be only an academic demand in the realization of which nobody believes, and a cause to which only few will seriously dedicate themselves.[4]

[1]*N.A.*, T 120-3270, Wedel to F.O., Dec. 10, 1918.
[2]*Ibid.*
[3]*Arbeiter-Zeitung*, Jan. 12
[4]*N.A.*, T 120-3270, Wedel to F.O.

One Regendanz, in a letter to the leading German industrialist and writer Max Warburg, confirmed Wedel's gloomy observations and attributed the "decline" of the desire for union to German radicalism, the "insanity in Berlin," and "the crazy people in Munich." The Entente appeared to have hinted also that, if Austria renounced the Anschluss, she would "get away with a black eye"; otherwise the Allies apparently had "the friendly intention [to] beat the brains out of the Germans" *(den Deutschen den Schädel einschlagen)*. And Riepenhausen, who had journeyed to Austria, pointed out the Austrian "counter-agitation" against the Anschluss which grew "day by day."[5] It received rich financial support from the Zentralverband der österreichischen Industrie; the opposition had also recently acquired influence in the *Deutsches Volksblatt*.[6]

On December 30, the French foreign minister Pichon squarely opposed the Anschluss in a speech in the Chamber of Deputies. His comments added strength to the Austrian opposition to the union; the *Reichspost* promptly pointed to the dangers of defying the Entente. Under the direction of Count Czernin, a group of aristocrats calling itself "Bürgerverein 1918" was organized. Czernin developed the program of this party as follows:

> No matter how attractive the old and beautiful idea of the political and economic union of all Germans is to me as a German, we are today harassed by most serious concerns and economic burdens and must devote ourselves fully to the reconstruction of our state. The economic problems cannot be overlooked.

From this point of view, Czernin favored Austria's establishing economic relations with Czechoslovakia, Hungary, and Yugoslavia, "to the exclusion of any political community," on the prior condition that guarantees will be given in regard to the independence and preservation of the German character of Austria.[7] At the first meeting of the Bürgerverein, Czernin insisted that a linkup with Germany was

---

[5]*B.A.*, Italics A.D.L., Beziehungen Öst., Regendanz, Jan. 20.
[6]*Ibid.*
[7]*Reichspost*, Jan. 2.

premature; it was necessary to await the decision of the Peace Conference.

Czernin's favorable comments on an economic Danubian federation paralleled French political views and represented the very opposite of the thought developed a few days earlier by Otto Bauer in the article "Zollverein" in the pages of the *Arbeiter-Zeitung*. Bauer had carefully pointed out the disadvantages for German Austria if a Danubian federation emerged. Not only numerically, but also economically, would German Austria trail behind the other member states, since with the loss of German Bohemia she would certainly also lose a great portion of her industry: and the fertility of the Alpine soil lagged behind that of the neighboring countries. "Our influence on the policy of the federal state would therefore be rather small. . . . The national struggles would continue. . . . We would not get rid of the old Austrian misery." [8]

But in view of the utter lack of interest in the project by the other nationalities of the Danubian Basin, Bauer questioned the usefulness of engaging in further discussion. "The federal state is a utopia; and therefore it is idle to debate whether it is a beautiful utopia."

The problem of Austria's economic and political future was also raised by Friedrich Austerlitz, editor of the *Arbeiter-Zeitung*, in the January issue of the party's theoretical journal *Der Kampf*. It was, he said, "a plain truth" that "we cannot exist by ourselves." The opponents of the union at home and abroad praised the mission of a "supra-national" state which would give the world "a shining example of peaceful living together and of cooperation among different nations" and claimed that the German Austrians would render a great service to the German people if they would only renounce German national unity.[9] Austerlitz and other Austrian Social Democrats were singularly unimpressed by the assignment to German Austria of a "mission" in co-existence of the different nationalities in Central Europe, the failure of which had just been so palpably demonstrated.

Like Friedrich Austerlitz, Otto Bauer and Karl Renner turned their guns against the domestic opponents of the

---

[8] *Arbeiter-Zeitung*, Dec. 25, 1918, Bauer, "Zollverein."
[9] *Der Kampf*, Jan. 1919; also *Arbeiter-Zeitung*, Jan. 11.

union with Germany. Addressing a voters' assembly on January 18, Bauer drew attention to the inconsistency of many of the great German Austrian industrialists. What actually disturbed them in Germany and German Austria was "socialism." The same theme was pursued in the *Arbeiter-Zeitung* editorial of January 21, "The Fatherland must be bigger." [10]

According to Karl Renner, only a minority in Vienna opposed the union, and they did so partly "out of love" for the Austrian capital and partly for special economic interests. Social Democrats, however, pleaded fervently for the Anschluss also on economic grounds. The old Austria of more than 50 million people employed numerous "officials, executives, engineers, chemists, technicians, and employees in industry, commerce and banks. What will happen to these thousands?" "Little German Austria" was not in a position to give them employment. In addition, thousands of Germans who had been employed in private industry in Slavic regions would soon be displaced. "German Austria with its vast super-abundance of intelligentsia can't absorb them. They can find employment only in the German Reich." [11] Thus a flurry of articles in December and January by Austrian Social Democratic leaders underlined the determination of Austrian Socialism to continue along the road leading to union with Germany and to disperse the gloom and despair spread by its opponents. The Austrian socialist leadership had high hopes of influencing the still fluctuating public opinion on the Anschluss among the Great Powers.

During the month of January the electoral victory of the German democratic parties and the Majority Socialists and the repression of the Spartacus revolt made a favorable impact upon the Austrian population and strengthened the Anschluss movement. The *Arbeiter-Zeitung* hailed what it called the victory of "red Germany," the "tremendous victory for democracy and Socialism." "If we emulate our German brothers, moved by the same will toward Democracy, Republic, and Socialism, if we are as successful on February 16 as the brothers on the other side were on January 19, then a red German Austria will unite with a red Germany." [12] In

---

[10]*Ibid.*, Jan. 19.

[11]*Ibid.*, Feb. 2: Feb. 4, "Wirtschaft und Zukunft."

[12]*Arbeiter-Zeitung*, Jan. 22.

spite of the revolutionary rhetoric, only moderate socialists were in uneasy control in the Reich. The more radical socialism in Austria was operating in an economically and militarily emaciated country which was at the mercy of the West. But the election results promised to give renewed impetus to the movement for union.

Knowledgeable people in the Austrian Foreign Office were quite critical of the German efforts made so far. An anonymous memorandum in the Auswärtiges Amt written in mid-January, "Zur Frage des Anschlusses an das Deutsche Reich," criticized "authoritative circles in Berlin" for having acted "in a timid and reserved manner." As a matter of fact, the author declared, "nothing at all has been done yet." [13] People still need passports with visas for travel between the two countries; mail from German Austria was still subject to censorship, and customs regulations, far from having been set aside, were instead strictly enforced. "Towering walls" still separated German Austria from the Reich.

On the whole German Austrians were plainly disappointed over Germany's inadequate interest and relative inactivity in the Anschluss movement. Later, in 1919, when the defeat of the movement was already evident, Michael Hainisch, later president of the Austrian republic, complained that the Reich's interest in Austria had been "strikingly small" and he blamed the lack of German interest in Austria for both the outcome of the war and the failure of the movement for union in 1919.[14] The Austrian physician Dr. Stransky similarly accused the Germans of being lukewarm and vacillating.[15] In the same vein the Austrian author Adam Müller-Guttenbrunn held that it was up to the German intelligentsia in the Reich to "make us welcome. This, however, has not been done." [16]

Though during the month of January 1919 under the new leadership of Ulrich von Brockdorff-Rantzau a more favorable wind seemed to speed the Anschluss movement, the German ambassador in Vienna, Count Botho von Wedel, advised Berlin not to rush headlong into what he feared were

---

[13]*A.A.*, Öst. 95, v. 26, "Zur Frage d. Anschlusses an d. deutsche Reich," Jan. 15.
[14]Hainisch, 1919: p. V.
[15]*Ibid.*, Stransky, pp. 14-15.
[16]*Ibid.*, p. 12.

insuperable obstacles. While he criticized the deputy Hugo Haase for what he called a timid attitude toward the union and welcomed in turn Brockdorff-Rantzau's positive statement on the Anschluss in the *Deutsche Allgemeine Zeitung*,[17] he warned the German foreign secretary not to become too closely identified with a vigorous pursuit of the Anschluss.

> *I would generally recommend to you not to make yourself an exponent in the Anschluss question, but to further the cause as far as it is politically useful and corresponds to the mood there. To support too strongly a cause which may not after all develop into anything is always an unfortunate matter. And the chances are not good.* The *volte-face* of the French and the counter-maneuvers of the press have not been without consequences. Ambassador Hartmann is an optimist and idealist and does not assess the situation cor-rectly, which in any case has substantially changed since his departure. *I recommend, therefore, that you support the cause, but do not become the champion of an idea whose realization is at the moment uncertain.*[18] [Italics mine, A.D.L.]

Wedel's position on the union was on the whole not incon-sistent. A partisan of the Anschluss, he opposed a vigorous campaign in its behalf since he was beset by doubts about the likelihood of an early success. On the other hand, he was afraid that the German government, by continued indif-ference and inaction, might let the Anschluss movement in Austria wither away.

But Germany should not and need not surrender her vital interests. Wedel cautioned Berlin that the German Austrian government was making greater claims than the German government could or should satisfy. "Our friends here," he wrote, were thinking that in offering Austria to the Reich they were presenting a gift to Germany and "that in principle we have to offer a present in return." German Austria would like to see Germany play the role of the suitor who "in his lovesickness is ready to anticipate and fulfill every wish of his lovely fiancée." [19] Though Germany would have to make concessions, he urged the Foreign Office to take a hard-

---

[17]*Deutsche Allgemeine Zeitung*, Jan. 5.
[18]*B.A.*, Akten betr. Beziehungen . . . , Wedel to F.O., Jan. 23.
[19]*A.A.*, Öst. 95, v. 27, Wedel to F.O., Report 18, Feb. 6, 1919.

headed view. It should be prepared to bargain during the impending negotiations and to "demand compensation for each point yielded." A tough bargaining position would also prevent a precipitate progress toward the Anschluss. And too rapid a progress was undesirable as long as the peace treaty was not concluded.

The general paralysis of the first few weeks after the Armistice and *Zusammenbruch* had affected German policy in all its aspects, including her relations with Austria. Secretary Solf had personally been a friend of the Anschluss concept, but his impending departure, which became known during the month of December, had further slowed down Germany's progress toward union. But when Brockdorff-Rantzau assumed the stewardship of the Foreign Office, he promptly took issue with the anti-union position adopted only a few days before by France's foreign minister Pichon and appealed to the Entente not to oppose the Anschluss.[20] Shortly after the elections to the National Assembly Brockdorff-Rantzau thus charged the assembly on occasion of an interview with Dr. Paul Goldmann, correspondent of the Vienna *Neue Freie Presse:* "I do not doubt that the National Assembly will consider it its first task to vigorously stress the unification idea." During these decisive and difficult days "all Germans, including the Germans in Austria," should not lose sight of the great historical goal of reunification.[21]

Brockdorff-Rantzau had disregarded his Austrian ambassador's advice for caution — at least publicly — and decided to identify himself strongly with the movement.

During the month of January the German Foreign Office notified Wedel of an impending journey to Vienna of Baron von Riepenhausen, who would inform him of a plan to lend more energetic support to the Anschluss movement. The contemplated project was to propagandize the union concept primarily through the Austrian press.[22] According to Riepenhausen's report, most Viennese newspapers, with the exception of the *Arbeiter-Zeitung* and the *Wiener Mittag*, were cool, if not hostile, toward the concept of union with Germany. To combat the "clever" anti-Anschluss propaganda

[20]Brockdorff-Rantzau, 1925: pp. 55-59.
[21]*Neue Freie Presse*, Jan. 24.
[22]*A.A.*, Öst. 95, v. 26, F.O. to Wedel, Jan. 14, Tel. 10.

Riepenhausen considered it necessary to purchase at least two new newspapers, and in view of the impending elections in Austria on February 16, he recommended that this be done promptly. His recommendation that the German Treasury immediately provide 2 million marks for this purpose was favorably acted upon within the next few days.[23]

Baron von Riepenhausen soon raised his purchasing goals from two to three newspapers, the *Wiener Mittagszeitung*, the *Sechs-Uhr-Abendblatt*, and the *Fremdenblatt*, and suggested that rather than representing a single political party they reflect different political points of view, namely those of the German Nationals, the Christian Socials, and the Citizen Democratic party, and that they be supported by their political friends and associates in the Reich. In the event that the union should fail to materialize, there would still be a need for a pro-German press in German Austria to continue to struggle for the Anschluss.[24]

In a later telegram Wedel informed the Berlin Foreign Office that private German Austrian circles had consented to advance three million crowns for the purchase of Austrian newspapers if Germany herself would be willing to supply two million marks. The German Austrian sources insisted, however, that they retain the entire control of the newspaper concern and that the investment of German capital in the undertaking be kept secret. Again the Foreign Office promptly wired the Vienna Embassy that two million marks would be made "immediately available for the suggested project." [25]

Dr. Walter Schotte, editor of the German magazine *Mitteleuropa*, and the German Major Fleck, who assisted von Riepenhausen in the attempt to purchase Viennese journals, were also instrumental in creating a German agency which was to play an important role in boosting the Austrian Anschluss movement, the *Deutsch-Österreichische Mittelstelle*. *Die Mittelstelle* was primarily thought of as a German propaganda and news bureau whose purpose was to enhance the appreciation of everything German in Austria. It was to be supplied with information by the Deutsch-Österreichische Arbeitsgemeinschaft, which was a corresponding Berlin

---

[23]*Ibid.*, Öst. 74, v. 2, Riepenhausen to Rheinbaben, Jan. 17, Tel. 41.
[24]*Ibid.* Jan. 23; *ibid.*, Wedel to F.O., Jan. 25, Tel. 46.
[25]*Ibid.*, Wedel to F.O., Jan. 26, Tel. 49: *ibid.*, Wedel to F.O., Jan. 30, Tel. 62.

organization headed by Dr. Schotte. The task of the *Mittelstelle* consisted not merely in supplying Austrian papers and agencies with pertinent information. It was also to gather material on the Anschluss in Austria and relay it via the Vienna Embassy to the Foreign Office in Berlin. It was to function partly under the direction of the Vienna Embassy and partly under that of the Foreign Office. The latter held the purse strings, authorizing it to spend 10,000 crowns per month, and also furnished the "guidelines" for its operation.[26]

Finally, the German Foreign Office also had a direct hand in the attempt to give support to the creation in German Austria of a middle-class Democratic party. Ideologically, it was to correspond to the Democratic party in Germany, and its guiding spirits were to be in favor of the Anschluss. It is difficult to perceive why the Foreign Office engaged in what clearly amounted to political intervention in German Austrian affairs, especially since two of the major parties, the Social Democrats and the German Nationalists, were Anschluss-minded. The Citizens' Democratic Party, in the view of the German Foreign Office, was apparently to attract new middle-class elements of liberal inclinations to the *Anschluss* concept. The party was to be led by the eminent Austrian jurist Dr. Franz Klein. He and Dr. Gustav Stolper, editor of the *Osterreichischer Volkswirt*, received considerable financial support from Germany for this purpose.[27]

On February 1, about a fortnight before the Austrian election of February 16, Riepenhausen notified Director Herzberg of the Depositenbank that one million marks would be transferred to him and were to be deposited on behalf of the Citizens' Democratic party. German financial support for the Anschluss propaganda was justified on the ground that anti-union capital was "at work" to an alarming extent, working feverishly against the Anschluss.[28]

While the German government was providing financial support for the Austrian Anschluss movement, individual

[26]*Ibid.*, Undersecretary of State to Wedel, Jan. 27, Tel. 39.

[27]*Ibid.*, Öst. 95, v. 27, "Richtlinien für den Betrieb d. deutsch-österr. Mittelstelle in Wien" Feb. 12, 1919; *ibid.*, F.O. to Wedel, Feb. 23, also Feb. 15; *ibid.*, "Skizze für Vorschläge und Richtlinien zu einem Gesellschaftsvertrag zwischen Herrn Dr. Walther Schotte und Herrn Major Fleck," Feb. 12; Stolper, 1960: p. 128.

[28]*A.A.*, Öst. 94, v. 2, Schotte to Riepenhausen, Feb. 1, Tel. 49.

Germans were exerting every effort to strengthen it. Early in 1919 a number of distinguished democratic leaders journeyed to Vienna and other places in Austria to boost the electoral prospects of the new Citizens' Democratic party. As it turned out, their efforts were in vain. Among them were Theodor Heuss (destined to become president of the German Federal Republic after World War II), Hjalmar Schacht, later noted for his financial wizardry and rightist sentiments, though at that time a Democrat, and the distinguished sociologist Max Weber.[29]

Above and beyond giving financial and political aid to the Austrian Anschluss movement, others in the Foreign Office pointed out the need for strengthening economic ties between German Austria and Germany and creating as many business, industrial, and financial ties between the two countries as possible. They recommend that German businessmen, industrialists, and bankers give financial and other support to union propaganda at their conventions, since the Foreign Office's funds were necessarily limited. They should openly announce their support for the Anschluss and use their powers of persuasion and their direct personal influence on their Austrian counterparts.[30]

Among non-political organizations most active in Germany in behalf of the Anschluss was the Deutsch-Österreichischer Volksbund, which represented the organization of German Austrians in the Reich. In mid-January it arranged a large

---

[29]Closely associated with Dr. Franz Klein, Gustav Stolper and his friends in the political campaign in early 1919 was also Dr. von Wettstein, professor of botany at the University of Vienna. Among Dr. Klein's supporters were also men such as the writer Walther Schotte, leader of the *Arbeitsausschuss für Mitteleuropa,* which had been founded by Friedrich Naumann himself, and the noted Austrian civil servant (Sektionschef) Richard Riedl. In his *Erinnerungen, 1905-1933* (1963), pp. 244-245, Theodor Heuss, president of the German Federal republic, recounted how he once came to the help of the scheduled speaker Dr. Franz Klein by climbing through a window into the crowded assembly hall, stepping on the table and beginning his oration by paying respects to the late Dr. Victor Adler and talking about the Anschluss of which he was an enthusiastic proponent. See also the account by Gustav Stolper's widow, Toni (Kassowitz) Stolper, 1960: pp. 127-129, about Heuss's and Schacht's activities in Austria. Toni Stolper, in this widely read book on her husband, an intellectual promoter of the party, revealed that a large amount of German money was spent in behalf of this electoral campaign in Austria, pointing to the close relations of the *Bürgerlich* Democratic party to the personnel of the diplomatic representations in Vienna and Berlin (p. 128).

[30]*A.A.,* Öst. 74, v. 2, Wedel to F.O., Jan. 26, Tel. 49, and Wedel to F.O., Jan. 30; also *ibid.,* Öst. 95, v. 26, Vienna Embassy to F.O., Jan. 26.

gathering in Stuttgart which was addressed by Austrian and German speakers, the latter representing various German political parties.[31] A month later a similar assembly in Frankfurt a.M. heard speeches in favor of Austria's Anschluss by various University professors, spokesmen of students' and workers' organizations, and a city official. Other German organizations exerting every effort in behalf of the union were the Grossdeutsche Vereinigung, which worked toward the Anschluss on several levels, and the Verein für das Deutschtum im Ausland which had numerous local chapters all over Germany and appealed to Berlin to lend support to Austria's union with the Reich.

During the month of January, German public opinion increasingly welcomed the thought of union with Austria and gave free vent to its pro-union feelings. There seemed particular concern that Germany had been too indifferent for too long toward Austria. On January 14, Georg Bernhard of the *Vossische Zeitung*, in the editorial "Die Politik der Entschuldigungen," attacked the dilatory and hesitant policy of Germany regarding Austria and the Anschluss, and also warned the West that the denial of self-determination to Austria would produce a sinister "hatred which will never disappear as long as Germans live on earth." The *Frankfurter Zeitung* joined the *Vossische Zeitung* in its criticism both of the policy of France and that of the German government on the Anschluss.[32]

In 1919 German hopes for the union were focused on the Constituent Assembly, just as in 1848-1849 they had been concentrated on the work of the Frankfurt Assembly. Thus the *Vossische Zeitung* warned its readers that the elected assembly would be only a "fragment as long as the ten million German Austrians will not be represented in it." "Every vote," the writer urged, "will contribute to the firm resolution that the first act of the *kleindeutsch* Assembly must be its transformation into a *grossdeutsch* Assembly."

On the eve of Germany's election, on January 17, the entire German press, responding to an earlier suggestion of Ludo Hartmann, unanimously called upon the German

---

[31]*O.S.*, K. 109, Deutschland, I, Seidler to F.O., Jan. 18, Report 5, also Günther to F.O., Jan. 18.
[32]*Frankfurter Zeitung*, Jan. 15.

government for the implementation of the November 12 resolution of the Austrian National Assembly to make German Austria an integral part of the German Reich. Virtually all German newspapers joined in the following appeal: "We demonstrate today with the entire German press for the right to self-determination of the German nation. . . . We salute our brethren in German Austria. They belong to us both in name and kind and wish to remain closely linked with us in an eternal union." According to the *Vossische Zeitung*, it did not happen every day that the papers of all sections and all parties of Germany found occasion to voluntarily demonstrate in a unified manner. The newspaper demanded the immediate implementation of the Anschluss of German Austria with Germany.[33]

In view of Germany's virtual unanimity it was hardly surprising that once the National Assembly opened its doors in Weimar on February 6, 1919, the voice in favor of the Anschluss was heard loud and clear.

[33]*Voss. Zeitung*, Jan. 17.

III. From the Weimar Assembly to the Presentation of the German Peace Treaty (February 6 – May 7, 1919)

1. THE WEIMAR ASSEMBLY AND THE ANSCHLUSS

"They [the German Austrians] belong to us, and we belong to them." Friedrich Ebert, February, 1919

T HE election for the German Constituent Assembly was to be held on January 19, 1919. The political programs of the German parties and their appeals to the electorate, however, were drawn up mainly during the month of December. They contained little about Austria and the Anschluss. Germans still stunned by defeat, revolution, and the further threat of social upheavals had not yet recovered from this sequence of blows enough to give their full attention to the fate of their brothers in German Austria.

The German National People's party, in its appeal to the electorate, had merely voiced the hope "that our German brothers in Austria, whose tribulations we feel like our own, will with the Anschluss to the German Reich gain security for their national existence." [1] The program contained no definite pledge obligating the party's candidates to work toward the union and implement it in the Constituent Assembly without delay. Equally vague was the German Conservative party in its platform of December 4, when it spoke out in behalf of the "unity of all German ethnic groups." [2] The German Democratic party in its appeal of December 15 came out more strongly in support of the "rights of the *Auslandsdeutschen*" and for national self-determination: "We shall always resist . . . any violation of this right to self-determination, which also belongs to the German Austrians." [3] Yet even this promise placed the burden of effecting the Anschluss on Austrian rather than German shoulders. A few days later, however, on December 20, the Democratic party called especially upon German Austria,

---

[1] E. Heilfron, 1919: **1:** p. 126; see also Salomon, 1926: **3:** p. 26.
[2] Salomon, 1926: **3:** p. 23.
[3] Heilfron, 1919: **1:** p. 141; also Salomon, 1926: **3:** p. 50.

pledging that her cultural and economic life would not be subjected to that of Germany, and asserted that the time to unite had arrived; without German Austria the new democratic German state would be "incomplete."[4] The Catholic Center party in its "Guidelines to Politics" had virtually nothing to say about the Anschluss of Catholic Austria.[5] The Bavarian People's party in its program of December, 1918, remained likewise strangely silent on the subject of neighboring Austria and the Anschluss.[6] The German Hanoverian party pledged in its guidelines support for the union of German Austria in accordance with its *grossdeutsch* convictions of long standing.[7]

The call to the polls issued by the Majority Socialists on December 28, 1918, made no reference to the Anschluss. The other parties of the Left likewise ignored the Anschluss in their programmatic declarations, concentrating on domestic issues and only touching on what they considered the most vital foreign policy problems. Policy statements of the Independents and of the Spartacist League in November and December of 1918 similarly failed to mention the German Austrian problem. In her pamphlet "What does the Spartacist League want?" Rosa Luxemburg demanded the elimination of all individual states and the creation of a "unified socialist republic."[8] She also urged the "instant resumption of negotiations with brother parties abroad," to place socialist revolution on an international basis and to secure the peace. In this context Rosa Luxemburg may have also thought of German Austria. And the Congress of the *Räte* (the Workers' and Soldiers' Councils) which met in Berlin between December 16 and 20 demonstrated the same lack of interest and concern in regard to Austria and the Anschluss.[9] European and world revolution rather than German territorial aggrandizement was on their mind. But the moderate and national-minded Left was by no means disinterested in the prospects for the Anschluss, as was clearly

[4] Purlitz, ed., *Deutscher Geschichtskalender* (Leipzig, 1918-), **1**: pp. 372-373.
[5] Salomon, 1926: **3**: p. 32.
[6] *Ibid.*, pp. 80-84.
[7] *Ibid.*, pp. 117-120.
[8] *Ibid.*, pp. 11-12.
[9] *Allgemeiner Kongress Arbeiter-und Soldatenräte Deutschlands* (Berlin), Dec. 16-20, 1918.

shown by the position of its leaders Friedrich Ebert and Philipp Scheidemann and that of the socialist press, led by *Vorwärts* itself. In their views, all Germans favored the union, and interest, even enthusiasm for it, transcended party lines. But burdened with the heavy responsibility of conducting affairs of state, the German Social Democratic party had to tread cautiously. Others in the political center and on the Right were fearful that in order to obtain the West's consent for the union, Germany would have to pay heavily in eastern territories.

Most German political parties, in contrast to their indefinite, if not evasive, campaign pledges on the subject of German Austria, were forceful and specific in their claims regarding such territories as Alsace-Lorraine, West Prussia, and Silesia. Yet all these lands had been German before 1914, while German Austria had not. It was quite apparent that the government would put up a vigorous struggle to retain prewar territories; it did not seem likely that she could successfully claim territories that had not been hers before 1914.

Yet Germany was to regain her balance after the psychological shock of military catastrophe and revolution. Once the doors of the Weimar Assembly opened, the representatives of all the German political parties were asking for the Anschluss of German Austria in increasingly confident, even strident tones.

Austria aside, the views of some German Cabinet members and of Germany's political and military leaders were in many respects far from encouraging in regard to international conciliation and peace. Ebert and Dr. David presented claims to Alsace-Lorraine, and the prominent General Groener, alluding on January 21 to differences between the Americans and the French, voiced the view: "I no longer have any fear of the West . . . I am convinced that in a very short time we shall be able to reconquer Alsace-Lorraine."[10] Ebert indicated the need to organize a force against the Poles, asked for the immediate entry of Germany into the League of Nations, and demanded the return of "our colonies."[11] And Erzberger warned his co-patriots not to trust their former enemies;

---

[10]*B.A.*, Reichskanzlei, Vorakten zu Reichsmin. 2b, v. 3, Groener, Jan. 21, E 627460.

[11]*Ibid.*

though among the latter the Americans stood "closest" to the Germans, still rumors about American friendship should not be believed.

When the German Constituent Assembly opened its first session on February 6, Friedrich Ebert—peoples's deputy and soon to be elected first president of the German Republic—presented the opening address. He protested most sharply against the projects of "our foes" which were based on vengeance, warning them not "to drive us to extremes."

> We cannot renounce the unification of the entire German nation within the framework of one realm (shouts of bravo!). Our German Austrian brethren, already proclaimed on November 12 of last year in their National Assembly that they were a part of the Great German Republic (applause). Now the German Austrian National Assembly, with impetuous enthusiasm, has sent us renewed greetings, expressing the hope that our two National Assemblies will succeed in refastening the tie which was torn apart by the violence of 1866 (renewed applause). Ladies and Gentlemen, I am confident that I speak for the entire National Assembly, when I sincerely and most joyfully welcome this historic demonstration (lively consent) and return the greetings with the same heart-felt friendship (renewed applause). Our racial kinfolk and companions in misfortune should be assured that we welcome them into the new Reich of the German nation with an open heart and open arms. (enthusiastic shouts of "Bravo!") . . . I may also be permitted to express the hope that the National Assembly will empower the future government of the Reich to negotiate as soon as possible with the government of the German Austrian People's State about the final tie-up. Then there will no longer be any border posts standing between us . . . (lively applause).[12]

Ebert's unusually strong speech, surpassing in commitment anything the German government and the German foreign minister had said since the November Revolution, was followed by a shorter but equally firm pledge by the Majority Socialist Dr. David, who had been elected president of the German National Assembly. "The reunion [with the

[12]Heilfron, 1919: **1:** pp. 3-7, 1. Sitzg., Febr. 6, 1919.

German Austrian brethren]," he developed, "touches the heartstrings of the entire German people. I express the hope that in the not too distant future I may be able to welcome the representatives of German Austria as colleagues in our midst (lively applause and clapping of hands)."

A few days later Brockdorff-Rantzau, minister of foreign affairs, assured the National Assembly—in a way directing his words also to Germany's immediate neighbors and the rest of the continent—that the new Germany was not pursuing any Pan-German goals. She did not wish to annex Switzerland, the Netherlands, or the Scandinavian countries. "But until the breakdown of the Holy Roman Empire, we and our Austrian brethren shared one and the same history. If at this point, after all the non-German races of the Hapsburg Empire have withdrawn their friendship, we unite with them again, it is because we are only making a belated correction of an error made in laying the foundation stone of the Reich, to which the Peace Conference will certainly not deny its sanction."[13]

Brockdorff-Rantzau also protested against the "wrong" which Czechoslovakia had committed against German Austria. The Czechoslovak state was attempting not only to subject the Germans of Bohemia and Moravia to its rule, but also to claim German-peopled territory in the Southeast. But he made it clear that the protest did not represent any direct claim on the part of Germany against the Czechs, but rather reflected his concern for Austria in general and the German Bohemian minority in particular.

The question arises why, after the relative calm and caution which had so far marked the political atmosphere in regard to the Anschluss, the German government and political leaders chose to make this unusual demonstration of their devotion and loyalty to the Anschluss concept at the time of the opening of the Weimar National Assembly. For one thing, the opening of the Constituent Assembly was certainly a grand opportunity to put forth Germany's claims and publicize German desires. They may also have reasoned that the Peace Conference in Paris might be influenced by a show of German determination and hopefulness rather than of

[13]*Ibid.*, pp. 147-155, 7. Sitzg., Feb. 14.

German despondency. Yet in an interview with a correspondent of the *Neue Freie Presse*, Ebert pointed his finger at the real cause, repeating a point he himself had previously made in a cabinet session late in December, 1918. He said as follows:

> We have so far softpedaled the Anschluss of German Austria *vis-à-vis* France. [This] has caused some concern in German Austria. We have only done this in order not to make it too easy for the Entente to wrest from us territories on the left bank of the Rhine. However, since Alsace-Lorraine is already being treated as French, we believe we do not have to take this into account any longer, and we have gone further and consented to the Anschluss of German Austria with Germany.[14]

The claims put forth in behalf of the Anschluss by some of the most influential men of the new Germany, Ebert, Dr. David, and Brockdorff-Rantzau, created concern abroad and had the effect of accelerating Allied countermoves. The evident alarm was clearly reflected in the contemporary French and English press, as for instance in *Le Temps* and the *Times* of London.

Le Temps paid the closest attention to the proceedings of the Weimar National Assembly, and especially to foreign policy pronouncements of its leading delegates as expressive of the mood and outlook of the German people. On February 9, it reported that Dr. David had asked simultaneously for Alsace-Lorraine and for the incorporation of German Austria. Two days later *Le Temps*, referring to Ebert's speech in the Weimar Assembly which had denounced the West's alleged policy of vengeance, *Le Temps* in turn energetically condemned the denunciation. "Never before had a vanquished nation scoffed in a similar fashion." The new German leaders voiced no regret, not a word of repentance, only threats and announcements of new conquests. Germany not only wanted to emerge from the war "unscathed," but to arise from it "a bigger power; already she is getting ready for annexations."[15]

---

[14]*Neue Freie Presse*, Feb. 11; also *Bohemia*, Prague, Feb. 13.
[15]*Le Temps*, Feb. 11.

The London *Times* showed no more trust in the new Germany than *Le Temps* and, because of the *Reich's* goals in regard to German Austria, no less concern. On February 12 the *Times* printed an article by Frank H. Simonds under the title "Germany's New Tricks, Plans to 'Win the Peace.'" According to Simonds, Germany, after her military collapse, planned to annex 6-7 million in Austria proper. "This means that even with Alsace-Lorraine lost Germany will gain at least 5 million people and an area several times as large as that of the Reichsland. She will acquire more territory and population than Prussia ever gained by a single war." With the absorption of Austria a greatly enlarged German empire of 75 million people would touch the middle Danube, enfold the new Czechoslovakian state, and also threaten the renaissance of Poland.

According to Simonds, the new German campaign in behalf of the Anschluss had found "converts in many American quarters. It bids fair to capture international socialism, as represented at Berne, and international finance, as represented elsewhere." With the annexation of Austria, Germany could "emerge the only victor, with all of Russia as her first international prey." On February 14, the *Times* restated its deep-rooted dislike and suspicion of Germany and the Germans: "They are almost as arrogant and quite as unrepentant as ever . . . the new Germany is the old Germany all over again."[16]

The bold German pronouncements on the Anschluss in the Weimar Assembly had clearly alarmed Western public opinion and awakened the hardly stilled fears and suspicions against Germany.

German statesmen, though initially blurting out their feelings in Weimar, soon regained their composure. And many German and Austrian political leaders again carefully scrutinized the emerging Western policy on the Anschluss and kept their fingers on the pulse of the Western press and of Western public opinion. But most German and Austrian representatives in Weimar and Vienna and the press of both countries continued to voice their desires and sentiments on the Anschluss without any diplomatic inhibition. The ses-

[16]*Times*, London, Feb. 12, also Feb. 14.

sions of the German Constituent Assembly became the
forum for the exchange of brotherly greetings between the
delegates of the peoples of Germany and German Austria,
who gave free expression to the far-reaching aspirations of
both countries to pool their economic, cultural, and spiritual
resources and join hands permanently.

Austrians deluged the National Assembly with greetings,
resolutions, and declarations pledging Austria's determination to effect the Anschluss and voicing loyalty to the
German nation and the Reich. A telegram from Mayor Weisskirchner of Vienna sent "warm salutations" from the City
Council of Vienna. The Council voiced its appreciation for
the "heart-warming words which were dedicated to us German Austrians in the National Assembly," words which had
found the "most ringing echo among the people of our city."
"We look forward to the day when a single Reich will be
created wherein we German Austrians too will be working
toward the welfare of our German nation." Also read was a
telegram from the acting president of the German Austrian
National Assembly, Karl Seitz, who promised that "the firm
united will of the German people on both sides will reunite
German Austria with the mother country."[17]

Among the numerous messages and felicitations reaching
the German Constituent Assembly from Austria were also
some which originated in threatened Carinthia and Styria
and others which were dispatched from neighboring
Salzburg, by the Academic Senate of the University of
Vienna and the German Bohemian Assembly in the Austrian
capital, the German Austrian National Democratic party, the
German Freedom party of Tyrol, representatives of the parties of South Tyrol, and numerous other organizations such
as the Verein für das Deutschtum im Ausland and the
various state chapters in Austria of the Deutsch-
Österreichischer Volksbund.

Delegates of virtually all the German parties, though
disagreeing on the solution of many a political, economic,
and cultural problem, seemed unanimous in their approval
of the Anschluss movement and responded to the Austrian
declarations by frequently giving loud expression to their ap-

---

[17]Heilfron, 1919: **2:** p. 670, 14. Sitzg., Feb. 24.

preciation of Austrian sentiments and Austrian loyalty to the "German spirit." Mrs. Baumer, a member of the German Democratic party, saw in the will of the Austrian people toward the Anschluss a sign of "renewed dedication of our Germandom and our German spirit," which would help the German nation find the strength to pass through difficult times. Koch, also a member of the German Democratic party, welcomed what he prematurely called the entry of Austria into the Reich as a real "source of joy": "This is an event which, in the midst of all the sorrow which has engulfed us, we ought gratefully to accept as one of the most beautiful gains in a very difficult time (persistent 'bravo!' on the left.)"[18] Dr. Preuss, minister of the interior and creator of the German constitution, referred to past differences between *kleindeutsch* and *grossdeutsch*—the Prussian and Austrian points of view — and voiced the hope that the Germany of the future would be a "German Germany." "And this German Germany, free from Austrian as well as Prussian hegemony . . . , is the task of the constitution."[19]

Friedrich Naumann, leading member of the Democratic party and great popularizer of the Mitteleuropa concept, was a natural proponent of the Anschluss. He voiced regret that for two generations the German Austrians had been separated from the German community, but expressed the fervent hope that "we and our German Austrian neighbors will abandon our status of prisoners of war and step forth into the new life as brothers who have been reunited in wonderful and difficult times. We greet the Austrian brothers. Come; we await you!"[20]

Two days later Hugo Haase, who in the early November days of 1918 had given only a cool reply to Dr. Bauer's plea for support of the union, affirmed that all German parties shared the same platform in regard to Austria and the Anschluss. If Germany will succeed in linking up with Austria, "we shall attempt to construct jointly with them the common political edifice which accords with our ideal . . . especially we Socialists, in close cooperation with the Socialists of Austria

---

[18]*Ibid.*, **2:** p. 966, Feb. 28.
[19]*Ibid.*, p. 681, Feb. 24.
[20]*Ibid.*, **1:** pp. 134-135, 6. Sitzg., Feb. 13.

('Very true!' from the Independent Socialists)."[21] The Social Democrat Wilhelm Keil looked upon union as the fulfillment of the "dream of August Bebel"[22] and Adolf Gröber of the Center party asserted that, judging by ancestry and history, the German Austrians belonged to Germany.[23] Professor Jakob presented a pro-Anschluss resolution on behalf of the German People's party. The only representative not mentioning the Anschluss was Count von Posadowsky-Wehner of the rightist National party who was more concerned over the anticipated loss of German territories in the East to Poland rather than in the West to France and over Austria.[24]

Finally, on February 21, 1919, the German Constituent Assembly passed a resolution, sponsored by all the German political parties, in favor of Austria's Anschluss with the Reich.[25] The resolution was the fitting climax of the pro-Anschluss speeches and demonstrations made in the Assembly since its opening session two weeks earlier, and at the same time a belated German reply to the demonstrative proclamation of the Austrian Provisional Assembly on November 12. The German resolution removed the obstacle which, in the view of the Austrian foreign secretary, Dr. Otto Bauer, made new initiatives by German Austria possible. Bauer now concluded that it had become feasible for a German Austrian delegation to journey to Weimar and Berlin for the purpose of entering into negotiations on the Anschluss with the German government.

Apart from such direct negotiations, German Austrians participated in the important work of the Committee on Constitution of the Weimar Assembly.[26] The March 20 session of this committee, according to the *Vossische Zeitung*, turned into an historic, memorable demonstration for the union of German Austria with the Reich. Friedrich Naumann submitted a resolution signed by the deputies Delbrück, Gröber, Haase-Berlin, Heinze, and Quarck, and supported by all parties of the National Assembly, which welcomed the participation of the two Austrian delegates in the negotiations of the commit-

[21]*Ibid.*, **1:** p. 253, 8. Sitzg., Feb. 15; about Haase also **4:** p. 2695.
[22]*Ibid.*, **1:** p. 179, 7. Sitzg., Feb. 14.
[23]*Ibid.*, **1:** p. 122, Feb. 13.
[24]*Ibid.*; see also **4:** p. 2677
[25]*Ibid.*, **2:** p. 667, 13. Sitzg., Feb. 21.
[26]*Ibid.* **2:** p. 681, Feb. 24.

tee. "We have no doubt that the German government may be certain of the approval of the entire nation if it will take into consideration the specific economic difficulties of German Austria."[27]

Thereafter von Körner, representative of the German Foreign Office, reported on the development of the negotiations for unity between the two governments.[28] Ludo Hartmann then assured the committee that German Austria did not demand any special rights such as the southern states had insisted upon when they joined Germany in 1871. Austria was asking for no special concessions ("keine Extrawurst"). The foregoing resolution was then unanimously adopted by the National Assembly, without further debate, and the following day it received the approval of the German government.[29]

Numerous speakers in the Constituent Assembly drew attention to the inconsistency of the Allied Powers who, while honoring the aspirations for national self-determination of the Italians, Czechs, Poles, South Slavs, Rumanians, and others, denied the very principle to the Germans and the German Austrians. They ignored the Allied contention that to permit a link-up between Germany and German Austria would amount to compensating Germany for anticipated territorial losses elsewhere. They also rejected the Allied assertion—expressed most loudly by France—that the Anschluss would give Germany vital strategic and geopolitical advantages in the very heart of Europe and lay the foundation for the very resurgence of vanquished Germany and the reassertion of her hegemony in Europe.

Only a few speakers bared their innermost thoughts on these matters. Dr. Spahn of the Center party admitted that the breakdown of the Austrian Monarchy had "deprived" the German Reich of the protection of her eastern flank and prevented her connection with the Danubian valley and her approach to the Adriatic Sea—disadvantages partly to be overcome by the expected Anschluss.[30] Another speaker held the Anschluss to be "perhaps the only ray of light" reaching

---

[27]*Ibid.*, **3:** p. 1512, March 20-21; also *Voss. Zeitung,* March 21.
[28]*Ibid.*
[29]*Ibid.*, March 22.
[30]Heilfron, 1919: **2:** p. 933, Feb. 28.

Germany.[31] He also advised that the German government should give its close attention to the borders of the Austrian territories which were to join Germany. "The undivided German South Tyrol and German Bohemia must be included in the German Reich (Very true!"). . . . If this occurs, if this is possible for us, then . . . the German race in Europe will find again the road to political and cultural greatness."[32] The Anschluss of the larger German Austria was to become the means for staging a quick comeback after the recent national catastrophe.

Yet these voices, though revealing, were rather unauthorized ones. Officially the German government, while speaking out in defense of her territorial and historical interests, showed on the whole remarkable caution and restraint in regard to German Austria. In the end, the German National Assembly failed to pass any resolution directed toward the actual implementation of the Anschluss.

It was rather the government of little Austria which came out strongly not only in defense of national self-determination and in particular of her right to move toward the Anschluss with Germany, but also in support of the larger German-inhabited Austrian territories — an Austria including the Bohemian lands, all of Carinthia and Styria, German South Tyrol, and West Hungary. On behalf of these territories Austria waged diplomatic battles and occasionally clashed militarily with Czechoslovakia, Yugoslavia, Italy, and even Hungary. In the defense of these interests she believed she could count on possible German support against Czechoslovakia, which alone of all these states bordered on Germany. But even this hope evaporated. Germany's primary concerns lay elsewhere, and her resources of power and influence were sharply circumscribed.

---

[31]*Ibid.* **3:** p. 1232, March 4.
[32]*Ibid.*

2. THE AUSTRIAN ELECTIONS. PREPARATIONS FOR THE AUSTRIAN VISIT

> "Ebert urgently desires the presence [at the Weimar Assembly] of a Social Democratic party delegate from Austria." Ludo Hartmann

EVEN before the Constituent Assembly opened its doors in Weimar on February 6, leading German statesmen were anxious to have an Austrian delegation attend its sessions. Hartmann had therefore recommended to Dr. Bauer that a delegation of the Austrian Council of State and the National Assembly be sent to Weimar to personally extend their fraternal greetings[1] to the Constituent Assembly. On January 25, Hartmann wrote again: "Ebert urgently desires the presence of a party [Social Democratic] delegate from Austria" and "regrets the delay caused by the Austrian elections." Referring to the circumstance that the Austrian elections were to be held on February 16, while the German Constituent Assembly, already elected on January 19, was to begin its work on February 6, Hartmann stressed that Ebert would like to have at least a solemn welcome extended at the Constituent Assembly in the name of the provisional German Austrian National Assembly.[2]

Ever since the German government had failed to respond in kind to the enthusiastic Anschluss proclamation of the Austrian National Assembly on November 12, the Austrian government had been handicapped in its quest for union. On January 23 Bauer had given his view that the German representatives in the Constituent Assembly "by formal resolution" would have to give their approval to the union. At the same time the German Assembly would have to invite German Austria to send her representatives to the legislative body of the German Reich, in accordance with treaty provisions still to be worked out. This would enable "us to

---

[1] *O.S.*, K 109, Anschlussfrage, Hartmann to Bauer, Jan. 23.
[2] *Ibid.*, Jan. 25.

proceed further." "For this purpose, I would myself be prepared to come to Berlin."[3] What Dr. Bauer expected was a belated favorable German response to the Austrian initiative, at least a mild encouragement.

Many Austrians had first thought of the Austrian delegation's proposed journey to Germany in the context of Austria's participation in the work of the Weimar Assembly, but the focus soon shifted from the joint deliberations in the Assembly to the conclusion of an executive agreement between the two foreign ministers. Yet the difference seemed to be only one of the means toward the same end which was widely desired on both sides of the border, the Anschluss.

Dr. Otto Bauer was prepared himself to head the German Austrian delegation to Germany to visit either Weimar, the meeting place of the National Assembly, or Berlin, the national capital and seat of the German Foreign Ministry. He was anxious to enter into direct negotiations with the German government, in order to obtain the best possible terms for Austria's entry into the Reich. While acknowledging the Anschluss resolution of the Austrian Assembly of November 12, 1918, the German Assembly, according to Bauer, should "enter into negotiations with us" concerning the actual implementation of this resolution.[4] It may have dawned upon Bauer that the November resolution about the Anschluss by the Austrian National Assembly, though demonstrating Austrian sentiments to the German people and the world at large, had actually weakened the hand of Austria's cabinet in its dealing with Germany. It had wrested from Austrian negotiators the lever with which to bring sufficient pressure to bear upon their German counterparts to force them to meet Austria halfway economically and financially.

The Weimar Assembly had failed to pass an Anschluss resolution which would have made union an immediate reality. Still there could be no doubt about the hand of welcome which it extended to Austria. Yet the Cabinet continued to maintain the reserved attitude which had so far characterized Germany's response and did not immediately take up Bauer's suggestion.

---

[3]*Ibid.*, Fasz. 5a, Bauer to Hartmann, Jan. 23; see also the anonymous "Anregungen für ein Programm der Besprechungen in Weimar," 89-92.
[4]*Ibid.*, K 261, Deutschland (Anschluss), Bauer to Hartmann, Feb. 5.

It was not before February 19 that Dr. Hartmann reported back to Vienna that "our" proposal had been debated in a recent session of the German Cabinet. Brockdorff-Rantzau had told him that a journey by Dr. Bauer would be "considered desirable" and that the Austrian foreign secretary would be expected in Weimar the following week. That the invitation was not extended in as cordial a manner as might have been expected was, Hartmann felt, probably partly due to the "old fear" of arousing the suspicion and ire of the Entente. Also when a resolution on the Anschluss had been pondered earlier in the German National Assembly, Hartmann reported that several members uttered "words of caution and warning."[5]

Still, it was surprising that Brockdorff-Rantzau had not sent a personal and direct invitation to Dr. Bauer. The foregoing "invitation," extended by way of the Austrian Embassy in Berlin, lacked real warmth. Brockdorff-Rantzau's studied coolness was probably designed to cut down Dr. Bauer's expectations.

Once the Austrian government had decided to send its country's delegation to Berlin and Weimar to reach a definite agreement on the numerous aspects of the Anschluss question, Austrian journals gave increasing attention to the need for solving the outstanding economic problems between the two countries, "The question of the Anschluss is discussed almost exclusively in connection with currency," reported Count Wedel in reference to an article in *Die Zeit*. The article pointed out that Germany would have to make sacrifices for German Austria; she would "have to present her with a national gift as France was doing in Alsace-Lorraine, and she would have to make generous investments if she wanted German Austria."[6] Weimar had declared that it did not look upon the Anschluss as an opportunity for making economic gains; neither did Austria, according to *Die Zeit*, have any such intention.

Economic considerations were similarly uppermost in the communications with Berlin of the well-informed German Embassy staff in Vienna. On the thirteenth of February,

---

[5] *Ibid.*, Hartmann to Bauer.
[6] *N.A.*, T 136-25, Akten betr. Beziehungen . . . , Wedel to F.O., Feb. 19.

Riepenhausen of the Vienna Embassy wrote to an acquaintance in Germany as follows:

> I would like to warn you not to say anything positive in regard to *nervus rerum* (the question of currency or loan). Utterances like these of von Richthofen and Payer may easily come to cost us dearly. The Anschluss will cost us enough anyway. Therefore, I am in favor of speaking often and heartily about the "engagement," while still remaining silent about the details of the "dowry."[7]

The election of February 16 gave the pro-union-minded Austrian Social Democratic party an impressive plurality, though no majority. The day after the election the *Arbeiter-Zeitung* celebrated the result as a "victory" for the "democratic republic." In this first comment, the socialist newspaper did not interpret the electoral outcome as a victory for the Anschluss: this issue, as a matter of fact, was not mentioned at all! Only after the interpretation placed on the Austrian election by reporters for American journals did the Austrian Social Democratic party insist that the election was a mandate for the union with Germany. Now Dr. Bauer could undertake the journey to Berlin.

Three days later Wedel prepared the German Foreign Office for Dr. Bauer's visit. It had been Dr. Bauer, he informed Berlin, who back in November, 1918, had pushed the resolution in behalf of the Anschluss through the German Austrian Council of State. But Dr. Bauer had since "changed his tactics. He had grown more cautious."[8] The discussions which Bauer planned for his impending visit to Germany, Wedel continued, would be limited to political and governmental matters; on the economic and financial aspects of the Anschluss question he could not negotiate. These problems would rather be reserved to a commission of experts which could assemble in Berlin or Vienna.

The German Foreign Office rushed its preparations for the Austrian visit. On February 24, the Bavarian minister in Berlin reported to the Bavarian minister of foreign affairs

---

[7] *B.A.*, Reichsmin. f. Ausw. Angelegenheiten, K 1064-K272188-K272319; Riepenhausen, Feb. 13.

[8] See 6.

that the impending visit of the Austrian secretary of state had prompted the German foreign secretary Brockdorff-Rantzau to invite various officials and experts for a discussion at the Foreign Office that afternoon. According to Count Brockdorff-Rantzau, Bauer was overly optimistic in regard to the prospective talks.

> He had voiced the opinion that it would be possible to reach agreement in Berlin on the Anschluss of German Austria in negotiations lasting about two hours! Brockdorff-Rantzau intends to take the point of view that Germany is unconditionally prepared to welcome Austria. However, questions of political economics which are tied up with the Anschluss cannot be rushed [über's Knie brechen]; he could not give his consent to the creation of a *fait accompli* prior to the Paris Peace Conference; we would have to be agreed on the Anschluss ourselves. He requested general guidelines which would be observed in the discussion with Bauer.[9]

Thus no implementation of the Anschluss before the peace treaty was signed! Economic questions affecting both Germany and Austria could not be solved from one day to the next. Given this framework, the success of Dr. Bauer's mission to Germany was bound to be rather limited, even under the most favorable circumstances.

While in Berlin, Bauer failed to achieve his economic objectives. As he revealed in *Die österreichische Revolution*, the Austrian government wanted to tie its fiscal unit, the krone, in a definite ratio to the German mark and also hoped to obtain a loan from Germany which would facilitate Austria's entrance into the German monetary union. Yet the German government did not find it possible to accept the Austrian proposal. In view of numerous uncertainties, the Reichsbank felt that the implementation of the Austrian proposal would impose an incalculably heavy burden on the Reich. And Bauer concluded: "The decision was postponed." The Reich had decided that the Anschluss would not be effected prior to the decision of the Peace Conference.[10]

---

[9] *G.A.*, MA 103022: Anschluss Deutschösterreichs . . . 1919-1927, Feb. 24, 1919.
[10] Bauer, 1923: p. 144.

In the days before the arrival of the Austrian delegation on German soil, Brockdorff-Rantzau plainly feared that Bauer would make the German government rush headlong toward the Anschluss. This concern may have been deepened by the following letter sent by Austria's aggressive envoy Ludo Hartmann to Brockdorff-Rantzau on February 24, the very day the aforementioned afternoon session was held in the German Foreign Office.

Hartmann wrote as follows:

> Most esteemed Herr Graf! In accordance with your wish, I am taking the liberty of transmitting to you my scheme for a law on the Anschluss of German Austria. I must once more point out that it is a purely private undertaking and I do not know what the [Austrian] Foreign Office would think about it. The draft will only serve to illustrate that it would be possible to complete the legal matters rapidly and decisively, so that in a short time a *fait accompli* could be created, while on the other hand some time would be gained for the more complicated economic negotiations. This way one could get under cover what can already be harvested today. I believe that you will agree with me that this would be of the greatest usefulness. I take the opportunity to add that I have received from two different sides extraordinarily favorable news about the likely attitude of the Entente.[11]

Though by this time Brockdorff-Rantzau undoubtedly knew about Hartmann's proclivity for exaggeration and extreme methods, the repeated emphasis on a *fait accompli,* in combination with the Entente's alleged change of heart and mind on the Anschluss, went straight against the more careful approach recently decided upon by the German government. Thus on the afternoon of the very day Hartmann made his far-reaching private propositions to Berlin, Brockdorff-Rantzau adhered strictly to the adopted policy and refused giving his consent to any *fait accompli* prior to the Paris Conference.

Actually, this caution was not needed as far as Dr. Bauer and the Austrian delegation were concerned. Bauer understood the political limits drawn by the West, which neither

---

[11]*A.A.,* Nachlass Brockdorff-Rantzau's 7/5, Österr. Anschlussfrage. Hartmann to Rantzau, Feb. 24.

German Austria nor Germany could safely transcend. Yet of the two foreign ministers of the German-speaking states, he was the greater driving force in making preparatory moves which, at the opportune moment, would prevent unnecessary delays and procrastination.

On February 25, Brockdorff-Rantzau gave a written statement to Chancellor Scheidemann, informing him of the German policy meetings of the foregoing day and outlining the course he intended to pursue *vis-à-vis* the Austrian delegation. He stated that Dr. Bauer's impending visit had the purpose of discussing the political aspects of the Anschluss as well as of "extracting [extrahieren] binding promises from Germany in regard to economic and financial questions." In anticipation of such procedure he had the other day invited representatives of the various bureaus for a debate on principles. They had reached a consensus that it would be advisable to give Austrian requests "a friendly and welcome reception," while leaving the more complicated questions to thorough examination by the departments. Brockdorff-Rantzau had also directed the officials to refer Dr. Bauer to him for the practical implementation of any suggestions he might make.[12] The German foreign minister was resolved to settle outstanding German-Austrian differences, but not quite as hurriedly as he thought Dr. Bauer would wish, nor quite as completely.

The stage was all set for the arrival of the Austrian delegation. German friendliness was rather subdued and the atmosphere on the whole somewhat marred by the extreme caution and reluctance of most members of the German government, including its foreign minister.

The Allied press was keenly aware of the preparations for the meeting in Berlin. It had followed the moves toward the *Anschluss* on both sides of the Inn river with close attention. *Le Temps* warned on February 14 that important developments had taken place during the last three months, moves on the part of Vienna and Berlin to come closer toward each other, with fusion as the ultimate goal.[13] According to *Le Temps*, the Austrian delegation's visit to Germany had been carefully planned and the conclusion of a treaty between the

[12]B.A., K 272198-100, Brockdorff-Rantzau to Scheidemann, Feb. 25.
[13]*Le Temps*, Feb. 14.

two German-speaking states was to crown the journey. Only the dire prophecy of the absorption of Austria into Germany by April, 1919, turned out to be in error.

Three days later, on February 17, *Le Temps* aimed its guns directly at both Dr. Bauer and Brockdorff-Rantzau who, because of their eminent roles, repeatedly became prime targets of the French press.[14] While the former was often criticized, both for so-called pro-Bolshevik tendencies and nationalist inclinations,[15] Brockdorff-Rantzau was attacked because of his alleged previous Pan-German sympathies and imperialist leanings and was especially criticized for having come out strongly for the Anschluss of Austria.

The repeated charges of Germany's "secret" diplomacy and of her policy of aggrandizement clearly reflected French fears, but they were at the same time also intended as a warning to France's allies, especially the United States and President Wilson. During the month of February, *Le Temps* repeatedly called for energetic decisions on the Anschluss question by the French government.[16] The threat of French action and the agreement which British and United States representatives reached on February 21 to oppose the Anschluss prior to the conclusion of the peace treaty — news of which was permitted to leak out — represented the sword of Damocles which hung over the Berlin and Weimar conference. And Brockdorff-Rantzau apparently believed that it might strike down at any moment.

---

[14]*Ibid.,* Feb. 17, "La spéculation de Brockdorff-Rantzau"
[15]Bauer, 1923: p. 153: "While the Paris press had so far denounced me as a 'Pan-German,' now it declared me a Bolshevik."
[16]*Le Temps,* Feb. 24, "L'Avenir de l'Autriche."

3. THE AUSTRO-GERMAN PROTOCOL, MARCH 2, 1919.

"[Otto Bauer] considered the implementation of the Anschluss prior to the conclusion of the peace treaty . . . inopportune. I concur with Dr. Bauer's view." Brockdorff-Rantzau

AUSTRO-GERMAN negotiations about the Anschluss were actually commenced in Weimar and continued in Berlin between February 27 and March 3. On February 28, Wolff's Telegram Bureau reported the following welcome speech by Brockdorff-Rantzau:

You will have observed the satisfaction with which the German public greeted the presence in Berlin of Secretary of State Dr. Bauer and his companions. The thought advanced by our fathers of belonging together will, I confidently hope, become a reality. It is a matter of extraordinary satisfaction to me to be permitted to take a leading role in working toward its implementation. As you know, I have lived in Vienna a long time. I know Austria, I have learned to understand and appreciate her, and in my thoughts I am often in Vienna, to which I am bound by the memory of the happiest years of my career. But the statesman must not judge matters in accordance with his feelings, as much as they have taken possession of him. . . . If the principle of nationality is raised as the first principle for peoples, there can and must not be an exception for the German nationality.[1]

---

[1] *A.A.*, Nachlass Brockdorff-Rantzau's, Presse 6/4, Wolff's Tel. Bureau, Feb. 28, H 233701. In his account *Die österreichische Revolution*, 1923, Dr. Bauer treated his journey to Weimar and Berlin rather sketchily (pp. 144-145). Writing at times apparently from memory, without consulting the diplomatic record and his own notes. Bauer erred in regard to the date of his departure from Vienna to Germany which he placed "in early March." The Austrian delegation must have left Vienna on February 24 or 25. After having stopped in Weimar where Bauer met Ebert and Scheidemann, the Austrian delegation continued its travel to Berlin where it commenced its work on February 27; it left the German capital on March 3. The journey to Germany has long been ignored in works on Austrian or, for that matter, German history. In the authoritative *Geschichte der Republik Österreich's*, Benedikt H., ed. (1954), W. Goldinger devoted four and a half pages to the entire Anschluss movement in 1918-1919 (pp. 94-98) and only eight lines to Bauer's

Turning to the economics of the Anschluss, Brockdorff-Rantzau emphasized that "a good marriage must also have a good economic foundation." Neither Germany nor Austria wished to "get the better of the other." "The personality of the eminent statesman who stands at the head of her [Austria's] mission is a guarantee that the negotiations will develop in the best and most friendly manner." It was one of the most positive speeches ever made by Brockdorff-Rantzau on the Anschluss. He was keenly aware of the historic role which he was called upon to play in attempting to bring the *grossdeutsch* solution of the German question, which had failed in 1848-1849 and 1866, close to fruition.

One of Dr. Bauer's first official meetings in Germany was with Chancellor Scheidemann. According to the latter's account, Bauer brought up the currency question, stressing that a solution to this difficult question could be found if one considered it "not purely as a business problem, but also as a political one in behalf of which Germany was ready to make certain sacrifices." Bauer also hinted cautiously, but ominously, at Austria's having been offered a loan by the Entente.[2]

According to Scheidemann, in his talk with Bauer about the currency question he had taken a merely theoretical position, remaining vague in practical matters and not making any definite promises. "Minister Eugen Schiffer told me," Scheidemann reported in the same vein, "that a discussion between him and the Austrians would hardly go beyond a few general phrases; he would, in any case, avoid giving assurances."[3] Apparently, the entire German Cabinet had

---

journey to Germany and the agreement reached there. Only recently, V. Reimann (1968) and O. Leichter (1970) have treated it in somewhat greater detail. There exists no scholarly biography of Brockdorff-Rantzau. The German historian Erich Brandenburg completed in 1932 a biography of Rantzau which is largely a collection of documents with connecting text, but the Auswärtiges Amt opposed its publication. This biography is to be found in the Nachlass Brockdorff-Rantzau's and is available in microfilm, serials 1690H, 1691H, 1692H, roll 1013, but contains few significant data on the Anschluss.

[2]At the very moment Bauer had come to Germany, another Austrian delegation, though of lesser stature, had traveled to Paris to plead for economic aid. But it returned empty-handed, since it was unable to give the French the necessary assurances that Austria would reject the Anschluss.

[3]*N.A.*, T 136-125; Scheidemann to F.O., Feb. 26.

taken all necessary advance precautions against the persuasive powers of the Austrian foreign secretary.

On February 28 Brockdorff-Rantzau wrote the following "secret note" about Bauer's utterances during their meeting:

> Secretary of State Bauer expressed himself in regard to the German Bohemian question to the effect that he would like to prevent unconditionally the Anschluss [*sic*] of German Bohemia with the Czechoslovak state. . . . He considered the Czechs enemies of German Austria, but hinted that he would not be disinclined to reach an agreement with them. When I indicated that in my opinion we ought to attempt to get along with the Czechs, Dr. Bauer acknowledged this and explained that he fully comprehended that the German Reich in its entirety had interests different from German Austria.[4]

Bauer voiced the wish to be kept informed about any negotiations between Berlin and Prague.

German-Czechoslovak relations, in spite of the recent occupation of German-inhabited regions of Czechoslovakia, were strikingly good, and Germany left Austria to fend on her own for the right of self-determination of her brethren. It was Germany's policy to remain aloof, unconcerned with their political and national fate. On the other hand, when the German foreign minister turned to the Polish question, an "object of particular concern" to Germany, Dr. Bauer replied that he fully understood his preoccupation: "German Austria, however, no longer has anything to do with Poland." The differences of national outlook and interest between Germany and German Austria could not be better illustrated than by Germany's relative lack of concern for the fate of German Bohemia and German South Tyrol and German Austria's relative indifference toward the fate of the German minority in the new Polish state.

Regarding the relations of Austria with Italy, Brockdorff-Rantzau described Bauer's position thus:

> Dr. Bauer informed me confidentially that for some time Italy had openly been attempting a rapprochement with Vienna. The question of the new border with Tyrol formed the major

---

[4]*A.A.*, Nachlass Br.-R.'s, 7/5, Akten betr. Anschlussfrage, Feb. 28, H234603-606.

bone of contention. Under no circumstances, remarked the secretary of state, could he accept the Brenner line as a boundary and permit the German parts of Tyrol to be ceded to Italy. He had done everything to present emphatically his point of view *vis-à-vis* Italy and hoped for success, especially since he sincerely entertained the wish to enter into neighborly relations with Italy. I confirmed him in this view.

Brockdorff-Rantzau gained the impression that Bauer "definitely" counted on the resumption of economic relations with the states of the former Habsburg empire. Bauer thought it out of the question that France would be prepared for any rational settlement in the foreseeable future. And Britain appeared to be moving toward the French point of view.

> England now appears to be attempting to prevent the Anschluss of German Austria with Germany in the final hour. I have gained the impression that Dr. Bauer does not entertain any illusions about the almost desperate situation of German Austria and that he tries with keen perspicacity to do everything he can to rescue what still can be rescued, and that in any case he was intent on acting toward myself with unreserved candor. We have agreed that in especially important cases we should be in touch with each other through private letters. Dr. Bauer has certainly an unusually strong mind and also left me with the impression of complete loyalty. This impression has been reinforced through the form in which he concluded yesterday's negotiations about economic and political questions.
>   Unfortunately, Dr. Bauer hinted that it was not impossible that he might resign in the foreseeable future. When I expressed my vivid regret about this possibility, he replied that the politics which German Austria would pursue toward the Reich would be continued independently of the person heading the Foreign Office. This was not a question of personality, and the mood in German Austria apparently had recently substantially changed in favor of an Anschluss with the Reich.

Recently the Entente had strongly supported the scheme of the Danubian confederation, Bauer informed Brockdorff-Rantzau.

Should the Entente exert pressure upon the Austrian government, he would formally enter into negotiations; he assured me, however, that they would not come to a positive result. He asked me therefore not to pay any attention to possible negotiations; he would soon succeed in carrying the concept of a Danubian confederation ad absurdum, especially since none of the other states really has any inclination to accept German Austria into the confederation.[4a]

Brockdorff-Rantzau was greatly impressed with Dr. Bauer. During the last years of the war the German aristocrat had come to understand the importance of the working class and had propagated a people's Kaisertum, if only for reasons of nationalism and Germany's survival as a world power. He had understood how to gain the confidence of the Majority Socialists and even of some of the Independents. Now he had also established a good working relationship with Dr. Bauer. Bauer himself appeared realistic in his evaluation of France's bitter opposition to the Anschluss concept and in his view that England was moving closer to France, likewise rejecting the Anschluss. Still, he believed that by pointing out the hollowness of the Danubian confederation concept, he might disarm the Western Powers and lessen their opposition to Austria's allegedly only other alternative, the Anschluss with Germany. Yet he also revealed his skepticism when he hinted at the possibility of his resignation as foreign minister in the near future.

After the lengthy initial conversation of the two foreign ministers on the European political situation and its implications for the Anschluss, Dr. Bauer and members of his delegation were asked to meet with members of the German cabinet, Havenstein, the president, and von Glasenapp, vicepresident of the Reichsbank, and other high-placed German officials. At the very opening of the negotiations, Dr. Bauer made it clear that the Austrian government could maintain its impetus in the matter of the Anschluss only if it were supported by the people. But Austrian public opinion could not be won over unless the country's "economic security" was assured. Since German Austria was economically by far the weaker partner, Bauer expected German consideration for

---

[4a] *Ibid.*

Austria's plight. When officials of the Reichsbank pointed out that the Anschluss would impose economic sacrifices on Germany, Bauer countered that in this case Germany would only be making "sacrifices for herself."[5]

In his meeting on February 27 with high-placed German officials Bauer had suggested that immediate attention be given to three problems which could be approached "without waiting for the juridical act of the Anschluss." These were: first, legal accommodation, second, social legislation — German Austria had a special interest in workers' rights, labor legislation, and insurance against sickness and old age — and third, the educational system. Bauer reminded his interlocutors of the main argument of the Austrian opponents to the Anschluss, the assertion that German Austria would be overwhelmed and suppressed by the much larger Germany. If he could obtain assurances in this regard, it would be possible to combat the opposition to the Anschluss more effectively.

If Germany and Austria were immediately united, Bauer continued, the Entente would be "insulted and German Austria would be subjected to vengeance." The Entente could not be challenged at this time. Yet in regard to "purely economic matters" it was possible to "act with speed." There were realities which the Entente could not ignore without causing chaos and dangerous social conditions. It was Vienna's intention, Bauer asserted, to clarify all problems in such a manner that the Anschluss could be effected "at the first opportune moment." He was thinking of accommodation of the two states along several lines, mutual adjustment in the areas of legal and educational development and social legislation.[6]

On March 2, ignoring numerous acts, anti-Anschluss declarations, and outright warnings on the part of the Allies, Brockdorff-Rantzau and Dr. Bauer signed a protocol on the union.[7] German Austria was to enter the federally structured

---

[5]*O.S.*, K 261, I, Deutschland (Anschluss), Protokoll d. Sitzung im A.A., Feb. 28, pp. 278-283.

[6]*Ibid.*, Protokoll d. Sitzg. d. deutschöst. u. d. deutschen Regierung vom 27. Feb. 1919: pp. 267-271; see also Protokolle v. 28. Feb. and 1. und 2. März, pp. 278-283, 302-303, 322-325.

[7]*A.A.*, Nachlass Br.-R, 's, Anschlussfrage, March 2.

Reich as a separate member state. Should individual Länder of German Austria wish to separate from Austria, either to enter the Reich as states of their own, or to join other member states, the government of the German Reich would effect their entry only in agreement with the government of German Austria. This was designed to discourage the then spreading separatist movement in some of the Austrian Länder, especially Vorarlberg, Salzburg, and Tyrol. At the same time German Austria could permit the Sudetenland and Northern Bohemia, from which it was geographically separated, to join neighboring German states. The agreement thus assured Austria a veto over "separatist" Anschluss movements of the individual Länder!

Article one, paragraph one of the Protocol stated that the governments of Germany and the German Austrian republic were agreed on quickly concluding a state treaty confirming their union, which would then be submitted to the two parliaments for approval and ratification. Thereafter, the delegates of German Austria were to be seated in the legislative assembly of the German Reich. Austria was given the right of special representation at the Vatican and was to receive papal legates in Vienna. For the transition period she was also to maintain relations of her own with the succession states. In the event that relations between state and church in Germany should be regulated by the former, Austria would, within limits, retain the right of special legislative regulation.

Austria recognized that the Reich would create an army of its own and its own railway system. There was agreement that a "suitable" portion of the former civil servants of the Dual Monarchy would be taken over by the Reich; details were jointly to be worked out later. With the entry of Austria into the Reich and the German economy, full unity of currency was to be established between the two countries. Union was to be prepared "immediately" through the work of commissions in such a manner that it became reality at the moment of the Anschluss. In order to facilitate the support of the rate of exchange of the German Austrian *krone*, the Reich would grant German Austria a *mark* credit. Negotiations would have to be undertaken for this purpose, but Germany assured Austria "utmost consideration." Germany also assumed the same obligation for German Austria which she carried for other member states. Austria on the other hand permitted the Reich to levy those revenues on her territory which were also raised on the soil of the other member states. The Reich also assumed the payment of interests and capital of a still to be determined portion of German Austria's public debts. But, a very anti-climax of the agreements reached, the treaty provisions were not published at that time.

In his surprisingly brief treatment of the Berlin Conference in his account of this period, *Die österreichische Revolution* (1923), Dr. Bauer explained the secretive character of the negotiations. The terms of the treaty, if published, could have powerfully strengthened the Anschluss movement in German Austria, but would have unfavorably influenced the peace negotiations. The German government for instance had conceded that German Austria, in the event of her incorporation into the Reich, should be treated financially as if she had belonged to the Reich since 1914. Since a great portion of Austria's debts would have been taken over by the Reich, it did not appear advisable to publish this treaty stipulation because it might have prompted the Entente to impose the entire war debt of the old Austria upon the German Austrian Republic. After her incorporation into the German customs zone, German Austria, according to the agreements, would also be permitted to continue to levy internal customs duties on German industrial products for a number of years, in order to protect her own industry, while Austrian industrial products could be imported into the former German territory free of duty. Again, Austria could not reveal these terms of the treaty lest the Entente insert commercial stipulations into the peace treaty which would make implementation of the agreement impossible.[8]

On March 3, the last day of the visit of the Austrian delegation, Brockdorff-Rantzau jotted down the following "secret note":

> Today, just before the departure of the Secretary of State, I had a fully confidential talk with Dr. Bauer. . . . He declared that he intended to cooperate with Italy in all circumstances and that he had found great willingness on the Italian side to meet Austria half-way. There existed there, without doubt, the

---

[8]Bauer, 1923: p. 145.

intention to cooperate with Germany and German Austria, and he would be happy if we too would support Italy. [What was apparently meant was support in the Italo-Yugoslav dispute]. As far as I was concerned, I did not commit myself.

Regarding Great Britain, Dr. Bauer remarked in reply to my questions that he had the impression that in London they intended to take a friendly position *vis-à-vis* Austria, partly out of traditional sentiments of former sympathy. He had always found understanding on the part of English representatives. How they felt in London about the question of the Anschluss he did not know for certain; it might be possible that England's friendly attitude had as its object the prevention of the Anschluss. In general there was undoubtedly great fear of Bolshevism in England; and therefore an inclination to save Vienna from extreme misery.... As far as America was concerned, so far she also had taken a friendly attitude *vis-à-vis* Austria.

In regard to France, according to the foreign secretary, any endeavor was in vain. In their fanatical hatred of Germany the French were completely deluded. To it must be added the old sympathy for the Czechs and the Poles, which now, after the victory of the Entente, had taken on almost grotesque forms.[9]

"I again had the impression," the German foreign secretary continued, "that the secretary of state, in clear and calmly calculating fashion and in spite of the political opposition, desires the initiation of normal ties and particularly of good economic relations, with Czechoslovakia."[10]

The last conversation of the two foreign ministers took place when Brockdorff-Rantzau accompanied Dr. Bauer to the Johannistal airport. The German foreign secretary was especially anxious to obtain "a clear picture" of Dr. Bauer's views regarding the timing of the Anschluss.

"[Dr. Bauer] declared that it was his view that we should not irritate the Entente, since both countries, especially German Austria, including Vienna, relied on them completely for the supply of food and materials. If they shut off the importation of coal and food to Vienna, a catastrophe would occur. Under these circumstances he proposed that the commissions for the consideration of the Anschluss convene as soon as possible,

[9]*A.A.*, Nachlass Br.-R.'s, Anschlussfrage, H 234603-606.
[10]*Ibid.*, March 3, H 234607-608.

perhaps in ten to fourteen days, and prepare everything so that the plebiscite, if necessary, could be decided upon at once. Contrary to the opinions of Dr. Hartmann and Ebert, president of the Reich, he considered the implementation of the Anschluss prior to the conclusion of the peace treaty to be inopportune. I concur with Dr. Bauer's view, and we both agreed that if the Anschluss were to be staged prematurely, we could easily be forced by the Entente into an embarrassing retreat.[11]

Bauer's views on the likely position of the Western Powers were, as might be expected, not different from those he had expressed four days earlier to his German colleague. As before, he was opposed to throwing down the gauntlet in front of the Entente, but wished to proceed with the economic and legal preparations for the Anschluss by establishing joint commissions, which would commence their work within the next few days. Strangely enough, he did not think that this would "irritate" the Western Powers or, if he thought so, he was prepared to take the risk. Brockdorff-Rantzau "concurred" with Bauer's views and, contrary to President Ebert's views, with the policy decision to postpone the juridical Anschluss until the peace treaty was signed!

The German-Austrian protocol of March 2, 1919, was basically an agreement between the two states to sign, at an indefinite time, a treaty which would make the Anschluss that Austria had earlier proclaimed a reality. It probably would have been unnecessary had the Weimar Assembly passed a formal resolution approving the Austrian Novem-

---

[11]*Ibid.* — There were other differences between German Austrian and German representatives about the question of a central bank and a German loan. German Austria favored having her separate bank of issue, but said she would follow German leadership in her currency and banking policy. The Germans insisted, however, that in the interests of political and economic unity the *Reich* required a single bank. No definite agreement was reached in these matters and none at all in regard to a German loan to Austria. In the field of taxation far-reaching concord was attained in principle concerning indirect taxes and state monopolies. Austria agreed not to demand financial rights exceeding those granted to all other German states. It was also decided to keep the question of war reparations of the two countries completely separated. German representatives did not reach a decision about the Austrian demand that the Reich assume all debts of the old Monarchy. The German members of the commission finally took under advisement the Austrian request for German financial aid to meet current expenses until such time when Austria would have adequate resources to pay for them (*N.A.*, T 136-25, Akten . . . March 12).

ber, 1918, union declaration forthwith, making it final and irrevocable. The opposition of the Entente had clearly intimidated Germany and Austria. In November, 1918, Germany, too dazed to make as bold and reckless an Anschluss proclamation as German Austria, could hardly be expected to come out openly for union when the Weimar Assembly began its work. By then Germany's dependence on the confidence and good will of the Paris peacemakers, mostly opponents of the Anschluss, had had time to penetrate the German mind. What was intended by the governments of both countries in signing the protocol in early March was to remove existing internal obstacles to the Anschluss. Thus union could be realized, if not immediately, "at the first opportune moment." Therefore the conclusion of the German-Austrian Protocol was still a challenge to the Western Powers.

But it was a subdued challenge. Not only was the Austro-German agreement not made public, but also in the weeks preceding the meeting in Weimar and Berlin, authorities in both states had apparently advised giving the conference as little publicity as possible. The Vienna *Arbeiter-Zeitung* and the Berlin *Vorwärts* virtually buried the journey of Dr. Bauer and the Austrian delegation in silence, a practice followed by many German newspapers. Others offered only the most meager reports.

Whatever actual achievement the Austro-German Protocol represented, from the Austrian point of view only a beginning had been made. About a week after his return to Vienna, Dr. Bauer penned the following letter to Count Brockdorff-Rantzau:

Most esteemed Count! Right after my return I took the opportunity to report to the Cabinet as well as the Council of State . . . about the agreement which I had the honor to conclude with your Excellency. My presentation in both bodies found a rather favorable reception, the more so since I could give the assurance that the intentions of the German government, as observed by me, permit one to expect with certainty that the negotiations which are still to be carried on will lead to a satisfactory result.

However, I would not render a useful service to my cause if I did not make it clear to your Excellency that considerable concessions of an economic nature and especially in the financial area, are in any case inevitable.

Two notions-first, that German Austria has made extraordinarily large sacrifices in the interest of the entire German nation and must therefore receive compensation, and second, that German Austria has suffered far greater losses than the German Reich—have put down deep roots here in the minds of many.

Bauer suggested to Brockdorff-Rantzau that the two foreign ministers provide the commission on currency problems and state finances certain basic guidelines, since the commission, if only for lack of sufficient authorization, would be unable to render a final decision. For this decision was a political one, and therefore could only be made through political agents. "However, the departmental patriotism on both sides leads to frictions and discords which perhaps . . . cloud the atmosphere of the entire negotiations . . . ." Granting credits alone, Bauer added, could not satisfy public opinion in German Austria. Other financial concessions should be granted.

"A calming influence," which was especially necessary in the financial commission, would also be desirable in the other commissions. Bauer himself planned therefore in all cases where a clash of some magnitude was to be feared to send a delegate to exercise a mediating influence. "I would be grateful to your Excellency if the Berlin Foreign Office also wished to contribute in a similar manner to facilitating the work of the commissions."[12]

One of those who were quite dissatisfied with the results of Dr. Bauer's negotiations in Berlin and Weimar was Ludo Hartmann. The day after Dr. Bauer left Germany, on March 4, Hartmann wrote him a letter as follows: He was driven by "duty of conscience to explain to you once more, after the conclusion of the negotiations, my views which deviate in some respects [from yours] and my doubts about the manner in which the question of the Anschluss is being treated."[13]

Hartmann was in favor of bringing about the legal Anschluss first and discussing economic principles later, while

---

[12]*Ibid.*
[13]*O.S.*, K 261, Berlin Protokoll v. 2. März, 1919, I, Deutschland (Anschluss), Hartmann to Bauer, March 4.

Bauer, "in reverse," put the economic discussions first. Bauer's procedure contained "dangers." True, the fear that the Entente might demand "compensations" in exchange for consenting to the Anschluss explained "the hesitant posture." But Hartmann had no sympathy for such policy and even blamed Dr. Bauer for having imposed it upon the German government: "I confess that, knowing the conditions, I have the impression that your conception of the [international] situation was decisive in regard to the hesitant course here."

Because of Dr. Bauer's views and his reluctance to act decisively in behalf of the Anschluss, Hartmann continued, Austria had missed,

> as Ebert in particular had stressed, the opportunity of working together in writing the constitution. I repeat: what is at issue now is not so much diplomatic finesse, but resolve and determination, the knowledge that a deed must be done. . . . The harm which may result from it appears to me relatively small compared to the goal that we all wish to attain.

"If we miss the right moment," he continued, the responsibility which "history has placed on our shoulders" would be tremendous, and "our children and grandchildren, owing to our current indecisiveness," would still have to cope with this question. In a telegram dated March 20 he again advised Bauer, who was rather tolerant of his German envoy, to complete the legal Anschluss "at once." [14]

The difference of opinion between Ebert and Hartmann on the one side and Bauer on the other—all Socialists of varying colors—had, however, no relation to the Marxist world view or their different interpretations of it. In Hartmann's view, Bauer put economic unification ahead of legal unity, while he himself was in favor of proclaiming the legal union first, being convinced that economic unity and every other kind would quickly follow suit. Their differences were based partly on their varying assessments of the international situation and the balance of power in Europe, and partly on temperament and the strength and recklessness of the national impulse.

---

[14]*Ibid.*, Hartmann to Bauer, March 20.

On the twelfth of March the German Austrian Assembly convened and heard Dr. Bauer's report about his journey to Weimar and Berlin.[15] He had gained the conviction that the entire German people, "without regard to party," was completely agreed on the union with Austria. But Bauer did not exaggerate the actual achievement. He made it clear that only a program for further, though elaborate, negotiations had been laid down. A series of commissions to consist of representatives of the pertinent offices in the Reich and the corresponding Austrian bureaus, both under the guidance of the two foreign offices, was to convene during the months of March and April, in Berlin and Vienna, and one each in Munich and Leipzig.

After approving Bauer's report, the Austrian National Assembly, taking account of the results of the recent mid-February elections, proceeded to form a new cabinet. The Austrian public was taken by surprise when it became known that Bauer wished to relinquish his office to devote his energy, as the *Arbeiter-Zeitung* put it, to "the great task of socialization."[16] Bauer's decision to shift his endeavors to socialization may have been related to a temporary setback of his and of the cause of the Anschluss in the councils of the Social Democratic party.[17]

Soon after the Austro-German treaty of early March had been signed, both sides had begun to make preparations for the work of the joint commissions for which the agreement provided. On March 31, the Bavarian ambassador in Berlin wrote to Munich about a "preliminary" German strategy meeting which was to lay the groundwork for the negotiations in the economic commission.[18] The desirability of creating a unitary economic realm was taken under consideration. About the length of the transition period pre-

[15]*Stenogr. Protokolle . . . konstit. Nationalversammlung*, Bauer, March 12.

[16]*Arbeiter-Zeitung*, March 15.

[17]*N.A.*, T 136-25, Akten . . . , Wedel to Rantzau, March 24. According to Wedel, an understanding had been reached between Chancellor Karl Renner and the editor-in-chief of the *Arbeiter-Zeitung*, Friedrich Austerlitz, to proceed more slowly in the *Anschluss* question. In the executive committee of the Party Austerlitz had asserted that the national point of view had harmed the Social Democratic party. Dr. Bauer had remained in the minority and Dr. Renner was allegedly searching for a new secretary of state.

[18]*G.A.*, Bavarian Embassy, Berlin, to Bavarian Ministry of Trade, March 31, "Anschluss Deutschösterreichs . . . ," Italics A.D.L.

ceding the complete unification, the ambassador reported, "they are not clear in Austria; they speak of one between six and twelve years."[19] On the fifteenth of April, in view of the "impending negotiations" with German Austria, another meeting of the German members of the commissions was held. The presiding officer von Körner stated in conclusion that the Anschluss should be prepared step by step in joint consultation so that it could be proclaimed as soon as the preliminary peace was signed.

> The desire to raise the status of Vienna was justified. The Reich Office of Patents could be moved to Vienna, in spite of opposition which had been advanced; also the Department of Health. Commissions for financial and economic affairs, for social security, and for the problems of the city of Vienna should soon convene and show that one could make progress and gain as firm foundations for the Anschluss as possible. The government of the Reich is prepared to welcome German Austria under conditions acceptable to us; the greater interest however is on the side of Austria.[20]

This view, shared by many Germans, was, however, voiced more frequently in internal discussions than in talks with the Austrians.

Financial problems had played a major role in the Austro-German talks in Weimar and in Berlin in early March. In the view of the German-Austrian Foreign Ministry, they represented the most difficult hurdles. Berlin wished that Vienna would avoid raising these problems. In a letter to Wedel, Langworth of the German Foreign Office criticized the Austrian government for attaching a cardinal importance to the financial problems and subordinating all others to them. Wedel was to impress the Vienna government to the effect that Germany would do "everything possible" to facilitate and hasten the Anschluss.[21]

---

[19]*Ibid.*; see also Bavarian Embassy, Vienna, to Bavarian For. Min., April 10; also April 28.

[20]*Ibid.*

[21]*A.A.*, Öst. 95, v. 29, Langwerth v. Simmern to Wedel, March 29; about the work of the various joint commissions on the *Anschluss*, see especially *O.S.*, Präsidialakte, Fasz. 5a, folios 23, 33, 79, 103-109, 205, 284, 296-297, 502-505, 512, 567-586, 619-622, 639, 644, 646-659, 672-674, 693f.

In a letter to Wedel, Brockdorff-Rantzau similarly repeated the stock-in-trade promises to do everything in behalf of union which was consistent with German interests; he prophesied, however, that the negotiations with Vienna would not lead to any agreement, "since the situation is not yet ripe." [22] It was a self-fulfilling prophecy. The German government was simply not prepared to drive full speed ahead.

The first meetings of the financial commission took place in Vienna between April 10 and 19. Among Austrian representatives on the committee was Gustav Stolper, editor of the *Österreichischer Volkswirt,* and among the German delegates were Havenstein, president of the Reichsbank, and von Glasenapp, its vice-president. The German representatives submitted to the German government an elaborate memorandum pointing to the dangers of an overevaluation of the Austrian crown in relation to the German mark. They underlined the danger of inflation and of the damage to Germany's balance of trade. The financial commission finally agreed that a definite exchange rate should be established only at a later date, and that in any case German Austria would not become part of the German currency system before January 1, 1920. [23]

In early March Dr. Otto Bauer had returned to Vienna from Berlin, a somewhat disappointed man. Nor did the subsequent discussions in the various committees encourage him. As he wrote bluntly to Hartmann: "In not a single point has any definite accord resulted, not even in those questions which had already been thoroughly discussed in my negotiations in Berlin. . . ." He found it especially disappointing that Germany refused to promise a loan. He also was both disillusioned and annoyed that the German representatives lacked the authority to make binding agreements.

The procedures of the representatives of the Reich completely failed to demonstrate that they were properly aware of the

[22] *A.A.,* Öst. 95, v. 29, Br.-R. to Wedel, Apr. 5, Tel. 198.
[23] *B.A.,* Reichskanzlei, R 43-I/104, v. 1, Reichsbank-Direktorium to Ebert, March 31 and "Denkschrift über d. Folgen einer Überbewertung d. Krone beim Eintritt in d. deutsche Währungsgebiet"; see also Instruktionen d. deutschöst. Referenten über d. Verhandlungen über d. Zusammenschluss mit d. Deutschen Reich, *Ö.S.,* Apr. 9, 1919, pp. 351-354.

urgency we had stressed. Thus they have now placed a lengthy questionnaire before us and have also requested more data. I ask now, why was this request not submitted to us on March 2, or at the latest, in mid-March?

Bauer urged Hartmann to point out to Berlin that a change in the method of conducting negotiations was imperative. He no longer disguised his impatience: "The dilatory procedure previously followed is politically extremely undesirable to me."[24] And he suggested smaller delegations which would be authorized to reach agreement within a few days.

At the same time, as if not even relying on the aggressive Hartmann, Bauer wrote directly to Brockdorff-Rantzau revealing his dissatisfaction with the progress made by the committees and voicing substantial criticism of German procedures. He had to confess, he wrote, that after the negotiations in Berlin he had expected "substantially more far-reaching results." He especially regretted the lack of authority of the German delegation to make a definite decision in regard to a loan. This "unexpected procrastination of an expected concession" could not remain unknown and would be interpreted as a "deliberately dilatory" move of the German government. While not denying that Germany was serious in her intention to aid German Austria and effect the union, Bauer reminded his counterpart that every mark spent at this time by the Reich in behalf of the Anschluss was likely to produce "incomparably greater political success" than was likely to be attained some weeks or months later.[25]

Again, nothing was more revealing of the different attitudes of the governments of Austria and Germany than their different assessments of the results of the work of the financial commission. While the Austrians were plainly disappointed and even bitter, the German representatives congratulated each other on what they considered achievements. Von Glasenapp conceded after his return to Berlin that no financial accord had been reached, but he seemed rather pleased. Körner of the Foreign Office expressed the same sentiments and judged that such

[24]*O.S.*, Präsidialakte, Fasz. 5a, Bauer to Hartmann, Apr. 20, pp. 647-648.
[25]*Ibid.*, Bauer to Br.-R., Apr. 20, p. 649.

preliminary work as the commission had been entrusted with had been successfully completed. The two parties had been brought closer together and the outcome, he claimed, had been "satisfactory" to both. Though Germany was prepared to resume negotiations with Austria at any time, he insisted that her representatives could not be given full powers to proceed on their own, since the problems were too "complicated and diversified."[26]

The commission on Vienna dealt with an agenda which listed goals suggested by the Vienna city government to the German Austrian Foreign Office. It included among other things German construction of a canal system in southern Germany in order to stimulate Danubian commerce and German support for preserving Vienna's leading position as an artistic and musical center. In response to Ludo Hartmann's entreaties, President Ebert declared himself ready to spend several months each year in Vienna. Furthermore, he did not anticipate any objections to the proposal that the Reichstag hold regular sessions in Vienna. Though others expressed opposition to the transfer of some government offices and departments to the German Austrian capital, Körner agreed with Ebert's view.[27]

Austrian delegates to the transportation commission journeyed to Berlin to hold discussions with their opposites. An unexpected difficulty arose when officials of the Prussian Ministry of Public Works presented their objections to the construction of a Rhine-Main-Danube canal, which they judged to be unprofitable. The Austrian representatives, however, considered the canal an "absolute necessity" for western and southern Germany. Nikolaus Post, German Austrian chargé d'affaires in Berlin, then wrote to Vienna that, if Germany wanted Austria's Anschluss, she should provide "a partially suitable substitute for the lost connections [with the Adriatic]" and should not favor the interests of eastern and northern Germany over those of the western and southern portions of the Reich.[28] Another Austrian, Gärtner,

[26]B.A., Reichskanzlei, R 43 I/104, v. 1, Glasenapp to Albert, May 4.

[27]O.S., Präsidialakte, Fasz. 5a, Weisskirchner to Bauer, Feb. 21; ibid., Memorandum, n.d.; ibid., Hartmann to Bauer, May 2, fol. 23; ibid., K 110, fol. 727, 735-736, 746-747.

[28]Ibid., Präsidialakte, Fasz. 5a, Post to F.O., May 12, Report 319; see also ibid., Pozzi to F.O., May 3, 532.

similarly criticized Prussian ministers for catering to "special interests. . . . This continuance of predominantly Prussian influence in Reich affairs" had been well noticed in Vienna.[29]

In talks between the German Austrian minister of war Julius Deutsch and the German General Cramon, preliminary agreements were reached concerning cooperation between the German and German Austrian armies, with the aim of eventual merger. Deutsch—who expected the union, if not now, "then in a year"—suggested that such measures as identical uniforms and rank badges, identical training, equipment, armament, and pay scale would facilitate the later absorption of Austrian military units into the German army. As a first step, the Austrian minister of war suggested that a German General Staff officer, one "completely familiar with the intentions of the Prussian minister of war," be assigned to Vienna to implement the projected military cooperation between the two German states.[30] In late March, the Prussian minister of war General Reinhardt proposed that in the near future German Austrian representatives be invited to Berlin to reach agreements before the beginning of peace negotiations. Brockdorff-Rantzau replied that an exchange of officers with German Austria would be "thoroughly useful," but stressed that there existed no immediate plans for the creation of a joint army.[31] The Anschluss movement, important as it was to him, apparently was not to complicate his main task at the Peace Conference, the defense of the interests of the German Reich.

By April of 1919 the work in the joint Austro-German commissions was well on its way. True, protagonists of the Austrian Anschluss movement like Dr. Bauer were disillusioned; fervent German vows of early implementation of the union seemed to be forgotten. But in principle at least the German members of the commissions were aware that long-range political advantages outweighed temporary economic

[29]*Ibid.*, Post to F.O., May 12; about railroads *ibid.*, Post to F.O., May 10, pp. 515-517.

[30]*A.A.*, Öst. 95, v. 28, Cramon to Min. of War, March 22, Report 7968/I.

[31]*Ibid.*, Gen. Reinhardt to Br. R., March 24; *ibid.*, Öst. 95, v. 29. Br. R. to Reinhardt, Apr. 17; about other sessions of the joint commissions, see *O.S.*, Fasz. 5a, Präsidialakte, Sitzg. im Min. f. Wissenschaft . . . , May 19 and 21, 573, Entwurf betr, Anerkennung der an d. Hochschulen d. Deutsch. Reiches zurückgelegten Studien . . . , pp. 574-575; Glöckel an Bauer, May 5, pp. 614-615.

difficulties.[32] Unlike the Austrian government, the German authorities may have procrastinated at times, but on the whole they seemed prepared to make some economic sacrifices during a transition period and were bent on making the Anschluss a reality. Several German members of the joint commissions mentioned the conclusion of the "preliminary" peace treaty as a suitable moment for union; one listed January 1, 1920, as a critical date.[33] If no Allied prohibition of the Anschluss had been forthcoming, there seems little doubt that the work of the joint commissions would have become the foundation for the union of the two German states.

---

[32]*G.A.*, Bavarian Embassy, Berlin, to Bavarian For. Min., Apr. 28, "Anschluss, . . ."
[33]*Ibid.*

4. DOUBTS AND OPPOSITION IN AUSTRIA AND GERMANY

> "It would have been a very good thing if this Austrian government which has compromised itself by its one-sided pursuit of the policy of union were advised to make room for another government which enjoys the confidence of the Entente." Ignaz Seipel, March 1919

IN the course of March and April, while the Peace Conference continued its work in Paris, fear and uncertainty gripped many minds in Central Europe. The specter of social revolution in Hungary and southern Germany , where Soviet republics were emerging, cast its shadow also over Austria. A good number of highly-placed Austrian politicians, leading industrialists, and professors suggested privately that one method of blocking the movements toward revolution or Anschluss would be for the Entente to dispatch troops to the unsettled areas and to send food and raw materials. They felt that the Entente should dissuade the Austrian people from seeking closer ties with Germany. One of these calls for British troops and supplies and for a differentiation in the treatment of Germany and Austria came from the eminent leader of the Christian Social party, Dr. Ignaz Seipel. His plea was directed to Professor Heinrich Lammasch, former prime minister of Austria-Hungary, who shared Seipel's views on these matters.

An appeal similar to that of Dr. Seipel was made by Professor Joseph Schumpeter, minister of finance and already a well-known theoretical economist, in a conversation with Professor A. C. Coolidge, head of the American mission in Vienna. Schumpeter asked the Entente to bring pressure to bear on the Austrian government — of which he himself was then a member — and in particular to disband the socialist-controlled Volkswehr. The conversation took place about ten days after the Bolshevik coup in Budapest. Schumpeter was apparently convinced that Vienna would shortly follow in the footsteps of Budapest, claiming that some of the Social Democrats were already negotiating with the Communists.[1] Schumpeter feared that "if things were allowed to drift, as at present, the result must inevitably be Bolshevism." Yet Schumpeter was equally concerned about the Anschluss with Germany. In his talk with Coolidge he pointed out that "the radical elements, if they came to power, would press for the union with Germany more urgently than ever, and all hope for a Danubian confederation would have to be definitely abandoned."[2]

To many of Schumpeter's conservative contemporaries in Austria and abroad, it appeared that the Anschluss movement and the radical socialist current were converging into the same stream and that its waters were becoming dangerously swollen.

The only party opposed *both* to Bolshevism and the Anschluss was the Christian Social party. As far as the Anschluss was concerned, it opposed it on grounds of Austrian patriotism and hostility toward socialism, then seemingly dominant in Germany. Yet at times the wind of the Anschluss movement blew so strongly that the party did not dare to unfurl its true flag of opposition. The party program of December 15, 1918, was conditional and ambiguous regarding the Anschluss. It read: "An essential prerequisite [of the return, *Wiederanschluss*], is that Germany succeed in transforming herself into a truly free commonwealth which does justice to the special character and the economic necessities of German Austria."[3] The attached conditions offered the party an easy way out to avoid its *grossdeutsch* and national commitments. In the midst of the revolutionary turmoil and on the eve of the Spartacist attempts to seize power Germany seemed a long way from developing into a "truly free commonwealth."

The Christian Social party's position on the Anschluss question had been rather equivocal from the very beginning;

---

[1]Such negotiations leading to communist seizure of power were the pattern in Hungary in March 1919 (Low, 1963: p. 31); a study, however, of the record of the relations between Vienna and Budapest (Low, 1960: esp. p. 178) shows clearly that Schumpeter's suspicion directed against the Social Democratic party and Dr. Bauer in particular was unfounded.

[2]*P.R.*, F.O. 606, v. 27, Intelligence Report B/493, A.C. Coolidge, March 31; about differences between Bauer and Schumpeter, see *O.S.*, K 212, 562-567.

[3]*Reichspost*, Dec. 15, 1918.

even the pro-union forces felt little passion for their cause. As the London *Times* remarked, the Christian Socials were "never eager for union at heart."[4] Trends favoring the Anschluss were stronger in the *Bundesländer*, while opponents of the union were prominent in Vienna. Yet the division of Christian Socials in regard to the Anschluss movement by no means strictly followed these geographic lines. In 1918 a Christian Social circle, opposed to the anticipated union, had already formed around the composer Ludwig Bittner; the author Hermann Bahr was also closely involved with this group. The writers Anton Wildgans, Robert Müller, and Oscar A. H. Schmitz spoke out against the union.[5] But the most important opponent of the Anschluss among the Christian Socials, although little known as such, was Dr. Ignaz Seipel.

Seipel was the most outstanding leader to emerge from the Christian Social party between the wars. Priest and professor of theology in Salzburg and later at the University of Vienna, he became a champion of political Catholicism. He did not conceal that at heart he was still a monarchist. In 1918 and 1919 Seipel was definitely opposed to the Anschluss which would bury any chance for the restoration of the Habsburg empire. Like numerous other German Austrians, he had earlier hoped that the polyglot empire could be saved. He had not considered the growth of the nation state the only possible form of modern development. Seipel had been, and still was, an Austrian patriot with a strong sense of German nationality and belief in the values of German civilization. But these views were tempered by his Christian universalism and his appreciation of Austria's polyglot historical tradition. Elected in February, 1919, into the Constituent Assembly as well as into the Presidium of the Christian Social Association, Seipel soon became the undisputed leader of the party to a degree which perhaps even Karl Lueger had never reached. In spite of the ideological gulf separating Ignaz Seipel from Otto Bauer, they had much in common. Both were looked upon as doctrinaires by some elements in their respective parties. Seipel was a statesman of "European caliber" (to use Bauer's words), but by force of circumstance he had had to

[4]*Times,* March 14, 1919.
[5]Wandruszka, Benedikt, 1954: p. 331.

confine his talents to the narrow political framework of a small country; this could also be said of Otto Bauer.

In 1916 Seipel had published his major theoretical work *Nation und Staat*. He concluded that since the beginning of the modern period, ethnic boundaries and political frontiers had largely coincided in Western countries such as England and France. But Seipel dared to question the historical necessity, absolute value, and inherent superiority of the national state, which seemed to him by no means the highest principle of political organization.[6] He criticized "the exaggerated belief that nationality, the fact of belonging to a particular nation, is man's highest good."[7] Seipel continued to cling to this idea even after the breakdown of the Habsburg monarchy. To him the polyglot empire not only had an important function; it had also a mission. It was the prototype of a state carrying a vital message for all of Europe and the world: the need for cooperation among different peoples and the establishment of peace.

Seipel's devotion to the old Austrian empire did not exclude love for the German nation or even a conviction of the preeminence of German culture and its educational value for non-German peoples. The German nation itself had reaped great advantages by being able to spread German *Kultur*, through the medium of the Austrian realm, to the East and South and into the Balkans. "If . . . the German Austrians," he wrote in 1916, "were to join the German empire, it would only gain a couple of million [sic] more inhabitants . . . Austria would have disappeared," and with it, by implication, the carrier of German *Kultur* and civilization.

On November 18, 1918, Seipel disclosed his views in the *Reichspost:* "The German Austrians have been members of a great state for so long that they cannot suddenly confine their spirit to the narrow interests of a small state." Seipel saw the only solution for Austria's problems in a link-up with a "great state," "but of course only as a fully privileged member of some confederation, not as a mere part." He thus clearly criticized the Anschluss resolution passed by the Provisional National Assembly on November 12 — just six days earlier.

[6]Seipel, 1916: p. 10.

[7]*Ibid.*, p. 14. "Indeed," he had written, "if human culture is not to take a retrogressive course, there must also be states which form a bridge from one nation to another, gathering numerous nations together so that they might learn to understand and love each other."

Seipel raised the point that Austrians "did not know yet" where they could best serve the German people. He reminded his countrymen of the historic German Austrian mission in Central Europe: to be Austrian was not merely to be German. Ignoring the Anschluss resolution of the Provisional National Assembly, Seipel pointed to the alternative, a link-up with other peoples of Central and Southeastern Europe in a new confederation, a new political structure which could become the heir of the Habsburg empire.

Yet the outcome of the war spelled doom for the multinational and polyglot state structure, while giving a fresh boost to the nation state. Still, though beset by doubts, Seipel held out against the union with Germany and was sympathetic to the Allies, who likewise combatted both the Anschluss and the threat of Bolshevism in Austria. Although Seipel, along with many others, had misgivings about the viability of German Austria, he was consistently critical of what he called a merely declaratory policy, which was not and could not be followed up by a meaningful deed. He therefore opposed the plebiscites on the Anschluss which were organized in some of the Austrian Länder. In 1926 in a talk to the Vienna Politische Gesellschaft he remarked:

> To us [Austrians] the nation, irrespective of citizenship, is the great cultural community; to us Germans it is dearer than the state. . . . If we see the life of our nation consumed in the creation of a unitary state, then somehow we can also find consolation in living in a German state which does not belong to the German *Reich*.[8]

This had also been very much his view in 1918-1919.

On January 14, 1919, Ludo Hartmann had forwarded to Secretary Bauer a letter which Seipel had confidentially written to a German friend. Though Bauer asked Hartmann on February 6 to obtain permission for the use of the letter, the request was denied and Bauer abstained from making political use of it. The letter, if published, would no doubt have been highly embarrassing to Seipel at a moment when proclaiming one's interest in the Anschluss was almost a political imperative.

---

[8]Quoted by Ward, "Seipel and the Anschluss," 1938: p. 48.

In the letter Seipel pointed to the absence of a German "echo" to Austria's offer for union and to the contrast between the interest displayed by Austrian journals in the Anschluss and the indifference shown by the great German newspapers toward the union and toward Austria in general. It was still uncertain, Seipel developed, "where the good Lord wanted to have us German Austrians." "Old Austria was by no means dead and the Danubian federation will certainly materialize and will invigorate Austria." It appeared that economic considerations as well as those of the interests of the entire German people would compel Austria to opt for the federation.

A union prior to the conclusion of peace would be "disastrous," resulting in the loss of German South Tyrol. The Anschluss movement in Austria had already led to the loss of German Bohemia to Czechoslovakia. Finally, Seipel expressed unwillingness to link up with "Germany of today in which there is the terror of soldiers' councils and a socialist dictatorship." Thus "we have every reason to use the brake." The Anschluss would only play into the hands of those who always had prophesied that Germany in the event of an unhappy end of the war would draw profit through the annexation of Austrian territories. "Only if Austria has definitely succumbed, shall we be morally free to find new associations."[9]

But another letter by Seipel, if known, would have become an even greater political liability. It was a letter written in March, 1919, to Professor Heinrich Lammasch, who had earlier gone to Berne at the invitation of Entente leaders, to inform him of the turbulent course of events and growing radicalization in Austria; both men had been ministers in the short-lived imperial cabinet in late October and early November of 1918. Describing in dark colors the situation in Vienna with its requisitioning, *Volkswehr* terrorism, general insecurity

---

[9]*O.S.*, Seipel, Dec. 17, 1918, Nachlass Bauer, K 261. The letter is also printed by Reimann, 1968: pp. 175-192 and by Klemperer in his important biography on *Ignaz Seipel* (1972). Neither Reimann nor Klemperer is apparently acquainted with Seipel's letter of March 25, 1919, which is of even greater importance and is to be found in the *P.R.*, London; it is listed in the following footnote. Klemperer must admit Seipel's "involved and ambiguous argument" in regard to the Anschluss and concedes that his position was bound to appear to contemporaries "devious and tortured." He concludes by saying that Seipel was no friend of the Anschluss (pp. 115-117).

and government weakness, Seipel told Lammasch that he anticipated an imminent upheaval in Austria more on the lines of the Russian Revolution than the German Revolution.

> A serious danger threatens the very moment when the government's policy of union collapses in the sight of all . . . Under Otto Bauer's leadership the government had . . . placed its entire stake on this one card [Anschluss]. When it becomes known that South Tyrol and German Bohemia have become separate states, without [Austria] having achieved union with Germany, then a most terrible despair will grip this people whose ideals have all been shattered and which is now a prey to hunger; not only will the government be overthrown, but doors will be flung open to Bolshevism which up to the present has not been able to obtain a firm foothold. . . .

In his letter to Lammasch, Seipel pleaded for aid:

> Under these circumstances help can only come to us from the Entente. In my opinion this is what should be done: (1) A clear and decisive position must be taken on the union question, and at the same time a strong differentiation made in regard to the treatment of Germany. It would be a very good thing if this government which has compromised itself by its one-sided pursuit of the policy of union were advised to make place for another government which enjoys the confidence of the Entente. In this case it may be presumed that the change in the Cabinet could be accomplished quite smoothly and it would not be necessary for the embittered masses of the population to be brought into direct touch with this matter. Thus, if the new government achieves success with its negotiations, a political consolidation will be promptly effected. (2) The safeguarding of public peace and order by means of a small contingent of British or American troops which could be transferred to Vienna. Some 3,000 men would suffice and would render the numerous guards harmless; the mere presence of the troops would suffice, and it is very improbable that there would be fighting of any kind. . . . All these measures of precaution must be taken before the Entente's decision on the Anschluss is made public.

Seipel's third request was for an adequate supply of provisions and his fourth for coal to be used for industrial purposes. "It is only by work that social revolution can be averted."[10]

These demands represented Dr. Seipel's minimum program to combat effectively the Anschluss movement. He was well aware that the dispatch of troops was advisable *before* the Entente made its negative decision on the Anschluss—a decision which was likely to swell dissatisfaction to a dangerous level.

Dr. Seipel emerged here as a determined opponent of the Anschluss movement in 1919 on the grounds that it was bound to fail and that failure in turn was likely to usher in Bolshevism. One wonders whether under different conditions in Germany, with no threat of social revolution on the horizon, Seipel might have looked favorably upon the union with Germany. How attractive could a predominantly Protestant, republican and moderately social democratic Germany be to the spokesman of Austria's political Catholicism, who still favored monarchist concepts?

Conservatives in Austria were on the whole basically cool toward the union with Germany. They were pinned between Hungarian and South German Bolshevism and fearful of Austria's own radical socialists who were pushing toward Anschluss with a Reich in which the Social Democrats were well entrenched. Though critical of the anticipated harsh treatment of Austria by the Western Powers, Austrian conservatives were dependent on the West for political, economic, and possible military support against the dangers from both East and West, Bolshevism and the Anschluss movement.

The man to whom Dr. Seipel had written, Professor Heinrich Lammasch, was a well-known and a widely respected authority on international law and organization. In the summer of 1918 he had been considered for the post of Austria's imperial chancellor and was finally chosen for it in the dark October days of 1918.[11]

---

[10]*P.R.*, F.O. 606, v. 27, Intelligence Report, Berne B443, March 25, 1919.

[11]During the war Lammasch had become an opponent of the alliance with Germany (*H. Lammasch. Seine Aufzeichnungen* . . . 1922: p. 207). Convinced of the need for a "separation of Austria-Hungary from Prussia and her orientation toward the Western democracies," he directed a memorandum to Emperor Charles in which he expressed his doubts regarding the alliance. When the historian Heinrich Friedjung learned about the memorandum, interestingly enough through Ludo Hartmann (*ibid.*, p. 143), he sharply attacked the author. Yet Lammasch believed firmly that working toward a separate peace would save

Lammasch considered pacifism a "Christian heritage." During the war, when waves of national antagonism lashed Austria continuously, he mercilessly castigated "national hatred." Author of a work entitled *Para Pacem*, he spoke out several times in the Austrian Herrenhaus in 1917 and 1918, pleading for a peace without annexations and for the equality of all nations. To further the cause of peace, he went in 1917 to Switzerland where he made close contact with several Americans. To him Switzerland was not only the neutral ground where peace could be attained, but also Austria's model for transforming the empire into a confederation.[12]

His conservatism, his interest in continued links with the peoples with whom the Austrian Germans had so long been associated, his opposition to German nationalism, and his Western orientation, all combined to make Lammasch oppose the Anschluss. In addition, one of his major aims was the salvation of German South Tyrol in behalf of which he had worked in Berne since March, 1919. He was convinced that Italy would be prepared to relinquish South Tyrol only as the result of "pressure" by the Entente and attempted to win over to his cause the American, English, and French envoys to Switzerland. Under these circumstances he considered Vienna's strident demand for the Anschluss as "untimely and menacing to the fate of South Tyrol." Later, as member of the Austrian delegation in St. Germain, Lammasch became fully aware of the contrast between his views and those of the leaders of his delegation who endorsed the union with Germany.[13]

---

not only the Austrian Empire, but also Germany (p. 210). While many German Austrians considered a wartime separation from Germany a break of faith and even outright treason, it was Lammasch's view that Austria had no obligation to support the far-reaching annexationist ambitions of her German ally. He thus incurred the hostility of the Austrian Pan-Germans and other German nationalists. His later interests in, and even enthusiasm for, the League of Nations deepened their enmity (Redlich, "Lammasch als Minister-Präsident," *ibid.*, p. 156). No wonder that in the strongly nationalistic academic circles Lammasch was seen as a solitary political thinker, "without any followers, without any sympathizers" (Sperl, "Im akademischen Leben," *ibid.*, p. 210). He was about as isolated in Austria as Friedrich Wilhelm Foerster was in Germany, but his courage and the purity of his conviction earned him respect both at home and abroad. About Lammasch see also Foerster, "Meine Erinnerungen an H. Lammasch," *ibid.*, pp. 215-218, Kann, 1950: **1**: pp. 209-212, and Fuchs, 1949.

[12]*Lammasch. Seine Aufzeichnungen . . . ,* 1922: pp. 186-196; contribution by G. Herron.

[13]*Ibid.,* F. Schumacher, "Lammasch in St. Germain," p. 200.

On February 24 Baron de Vaux of the Berne legation reported to Vienna that some British and American political leaders had expressed the wish that Professor Lammasch visit Berne and added: "This way the Entente's prohibition of negotiations, which is so harmful to our interests, could be broken for the first time."[14]

Dr. Bauer wrote to the Austrian envoy in Berne on March 7, immediately after his return from Germany. Bauer considered Lammasch to be loyal, though a monarchist, and mistakenly thought him sympathetic to the Austrian government's pro-German orientation. He suggested that Lammasch, aside from treating questions of the law of nations, use his influence in behalf of German Bohemia, the Sudetenland, German South Tyrol, and the threatened border regions in Carinthia and Lower Styria. Lammasch should also speak in behalf of the Anschluss and a plebiscite in Austria and against the Danubian federation.[15]

On the eighteenth of March a disappointed Baron de Vaux replied to Dr. Bauer. Lammasch, he claimed, was badly informed about the national composition of German Bohemia; he was apparently unwilling to present Austria's claims. Lammasch's sympathies, de Vaux continued, belonged to the Danubian confederation. He was also favorably disposed to the project of the neutralization of the Alpine republic and resigned to the loss of German Bohemia. If neither the Danubian confederation nor Austria's neutralization were feasible, he would favor the Anschluss with a South German republic—a concept which Dr. Bauer earlier had sharply rejected.[16]

It was evident that the scholar, great individualist and conservative Lammasch, who had been suggested by Entente politicians as a middleman, was not cut out to be Dr. Bauer's diplomatic agent or a spokesman for German national demands. Convinced of the necessity of building some

---

[14]*O.S.*, K.261, "Lammasch," de Vaux to F.O., Feb. 24, p. 446.

[15]*Ibid.*, Bauer to de Vaux, March 7, pp. 451-452. Lammasch wrote to Bauer in the foregoing matter, promising that in his talks with Entente representatives he would preserve complete neutrality on the Anschluss (*ibid.*, March 3, Berne, pp. 457-458). In his reply Bauer assured him again that he did not mistrust him in any way and that the area of mutual agreement between them was even larger than he had assumed (*ibid.*, Bauer to Lammasch, March 28, p. 456).

[16]*Ibid.*, de Vaux to Bauer, March 18, p. 454.

multinational structure at a time when nationalism was rampant, he was unsuited to represent the foreign policy of the new socialist, republican, and above all Anschluss-minded Austrian government.

It was hardly surprising that the widespread despondency which affected high-placed Austrian officials and political leaders of the caliber of Seipel and Lammasch during the months of March and April of 1919 also seized the German ambassador in Vienna, Count von Wedel. Wedel, a moderate and at no time a fierce partisan of the Anschluss concept, was sporadically plagued by serious doubts about the union. It was, strangely enough, soon after Dr. Bauer's return from Berlin that he became once more thoroughly skeptical about the Austrian link-up. His doubts were deepened by several circumstances, most of them predictable: the continued resistance of the Entente, the alleged diplomatic errors committed by Dr. Bauer, the impoverished condition of Austria, the questionable benefits Germany would reap from incorporating the country, and the territorial losses elsewhere which she probably would have to incur in return. Wedel burst out bitterly against the Viennese, who were "without character and unreliable" and against Dr. Bauer who was much blamed by von Wedel for his precipitate actions:

> The matter [Anschluss] may easily end in disappointment. In fact, it is impossible for us to make any territorial sacrifices for German Austria; it would be a bad deal, for we would get nothing but an empty barrel. . . . Northern Bohemia is another matter, almost independent of the question of the Anschluss, and by far the most valuable. What else do we get? The Alpine countries, charming as they are, don't have much more to offer than water resources, and Vienna with her two million inhabitants of which at the most 500 are fit for something. We cannot surrender any German soil in exchange for this. If the Anschluss does not get off the ground, perhaps it will still be possible to gain something for abandoning it—for instance we might succeed in having the enemy powers renounce the Saar and Upper Silesia, perhaps also North Bohemia. German Austria is bound to seek to lean toward us in any case.
>
> I quite understand that many Germans like to look on this solution as the only ray of light, but if it cannot be done without unreasonable sacrifices, we shall have to do without it. Bauer stays for the moment. This is favorable for us, because

he is trustworthy and more cautious than he used to be; and also he has the Party behind him.[17]

On April 29, about six weeks after the foregoing letter was written, the German ambassador again raised the question of the advantages of the Anschluss for Germany, this time in connection with his fear of the alleged Bolshevization of Austria under "radical" socialist leadership. He sent the letter to his cousin Langworth, leaving it to his judgment whether to forward it to Foreign Secretary Brockdorff-Rantzau in Paris or not. In the latter case, however, he wished the letter placed "not ad acta, but into the fire!" Considering the emotional and exaggerated character of the letter, the request was perhaps understandable.

According to Wedel, Dr. Bauer had recently taken over also socialization. "His recent plans have revealed him to be a real theoretician," and he represented "a radical point of view, perhaps like our Independents." He wished to nationalize castles, palaces, and other stately homes, compensating the owners and using the buildings for invalid care. Larger communities would be given the right to socialize factories without compensating the existing owners.

German Austria faces bankruptcy, it faces sure ruin. . . . A radical socialism rules here almost dictatorially, though it does not have majority support; the bourgeoisie is completely intimidated. Economic circles are in complete despair. In spite of the Anschluss, they are negotiating . . . with the Americans about exploitation of water power. . . . Under such circumstances can we desire the Anschluss? There is great danger of infection which is spread here by the Bolshevik disease. Can we afford such a luxury? . . . Many in Germany were skeptical at first regarding the Anschluss, but then turned from a Saul into a Paul. The reverse is happening to me. Of course we must remain loyal to the Anschluss and leave it to others—the Entente and its opponents here—to torpedo it; but we can be grateful to them, as they are rendering us a good service. The evolution will probably still lead to the Anschluss one day, but under better conditions, especially when we can afford the burden and when the Bolshevik phantom can no longer do us any harm. It is possible that some crown-lands will tear themselves away, for the disgust against Zionist-Communist [!] Vienna is

---

[17]*Ibid.,* Wedel to F.O., March 14.

great. The peasants of Styria and Upper Austria have armed themselves to the teeth, in order to receive the Viennese communists as they deserve.

Considering the development here, I believe the following policy to be correct for us: *We must fight for the Anschluss, but fight to lose the battle.* [Italics mine, A.D.L.] I believe incidentally that the matter can't be pulled off here. The movement has greatly declined, here and also in the crown lands as well. Perhaps we still can, with a great deal of shouting, obtain compensations by renouncing the Anschluss. I have the feeling that the Anschluss question has fanned hate against us among the Entente and has increased the demand to squeeze us for it elsewhere.[18]

Generally a keen observer, Count von Wedel shared the widespread anti-socialist and anti-semitic prejudices of his class and of many Germans. While national-minded and in general in favor of the Anschluss, he was prepared to postpone it until the day when conservative nationalists rather than "radical" socialists would be at the helm of the Austrian ship of state. In the eyes of the nineteenth-century Prussian conservatives the unification of Germany was "wrong" in the years 1848-1849, but "right" in 1870-1871. Similarly in 1919 many German conservatives thought it better to postpone the Anschluss, until the day when the conservatives were in power. Yet in view of the strength of Anschluss-sentiments in both German states, this could not be suggested publicly. An Anschluss in 1919, in the opinion of many German conservatives, might not only impoverish, but also radicalize Germany.

In the midst of his emotional outburst during which he bared the less attractive aspects of his political philosophy, Wedel, while minimizing the concrete benefits to Germany of Austria's incorporation, did by no means overlook the bargaining potentialities of the Anschluss policy. The diplomat fighting for the noble principle of national self-determination was not above resorting to Macchiavellian tactics, and not for the purpose of deceiving the national opponent but his very own people and the Austrian brethren; while claiming to fight a national battle, he actually hoped to lose it!

[18]*Ibid.,* italics A.D.L., Wedel to F.O., Apr. 29.

In any case, the second thoughts of the German ambassador in Vienna, combined with Allied pressure from Paris, were likely to have considerable influence on a German government already cautious and fearful of having to pay an inordinate price for the union.

5. THE FRANCO-GERMAN "CONTEST"

> "Could contemporary Austria [like Switzerland] not
> be a neutralized state?" *Le Temps*, February 24, 1919

AFTER Bauer's return from his German journey in early
March, France began to mount a vigorous campaign
against the Anschluss. As Wedel concluded, the Entente had
left the field of propaganda largely to its Austrian and German proponents. But when their success suddenly
threatened to create a new balance of power, the Entente in-
terceded and blocked their way.

The agitation against the Anschluss was fostered in particular from Switzerland, which, according to Wedel, had
become the "center for the machinations" of the opponents
of the Anschluss.[1] A very skillfully conducted and well-
financed correspondence bureau, called the Agence Centrale, had been established there under the guidance of
Prince Ludwig Windischgrätz, former Hungarian minister of
food, and Prince Schönburg, former Austro-Hungarian envoy at the Vatican, and probably also Count Leopold von
Berchtold, former minister of foreign affairs. This agency
was placed under the direction of the well-known Austro-
Polish writer Otto de Forst Battaglia. Friends of the Anschluss suspected that French money kept the anti-union
propaganda alive.

A more important instrument of French influence was the
resumption of direct diplomatic relations between Paris and
Vienna. On March 19 the *Petit Parisien* reported that the
French government was contemplating the establishment of
at least semi-official relations with German Austria and that it
proposed to send Henri Allizé, then minister at The Hague,
to Vienna.[2]

---

[1]*N.A.*, Akten . . . Austrian Embassy, Berlin, Apr. 7, "Die deutsch-österr.
Anschlussfrage," (6 pages).

[2]*Petit Parisien*, March 19. On the twenty-fifth of March the French ambassador
H. Allizé arrived in Vienna with two assistant attachés (*P.R.*, F.O. 608. v. 16,
Adam, Apr. 2). The *Neue Freie Presse* connected the event not only with German

Soon after his arrival in Vienna, Allizé presented his credentials and visited Chancellor Karl Renner, promising the early arrival in Vienna of French businessmen and industrialists who would resume commercial relations with German Austria. According to the *Neue Freie Presse*, Chancellor Renner pointed out to Allizé that the Austrian government hoped to be able to preserve order in the country, but only "if German Austria were no longer drawn into the maelstrom of international politics and if her territory were not used as a base for Entente operations against Hungary." Allizé denied that such had ever been the intention of the Entente, but promised to pass the wishes of the Austrian government on to Paris.[3] The French envoy mixed and mingled freely with Austrian politicians, journalists, and writers[4] and displayed great adroitness in wooing them in behalf of friendship with France.

Early in April the German ambassador Adolf Müller reported from Berne to the Berlin Foreign Office that Allizé's maneuvers in Vienna should fall on fertile soil, since the territorial assurance held out by him had many attractive aspects.[5] Allizé apparently went surprisingly far in making dazzling promises to Austrian official and semi-official cir-

---

Austria's desire to join Germany — a nation beaten to the ground but before which France "still trembles" (morning ed., March 25) — but also with the recent emergence of a Soviet Hungarian republic; as the latter had come into existence on March 21, it could only have had the effect of speeding Allizé's departure from Paris. For the first time in five years, the newspaper wrote, a diplomatic representative of the French republic had been assigned to Vienna. He was "a vivacious, sensitive and imaginative diplomat," who had served in Bavaria for five years before the war and had had the opportunity to learn the difference between the North and South German characters. The *Neue Freie Presse* observed that since Allizé's arrival the French press, while remaining opposed to the *Anschluss*, had become distinctly more friendly toward Austria.

[3] *Neue Freie Presse*, Apr. 29.

[4] *Ibid.*; Allizé's account of his activities in Vienna is given in his book *Ma Mission à Vienne*, 1933. The archives of the French Foreign Ministry, Quai d'Orsay, contain his correspondence with France's foreign minister Stephen Pichon which is drawn upon in the chapter on French policy on the Anschluss of this work. This correspondence reveals much that is not covered in his book.

[5] *N.A.*, T 120-35, Akten . . . , A. Müller to F.O., Apr. 4; a year later, on June 9, 1920, L. Hartmann was still convinced of the "danger of this personality [H. Allizé] to our policy" and asked for "authentic material about the relations of Allizé to the Germanophobe circles" (*O.S.*, K 465). The Austrian Foreign Office regretted to be unable to furnish him with pertinent material since "nothing authentic" of any compromising nature was known. Allizé's views about Germany "were similar to those of French diplomacy in general."

cles, though some Austrians might well have inflated them. The peace of St. Germain punctured their dreams about holding on to German South Tyrol and somehow retaining part of German Bohemia. Their disappointments and frustrations found expression in bitter criticism of the alleged deception perpetrated by Allizé. To some degree it was a self-deception, nurtured by a months-long barrage of propaganda to which in the end some of the originators themselves succumbed. Yet Allizé was by no means innocent of the charges leveled against him.

To a lesser degree this also held true of Colonel Thomas Cunninghame, British representative in Vienna since January of 1919. As he candidly disclosed, he was at first unaware of what British and Allied policy toward Austria and the Anschluss actually was. Like Allizé he appears to have made sweeping promises about the peace settlement to the Austrian government in the hope of saving Austria from plunging down the precipice to the Anschluss. His apparent generosity to Austria aroused the suspicion and ire of both Czechoslovakia and Italy. On the twenty-second of May, Gosling, British representative in Prague, relayed to the London Foreign Office a protest by the Czechoslovakian government concerning Cunninghame's alleged promises to Austria.[6] A report to the *Reichspost* caused also an Italian protest centering on Colonel Cunninghame's pledge concerning German South Tyrol; the note was presented by Marchese Imperiali, Italian ambassador in London, to Lord Hardinge. It is also possible that Colonel Cunninghame, like Allizé, sensed the lack of a clear British and Allied policy toward Austria and the Anschluss and, by taking the initiative, attempted to force the Western governments to make a definite stand without further delay.

While Allizé and Cunninghame raised the hopes of many Austrians, they actually made little impact on the Austrian government itself. In his recollections Julius Deutsch, Austrian secretary of war in the crucial postwar year, wrote that by mid-April, 1919, Colonel Seiller, the officer of the Defense Ministry assigned to the British Military Mission, came to him with Colonel Cunninghame's confidential communication.

---

[6]*P.R.*, F.O. 608, v. 16, Gosling to F.O., May 22.

The chief of the mission wanted to let me know that at the conclusion of the peace treaty Austria would be better treated and
might perhaps even gain South Tyrol and portions of the
Sudetenland as well as West Hungary, if she only renounced
the Anschluss with Germany. The French envoy Allizé spoke
several times along similar lines. Yet one could not come to
grips with these casual utterances of the diplomats. A concrete
proposal of the Western Powers was unobtainable, and on the
mere hints of their representatives, whose full powers we did
not know, we could not build the foreign policy of our country.[7]

In its fight against the Anschluss movement the French
government operated on several levels and moved in several
directions. During the months of February and March, 1919,
it intensified its propaganda for a Danubian confederation
and began vigorously to advance an alternative project, the
neutralization of Austria.[8]

On February 24 the French foreign ministry launched the
project of the neutralization of Austria through the pages of
the influential newspaper *Le Temps.* The example of the Swiss
Confederation which enjoyed a permanent neutrality was offered to Austria as such a solution.

The German Swiss have developed a spirit of independence,
an aspiration for the democratic ideal, and a desire not only for
the greatest welfare of the state they inhabit but also for the
greatest good of Germany, a state which in the worst days of
Prussian militarism offered a home for free civilization. . . .
Could contemporary Austria not likewise be a neutralized
state? The entire world would thus gain, with the exception of
the incorrigible annexationists of Germany. What do they
think about this in Vienna?

The *Times* of London, quickly taking up the French
paper's suggestion, spoke favorably of according Austria a
guaranteed neutrality with the help of the League of Nations
and under its auspices. While encouraged by the English
response, *Le Temps* was disheartened by the lack of any immediate Austrian reaction, though it charged that the silence
was imposed by the Vienna government.[9]

---

[7]Deutsch, 1960: p. 129.
[8]*N.A.*, Akten . . . , Wedel, March 16.
[9]*Le Temps,* Feb. 24.

While some Austrians proposed a temporary Allied occupation to save Austria's independence, the French scheme of neutralization was aimed at a long-range guarantee of Austria's independent existence. Neutralization of German Austria would of course require the permanent renunciation of the Anschluss by the people of Austria.

While earlier articles of *Le Temps* were in the nature of a trial balloon, on March 14 the newspaper went several steps further with the publication of an article by none less than France's foreign minister Stephen Pichon in which he elaborated on the neutralization of an independent Austria. In return for Austria's consent the Allies would offer her substantive advantages to enable her to lead an independent existence. Pichon opposed holding a plebiscite in Austria, since in view of the troubled conditions it could not reveal the country's true sentiments and interests.[10] With the publication of this article France made an official bid to the Austrian government and people to abandon the course leading to union with Germany and to link itself diplomatically, economically, and ideologically to the West.

The French propaganda had clearly made an impact in Vienna.[11] According to Wedel, France's neutralization project had aroused greater confidence in Vienna than the earlier plan for a Danubian confederation. But he discerned the common denominator in both projects, the intent to "prevent the Anschluss . . . under the benevolent patronage of the Entente."

On March 17, in the opinion of the *Vossische Zeitung*, "the battle against the Anschluss began on the entire front."[12] The following day the *Neue Freie Presse* in Vienna echoed this view: "On account of the Anschluss" a "struggle" had now begun between France and Germany. This diplomatic contest reached a new height when the *Neue Freie Presse* opened its pages to eminent German officials for a critical assessment of the French propositions to Vienna. First, on March 21, German Minister of Justice Georg Gothein assured the Austrian reading public that the French endeavors to pre-

---

[10]*Ibid.*
[11]*Neue Freie Presse,* March 17, "Neutralisierung von Deutschösterreich. Der Plan des französischen Ministers Pichon."
[12]*Voss. Zeitung,* March 17.

vent the Anschluss of German Austria with Germany and to
transform her into a neutral state "need not discourage
anyone."

> It is the business of German Austria alone to make this
> decision. . . . [Germany] exerts upon them [the Austrians]
> neither political nor moral pressure. If they want to come to us,
> we shall accept them with open arms, and we are prepared to
> share with them in love our concerns and our joys. Of the for-
> mer there will of course be more for the moment than of the
> latter.[13]

Gothein dismissed Austrian and German fears of an Allied
military move against Germany as a possible penalty for any
Anschluss coup.

An "Aufruf an Deutschland," made in the *Neue Freie Presse*
on March 10, was from the pen of none less than Mathias
Erzberger, leader of the Catholic Center party and influential
member of the German Cabinet. The German government
and the National Assembly would do everything to take
simultaneously with the political the economic interests of the
German Austrian population into most careful consideration.
"In regard especially to financial questions, particularly the
problem of currency, we know that we must make sacrifices,
and we are prepared to make them."[14]

Two days later, Freiherr von Richthofen, a prominent
member of the Democratic party, held in the article
"Deutsch-Österreich und die Entente," that Austria had
reached a "turning point."

> The entry of German Austria into Germany, if it comes about,
> will coincide with the saddest period in the history of our
> fatherland. . . . we also know that one rarely finds voluntary as-
> sociates in misery. For this reason perhaps, the reluctance of
> the political leaders of Germany was greater than was
> justifiable from a practical point of view.

German Austria held her fate in her own hands; she knew
that Germany would accept the German brethren from all

[13]*Neue Freie Presse*, morng. ed., March 21, G. Gothein, "Deutschland u.d.
Bestrebungen gegen d. Anschluss Deutschösterreichs."
[14]*Ibid.*, March 23, M. Erzberger, "Die ökonomischen Voraussetzungen d.
Anschl."

corners of Austria with open arms, "though with us too, purely economic considerations do not necessarily speak in favor of the Anschluss of German Austria." [15]

The unequal Franco-German "contest" of March, 1919, continued during the following months, widening into a struggle for influence in Austria between the Entente and Germany. But the Reich, aware of the limits of its power and having already set its eyes on Versailles, was reluctant to press the issue. The German Cabinet had earlier postponed the "marriage" between Austria and the Reich until after the conclusion of the peace conference. But the Western Powers, especially France, were intent on breaking up the romance and on preventing the union.

---

[15]*Ibid.,* March 25, Freiherr v. Richthofen, "Deutschösterreich u.d. Entente"; see also March 30, J. Giesbert, "Anschluss und Deutschland."

IV. The Anschluss and the Policy of the Great Powers

1. THE SHAPING OF BRITISH POLICY ON THE ANSCHLUSS, 1918-1919

> "Once Germany has reached Vienna, she is again on the high road to the Balkans and Constantinople and will resume her *Drang nach dem Osten* policy, one of the causes of this war." Memorandum of the British War Cabinet, 1919

D URING the war British postwar planners had contemplated the possibility—and toward the end, the desirability—of the dissolution of the Habsburg empire, and pondered about the Anschluss of German Austria. Some advisers to the Foreign Office had recommended Austria's union with the Reich. When the war ended, the pro-Anschluss view seemed still to have its partisans in the Foreign Office, though the government had made no definite decision of any kind on the future of Austria. The pro-union view found its crystallization in the position paper "South-Eastern Europe and the Balkans" which contained a chapter on German Austria.[1] The paper bore no date but was presumably considered by the members of the British delegation during the months of December, 1918, or January, 1919, before the opening of the Paris Peace Conference.

In the view of the writer of this essay, British interests categorically required the destruction of the Habsburg empire and forbade its restoration in any form, including that of a Danubian confederation. Though Great Britain was known in 1918 and 1919 to be favorably disposed toward a Danubian confederation, the point made in this paper was that a federation with German Austria as the center would in the long run merely amount to a resurrection of the old Austrian empire and would be contrary to British interests "as well as to the interests of the Czechoslovaks and Yugoslavs." The German Austrians themselves no longer

---

[1] Public Archives of Canada, Foster Papers (M.G. 27, II, D7, v.56, file 119), "Southeastern Europe and the Balkans," pp. 43-55.

desired the reconstitution of the former Austria. A separate political existence of German Austria, on the other hand, would be "the worst of all possible solutions." Thus, the Austrian Germans had no alternative but to join Germany. The author of the paper was by no means either pro-Austrian or pro-German, but had rather a pro-Czech bias.

In the author's view, the Anschluss could no longer be prevented.

> We cannot exterminate the German Austrians; we cannot make them cease to feel as Germans. They are bound to be somewhere. Nothing would be gained by compelling them to lead an existence separate from that of Germany. Such enforced separation would only stimulate German nationalism, but could not prevent cooperation between the two branches, nor their final reunion.

The writer even claimed that the inclusion of German Austria in Germany was "not altogether disadvantageous" from the British point of view, since it would restore the balance between the Catholic South and the Protestant North and might help to check Prussianism in Germany. He dismissed the idea of preventing German Austria from joining Germany, even if both parties concerned seemed to wish it, "both on grounds of principle and expediency." Other British leaders were to admit the strength of the principle of national self-determination, while not prepared to consider the Anschluss as a demand also based upon expediency.

Some of these views had been also expressed by the authors of the wartime memorandum on Austria in 1916 which had been so highly praised by Lloyd George.[2] If the writer of the foregoing position paper was not one of the authors of the earlier document, he was certainly familiar with its main lines of thought. In any case, the authors of both the foregoing wartime and post-war documents on the future of Austria were agreed on the desirability of the Anschluss option, especially when compared with the other alternatives, and tended to look upon the Prussian rather than German power as a source of concern for Great Britain and Germany's neighbors. They also considered the

---

[2]Lloyd George, 1936: pp. 17-19.

restoration of the Austro-Hungarian empire, even with a new political label and a different content, as detrimental to the interests of Britain and all of Europe.

Yet this view of Central Europe was at no time undisputed in the British Isles. Others entertained the most serious doubts about any aggrandizement of Germany, their recent enemy, and were fearful that the Balkanization of Central Europe in the wake of the dissolution of the Habsburg empire would play into Germany's hands. They felt the need to stabilize Central Europe and endorsed the concept of a Danubian confederation of which German Austria would become a part. In the end British public opinion hardened in regard to the Anschluss and the British Foreign Office stiffened its policy, finally moving toward the French view of outright prohibition of the union.

But toward the end of the war British opinion was still uncertain in regard to the Anschluss. The writer of the foregoing pro-union paper was not quite alone in his opinions. In the days before the Armistice some influential voices were raised in England which were anything but adverse to the concept of German Austria's Anschluss with Germany. Lord James Bryce, scholar and statesman and former ambassador of Great Britain in Washington, D.C., declared in his book *Essays and Addresses in War Time* (1918) that the nationality principle ought also to be acknowledged without qualifications for the German nation.[3] On October 17, in an article, "Our Peace Terms," *The New Europe,* which pursued a pronounced pro-Slavic and anti-German course, demanded no interference with German unity and asked that the "German provinces of Austria must also be free to unite with the German empire."[4] On November 4, Lord Northcliffe, who was in charge of British wartime propaganda, wrote an article in the *Times* developing thirteen theses for the peace. The fifth of these said: "All peoples of Austria-Hungary must be secured a place among the free nations of the world and their right for entry into a league with their kinsfolk beyond the border of Austria-Hungary." It was obvious, he continued, that "the same right of self-determination cannot be denied

---

[3]Bryce, 1918: pp. 156-157.
[4]*The New Europe,* Oct. 17, 1918, pp. 9-10.

to the German provinces of Austria should they desire to enter Germany as a federal state."[5]

On November 9, *The New Statesman*, which was considered
close to Lloyd George, stressed that in the event of the
breakup of the Austrian monarchy it befitted German
Austria to link up with the Reich. The former nationalities of
the Dual Monarchy no longer wanted German Austria. All
the German Austrians asked for now was "to go home" and
reunite with the German people of the empire. "This is a
desire which we must fully respect and acknowledge."[6] These
views were quite in line with those of the authors of the 1916
Memorandum on the Dual Monarchy and of the aforementioned position paper "South-Eastern Europe and the
Balkans," probably written in December, 1918.

Even though the war had ended, suspicion of Germany
continued to run high in Great Britain. On November 5 the
London *Times* spoke of "German schemes for the Peace Conference," saying that there were significant indications that
Germany hoped to "gain by negotiations no small part of the
objects which she sought and has failed to win by the
sword."[7] As the paper stated further: "A large part of the
German press, is now much exercised by a question of de-
portment, the question whether it is wise or profitable for
Germany to wear sackcloth and ashes, and whether it is worse
for her to appear impenitent or cowed."[8] About a week
earlier, the German press was criticized for keeping up a
"persistent and impudent propaganda": the German public
was encouraged to believe that a few military leaders,
especially Ludendorff, were alone responsible for Germany's
defeat, that Germany had now completely purified herself
through revolution, and that the world's great trouble now
lay in the chauvinism of the Great Powers.[9]

But in spite of this sharply anti-German position and the
general expectation that Germany would suffer large territorial losses, there were several indications that the *Times*
was not definitely opposed to the union of German Austria
with Germany. It held that most Germans favored such a

[5]*Times*, Nov. 5.
[6]*The New Statesman*, Nov. 9.
[7]*Times*, Nov. 5.
[8]*Ibid.*, Dec. 18.
[9]*Ibid.*, Dec. 10.

union.[10] On December 18, in the editorial "The Coming Peace Discussions" it pointed out that Germany would have to respect the independence and integrity of the new states in the East, including restored Poland. "She will have enough to do in working out her unification with German Austria and in effecting her own internal unity on the democratic lines which she attempted in 1848."[11]

Written in a vein similar to the foregoing editorials was an article on Austria in *The New Statesman* of December 28, 1918; it stressed that Austria was incapable of leading an independent economic existence. Since it had been British policy to dismember the empire and to encourage the rise of new national states, the German provinces of Austria should be given the same right of national self-determination, of union with Germany. The author rejected a French argument that self-determination meant only freedom from oppression, but not the right of one nation to join another. Union must also be permitted on the pragmatic ground that it would be impossible to prevent it in the long run. If deprived of the right to self-determination, Austria would become a new center of national discontent. The author discarded the possibility that the Anschluss would change the balance of power. The union of Austria with Germany might also have a moderating influence upon the latter.[12] These considerations aside, even an independent Austria could not be prevented from collaborating with Germany or even becoming her active ally in time of war.

These views reflected Great Britain's official position on the Anschluss. This position was given expression by Bonar Law, chancellor of the exchequer, in the House of Commons on November 20—eight days after the Anschluss resolution was passed in the Austrian Provisional National Assembly. On that day Colonel Wedgwood asked in the House of Commons whether the government was aware that attempts were being made by German agents to drive German Austria into union with Germany. Whereupon Bonar Law replied:

Yes, attention has been called to the matter. . . . Rumors seem to have spread in Austria by German agents alleging that Great

[10]*Ibid.*, Dec. 14, "Through German Eyes."
[11]*Ibid.*, Dec. 18.
[12]*The New Statesman*, Dec. 28.

Britain proposes actually to force Austro-Germans into a Danubian confederation and prevent them from joining Germany should they wish to do so. These rumors have no foundation in fact (hear, hear).[13]

The British declaration did not necessarily disavow British interest in Austria's voluntarily joining a Danubian confederation then or later. Nor was it by any means certain that Great Britain recognized the resolution of the German Austrian Provisional National Assembly, composed as it was of members elected many years before, as duly expressing the wish of the Austrian people on the union issue. The British statement, aimed at quenching "rumors" spread by the enemy, could not properly be considered a British endorsement of the Anschluss, though, understandably enough, Dr. Otto Bauer and Ludo Hartmann gave it this interpretation. Shortly afterwards Bauer admitted that he was not clear what British policy on Austria's union with Germany actually was.

Bonar Law's declaration that Britain might not oppose Austria's union with Germany if she were persuaded that German Austria genuinely wanted the Anschluss did not preclude Britain's using diplomatic powers of persuasion against such a move. However, taken in conjunction with Lord Northcliffe's suggested peace terms of November 4, it must be concluded that the British government was by no means hostile to the *Anschluss* concept. In any case, such real or apparent pro-union voices were to become largely muted during the following months.

The British press, however, continued to reflect a division in British public opinion for some time. Its attitude on German Austria and the feasibility of the Anschluss can be gauged from occasional articles and references in the conservative *Times* and the liberal *Manchester Guardian*. On the whole, specific references to the Anschluss were very meager in the pages of the latter newspaper[14] until about the end of May, at which time the first draft of the peace terms was submitted to Austria; the references were only slightly more frequent in the *Times*. The *Manchester Guardian*, though

---

[13]*Great Britain. House of Commons.* Parliam. Debates, Fifth Ser., v. 110, 3430-31.
[14]*Manchester Guardian,* March 27; also Apr. 7, 1919.

giving full attention to Germany, appeared little interested in the Anschluss; it was much more concerned with the problems of Persia and Afghanistan, Egypt and Turkey, India and the Far East, which were treated repeatedly and in detail in its pages.

On January 13 the *Manchester Guardian* took critical note of the statement made by the French foreign minister Pichon in early January, according to which German Austria was not to be allowed to join the German republic, "however much she may so desire." "That can hardly be the view of the Allies," asserted the *Guardian*, and castigated the lack of respect for the right of self-determination which it revealed. On February 1, on the other hand, the *Manchester Guardian* drew attention to the *Frankfurter Zeitung*, the "old exponent of the Mitteleuropa scheme" — a rather suspect German wartime objective — as leading the Anschluss movement.

On May 12, commenting on the peace terms submitted to Germany, the *Manchester Guardian* printed a long letter signed by several very distinguished Englishmen, including Arthur Ponsonby, J. Ramsay MacDonald, Charles Trevelyan, and Ethel Snowden, criticizing the peace treaty in detail, but omitting in this context any special mention of German Austria. Not before May 22 did it refer to the independence of German Austria, a point in the treaty which was "of great importance." And only on May 26 did the *Manchester Guardian* call the Versailles Treaty "a bad peace" and blamed the government for not yet having published the treaty terms in full, referring at the same time to the prohibition clause concerning the Anschluss. This provision was considered a "glaring negation of liberty and of the right of peoples to determine their own allegiance. It is a sorry business." [15]

In early June, in connection with the Treaty of St. Germain, the *Manchester Guardian* renewed its criticism of the prohibition of the *Anschluss*. It would be a natural course for German Austria to throw in her lot with Germany. Yet, "by one of the strangest and least defensible provisions of the treaty with Germany," she was prevented from doing so. [16] In spite of this criticism of the Treaty of St. Germain, the *Manchester Guardian* was not irreconcilable. It found features

[15]*Ibid.*, May 26.
[16]*Ibid.*, June 4.

in the Austrian treaty "which suggest hope," namely the provisions for giving Austria access to the Adriatic, and those relating to the minority treaty which offered protection to minority groups. Clearly, the liberal *Manchester Guardian* was prepared to acquiesce to the terms of St. Germain.

The *Times*, on the other hand, moved from its early pro-*Anschluss* position to one opposing the union. It had remained fearful of and hostile to militaristic Germany and judged that in spite of the November Revolution the German world outlook had changed but little. Therefore, the change of position on the part of the *Times* was not surprising. No persuasion was needed to reach a common front on the Anschluss between the *Times* and the French government.

The *Times* was most understanding of France's interests and position and that of England's and France's Central European friend, Czechoslovakia. The *Times's* special correspondent from Prague praised "Bohemia" (Czechoslovakia) as a "bulwark against anarchy," while simultaneously pointing out that Bolshevism was rampaging throughout the enormous expanse of the rest of the former Austro-Hungarian empire.[17] "German Austria on the other hand, while not inherently subject to the dread disease, is inoculated with a virus almost equally deadly, which is the Pan-German mentality, utterly unrepentant and feeding on lies."[18]

During February, the *Times* continued its criticism of the new Germany. On February 1, the American journalist Frank H. Simonds wrote in its pages: "German propaganda is at work; the German, although beaten, is using his teachers and his preachers to deny defeat, responsibility for the war — everything."[19] On February 12, the newspaper printed another article by Simonds in which the writer specifically spoke out against the union of Austria and Germany. This would "mean that even with Alsace-Lorraine lost, Germany will gain at least 5 million people and an area several times as large as that of the Reichsland." What would emerge would be a "greatly enlarged German empire with 75 million people, touching the Middle Danube (including Vienna), enfolding the new Bohemian state, threatening Polish renais-

---

[17]*Times*, Jan. 10, 1919, "Bohemia."
[18]*Ibid.*, Jan. 15.
[19]*Ibid.*, Feb. 1.

sance." There was a danger that the new German campaign might find "converts" in many American quarters.[20] Early in June, on the occasion of the presentation of the peace terms to the Austrians, the *Times* insisted that "Austria, like Germany, must sign or take the consequences." Austria's signature signified, of course, renunciation of the union with Germany.[21]

While torn between public opinion at home, which was still anti-German, and the theoretical appeal of self-determination, Great Britain's policy was also shaped by concern for the security of Europe as a whole, by consideration of the interests of her French ally and of her Central and East Central European friends and the wartime promises made to them, and by plain fear of strengthening a vanquished and seemingly unchanged Germany.

In *Die Österreichische Revolution* (1923) Dr. Otto Bauer attempted to justify his foreign policy course as one not devoid of a reasonable chance of success. But he had to admit that in England the German Austrian government faced an opponent to the Anschluss which was hardly less determined than France. "The idea that Germany's defeat should result in the increase of the Reich's population was disliked by English policy makers."[22]

Of the possible alternatives before Austria, Great Britain favored Austria's independence, but thought the establishment of a Danubian confederation even more preferable. The latter project would embrace the newly established independent national states; it promised them as well as German Austria the great economic benefits of a wider region, one more or less identical with that of the former Austro-Hungarian monarchy. Since the formerly oppressed

---

[20]*Ibid.*, Feb. 12, Simonds, "Germany's New Tricks. . . ."

[21]*Ibid.*, June 3.

[22]Bauer, 1923, p. 146. The contributor to the *Cambridge History of Foreign Policy* **3** (1866-1919), 1923, however, like D. Lloyd George in the foregoing, apparently wished to pass the buck to France. At a time before British records relating to the Peace Conference could be examined, he held that the victors, including Great Britain, vetoed Austria's union "at the instigation of France" (p. 357). Paralleling this statement of a British historian are the remarks of André Tardieu made long after the event, in 1921, in the Chamber of Deputies (*Annales de la Chambre des Députés. Débats Parlementaires,* pp. 2122-2125) for which, however, no evidence was produced. According to Tardieu, Clémenceau won Britain's consent for the prohibition of the *Anschluss* in return for concessions over spheres of influence in the Near East.

nationalities had obtained their political and national objectives, there seemed to be little danger that the new confederate structure would be dominated by its German neighbor, as the old Dual Empire had been.

By February, 1919, some experts in the British Foreign Office held that it was no longer possible for the Paris Peace Conference or for the British government in particular to postpone serious consideration of the Austrian question. To Sir Eyre Crowe the responsibility for delaying a solution of the Austrian question lay with his foreign colleagues and the diplomacy of France and Italy. He warned "that the longer a decision is delayed, the greater will become the difficulty, if only because, whilst we do nothing, the enemy is likely to act and present the allies with *faits accomplis*."[23]

One of Sir Eyre Crowe's colleagues did not share his fears. He held that, once Germany's frontiers had been "irrevocably fixed" by the Conference, it would be comparatively easy to settle those of the remaining states.[24] But he hardly came to grips with the main thrust of Sir Eyre Crowe's argument. A prolonged silence on the Austrian question, particularly on the Anschluss of German Austria, was bound to arouse hopes in Austria and Germany, to give encouragement to the friends of the Anschluss in both countries, and thus to affect the settlement with Germany. While Sir Eyre Crowe feared a "do-nothing" policy which would merely encourage the enemy's policy of a *fait accompli*, he was prepared to recognize Austria's right to self-determination in the long run and was critical of the French scheme of prohibiting the Anschluss, "a plan against which much is to be said." Nevertheless, Sir Eyre Crowe himself apparently favored at least a temporary prohibition. Clearly, by mid-February British policy on the Anschluss was still being shaped and had not yet taken a definite form. But its outlines had begun to be written.

In the spring of 1919, British and French policy was based upon prevention of the immediate Anschluss by Germany and on discouraging and even halting the Anschluss movement in Austria while not closing the door for all time to come. One means of preventing the Anschluss was the improvement of relations between Austria and the succession

---

[23]*P.R.*, F.O. 608, v. 16, Sir Eyre Crowe, Feb. 18, 1919.
[24]*Ibid.*

states and thus eliminating the obstacles in the way of establishing a Danubian confederation. In March, Colonel Thomas Cunninghame proposed the dispatch of an inter-Allied commission to Vienna to promote cooperation between states in the area of the former Austro-Hungarian monarchy.[25] With the Austrian peace settlement delayed in favor of writing the German peace treaty first, a clash between the former nationalities of the Habsburg empire and the German Austrians was not unlikely.

The danger of further delays in writing the peace settlement was also recognized by Harold Nicolson of the British Foreign Office. To prevent a possible agitation in German Bohemia in favor of a union with Germany, he suggested that simultaneously with the publication of the German treaty the British and the Allies make a declaration about German Bohemia to the effect "that the decision not only is final, but also that their [the Germans'] rights and privileges will be remembered and safeguarded."[26]

The difference between Cunninghame's plan and Nicolson's recommendation lay in that the former was based upon a preliminary agreement between the disputing parties arrived at under the guidance of an inter-Allied commission which had traveled to Central Europe, while the latter suggested an authoritative Allied fiat to be decreed in Paris and valid until such time as the Peace Conference would elaborate upon it and make it final.

Nicolson's suggestion also to publish this document in Vienna—not in Berlin—was indicative of how much in his view Vienna had made itself the spokesman and champion of the rights of the population of German Bohemia.

British policy seemed primarily concerned with calming the aroused passions in Central Europe, preventing the outbreak of hostilities between the nationalities of the former Dual Monarchy, and even helping them to cooperate. Thus the old territorial realm might even re-emerge, though under new political auspices. This new Danubian confederation would be based upon a just and realistic balance of power between the nationalities and the grave would be dug for the Anschluss movement. The Austrian people in the very exer-

---

[25]*Ibid.*, v. 6, No. 1473, Cunninghame, March 18.
[26]*Ibid.*, No. 62, H. Nicolson, Apr. 11.

cise of national self-determination—a principle which plagued the Allies although, or because, they had just curtailed it—would join a Danubian federated bloc.

Dr. Bauer wrote later: "The unclear plans for a federation of the succession states had most adherents in England."[27] Actually, French interest in a federation in Central Europe was by no means lagging. The program never attained the level of a well thought-out and systematic project which was fully and actively supported by the Allied governments. But projects relating to a Central European confederation never ceased to crop up during the immediate and even later postwar period.

In mid-February, Adam Müller, German ambassador in Switzerland, reported from Berne to the German Foreign Office that he expected the Entente to call a conference of several states which was to be held in Vienna and to discuss the possibilities of creating a Danubian confederation. A few days later, Wedel pointed his finger at the real obstacle to the realization of the project: "The Entente has concentrated its work toward it [the Danubian confederation] in Vienna and has overlooked the fact that the main resistance to it is to be found in Prague, Laibach, and Agram."[28] The very opposition of Austria's neighbors to a Central European confederation made Sir Headlam Morley of the British Foreign Office suggest on March 2 that the Entente insist on postponing the final decision on Austria's future until after the signing of the peace treaty, at which time the question of the establishment of a Danubian confederation should be definitely considered.[29] The confederation seemed to be the means with which to torpedo the Anschluss project.

During the year 1918-1919, English and French policies toward Austria and the Anschluss became increasingly similar. But the prohibition of the Anschluss until after the signing of the peace treaty was a minimum program for the French. While they wished to make it permanent, the British instead stressed its temporary character. Some Englishmen wanted the French to bear the "odium" for any violation of the principle of national self-determination. But everything

[27]Bauer, 1923: p. 146.
[28]*N.A.*, T 136-25, Akten . . . , Müller, Berne, to F.O., Feb. 14, 1919.
[29]*P.R.*, F.O. 608, v. 16, Headlam Morley, Feb. 17.

considered, the British government and British public opinion were as opposed to strenghtening vanquished Germany as the French were. By favoring the project of a Danubian confederation and the neutralization of Austria,[30] and even occasionally hinting at the possibility of joining parts of southern Germany to Austria, the English moved in channels which the French had started to dig.

The Austrian election results in mid-February and the wave of pro-Anschluss sentiment which swept through the Weimar Constituent Assembly immediately after its opening provided the catalyst which made the Allies move rapidly toward adopting an Anschluss policy. The day following the Austrian elections a member of the British Foreign Office recommended that, if Austria's incorporation in fact were to take place, it would be essential that the Allies should insist on its postponement until after the conclusion of the peace both with Germany and German Austria.[31]

A few days later this policy became accepted in London and Washington, and was quickly adopted by Paris. At a meeting on February 21 British and American delegates definitely agreed that no union between German Austria and Germany could be recognized until the peace treaty had been signed. At the same time they decided that Allied representatives in Austria should be instructed to suggest to the inhabitants the desirability of "not taking any hasty action in this matter."[32] Soon after the British and American delegates had agreed on this temporary prohibition of the Anschluss, a parallel recommendation on it was made by a joint group of French and American experts.[33]

While the policy was prohibitive, the prohibition was clearly limited to the present and the immediate future. For the more distant future this first policy statement, and later others, held out the hope that the Anschluss might be permitted under certain conditions, depending mainly on the con-

---

[30]N.A., T 136-25, Akten . . . Müller to F.O., Apr. 25.

[31]P.R., F.O. 608, v. 16, Gen. Secretary of the Peace Conference to the Secretary of the British Peace Delegation; Headlam Morley, Feb. 17.

[32]Ibid., Minute by W. Tyrrell, Feb. 21, 1919; docket: Attitude of Allies towards proposals for union between German Austria to Germany.

[33]Ibid. Report of the Central Committee on Territorial Questions to the Supreme Allied Council. Communicated by Secretary General, March 16; see also Woodward and Butler, 1946: 1: pp. 183-184.

sent of the Council of the League of Nations. As it turned out in later years, the built-in veto could not be overridden. But the Entente's emphasis during the crucial months of 1919 was on possibly allowing the union between Germany and Austria once the treaty was signed, provided the Anschluss was still strongly desired by the people of Austria.

The relations between victors and vanquished were regulated by the armistice terms. Any attempt to bring about an immediate union between German Austria and Germany would have amounted to a violation of the armistice agreements. In addition, news of the foregoing new policy as agreed by Great Britain and the United States was leaked to the Austrian government. Berlin and Vienna also became fully aware of the French position, which was openly discussed in the French press. Thus both German Austria and Germany were now clearly forewarned.

The warning came just in time. It was probably designed to be transmitted to Vienna before Dr. Bauer left for Weimar and Berlin in late February at the head of the Austrian delegation. The Allies wished to bring the Anschluss movement in both Austria and Germany to a grinding halt.

On March 3, at the very time Dr. Bauer and the Austrian delegation were in Germany, E. L. Dresel of the United States Peace Commission, fearing that time was running out, drew up a memorandum on the Anschluss which was to play an important role in the development of both American and Allied policy on the union issue. Dresel and his colleagues recommended that the Council of Ten of the Peace Conference make a public statement to the effect that any attempt to bring about the union of German Austria with Germany would "under present abnormal conditions" be considered "premature and precipitate" and therefore be disapproved by the Council.[34] It must be assumed that Dresel knew of the foregoing Anglo-American agreement on the Anschluss with which his memorandum was in consonance. Yet the memorandum went beyond it; its adoption by the Council of Ten and by the Peace Conference in general

---

[34]P.R., F.O. 608, v. 16, Dresel, memorandum, March 1, 1919. Dresel had discussed the *Anschluss* question with his compatriot General Bliss and left him with the memorandum for a projected declaration of the Council of Ten (*F.R.U.S., P.P.C.*, 1919, **9:** pp. 87-88; Minutes of the Daily Meeting of the Commissioners Plenipotentiary, March, 1919).

would have given it a much wider basis and support, including the active endorsement of both Latin powers, France and Italy. What Dresel proposed was not merely a bilateral understanding or a diplomatic note of the Entente formally addressed to the political leaders of Austria and Germany, but a proclamation and direct appeal of the Peace Conference over the heads of the German and Austrian leaders to the peoples of Germany and Austria themselves.

Dresel not only urged the Peace Conference to issue a statement which would prevent an immediate *fait accompli*, but also advanced numerous rather persuasive arguments against the Anschluss as a long-range project. First of all, there was in his view no evidence of a numerical majority of Austrians being in favor of a union with Germany. Pressure from Germany, socialist propaganda, and temporary economic and financial difficulties were the factors which were controlling the present pro-Anschluss agitation.

"As far as the final resolution of this question is concerned," the memorandum said, "the principle of self-determination should undoubtedly be the decisive factor. On the other hand, arguments against the union are so convincing that any over-hasty determination of the question seems highly unfortunate." The Anschluss would have the following consequences:

1. It would more than compensate Germany for the loss of Alsace and Lorraine.
2. Switzerland would be bound to fall under "preponderantly German influence."
3. Bohemia would be "encircled."
4. Politically and economically, Vienna would be doomed to decline.
5. The incorporation of Austria would give Germany "a new starting point for political and economic penetration of the Near East."
6. Germany would come within "striking distance" of the Adriatic Sea and the Mediterranean.
7. The union with Austria would "render difficult the realization of either a Danubian or a greater Balkan confederation which may prove the most satisfactory solution of the present Austro-Hungarian problem."

On March 13 Dresel forwarded this memorandum to Sir W. Tyrrell of the British Delegation, warning him of the dangers of procrastination and inaction: "Absence of declaration by Allies is considered tacit assent to Union. Action should be immediate as negotiations are complete." If the Entente did not act, Germany and German Austria could be expected to make their moves. This would force the hands of the United States and of the Entente in their policy towards Central Europe and the Balkans and would present them with a *fait accompli.* Dresel's memorandum strengthened British opinion that the union should be prohibited until, as Sir Eyre Crowe remarked, "after the final peace had been signed and ratified."[35]

British and Allied policy was preponderantly in favor of an independent Austria, or better, of a Danubian confederation, and against the union of Austria with Germany. Yet the policy adopted was one of mere delay. This attitude also appears in the recommendations drawn up on March 18 by W. Douglas of the British Foreign Office[36] for the British ambassador Gosling in Prague. According to Douglas, the Allied and Associated Powers should under no circumstances permit the Anschluss to take place until after the conclusion of the final treaty of peace. Furthermore, postponing the union would "give time to see how things work out between the Danubian states." It would give the Czechoslovaks an opportunity to "cooperate" with German Austria and Hungary in settling the very difficult financial and economic problems with which the three states were jointly confronted. Foreign Minister Balfour specifically approved Douglas's recommendations.[37]

While British policy regarding the Anschluss appeared adamant for the moment and indeed for the next few months, it actually opened wide the doors to certain Austrian hopes that it might be possible later to bury the very national independence which the peace treaty was to assert. What British policy aimed at was gaining time and hoping for the best — under the circumstances also the most unlikely to

[35]*P.R.,* F.O. 608, v. 16, Dresel's letter to W. Tyrrell, March 3; also Eyre Crowe's comment on Dresel.

[36]*Ibid.,* Douglas, Memorandum, March 18.

[37]*Ibid.* Balfour's approval and comment by B.W., March 25.

happen—namely the emergence, according to Douglas, of a "wish" among German Austrians to remain independent. And this was to arise out of their "cooperation" with Czechoslovakia and Hungary on the solution of indeed most "difficult" questions; graver ones than had separated these nations in the prewar period when they were still members of one state and no irreparable step—the dissolution of the empire—had yet been taken.

The aforementioned British policy, subsequently adopted by the Allies, was widely felt to be contradictory and confusing. In his message from Prague dated March 14 the British envoy Gosling reported the following remarks of President Masaryk: "The Czech government will, of course, shape its policy towards Austria and Germany in complete accord with the Allies. But the great difficulty lies in the fact that the Allies apparently have no clear and firm programme in this matter."[38] The president of Czechoslovakia had hit the nail on the head. Similarly Rumbold, the British envoy in Berne, who had repeatedly reported that the Anschluss was most undesirable to the Swiss government, informed the Foreign Office that he had been asked point-blank by the president of the Swiss republic "what view His Majesty's Government takes of the matter [Anschluss]." "I replied that I did not know."[39] Neither did the British representative in Vienna, Colonel Thomas Cunninghame, and Dr. Otto Bauer, Austria's foreign secretary.

On February 16, 1919, came one of the most urgent calls for clarification of Entente, particularly British, policy. It originated with Colonel Cunninghame, head of the British Mission in Vienna, who revealed that he was not aware of the attitude of the Entente Powers towards German Austria. Nor did anyone else know the Entente's goals in regard to Austria, "the result being hesitancy and the withholding of energetic measures calculated to help the state out of the quandary in which it is at present." He also urged the Entente to make "a clear statement of [its] wishes in regard to the Danubian confederation."[40]

---

[38]*Ibid.*, Gosling to F.O., March 14.
[39]*Ibid.*, Rumbold to F.O., March 21.
[40]*A.A.*, Nachlass Br.-R.'s, Cunninghame, H 234604-605.

This widespread lack of knowledge of the British and Allied position on the Anschluss was plainly linked with the British and Allied failure to come to grips, in theory and practice, with the widely recognized principle of self-determination and its possible limitations. In regard to self-determination in general and the Anschluss in particular the Allies were indecisive and inclined to procrastination. The decision not to permit the Anschluss prior to a certain date — until after the peace treaty was signed — but to allow it thereafter, was bound to court a charge of inconsistency. It raised opportunism, the lack of clear vision and resolve, and the consideration of the moment, to the level of a policy. It was a compromise which could not but confuse public opinion at home and abroad.

Uncertainty about Allied goals played right into the hands of the friends of the Anschluss. They were encouraged when during the first critical months after the disintegration of the Dual Monarchy the Allies made no clear-cut policy statement against the Anschluss. The Austrian minister in Berne, an ardent adherent of union with Germany,[41] confided to Rumbold, British envoy in Switzerland: "Had the Allies made clear to German Austria their wish for a Danubian confederation, such a confederation might have been possible, and that would have been a better solution."[42]

What lay behind the weak policy of the Allies — their delay, and playing for time — was their unwillingness and inability to dispatch troops to Central Europe. Even the rise of a second Soviet republic in Hungary in March of 1919 failed to rally the Great Powers. At a time of intervention in Russia, it was apparently not so much considerations for international law and propriety, but rather shortage of troops that made the British shy away from intervening against Soviet Hungary. And France rejected the thought of intervening without the support of British or American troops.[43] Early in April, in the wake of Béla Kun's and the Bolsheviks' seizure of power in Hungary, the Italian delegation to the Peace Conference sent a memorandum to the foreign ministers of the Great Powers suggesting as a matter of highest urgency an inter-Allied oc-

---

[41]*P.R.*, F.O. 608, v. 16, March 25.
[42]*Ibid.*, Rumbold to Balfour, Tel., Apr. 2.
[43]Low, 1963: p. 89.

cupation of Vienna and other cities in German Austria "to avoid the gravest consequences in relation to public order"[44]—in other words, to secure Austria against Bolshevism, which threatened from Budapest, rather than against any annexationist move from Berlin. The British Foreign Office declined for the reason, as one official put it tersely: "We have no troops to send to Vienna."[45]

As mentioned above, in February and March, 1919, both a British-American agreement and a Franco-American understanding on the Anschluss had been reached. Yet the English and the French were also discussing the Anschluss with each other and were seeking a broader area of agreement and a larger measure of cooperation and coordination.

The French point of view had found expression in a position paper which André Tardieu considered of such intrinsic importance that he brought it personally to the attention of the British foreign minister Balfour on April 25, 1919.[46] The note, called "Memorandum Concerning German Austria," had been written in February of 1919; it stated that the Central Committee on Territorial Questions had presented to the Supreme Council the following recommendation relative to the German Austrian frontier with Germany: "The American and French delegations to the Committee on Territorial Questions suggest that it would be expedient to impose on Germany in the peace preliminaries the obligation to undertake nothing, politically or economically, which might encroach upon the independence of Austria. . . ."

---

[44]P.R., F.O. 608, v. 16, Delegazione Italiano all Congresso della Pace, Marchese Imperiali, Apr. 7.

[45]Ibid., Comments of H. on Imperiali. A few days later, the American Professor George D. Herron similarly telegraphed to Sir W. Tyrrell a copy of a message sent by H. Lammasch. In an appeal to President Wilson, Lammasch had pleaded for the dispatch of Allied troops "for the protection of an unbiased plebiscite on the question of the attachement to Germany" and "at the same time" securing Austria against the spread of Bolshevism. A force of 14,000-15,000 for all of Austria would be "entirely sufficient" (P.R., F.O. 608, v. 16, Herron to Tyrrell, Apr. 10). Harold Nicolson of the Foreign Office then added the marginal comment: "It is no use going on crying as to sending troops when we have none to spare" (ibid., Nicolson, Apr. 10; also Swiss government to Curzon, Apr. 14).

[46]P.R., F.O. 608, v. 9, Note relative à l'Autriche Allemande. Proposition Française. Communicated by French Delegation, Apr. 25, 1919 (eight pages); also to be found in Ministère des Affaires Étrangères Archives, Paris, Aff. Étrang., Europe, A-Paix, Photos Allemandes, A 1056, Bureau de Mlle Duval, pp. 220-229.

But the French were prepared to go further. They wanted to prevent not only Germany but also German Austria, which tended to take the initiative on the union issue, from moving toward the Anschluss.

> The French government demands that under present conditions the union of German Austria with Germany be forbidden in the preliminaries of the peace. Objections had been raised that such a prohibition would deprive Austria of the right of self-determination. The French government disputes *(a)* that in the present circumstances this right can be legitimately exercised by German Austria. and *(b)* that, even if it could, the decision of the Powers should be influenced by it.

According to the French memorandum, there was no justification for a plebiscite:

1. The movement in German Austria was "purely artificial" and had an "extraneous" character. The vote of the Austrian National Assembly could not be considered valid, since its members had not been elected for the purpose of making a decision about the union with Germany. All information indicated that, with the exception of the Socialists who pursued a political goal, all German Austria really wanted was "economic guarantees, neutrality if possible, and the preservation of Vienna as a capital, either as the center of a Danubian confederation or as the seat of international organizations."
2. The Anschluss movement in Austria had actually originated in Germany. "This is a Pan-German and socialist movement imposed on the Vienna confusion by German determination and by the silence of the Great Powers." In the past, neither German Austria nor even Germany, though an ally of the Dual Monarchy, had dared to demand this union.

> Today, the Pan-Germans, profiting from their defeat, claim it [the Anschluss] so that one of their principal war goals may be attained. The Socialists demand it to augment the total strength of their party. . . . Pan-Germans and Socialists present a common front in a government which associates Ebert, Scheidemann, Brockdorff-Rantzau, and Erzberger. . . . this is the government which has "created" the Austrian affair, in ac-

cordance with the classical methods of Germany's unitary and expansionist Socialism.

3. It was known that Pan-Germanism had always taken advantage of the argument for a fusion which was based on common nationality and community of language. Nor was the argument valid that union between the two German states was inevitable. The annexation of Canada by the United States or of Belgium by France would be equally "inevitable."

The French government held that the rule of self-determination was presently not applicable to the Austrian question. A plebiscite would be dangerous and would contradict the general principles of peace.

Austria-Hungary was the first country to declare war and has waged war at Germany's side for four and one-half years. German Austria, the remains of Austria-Hungary, is still an enemy country just like Germany herself. Is the peace treaty's goal to encourage or restrain the political ambitions of enemy countries? This is the question. Pan-Germanism of which all the leaders of the present German government have been active agents for five years has always maintained that Germany, even if defeated, would emerge from the war bigger and stronger, due to the annexation of German Austria. Do we want to give a basis to this hope and assure German imperialism the revanche which it cynically anticipates? To act thus would mean giving an immoral reward to the enemy countries which are responsible for the war.

At the same time it would mean creating a danger to peace in Europe. At the very moment when the conference is imposing upon Germany military clauses whose justification is general security shall we wish to augment the numerical strength of this country by seven million German Austrians?

At the moment when the conference calls the Czechoslovak republic into being shall we condemn it to live in a state of suffocation, between Germany on three sides and Hungary on almost the entire fourth side? — Switzerland, on the other hand, has already protested against the union in the name of her security and her internal peace. Besides, if one acknowledged that Austria has the right to union with Germany, what should we do if, for political, financial or monetary reasons, Hungary claimed the same right? And in this case it would be the Allies themselves who had reopened to Germany the road called *Drang nach dem Osten.*

The Peace Conference had the overriding duty to prevent aggression and to make enemy countries innocuous.

> Before consulting them about their political preferences, one must first guarantee the general interests of peace against them. Must we abandon this principle in the question of German Austria? France, which has one half the population of Germany, considers this rule of prudence to be of vital interest to herself. But she is at the same time convinced that it also conforms to the general interest.

The note attempted to brush aside the argument that by prohibiting the union the Conference would sacrifice Austria's future. Having been subjected to intensive German pressure for more than four months, German Austria was presently not in a position to express her own desire freely.

> To permit the [free] exercise of this will, independence must, for the moment, be imposed upon the country. This way, and this way alone, will Austria be able to assess calmly different alternatives and prepare herself to choose among them the one she prefers: independence, entry into a Danubian confederation, or even union with Germany. Assisting toward a German solution today would not signify preserving the future, but pawning it away. The only solution which would preserve it is independence. Besides, the foundation of peace is the League of Nations, that permanent organization always ready to make readjustments of treaty provisions.

In the future nothing would be forbidden to Germans and German Austrians, but at present no advantage could be granted to them which would constitute a factor of insecurity in Europe. In spite of the weight attached to the arguments against the Anschluss, the claim to national self-determination was considered so strong an argument that even the French document did not go so far as to deny German Austria the right to union for all time to come.

When on April 25 Tardieu submitted to Balfour the French memorandum asking for the prohibition of the Anschluss in the peace preliminaries, he informed him that

Clémenceau hoped to submit the draft clause prohibiting the union of Austria with Germany "very soon, probably this afternoon." He also expressed the "earnest hope" that France would not be left alone as the only power to insist on such a clause.[47] The French government thus wanted to enlist the English in its campaign to outlaw the Anschluss. It claimed that it wished primarily to strengthen the Austrian opposition against the union with Germany, yet its main endeavor, prohibition of it in the peace treaty, went considerably beyond this objective.

While, according to Tardieu, the Council of Four had made no decision on the Anschluss,[48] this was not Balfour's opinion.[49] Actually, the French found the agreed formula on the union too weak and ineffective and suggested tightening the prohibition clause by inserting the word "inalienable" before "independence."[50] Sir Eyre Crowe thought it doubtful "whether even this, either in theory or practice, would prevent union with Germany," if it was really desired by the entire Austrian population. But it would serve to encourage the Austrian opposition to the Anschluss. And one way of doing this was indeed to insert a properly worded clause in the treaty with Germany.

> If I may express an opinion, I would urge that we should avoid any form of words which would oblige us, in the event that Austria at some future date would wish to unite herself with Germany, to oppose such union by force of arms as contrary to a solemn treaty. Anything, however, that, whilst avoiding such obligations, would help to keep Austria and Germany apart, deserves encouragement; and we ought to go as far as we possibly can to support any French proposals to this end.

It might perhaps be possible to extract from Germany the pledge that she would not work for an alteration in the territorial *status quo* as fixed by the treaty of peace.

In the end a clause of the foregoing nature was indeed inserted in the peace treaty with Germany. It clearly grew out

---

[47]*P.R.*, F.O. 608, v. 9, British Delegation in Paris to F.O., n.d., probably written late April, 1919.
[48]*Ibid.*, see comment by M. Hankey on the French memorandum.
[49]*Ibid.*, British Delegation to F.O., n.d.
[50]*Ibid.*

of the joint Franco-British effort in 1919 to keep Germany and Austria "apart," then and for an indeterminate future.

If there was anything new in Sir Eyre Crowe's recommendations, it was his guidelines for British policy on the extent of the support to be given to France. They caught Balfour's fancy and contributed substantially not only to British, but also to Allied policy on the Anschluss. But Sir Eyre Crowe's recommendation fell short of the French proposition to prohibit the Anschluss outright, and to prevent Austrian as well as German initiatives and moves toward this objective. Balfour and the British Foreign Office rejected the future use of force to oppose a union between Germany and Austria, but thought the French ought to be supported in their drive to keep Austria out of Germany's grip and prevent her from moving into Germany's orbit. Since, in the view of the Foreign Office, British interests demanded Austria's independence, the foregoing position was based on contradictions. Yet the use of British troops in Central Europe was rejected, partly out of conviction that the most vital British interests were not affected, partly out of deference to the right of self-determination, and partly for pragmatic reasons, the temporary shortage of troops and the fear of being drawn into confrontation and conflict.

In early May and early June of 1919 respectively the drafts of the German and Austrian peace treaties were submitted to the German and Austrian peace delegations which had traveled to Paris. But even thereafter, in the summer months, the questions of the Anschluss and the future of Austro-German relations continued to preoccupy Britain's political leaders. On June 3 and June 20, at the request of the chancellor of the exchequer, Sir Francis Oppenheimer wrote two memoranda on Austria and the Anschluss, which subsequently were also endorsed by the Foreign Office and the War Cabinet.[51] The memoranda thus closely reflected the opinions of the British government on the Anschluss during the summer months of 1919.

Sir Francis Oppenheimer criticized the peace terms as then drafted and made certain recommendations for the recon-

---

[51]*P.R.*, F.O. 608, v. 20, memoranda by Sir Oppenheimer, printed for the War Cabinet, July, 1919. The memoranda are also printed by Woodward and Butler, 1956: **6:** pp. 40-56.

struction of German Austria which would spare her having to seek assistance from Germany, an assistance which was likely to lead to the Anschluss. After stressing the new Austria's desperate situation, Oppenheimer pointed out that help could either come from the Allies or from Germany. Since the Allies had prohibited the fusion of Austria with Germany, they were under a moral obligation to assist Austria in the present crisis. So far there was no indication that the Allies were really willing to help Austria. Their "policy of drift constitutes a terrible danger. The present indecision on their part may become responsible for a reign of terror which could easily spread beyond the borders of Austria."

Oppenheimer continued:

[There is] little doubt that on political grounds an Austrian fusion with Germany should be prevented. . . . The great political dangers resulting from such a fusion have been pointed out earlier, especially in the Paris memorandum on June 3. A link-up of Austria with Germany would give great impetus to German expansion toward the Near East. It would lead to the establishment of a German-Italian bloc which would divide the European continent and thus isolate France from possible eastern allies. The Anschluss would also prepare the isolation and destruction of Czechoslovakia. . . . These arguments should weigh heavily if the question is being considered whether the Allies should make a special effort to assist Austria. and thus prevent her drifting into the arms of Germany.

In addition to the foregoing political and military arguments, Oppenheimer said, arguments of an economic and sentimental nature should also determine Allied policy toward Austria. Excellent investments were possible in Austria, and it would hardly be in the Allied interest to allow these plums to fall into enemy hands. From a sentimental point of view, there was much worth saving in Austria, one of the oldest surviving centers of European culture. "If the country is not saved, it will disappear into the German melting-pot or become a prey to Bolshevism."

Unfortunately, Oppenheimer continued, in regard to Austria there appeared to be less harmony among the Allies than might be expected. An inquiry by an inter-Allied committee was urgently needed. And the British, "at present by far the most popular foreigners in Austria," should take the lead in appointing a committee of experts and invite the other Allies to join it. "The fundamental question before the committee will be: 'Can we save Austria or can't we save her?' " If it should be found that the necessary assistance could not be granted, then His Majesty's Government should withdraw the prohibition of the Anschluss. Only such a step would "absolve us from any responsibility for whatever the consequences of our inability may be." But drift was the "worst possible" of all courses, it was "unworthy and pernicious."

Foreign Secretary Balfour then requested Philip Kerr, Sir Headlam Morley, and others of the Foreign Office to comment on Sir Francis Oppenheimer's suggestions for a possible modification of some provisions of the Austrian peace treaty.[52] A penetrating criticism of Oppenheimer's memorandum came from the pen of Sidney Peel who warned that, "if an attempt was made of trying to settle too much by this treaty, if we are too ambitious, the treaty would never be finished." "If the Austrians like to ask the Allies for help in their internal affairs, let them do so, and let us consider their application on its merits, but let this be a separate negotiation."[53] According to Peel, Oppenheimer's appeal for economic assistance was valid, but his case for making it part of the peace treaty was not. Harold Nicolson remarked in similar fashion about Oppenheimer's memorandum: "Oppenheimer's views, voiced earlier, have always had the support of the political section—the question is, however, entirely a financial and economic matter."[54]

Finally, the Foreign Office sent an official reply to the Treasury, strongly supporting Oppenheimer's main thesis.

His Lordship feels that unless some action of this kind is taken at an early date, the fusion of Austria with the German empire cannot be prevented and that such fusion would have a direct and unfortunate effect upon the position of the new states of

---

[52]*P.R.*, F.O. 608, v. 20, Memorandum, July 9, No. 4577; see also Aug. 15.
[53]*Ibid.*, S. Peel.
[54]*Ibid.*, H. Nicolson.

Czechoslovakia and Yugoslavia whom His Majesty's Government are morally bound to support.[55]

Oppenheimer's memoranda, written in June and labeled "secret," were printed by the Exchequer for the War Cabinet in July of 1919. Shortly thereafter, the War Cabinet in a three-page printed policy statement commented on Oppenheimer's second memorandum.[56] According to the Memorandum of the War Cabinet, his proposal offered a favorable market for Great Britain in Austria.

> If we obtain a strong position in Vienna, we immediately strengthen our position in Bohemia, in Hungary, and even in Yugoslavia. All these countries wish to trade with us, and we also shall be able to facilitate regular interchanges between the various states, thus helping to solve one of the great problems of Central Europe, while profiting ourselves at the same time. The commercial aspect of the question aside, the political advantages of the proposal are even more important.

The memorandum continued by saying that Vienna would either fall to communism or be absorbed into Germany. But the political dangers of a fusion with Germany were obvious. "Once Germany is in Vienna, she is again on the high road to the Balkans and Constantinople and will resume the *Drang nach dem Osten* policy, one of the causes of the war." The problem of the German minority in Bohemia would then become acute, and the survival of the Czechoslovak republic would be "definitely threatened." Furthermore, Italy and Germany would become direct neighbors and, "in view of Italy's present state of mind, it should not be too difficult to picture the dangers to which such association might give rise." A renewal of Italo-German friendship was likely to spell doom for both Czechoslovakia and Yugoslavia. The War Cabinet saw the dangers of the Anschluss with prophetic clarity.

If on the other hand, the memorandum continued, Austria could rehabilitate her trade and feed Vienna, she would set her face against union with Germany and would want to

---

[55]*Ibid.*, F.O. to Treasury, July 10.
[56]*Ibid.*, Memorandum of War Cabinet, July 9, No. 4577, and Aug. 15.

remain independent. "We thus have at the same time a buffer between Germany and Italy and a bar to German designs in the Balkans. It would then be possible for Britain to create for herself an eminent commercial and political position in Central Europe." Having secured the friendship of Austria, it should not prove to be an insuperable task to settle the differences which divided the states in Central Europe. The Memorandum of the War Cabinet ended on a note of special urgency: Time was running short and, if nothing were done by Great Britain and the Allies, Austria inevitably might go elsewhere. Therefore, the proposed commission should be sent without delay.

Thus the War Cabinet and the Chancellery of the Exchequer joined the Foreign Office in its determined opposition to the Anschluss. A the same time they saw clearly that this negative attitude had to be balanced by granting extensive economic assistance to Austria.

Though the peace treaty had already been presented to the Austrian delegation, several British departments were still pondering the future of Austria. They realized the need for rapidly improving her economic situation and the political atmosphere of all of Central Europe to instill life-blood into the independence of Austria, an independence which the treaty would only legally insure. British concern at this late stage was a clear indication that in their view the treaty submitted to Austria was not the ultimate solution and that it needed economic and political supplements of a vital nature. Even if Western economic help were provided in adequate measure, there seemed to be some doubt that the chasm separating Austria from the new succession states could be bridged in the reasonably near future. But if it was not, Austria's continued economic, national, and political isolation and the attraction of belonging to a Greater Germany were not likely to lessen.

2. FRENCH PUBLIC OPINION AND POLICY ON THE UNION OF AUSTRIA WITH GERMANY

> "I have become more convinced than ever that the course of France is identical with that of justice and the best way to be a good Frenchman while solving the Austrian question will be to be a good European."
> André Chéradame

FRENCH political thought about the Austrian empire, its role in Europe and its importance for the equilibrium among European powers in the late nineteenth and early twentieth centuries has been dealt with already, including the preceding pages. Before 1914, France's "first interest" had been "the preservation of Austria," at least in its historic core.[1] When the Austrian empire disintegrated and Germany went down in defeat, the French government, victorious but haunted by fear for France's security, was determined to prevent Germany from annexing German Austria and thus to compensate for expected losses elsewhere.

During the days when the aged structure of the Habsburg empire broke to pieces, French public opinion, however, was clearly divided on the question of the Anschluss. The pace of events took also the victor by surprise. On October 27, 1918, the nationalist journal *Victoire* held that it would be impossible to oppose the union of Austria with Germany "after invoking democratic principles all throughout the war." A few weeks later *l'Oeuvre*, admitting the danger of applying the principle of national self-determination in all of Central Europe, nevertheless opposed French intervention to thwart the union.[2] In the rightist and royalist *Action Française*, however, Jacques Bainville, pointing to France's long-range interests in Central Europe, warned against permitting the Anschluss. In that case forty million Frenchmen would face a bloc of eighty million Germans, and at a moment when due to the Russian Revolution no effective counterweight existed

[1]R. Henry, 1903: p. 72.
[2]*Victoire,* Oct. 27, 1918, *L'Oeuvre,* Nov. 21, 1918, quoted by Noble, 1919: p. 224.

in the East. Bainville favored some kind of federation of the Central European peoples for which German Austria, the remaining "skeleton of the Austrian state" was needed. President Wilson should demand that German Austria become the pillar of the "federalization" project in the center of Europe. Bainville clearly mistrusted the emerging German republic and was convinced that the nationalist spirit would be promptly revived across the Rhine.[3]

As a sharp opponent of the Anschluss concept in the last days of the dying Habsburg empire appeared also the influential *Le Temps* which was known to express views closely akin to those of the Quai d'Orsay. Commenting on October 19 on "Le Manifesto de Charles I" of October 16, *Le Temps* left no doubt as to its hostility to the union:

> At no price and under no circumstances can we approve that the Germans of Austria enter the empire of the Hohenzollern or any other democratically camouflaged structure which some people would attempt to substitute for the empire of Bismark. . . . Whether the German government is in the hands of Ludendorff or Scheidemann, whether it practices the doctrine of force in the name of Bismark or in the name of Karl Marx, it does not represent national unity but subjection of the different German ethnic groups to the Prussian state. We shall not allow that the number of subjected people be increased.[4]

Under these circumstances it was hardly surprising that French officials and the French government paid closest attention to any suggestion to salvage the unity of the Austro-Hungarian realm in any form, perhaps save even the Habsburg dynasty, and to prevent the otherwise inevitable German aggrandizement. On November 2 Dutasta, then French envoy in Berne, reported about the ideas of Choumecki, German Austrian deputy in the Reichsrat and friend of Emperor Charles, who was then attempting to contact the Entente from Swiss soil. Choumecki warned the Allies not to overthrow the Habsburg dynasty, since its disappearance would ultimately deliver the new independent states to German domination.[5]

---

[3]*L'Action Française,* Oct. 21, 1924, J. Bainville, and Oct. 26, 1918.

[4]*Le Temps,* Oct. 19, 1918.

[5]*A.E.,* Europe 1918-1929, Autriche Z 88 I, Politique Étrangère, Dossier Général I, Dutasta, Berne, to F.O., Nov. 2, pp. 96-97.

Two days later, on November 4, Dutasta sent a telegram to Paris designating his message "urgent." He had learned that an imperial Austrian mission headed by Prince Ludwig Windischgrätz had arrived in Switzerland. Windischgrätz was going to invite the Entente to occupy militarily Vienna, Budapest and other cities to maintain order. The emperor was allegedly terrified by the state of mind of the Austro-Hungarian troops who were returning from the front and committing acts of pillage and violence. He feared equally German troops who were retreating from Rumania and prepared to cross Austrian territory; they leaned strongly toward Bolshevism. This withdrawal could result in the occupation of Vienna and of German Austria by German troops and would strengthen the partisans of Austria's annexation by Germany; the emperor was concerned that certain German Austrian elements of Austria-Hungary might go over to Germany's side. Also Pan-German propaganda might be "redoubled" in the German provinces of the monarchy, and even civil war might ensue.[6]

In early November the French government came close to seriously contemplating the occupation of German Austria.[7] A discussion of the advantages of a possible French occupation of Austria-Hungary, written probably at that time, dealt only with the pros of such a move; it did not discern any possible disadvantages in it. The anonymous author of "De l'utilization politique de l'occupation Française en Autriche-Hongrie," a position paper of the French Foreign Office, saw in a possible French occupation only an "excellent opportunity of France establishing herself in these countries and taking definite roots." The Italians were hated in this region, the English were considered being ignorant of the area and haughty and the Americans being distant and indifferent. "We have working for us the revolutionary tradition, the memory of Napoleon, our loyalty to the principle of nationality, the aid which we have lent to the oppressed peoples during the war and especially the prestige of a victory which, in their eyes, is first of all our victory."[8] French policy toward German Austria and Hungary ought to be "firm and

[6]*Ibid.*, Dutasta, Berne, to F.O., Nov. 4, 1918, pp. 116-117.
[7]*Ibid.*, Dutasta, Nov. 5, Tel. 2030, 118.
[8]*Ibid.*, Doss. Gén. I, "De L'utilization politique de l'occupation . . . Française en Autriche-Hongrie," p. 107f.

just," with a marked nuance of severity toward the Germans, of tolerance toward the Magyars. "Our political objectives in regard to the German Austrians must be negative to keep them away from Germany, to make them understand the advantages which they will find in an independent state, in economic relations with the new Slavic neighbors."

After the breakup of the Dual Empire and the Revolution of November 12 in German Austria, Franklin-Bouillon was one of the first Frenchmen who raised his voice loud against the Anschluss. Chairman of the Foreign Affairs Committee of the Senate and one of the outstanding leaders of the Radical Socialists, then the largest party in the Palais Bourbon, he warned an Executive Committee meeting of his party of the danger of Austria joining Germany.[9]

The French official position was categorically stated also by France's foreign minister Stephen Pichon in the Chamber of Deputies at the end of the year. In his foreign policy talk of December 29, 1918, Pichon pointed to "Bohemia [sic], Poland and Yugoslavia" as three states which would strengthen the coalition among the Slavic peoples and would also give France a "particularly strong military support and new guarantees of security." The debate was lively, as a verbatim report shows.

> There remains the question of the Germans of Austria. It is a serious one, but it must not alarm us. There exist means, as we know, to solve it in such a manner that it does not offer our enemies compensations and resources which they would like to obtain. . . . In regulating the new situation of Germany and of the remains of Austria, it will depend on the Allies to take measures which, by strictly reducing Germany's power to her proper limits, will deprive her of the possibility of recovering by means of the Austrian population . . . what she will have irrevocably lost through the consecration of our victory. . . .
> It will be necessary that in the first place our victory, through the exercise of rights which it gives us in regard to the vanquished, be translated into reality . . . in order to eliminate the possibility of their imperiling again the security of the freedom of the world [applause]. *Pierre Renaudel:* What if the German Austrians themselves proclaim the union? *Foreign*

---

[9]Bulletin du parti républicain radical et radical socialiste, Dec. 14, 1918, quoted by Mayer, 1967: p. 179.

Minister: Don't you believe that the victory gives us these rights in regard to the vanquished? [applause — lively interruptions at the extreme left.] *Renaudel:* Not those! At the extreme left: This is not Wilsonian doctrine. M. *Marcel Cachin:* The chamber has not applauded those Bismarckian words. M. *Jean Longuet:* M. Clémenceau you yourself have once said: "Let us be strong in order to be just."[10]

France's policy, notwithstanding protesting voices on the Left, was based on the rejection of the Anschluss. This policy was to remain unchanged during the following months and years. The French government opposed squarely that Germany, through the backdoor of the Anschluss, was to gain "compensations" for losses which she might incur elsewhere and that French and European security once again be endangered.

But the parliamentary debate had revealed some doubts and even opposition on the moderate and extreme Left. Sharp criticism of the Austrian policy of the French government and of Pichon in particular was uttered in the then socialist *L'Humanité* and continued in the following months.[11] The militant daily pleaded for French demobilization, fought intervention in Russia, and contrasted France's rigidly chauvinistic and imperialist policy with what it considered occasional "words of wisdom" on Central Europe voiced in the English and Italian press.[12] On the whole the socialist press was equivocal. After Austria's mid-February election of 1919 *Populaire* offered the curious comment that the Socialist triumph meant that German Austria would abstain from joining the Reich.[13] And though *L'Humanité* repeated its faith in the principle of self-determination, it candidly admitted that it considered the union "dangerous."[14] Yet during the month of March it published several articles on Austria by Jean Longuet, grandson of Karl Marx, particularly "The Socialists and the Austrian Problem." Longuet repeated herein many of Otto Bauer's theses, praised Austrian Socialism for having achieved "magnificent success," and

[10]*France. Débats Parlementaires.* Annales de la Chambre des Députés. Pichon, Dec. 29, p. 3334.
[11]*L'Humanité,* Jan. 12, 1919.
[12]*Ibid.,* Jan. 13.
[13]*Le Populaire,* Feb. 20.
[14]*L'Humanité,* Feb. 23.

warned against the "Balkanization" of Central Europe.[15] Bauer's attempt, made already in November, 1918, to win Longuet over to his point of view, had paid dividends. Since, as Longuet pointed out, the new states of the region rejected the concept of confederation, Austria had no choice but the Anschluss. English and American public opinion — a point also repeatedly made by Otto Bauer — were, however, opposed to accepting the confederation project, since they could not object to the Anschluss wishes "so clearly voiced by the Austrian people." French policy, however, Longuet concluded, was the stumbling block, since France was "agitated by integral nationalism."[16]

Whatever France's motivation, early in 1919 French policy began definitely to stiffen in regard to the Anschluss. It appeared to many Frenchmen that occasional vigorous pronouncements against the union would deter neither German Austria nor the Reich and that energetic action was urgently needed. But they were plagued by doubts whether they were not too late already.

By mid-February the Central European situation appeared to *Le Matin* hopeless; it considered that France had already lost the battle over the Anschluss. *Le Matin* merely wished to soften the blow; Austria was to remain administratively a separate state and was not to be divided between Saxony and Bavaria. Germany was not to gain the right either to levy troops in Austria or to construct fortresses on her soil. "Briefly, we shall propose for it a regime of the type that the Entente wishes for the left bank of the Rhine." Germany's loss of Alsace and Lorraine and Prussian Poland would, unfortunately, be outweighed by the gain of Austria. "And all this in the name of the principles of President Wilson!"

Le Matin held that French postwar diplomacy in Central Europe had failed:

Let us admit our error. On the morrow of the armistice it was extremely easy to shackle German propaganda in Austria. This country belonged to whoever wished to aid and advise it. We

---

[15]*Ibid.*, March 5.

[16]See also Longuet's articles, *ibid.*, March 22 and March 23; in the latter issue also Edgar Milhaud, "Le Temps and Neutrality." See the editorial of May 11 against the Versailles treaty.

did not go there, and our diplomacy will bear responsibility for having been absent from Vienna at the moment when presence there was indispensable. . . .[17]

Le Matin did not stand alone. The entire French press was deeply concerned. It accused French statesmanship of having failed to stop the movement toward the union of Austria with Germany, doubted that Germany had had a change of heart and mind and that she now embraced sincerely democracy, peace, and international conciliation, and denounced Germany for continuing the imperial German foreign policy of annexation, militarism, and expansion. It suspected German and Austrian statesmen of plotting the Anschluss and the former of exploiting the issue to recoup anticipated losses.

Like the London *Times*, *Le Temps* questioned throughout these months whether a new Germany had arisen. German organizations abroad, particularly in Switzerland, had transformed themselves into Socialist or Bolshevik agencies and carried on "an active propaganda of false news, calumnies and threats against the Entente." While the goals were declared to be revolutionary, the German and Austro-Hungarian legations in Berne had entirely perserved their old personnel.[18] Nationalism and Pan-Germanism in the Reich were as strong as ever, in spite of the wave of revolution which was sweeping Central Europe.

The opening days of the German Constituent Assembly in Weimar witnessed the strength of German national feeling. Germany presented her claims for the preservation of her territorial integrity and also bared her sentiments in favor of the Anschluss. In France, the repeatedly avowed proclamation of interest in the Anschluss was taken as sure proof that Germany, in spite of the revolution, had not changed her outlook, would not work toward a "pacific rehabilitation," and not repudiate "the cult of force and vengeance." "Will she definitely renounce conquests or will she seek . . . ersatz-annexation? One will soon know what to think of it, seeing what is going on between Vienna and Weimar. . . . By taking over German Austria without striking a blow, Prussian im-

---

[17]*Le Matin*, Feb. 16, "L'Autriche sera-t-elle abandonnée à l'Allemagne?"
[18]*Le Temps*, Dec. 31, 1918.

perialism will certainly not be weakened."[19] It would only prosper under a new label.

Concern about the "scheming" of German and Austrian statesmen for the aggrandizement of a Germany which was considered still unrepentant, nationalistic, and eager for revenge, dominated French thinking.[20] The aggrandizement of Germany was not going to stop with the incorporation of Austria. Germany, emboldened by it, would merely turn avidly to other German-inhabited territories across Europe and make the idealistic structure of the League of Nations crumble.

On February 15, 1919, *Le Temps,* pointing to Allied plans for a League of Nations, reminded France that Austria and Germany were building "another structure."

> Thus the new Germany extending to the Drave and to the Leitha, would encircle Bohemia, threaten Italy, reach Yugoslavia, stretch out her hand to the Magyars, and through them to anyone who will enable her to resume the *Drang nach dem Osten.* This new Germany would be much more united than the old one. The fall of the dynasties and the accession of Social Democracy to power will have leveled particularism everywhere. The critics from Alsace-Lorraine and those of Polish and Danish national background will have been replaced by an equal or larger number of German Austrians who too will have learned Prussian methods as easily as the Bavarians have done. Once unshackled, the principle of German unity will not allow itself to be stopped. From the moment of the recognition of the right of all German-speaking groups to unite with Great Germany, capital Berlin, an unheard-of irredentism will spread among the German isles of Kurland, Livonia, Lithuania, and Poland, of Bohemia and of Transylvania. This irredentism, richly cultivated by the German government, one day will dare to attack Alemannic Switzerland

---

[19]*Ibid.,* Feb. 14; the close ties of *Le Temps* to the Quai d'Orsay were a matter of common knowledge. The daily was considered, if not a mouthpiece of the French Foreign Ministry, an organ expressing views in consonance with official policy. Foreign Minister Pichon himself used its pages to expound French foreign policy. The views of Henri Allizé, as expressed then in his correspondence with Pichon, were on many points, including economic assistance to Austria, virtually identical with those voiced in *Le Temps.* Professor Louis Eisenmann, a scholarly expert on Austrian history and politics, suggested to L. Hartmann that the *Ballhausplatz* follow the development of French public opinion in well-informed and influential French papers such as *Le Temps* and *Journal des Débats.*

[20]*Le Temps,* Feb. 8.

and perhaps even the Lowlands, as absurd as this may appear now. It will agitate the Germans who live in compact groups in South America.[21]

The French press accused the leading politicians of both Germany and Austria of resorting in their pursuit of the Anschluss to dubious methods, diplomatic maneuvers, double-dealing, and surprise tactics. On January 3, *Le Temps*, editorializing on "German Problems," leveled the charge of deceptive tactics against the government of German Austria. While Vienna had sent an emissary to Berne to assure the Allies of its interest in a Danubian confederation—turning thus her back at Germany—at the same time the Austrian government explained in the *Fremdenblatt*, why it could not be a party to such a confederation. "Let us relinquish guessing when the government in Vienna is sincere."[22] On January 5, *Le Temps* reverted to the theme that the Austrian government engaged in double play and denounced the "maneuver of Otto Bauer."

The thought of the continuity of German goals from the Hohenzollern, Bismarck, and the Pan-Germans to the followers of Marx was repeatedly voiced, often in combination with criticism of the questionable means employed by all of them: "Intimidate, create the *fait accompli*, this is the unchangeable method of Pan-Germans, whether they are Marxists or disciples of Bismarck."[23] One week after the Austrian election *Le Temps* criticized remarks of a prominent leader of the Austrian Social Democratic party, Friedrich Adler, who insisted on the "indivisibility" of Germany and of Austria. Thus operated the machine for annexation "under the eyes of the Allies who bring them their grain."[24]

On February 8, *Le Temps* pointed to the urgency of making prompt policy decisions. Three days later the French daily criticized the lack of Allied policy in regard to Austria and the Anschluss. The Paris Conference had been unable to indicate "either its reservations or its opinion" on this major point. "Since it has not pronounced any 'non volumus,' Germany has said herself that she could without impunity put the Al-

[21]*Ibid.*, Feb. 15.
[22]*Ibid.*, Jan. 3
[23]*Ibid.*, Feb. 22.
[24]*Ibid.*

lies before a *fait accompli*."[25] As late as May 21 *Le Temps* denounced French "politics toward Vienna which had resulted so far in our being treated as donkeys and in our being scoffed at at the same time."[26]

The French press turned its attention also to the "why" of France's opposition to the Anschluss. On March 3, *Le Temps* dealt editorially with "The Question of the Rhine," and on March 7 it raised once more the question: "What are we doing in Austria?" The editorial in the March 11 issue "The Rampart in the West," established with unusual frankness the common denominator of French policy in these two regions which were geographically rather far apart, namely: security for France, Belgium, Switzerland, the Netherlands, as well as for the rest of Europe. "We still remain stationary as far as the natural increase of our population is concerned," while "our enemies think of augmenting the 66 million Germans" who comprise Germany today "with seven million Germans of Austria and two [*sic*] million Germans of Bohemia. . . . One may say that the word of the old Moltke about the 'invisible battle' which the French lose every year has not lost anything of its cruel force." France would, no doubt, experience an awakening of her vitality, but before this was going to happen she would have to seek other safeguards. This has become urgent in view of the apparent "tendencies" of official Germany, the blunt utterances of the German foreign minister Brockdorff-Rantzau, and the voices from the National Assembly.[27]

In view of France's traditional preoccupation with the Rhine frontier and with security the importance of the independence of German Austria for the French could hardly be shown more clearly than in the frequent comparison between the Rhine region and Austria. Both, in the view of *Le Temps*, were equally essential for French security.

Le Temps was not alone in linking the problem of the Rhine with the Anschluss question, though the anonymous author of the following position paper seemed somewhat less unyielding. The paper, bearing the title "L'Autriche, Le Rhin et Dantzig" and dated April 9, 1919, was apparently written in the French Foreign Ministry. Its author was not prepared to hold firm both on the Rhine and in Austria, but objected to yielding in both regions. Referring to a telegram by Henri Allizé, French envoy in Vienna, of April 7, the writer revealed the still prevailing skepticism of the French in regard to the Austrian government. Vienna clearly aimed at "the immediate and unconditional union." As the author wrote,

I am persuaded that it [the union] will surely come about in the future. But at a later time it can be arranged so as to minimize the dangers. In any case, the problem of German Austria must continually be in our mind when we discuss the other boundaries of Germany. . . . If one permits the union of Austria with Germany, one asks in vain for guarantees concerning the Rhine and Danzig. If one yields in regard to the Rhine and Danzig, one must clearly take position against the union of Austria with Germany.

Though the French government pondered about numerous territorial and other questions of the German treaty, the Austrian question frequently loomed large in the background.[28]

In a subsequent "Note," likewise anonymous and also originating in the French Foreign Office, dated April 12 and bearing the caption "Autriche-Allemande et question du Rhin," the writer, returning to this theme, insisted that one could not settle the question of the Rhine either "at present or in the future without coming to grips with the Austrian problem." If the left bank remained German, though occupied, the interests of France and Belgium must be guaranteed in such a manner that their position in this region be made contingent on that of Germany *vis-à-vis* Austria so that, if one day Austria should unite with Germany, the Rhineland will be detached in return.[29]

The theme of France's security depending not only on what happened on the Rhine but also in Central Europe was

---

[28]*A.E.*, A Paix, A 1065, Bureau de Mlle Duval, "L'Autriche, le Rhin et Dantzig," Apr. 9, 1918, pp. 26-27.

[29]*Ibid.*, "L'Autriche-Allemande et question du Rhin," Apr. 12, 1919, p. 28.

dealt with again in *Le Temps* on June 28, in the editorial
"L'Adieu du Président Wilson":

> If Germany were to remain free to upset Central Europe, as
> Bismarck did in 1866, France would soon be in peril even
> though no German cannons threatened Strasbourg. And
> without help from overseas such danger would in-
> crease. . . . France would then face the prospect of finding her-
> self *vis-à-vis* a Germanic Central Europe.

And sooner or later the Americans would be forced to
resume the enormous effort of breaking the new German
hegemony.[30]

The annexation of Austria by Germany would, according
to another editorial of *Le Temps*, "The Austrian Delegates in
St. Germain," have disastrous results in every respect. For
Italy, which at times did not seem to object too strenuously to,
and at times even looked favorably upon, the annexation
which would establish a common Italo-German border, *Le
Temps* had dire warnings. "The power of the German Reich
in its entirety would bear down upon the Alpine frontier."
"Every German would believe that he had inherited the
rights which the Habsburgs possessed in the Adriatic," and
Germany then would turn to further expansion in the
Mediterranean. The annexation of Austria would also be a
"misfortune" for Czechoslovakia and for Austria herself.
Germany could not support two capitals, and Vienna would
decline to the advantage of Berlin.

And "what would be the position of France? She would be
the neighbor of an aggrandized Germany." The peace would
be unstable. Every minor local success of Germany would upset the fragile equilibrium of Europe and would translate itself in a growing danger on the Rhine. It would then be
necessary to intervene incessantly to frustrate all the German
maneuvers the pivot of which would be Vienna. It would be
necessary perhaps to intervene by arms and to mobilize the
League of Nations.[31]

In the spring of 1919 France realized that a mere negative
policy toward Austria and the Anschluss question was not

---

[30]*Le Temps*, June 28, 1919.
[31]*Ibid.*, May 13.

enough. *Le Temps* in particular attempted to develop the outlines of more attractive alternatives to the union for the benefit of the Austrian people. And spurred by the real threat of the Anschluss, French diplomacy in February of 1919 began to work frantically on the projects of a Danubian confederation, of neutralization, and of more extensive and permanent economic assistance to Austria, especially after the arrival of Henri Allizé as France's envoy in Vienna.

While the French had few kind words for the Germans, whose reaction to the peace terms and demands for the restoration of the *status quo ante* increasingly alarmed them, they attempted to woo the Austrians. Meaningfully they suggested that the Austrians needed time to "reflect" on their future and their "true interests" and to consider both the benefits which they might gain from the Allies and the burdens which, in the event of the Anschluss, they would have to share with Germany. They also reminded them of their precarious situation and their dependence on the Entente for food, coal, and raw materials; they warned, cajoled, and threatened.

The proponents of the Anschluss maintained that only Germany could save the situation for Austria. Yet *Le Temps*, evidently skeptical, asked some pointed questions designed to reverberate throughout Central Europe:

> Would it not be necessary to inform Germany that she would have to pay hundreds and hundreds of billions? Should one not have to explain that, if German Austria would permit her annexation, Austria would run the risk of a double charge: that of reparations which she would have to pay in her capacity of being Austria, and that which she will have to assume in being part of Germany, herself burdened with enormous reparations? Would it not be necessary finally to show that the Allies can remedy the Austrian crisis if German Austria takes account of these true interests?[32]

When, late in May, France was impatiently waiting for the German signature to the peace treaty, *Le Temps* in an editorial "Utilisons l'Autriche," urged the Allies to develop an enlightened policy toward Austria, namely to "treat the new

---

[32]*Ibid.*

Austria equitably, humanely."[33] It was imperative to secure Austria's and the Austrians' future. "To confer independence upon them and at the same time refuse them the means of livelihood, that would be a contradiction which would turn quickly to the disadvantage of the Allies." The Entente's Austrian policy was closely tied up with her German policy, and success of the former would ensure success of the latter. A wise policy of the Entente *vis-à-vis* Austria will encourage German "particularism." But "German particularism, which can be so useful an element for maintaining the European peace would run the risk of hopelessly sinking into the whirlpool produced by the Austrian shipwreck." Traditional French policy of encouraging "particularism," if not separatism, across the Rhine and in southern Germany saw a revival at the war's end; it was clearly incompatible with permitting the Anschluss.

According to *Le Temps*, some "rough decisions" were necessary if the new Austria was to be saved from "total ruin." The debt contracted during the war by the old Austrian empire should not be borne by the six million contemporary Austrians alone, but would be distributed among the various states created or aggrandized at the expense of Cisleithania. In order to save Austria, basic economic help from the West was essential.[34] Yet while economic help for Vienna was contemplated, French policy-makers considered prohibition of the Anschluss by the Entente a *sine qua non* of any short-range or long-range policy toward Austria and Germany.

Austrians and Germans had every reason to take *Le Temps's* warnings seriously. In the same month, February, 1919, in which the distinguished newspaper had earnestly resumed its struggle against the Anschluss, a joint group of French and American experts on the Central Committee on Territorial Questions, addressing the Supreme Allied Council of the Peace Conference, had suggested that Germany in the preliminaries of peace promise not to undertake anything "politically or economically which might encroach upon the independence of Austria."[35]

It is most likely that this meeting of French and American experts took place soon after February 22. On that day

---

[33]*Ibid.*, May 24.
[34]*Ibid.*, May 13.
[35]*P.R.*, F.O. 608, v. 16, communicated by Secret. Gen., March 16, 1919.

Clémenceau had brought strongest pressure to bear upon Colonel House in regard to the prohibition of the Anschluss. At Clémenceau's request Colonel House met the French premier in conference. During this meeting Clémenceau presented to Colonel House several demands from which France could not retreat. Point Four stated Clémenceau's belief that, unless the Allies would make known to German Austria that they looked upon the Anschluss with disfavor, German Austria would press for the union. He insisted therefore that the Allies issue such an intimation to Austria.[36] The French position in February, 1919, was finally crystallized in the already discussed "Memorandum concerning German Austria," authored in February and transmitted by André Tardieu to the British Foreign Minister Balfour on April 25.

Throughout the winter and spring of 1919 as well as thereafter it was French tactics to hold out promises of generous treatment to Austria, of "far-reaching concessions . . . in economic matters," if she would only renounce the Anschluss, and to threaten the most harsh peace terms in case she should stubbornly insist on implementing her plans for union with Germany. At the same time the Austrian and German people and their governments were also to be impressed with the unshakable opposition of France to the union concept. In an interview on February 16 Pichon repeated the French government's unaltered position in regard to the Anschluss, though he added that it was possible that the other Allies might have a "different opinion" about it.[37] In a subsequent interview on March 9 he warned in a more stringent tone that the union of Germany and Austria could not be decided on the basis solely of the desire of the people of these states or their governments, "but it was for the Conference to make the decision. He was certain that it will decide contrary to the wishes of the Germans."[38] Unknown to the public at large, agreements on this issue had in the meantime been reached between Paris, London, and Washington, D.C.

When on March 21 Béla Kun and the Hungarian Bolsheviks seized power in Hungary, German Austria's

---

[36]Seymour, 1928: **4:** pp. 334-335.
[37]*Lyon Republicain,* Feb. 17, quoted by Noble, 1935: p. 226.
[38]*Nouvelliste de Lyon,* quoted *ibid.*

diplomatic situation improved temporarily. Now the Entente wanted German Austria not only to continue to resist Germany and the demands of her own proponents of the Anschluss, but also the Bolshevik lures from Budapest. On March 27, Baron Haupt of the Austrian Embassy in Berne reported thus to Vienna: "Monsignor Brulei had yesterday a talk with Lammasch. The French are heavily under the impression of events in Hungary. At the direction of the French ambassador Clinchaut, Brulei requested a quick formulation of our conditions [!] for the effective struggle against Bolshevism." Haupt had demanded that a plebiscite under international auspices should be arranged on the political future of all territories of the former Austrian monarchy which were settled by Germans.[39] The demand for the plebiscite was ignored, but France promptly lifted the blockade against Austria, while continuing it against Germany and Hungary.

On March 29 Henri Allizé arrived in Vienna as French envoy. In his first days already he was preoccupied both with Hungarian and German developments and their bearing upon the new Austria.[40] On April 6 he reported that soon after his arrival in Vienna he had arranged interviews with political leaders, members of the government and writers, every day and virtually every hour. In addition, he had visited Chancellor Dr. Renner and Foreign Secretary Dr. Bauer, had outlined to them the scope of his mision and had impressed upon his interlocutors "that we were disposed to examine the conditions under which German Austria could secure her political and economic independence." Chancellor Renner, Allizé informed Pichon, wished to pursue a democratic policy, was a convinced opponent of the Austrian Räte (Soviets), but blamed the Entente for having, through a mistaken policy, foisted the Soviet type of government upon neighboring Hungary. Renner was still determined to pursue the Anschluss policy and in this respect was encouraged by the circumstance that the Entente had not yet taken any definite decision in regard to German Austria and to the frontiers of German Bohemia.[41]

[39]O.S., Fasz. 262, Präsidialakte . . . 1918-1919, Haupt to F.O., March 27.
[40]A.E., A Paix, A 1056, Allizé to Pichon, Apr. 1, pp. 12-13.
[41]Ibid., Europe 1918-1929, Autriche Z 881, Pol. Étrang., Doss. Gén. I, pp. 231-232. The archives of the French Foreign Ministry contain many letters of

According to Allizé, Austria was threatened by a twofold danger, "the danger of Bolshevism and the union with Germany."[42] Bolshevism was desired only by a very small but active minority. To counter it effectively and to assure that the intimidated majority would be strengthened, it was necessary, he held, to dispatch a few French regiments to assure freedom of transportation and communication in Austria.[43] It could hardly escape Allizé that these regiments, once in Austria, would be able to defend the country, if necessary, not only against any threat from Budapest but also against any originating in Berlin.

As far as the Anschluss was concerned, it could be prevented if France displayed "a little initiative and energy" in her plans. Taking proper safeguards, he was confident that a great majority in Austria would vote against the union. Allizé seemed perhaps startled by the emotional depth which the South Tyrolese question aroused not only in Tyrol but among the entire population of German Austria and over the circumstance that a movement was on the way even to renounce the Anschluss in exchange for keeping Tyrol intact.[44] Once in Vienna, he was perhaps more keenly aware of Italy's impact upon the Austrian population than he had ever been and reported accurately the anti-German as well as pro-German currents in Italian policy which could be observed from the Austrian capital.[45]

Allizé was never misled by the tactics of the German ambassador Wedel in Vienna and those of his superiors in Berlin. According to Allizé, the Germans, though keenly interested in union, gave the deliberately misleading impression that the Anschluss was merely a question of secondary importance

Allizé to Pichon, but few of the foreign minister to his ambassador. Pichon probably was too deeply absorbed in preparation for the Peace Conference to spare time for correspondence with his ambassadors. As a result, French envoys in both Prague and Rome complained about being inadequately informed about France's policies in Central Europe and Austria. (See Clément-Simon, envoy in Prague, to Allizé, *ibid.* May 14, 1919, pp. 201-216). Likewise, Barrère, envoy in Rome, reprehended Paris for having received only "very little indication of what our [France's] policies were in this part of the world [Austria and Central Europe], though it is not far from where I am stationed" (*ibid.*, June 2, Tel. 1264).

[42]*Ibid.*, Doss. Gén. I, p. 233.
[43]*Ibid.*, A Paix, A 1056, Apr. 8, 1919, p. 23.
[44]*Ibid.*, Autriche Z 88 I, Doss. Gén. II, pp. 590-592.
[45]*Ibid.*, Allizé to Pichon, Sept. 20, 1919, pp. 627-630. Allizé also warned later that the new Italian envoy in Vienna, Prince Livio Borghese, was a leading

to them and adopted an air of indifference about it.[46] Allizé was convinced that Brockdorff-Rantzau followed a line of policy recently agreed upon between him and Bauer in Weimar.[47]

One of Allizé's striking impressions in Vienna was the "very great intensity" with which German propaganda was carried on in virtually all fields. Maps of Austria were displayed in all libraries, and explanations eagerly offered to visitors about the resources which the Reich and German Bohemia would furnish to Upper and Lower Austria to guarantee their existence. The Germans organized an oral propaganda—which Allizé had already seen at work during the war in Holland where it had been aimed against the blockade—with "extraordinary," with scientific efficiency. Of course, Allizé was bound to be disturbed by the meeting of the Austro-German joint financial commission in Vienna which in April began its preparatory work, aiming at unification. He concluded with the warning that German assurances that the Reich was disinterested in the Austrian question were meaningful only for the period of peace negotiations.[48]

Allizé considered Bauer the "most ardent and obstinate partisan of the concept of union with Germany."[49] On the eve of the departure of the Austrian delegation for Paris on May 11 he appeared to be pleased with the appointment of Renner as its head. Allizé was convinced that Renner even shared the concerns of the Christian Social party about the union. "He has informed me . . . that he would abandon the policy of union with Germany if he would reach the conclusion that it was not feasible."[50] Allizé was hopeful that his policy recommendations, if accepted by Paris, would give satisfaction to Renner and "definitely swing Austria over to our side."[51]

---

spokesman of the pro-German wing in Italian foreign policy, but set his hopes upon those in Italy who dreaded having a common frontier with Germany.

[46]*Ibid.*, A Paix, A 1056, Allizé to Pichon, Apr. 14, 1919, p. 31.

[47]*Ibid.*, pp. 32.

[48]*Ibid.*, pp. 32-35.

[49]*Ibid.*, Allizé to Pichon, May 1, p. 120.

[50]*Ibid.*, Allizé to Pichon, May 11, p. 168.

[51]*Ibid.*, p. 169.

Allizé's report, dated May 14, reflected the deep disappointment of all Austrian circles with the Austrian peace terms which had been published in *Le Journal* and *Le Matin*, but also his own. A telegram sent by Allizé on the same day underlined two issues which, as he remarked, had to be solved, "if we want to assure the success of the policy which we have inaugurated here."[52] All debts, including war debts, should be proportionately distributed. Otherwise Austria would go bankrupt and French interests too would suffer. "There are several billions at stake, as you know." Secondly, there is also the most difficult territorial question, the one of South Tyrol. If these matters were not satisfactorily disposed of, disintegration of the new Austria and final union with Germany was unavoidable. It was of course understood that any concession in South Tyrol would be one made by Italy, not by France.

When later the French Commission of the Budget refused Austria a credit of 45 million francs, representing part of a promised loan, Allizé again was deeply disturbed and clearly critical of his country's Austrian policy: "More than any other power in the world we seem convinced of the necessity of preventing the establishment of German power on the Danube. It is therefore surprising that we would refuse, on financial grounds, to consent to initial payments which not only America, and Great Britain but also Italy have already promised."[53]

No doubt, Allizé feared the new Austria's disintegration. Four days after his warning in mid-May, he again impressed upon Foreign Minister Pichon the necessity of protecting oneself in the treaty with Germany against the results of a disintegration of the provinces which composed the new Austria. Allizé was concerned that Germany through the backdoor of Austrian particularism might gradually arrive at her goal, by endorsing the Anschluss of one province after the other. Therefore, a clear prohibition of the Anschluss of the individual Austrian *Länder* was imperative.[54]

---

[52]*Ibid.*, Mission Pernot, May 14, pp. 191-192, and Embassy, Vienna, Tel. 101, May 14, p. 199.
[53]*Ibid.*, Allizé to Pichon, May 22, pp. 239-240.
[54]*Ibid.*, Allizé to Pichon, May 18, pp. 230-234.

The threat of particularism to the new Austria was tied up with the country's peculiar history and the strength of provincial sentiments. This strength in turn was embodied in the Christian Social party, "the core of the particularist movement"[55] in Austria. The party played unwittingly into Germany's hands by undermining the necessary cohesion and integrity of the new republic. There was, according to Allizé, deep irony in the circumstance that the Christian Socials, indifferent, if not hostile to the union concept, and providing spokesmen for Austria's independence, thus weakened the chances for Austria's political recovery. At the same time Allizé discerned — which was also ironic — that the Social Democrats, though "devoted to Berlin body and soul," combatted the federalist conception at home, thus working, at least for the immediate future, for the preservation of the new Austria.

Allizé's most detailed recommendations for an Austrian policy were contained in his report to Pichon, dated April 17, and are also summed up in a "Résumé" which bears the date of April 23.[56] They reveal him not only as an astute diplomat but also as a far-seeing statesman. Allizé's report, written in response to instructions given him by Pichon,[57] was the result of interviews of some of the most influential people in the new Austria. Pichon had narrowly circumscribed the scope of Allizé's task by specifying as purpose of the inquiry "the prevention of the union of the new Austrian state with Germany and to assure to that neutralized state means of normal existence." In its ultimate form, however, the replies gathered by Allizé bore the stamp of his own interpretations and the report contained his personal views and recommendations.

In regard to territorial provisions Allizé recommended to leave Klagenfurt to the Austrians and Marburg to the Slovenes. He supported the neutralization of South Tyrol and advised that the area be left with Austria. If Czechoslovakia would accord autonomy to the Bohemian

---

[55]*Ibid.*, p. 232.

[56]*Ibid.*, Allizé to Pichon, Apr. 17, pp. 36-45, and Résumé du rapport de M. Allizé, Apr. 23, pp. 84-89.

[57]*Ibid.*, Allizé to Pichon, Apr. 16, p. 36, referring to Pichon's instructions, Apr 13.

Germans,[58] the "germs of irredentism" would be eliminated.[59]

Allizé stressed especially the need for the establishment of commercial relations between the new Austria and Czechoslovakia, not only for the purpose of guaranteeing to the former coal, sugar, and metallurgical goods, but also to provide for her economic expansion.[60] The Conference could help Austria to become a major commercial power. Her "new mission" would then conform to her old history. Austria once again would turn to the Levant and also would "guard the river Danube against Germanism." "This project would have the great advantage of giving Vienna . . . a reason for existence."

Various personalities had ambitiously projected an important international role for Vienna. The city, according to Pichon, offered "deserted palaces . . . , her army of civil servants of the old monarchy." One can conceive that she will become the seat of the international Danubian Commission as well as of a great number of other international organizations which the League of Nations might create.[61]

Sanctions were necessary to prevent the new Austria, though neutralized, from later falling into the German orbit. Such sanctions which were to hinder the fulfilment of Pan-German aspirations would spell out the advantages which would accrue to Austria if she preserved her independence. If, on the other hand, Austria should manifest a wish to unite with Germany, the League then would grant Italy the right to occupy Tyrol up to the Brenner Pass and the Yugoslavs the right to occupy mixed regions in Styria and Carinthia. Vorarlberg then would become a Swiss canton, autonomy to the Germans of Bohemia would be withdrawn, and the remaining Austria would have to make payments for war damages which had been canceled only on condition that she would remain independent.[62] Yet Allizé seemed confident that Austria, once cured of German irredentism in Bohemia and Tyrol would find again her "Danubian mission."[63]

[58]*Ibid.*, Résumé, Apr. 23, pp. 84-85.
[59]*Ibid.*, Allizé to Pichon, Apr. 17, p. 38.
[60]*Ibid.*, p. 41.
[61]*Ibid.*, p. 42.
[62]*Ibid.*, Résumé, p. 89.
[63]*Ibid.*, p. 74.

The French, Allizé continued, should transmit the Allied decisions to the Austrian government and people of the new Austria and also present them "as the result of the deliberations of the Council of the Allies." Otherwise Germany would continue trying to drive wedges between the Allies, "denounce the initiatives of France, underline the silence of London, point to the indifference of Washington and exploit the articles of *Corriere de la Şera* as proof that Italy's views in the Austrian question did not conform to ours."[64] The Allies would have to declare that the Conference held that the union of the new Austria with Germany would under no circumstances be permitted. This proclamation should be followed, at short intervals, by the publication of general Entente projects aimed at guaranteeing the new neutralized Austria an independent existence by assuring her economic and financial advantages and enabling her to survive.[65]

Allizé, while pursuing a policy which was clearly negative in regard to the Anschluss, was in form at least diplomatic, polite, and even amiable. He understood the need for meeting basic economic demands of the new Austria both on humanitarian and political grounds and did not refrain from criticizing occasionally policies of his own government in the hope of modifying them.

Recommendations for policies which France should pursue *vis-à-vis* German Austria were also presented by the writer of an unsigned note, dated April 24 and originating with Mission Pernot, Vienna. It was similar in tone and authority to Allizé's recommendations, but differed in occasionally almost offensive bluntness from his more tactful conclusions.[66]

The "Note" was an attempt to persuade Paris authorities to permit French representatives in Vienna to present the neutralization project in a more inviting and "less repulsive" fashion. The Austrians, admittedly, would have to be reminded that they had lost the war and that their monarchy had floundered with no hope of reconstruction. One has to say to them:

---

[64]*Ibid.*, Allizé to Pichon, Apr. 17, p. 44.
[65]*Ibid.*
[66]*Ibid.*, Mission Pernot, "Note sur la politique à suivre vis-à-vis de l'Autriche Allemande," Apr. 24, pp. 90-94.

You will no longer be a great nation. It is necessary for you to renounce grandiose policies from now on; incidentally, Great Power politics has not done anything for you. . . . We in turn don't condemn you to die, to the contrary. Through neutrality which we recommend to you . . . we offer you effective guarantees against your neighbors, small or great ones. You will have to abandon every hope for political and territorial growth, but you will retain possibilities for economic development — and we shall aid you to realize these possibilities. You have had the lazy habit of living on the resources of Bohemia and Hungary. Now you will have to live on your own resources: we shall give you the means to put them to work. To an extent which remains to be agreed upon, our capital, our technical experts will be at your service. . . . We are prepared to make customs, economic and financial arrangements which will permit you to rebuild your country and even to assure it a certain prosperity.[67]

The writer seemed to be under the illusion that his perhaps generous, but clearly patronizing, approach was likely to win friends in Austria.

It was hardly surprising that a sharply critical position on the Anschluss was taken by a military man, General Hallier, chief of France's Military Mision in Vienna. On May 1 he wrote thus to the minister of war in Paris: "If there exists at this moment for France and for the peace of the world a fundamental question it is that of the union of Austria with Germany. People have said correctly that if Germany would annex the German population of the old Austro-Hungarian monarchy, she will have won the war in spite of all her defeats." In effect she would not only have recovered her losses in Alsace and Poland, but even made gains. She would have acquired a glacis from which to move both toward Italy and the Mediterranean and toward the Near East, "while still encircling . . . Czechoslovakia, cutting her off from the West and from her bases of support and thereafter making of Poland an easy prey."[68] Owing to widely disseminated German war propaganda which had infiltrated everything and had been combatted only since the arrival of the French Mission, the Austrian people, the general held, remained still impressed by German power.

---

[67]*Ibid.*, p. 92.
[68]*Ibid.*, Gen. Hallier to Minister of War, May 1, p. 114.

Clément-Simon, French minister in Prague, while embracing the Czechoslovak point of view, was, like General Hallier, quite critical of the Austrians. The new Austria was, in his words, a "small country," of "little productivity" and tributary to neighbors in regard to food and other basic resources. Vienna will probably be reduced to the size of the city of Stockholm with its 600,000 inhabitants. He admitted that, if the trend toward rapprochement between the two German states was serious, "deeply rooted in the people's mind, nothing will stop it," though the consequences of these sentiments will perhaps be deplorable. But he apparently did not believe that the Austrian character was "forged of such steel"[69] as not to make it bend.

The Austrians, French policy-makers hoped, could be bent by adopting, if not independence, other plans which would force Germany to halt at her borders. Among them loomed large the neutralization project. By means of neutralization France hoped to keep German Austria politically apart from Germany. The French foreign minister Pichon's initial instructions to Allizé and General Hallier's remarks in his memoir "Paix avec l'Autriche" showed clearly how large a role neutralization played in France's Austrian plans. General Hallier felt that the Austrian bourgeoisie at least understood "without enthusiasm perhaps, but quite clearly [that] neutrality was the only possible policy for contemporary Austria."[70] The French policy of Austrian independence scored triumphantly in 1919, but that of neutralization was to fail, though it would have made the country's independence more secure and permanent. It was not to be revived until after World War II when it was applied in the Austrian State Treaty of 1955.

The project of neutralization was presented on its own merit, but at times was coupled with another favorite Allied project, the scheme for a Danubian confederation. Linking Austria with the peoples with which her inhabitants had been associated in the past, though now on a new basis, would make the Anschluss both impossible and economically superfluous. As Ludo Hartmann revealed,

---

[69]*Ibid.*, Clément-Simon, Prague, to Pichon, May 14, pp. 201-216, espec. p. 209.
[70]*Ibid.*, p. 209.

In regard to the Danubian confederation, E. [the French professor Louis Eisenmann] held that the plan really originated with Reinach, but in France it was by no means a precise and carefully thought-out plan. People were indeed fearful that in the event of the Anschluss of German Austria the great German mass would press upon South-East Europe and that this would lead to the resurgence of Mittel-Europa. In this direction, in his opinion, operated in general conservative thinking, which had not come to terms yet with the disintegration of the Austrian Monarchy, the Catholic interest, a lack of confidence still existing toward the Slavs, and finally certain financial interests.[71]

Thus the Danubian confederation was not merely to counter the Anschluss, but also to prevent an extension of Germany's influence via Austria's territory into the Adriatic, the Mediterranean, and the Balkan peninsula.

The Austrian Social Democrats suspected, not without reason, that the House of Habsburg hid behind French plans for a Danubian confederation. Late in 1918 the British representative Lord Acton in Berne had thus notified Earl Curzon:

Emperor Charles had approached French Embassy here in the following manner: His Majesty states that although . . . France, being a democracy, can feel little sympathy for his cause, he submits that he constitutes sole possible link which could be utilized by Allies for the purpose of effecting an . . . economic union between portions of former Austro-Hungarian Empire. Connection is rightly interpreted by French colleague equivalent to a demand for restoration under some form. There is a strong current of opinion, though not unanimous, at French Embassy in favor of recommending appeal to French government. France's Chargé d'Affaires however, prefers to await return of French Ambassador to Berne before taking action.[72]

Monsieur Dutasta, French ambassador in Berne, was then serving as secretary general of the Paris Peace Conference.

While the former emperor Charles obtained a sympathetic hearing and some support in French and English circles,

---

[71]*O.S.*, K 109, Anschlussfrage, Hartmann to Bauer, Jan. 7 and 24, 1919.
[72]Woodward and Butler, 1946, first ser., **1:** p. 24, No. 13.

France's and England's endorsement of the concept of a Danubian confederation did not hinge on its being linked with a Habsburg restoration.

The objective of preventing Germany's territorial growth from reaching a menacing level could be achieved not only by blocking the Anschluss through a Danubian confederation but also could be gained by other schemes. One of the plans which frequently emerged was to separate one or several South German states from Germany and link them with Austria. On March 22 Baron de Vaux reported from Berne to the Austrian Foreign Ministry that propaganda was made in Switzerland for the Anschluss of Austria with a South German republic.[73] In March of 1919, Haupt of the Austrian Embassy informed Dr. Bauer that, according to Professor Lammasch, Lord Acton, British envoy in Switzerland — "half a Bavarian, his mother was a Countess Arco" — was not in favor of a union of German Austria with the German republic in its entirety but of a link-up of Austria with all of Bavaria,[74] though not with Württemberg and Baden. Similarly, Hartmann reported also a conversation with the French professor of history Morize and the French prelate Bruley. Both had come out in favor of a neutralized Austrian republic. Morize, a man with excellent connections with the Quai d'Orsay, hinted at the possibility that German Austria "could be strengthened by a portion of Bavaria." "Eventually there might be established a South-German republic (German Austria, Bavaria, Württemberg, and Baden)."[75] According to André Tardieu, the French royalist writer Jacques Bainville disseminated propaganda in favor of the link-up of Bavaria and Austria.[76] And the Austrian chancellor Karl Renner referred to Allizé as having wanted Austria "to combine with a Bavaria emancipated from Prussian control," a policy which had been strongly supported in Catholic circles.[77] It is of in-

---

[73]O.S., K 109, Anschluss, I-2464/2, de Vaux to F.O., March 22, 1919.

[74]Ibid., Haupt to Bauer, March 4.

[75]Ibid., Hartmann to Bauer, I-2625.

[76]Tardieu, 1921: pp. 414-415.

[77]Bonsal, 1944: p. 124. See also Allizé's account of a private conversation with Renner, Apr. 23, 1919, when the Austrian Chancellor rejected the link-up of Austria with Bavaria, in apparent response to a suggestion by Allizé (A.E., Europe 1918-1929, Autriche Z 881, Pol. Étrang., Doss. Gén. I, Apr. 23, 242). Allizé himself reported fondly of the growing movement in Bavaria and the new Austria for a union between both countries (ibid., Doss. Gén. II, July 1, 1919, p. 11).

terest to observe in this context that Allizé, having served
before the war as France's envoy in Munich for several years,
was long acquainted with and interested in South-German
and Catholic groups which hoped for some tie-up with
Austria. Some Bavarian circles around Dr. Held, segments of
the Bavarian People's party and others were quite receptive to
schemes of this kind.

French traditional policy of encouraging German particularism and separatism played a distinct role in shaping
France's position on the Anschluss. Through an ingenious
solution of the German Austrian problem Germany might be
reduced in size and even split in two. This would diminish
the danger of a German revanche.

Anxieties over the size of Germany's population as compared to that of France and the related concerns of security
and of the "purpose" and meaning of the last war lay heavily
on the French mind and determined France's policy toward
the Anschluss. Commenting on a speech in Mainz by the
leading majority Socialist David, a delegate also to the Weimar
Assembly who once again had put forth a claim to German
Austria, *Le Temps* wrote: "Here is revealed the deep and
secret thought of all German statesmen without exception.
Yet this thought has another aspect. If Germany is much bigger and stronger than before the war, will this war not have
been without purpose? Then it will be in vain that France,
serving as rampart of civilization, will have lost in its defense
1,400,000 of her best sons."[78]

British interest in the balance of power and French concerns over Germany's "numerical imbalance" in relation to
her neighbors and to herself outweighed in the end primarily
British considerations for the principle of national self-
determination.

[78]*Le Temps*, Feb. 11.

3. ITALY, THE DANUBIAN CONFEDERATION, THE ANSCHLUSS, AND GERMAN SOUTH TYROL. ITALIAN INTERESTS AND POLICY

"Italian interest in Austria's Anschluss with Germany has substantially declined since the project of a Danubian confederation could be considered definitely abandoned." Paulucci (Italian ambassador in Berne), 1919

WHEN war broke out in the summer of 1914, Italy remained neutral. Though under the terms of the Tripartite Pact she was free to do so, she soon faced the dilemma of choosing whether to intervene on the Allied side or maintain her neutrality. Those who favored the latter course, like the Italian statesman Giovanni Giolitti, hoped to wrest concessions from Austria and thus gain the fruits of war without incurring its risks. But Vienna refused to make major territorial concessions. In the end the Allies, holding out promises of Austrian territory to Italy, were more generous to the latter than the Dual Monarchy could possibly have been, and this very circumstance clinched Rome's decision. But the Allies too felt that Italy had pushed her bargaining power to the very limit.[1] Italy's military setbacks during the war tended to stiffen the resistance of the Western Powers to her territorial demands, though they did not question the validity of the Treaty of London in 1915.

Italy's territorial objectives lay in the Austro-Hungarian empire. And it was this empire, not Germany, which was Italy's traditional enemy. When Italy declared war on Austria-Hungary on May 23, 1915, she merely severed diplomatic relations with imperial Germany. An entire year elapsed before she succumbed to Allied pressure and finally declared war on Germany.

---

[1]Albrecht-Carrié, 1950: espec. pp. 94-124.

At the end of the war the major goal of France's diplomacy was to prevent Germany from once again becoming an overpowering force on the continent. Germany was to be weakened, surely, not strengthened by being allowed to expand into Austria. Italy, on the other hand, had in the past fought mainly against the Austrian empire which had held Italians under domination in the Alpine region, the Po Valley, and along the Adriatic. Though the Austrian empire had been dissolved, the fear of its resurrection haunted its former subjects and neighbors, including Italy. Many Italians could not eradicate ingrained patterns of thought and still feared the danger emanating from Vienna. On the other hand, they no longer considered vanquished Berlin an immediate or potential threat.

A reading of the contemporary Italian press gives a good idea of Italian public opinion in general and the prevailing sentiments and lines of thought about Italy's new foreign policy toward Austria and Germany, her attitude toward the Anschluss and a Danubian confederation and policy toward France and Yugoslavia and related questions. Even the most influential papers, among them the Milan daily newspaper *Corriere della Sera*, were of course not spokesmen for the Italian government and did not make policy; but they clearly reveal the hopes and anxieties of the Italian people and the postwar political atmosphere in which the country's policy was shaped.

On October 19 and 20 *Corriere della Sera* came to grips with the problem of the dying Austro-Hungarian empire and the future of German Austria. It attempted to refute an article in the *Action Française* by Jacques Bainville who had asserted that it was necessary to preserve the Austrian empire to prevent Germany from absorbing the Germans of Austria. Italy, however, the Italian paper countered, would prefer the solution of becoming through the Anschluss a neighbor of Germany, such as France was, "to the preservation of the Austro-Hungarian monarchy for the destruction of which she has shed her blood."

The Franco-Italian press dialogue on the problems of Central Europe and its future was to continue. On October 29 the journal *Secolo* felt called upon to enlighten *Le Temps* and *Le Matin* which were concerned about the aggrandizement of

Germany in Central Europe. *Secolo* voiced concern that *Le Temps* listened only to the pacifist proposals of the Austrian clergy and of neutrals and of those who hoped to save the Habsburg dynasty. The Milan journal, however, was working hard toward the disintegration of the old Habsburg monarchy and was convinced that its breakup would remove a major obstacle to domestic and international peace.

But Italian opinion on the future of German Austria which might emerge from the catastrophe in Central Europe was divided from the beginning. Sonnino and many other Italian political leaders were opposed to the aggrandizement of Germany at German Austria's expense. As the French consul in Milan reported, many Italian lawmakers were

> converts to the ideas of Sonnino and estimate that in the last analysis Italy would badly accommodate . . . to the annexation of German Austria by Germany. The perspective of having Germany as a neighbor is little enticing. . . . It would be better for Italy if she remained separated from Germany through a confederation of the Austrian Länder.[2]

On November 15, only three days after the proclamation of the German Austrian republic and the simultaneous disclosure of her desire for union with Germany, *Corriere della Sera* grappled again with the German Austrian problem. It rejected the idea of intervention by the Great Powers in the area of the former Austro-Hungarian monarchy, upheld the principle of national self-determination, and favored German Austria's Anschluss with the Reich. It clearly stated its opposition to a Danubian confederation and to German Austria's inclusion in it. The paper, while rejecting crude interference in Central Europe, staked out Italy's own claim to extend her influence beyond the Brenner pass.

With the article "La federazione Danubiana," *Corriere della Sera* turned its sharpest criticism against the Danubian confederation.[3] A month later, on the occasion of Dr. Bauer's journey to Berlin and Weimar, the Milan daily voiced the view that the union with Germany appeared "inevitable and

---

[2]*Corriere della Sera,* Oct. 19 and 20, 1918, and *Secolo,* Oct. 29, both quoted in *A.E.,* Europe 1918-1929, Doss. Gén. I, Consul, Milan to Pichon, Oct. 29, 1918, pp. 88-89; *ibid.,* "Dynastie des Habsbourg, Renseignements provenant du Cabinet de M. Sonnino," (Nov. 11, 1918, p. 123).

[3]*Corriere della Sera,* Nov. 15, 1918; also Jan. 28, 1919.

desirable. Inevitable, since the border of Austria, created in the Middle Ages to defend Europe against Slavic barbarism, no longer has a reason for existence; . . . desirable since the peace and progress of the world depend to a great extent on a definite political emergence of the various national groups and also of the German Austrian ethnic group.[4] The German Austrians were an integral part of Germany, no less so than the Bavarians or Hanoverians.

The idea that a Europe based on national groupings was just and most likely to provide a lasting basis for peace and progress was rooted in Italy's own political and intellectual past, the tradition of the Risorgimento, its victory in 1870, and its definite fulfillment in 1918 when the Italians under former Austrian rule were liberated. A nationally united country, *Corriere della Sera* and many others in Italy held, was likely to be satiated. Therefore, European peace was best secured by permitting the union of Austria with Germany.

> The reorganization of Central Europe on an ethnic basis should be especially desired in Italy. . . . In an international society of free peoples, Italy has nothing to fear from a completely united nation, even if it is twice as large and much wealthier, in the same way as the citizen has nothing to fear from the fellow citizen. . . . But on the contrary, Italy would have everything to fear from a Danubian Confederation.[5]

Corriere della Sera and a sizable segment of Italian public opinion could not be persuaded by any argument pertaining to the military balance of power that the aggrandizement of Germany was a potential threat to Europe in general and to Italy in particular. A significant sector of Italian public opinion was so obsessed with the past, the centuries-old danger which had emanated from the Austrian empire, that fear of its reemergence in any form blinded it to the obviously greater danger of the German colossus pressing upon her from the north. The historical past, rather than sharpening the view into the future, actually warped it.

Since *Corriere della Sera*'s views on the Anschluss and the Danubian confederation were for a time widely shared in

[4]*Ibid.*, Feb. 27, 1919.
[5]*Ibid.*, Nov. 15, 1918.

Italy, it is hardly surprising that the Italian press was engaged in a running battle with French journals over these very issues. The then prevailing Italian point of view was one of unmitigated hostility to the confederation project, and many Italians looked favorably upon the Anschluss. At the same time the French supported the Danubian confederation as the means to defeat the Anschluss project. Many Italians did not believe that Austria could survive on her own and saw in Austria's Anschluss the only means of blocking the hated Danubian confederation scheme. The French, on the other hand, saw in the confederation a welcome assurance that Austria's manpower and resources would not be added to those of Germany, thus strengthening, as they feared, a still expansion-minded people.

Corriere della Sera frequently claimed that its views on the Anschluss and the Danubian confederation had produced "unanimous consensus in the press and our Italian public opinion."[6] It never considered Austria's existence as an independent state a viable alternative to either the Anschluss or the hated and bitterly opposed confederation.

> It was and is evident that Austria cannot live on her own, that neutralizing her is a dilatory maneuver to force her sooner or later to enter into a Danubian confederation, that this confederation will not be able to subsist unless it espouses a program of foreign policy which links German irredentism against the Alto Adige with Slav irredentism against the Adriatic.

The view was repeatedly expressed that even a satisfactory solution of the frontier along the Alpine crest and the Brenner pass would be outweighed by the harm done by the creation of confederate state structures to the north whose very existence would pose an irredentist threat to the new Italy.

On May 15, 1919, in a first-page editorial *Corriere della Sera* uttered the warning that Austria was staging a comeback in St. Germain-en-Laye. The newspaper was also greatly disturbed by the Entente's conversation in Paris with the Yugoslavs and critical of the Italian delegation's behavior at the

---

[6]*Ibid.*, May 4, 1919.

Peace Conference. "The peace with Austria belonged to Italy, as the war with Austria belonged to her. She should have been the inspirator and peacemaker," since it was Italy which had stopped Austria at the Piave and swept the Austrians back from Italy's mountains and rivers.[7]

French policy in Central Europe was mercilessly castigated in *Corriere della Sera*'s editorial of May 17:

> France is dragging herself behind this corpse [of Austria-Hungary], trying at great expense of money and time to breathe life into it. Step by step we are regressing to the previous state of affairs. First they prohibit the union with Germany, then they work to reconstitute the disjointed parts of the old organism, and now they are already speaking of placing a Habsburg prince at the head of the remade monster. . . . Italian resentment of the reception given to our future enemies is deep and burning.[8]

While France feared an Austrian and German *fait accompli* in the form of the Anschluss, Italy was alarmed at the prospect of the *fait accompli* of a French-sponsored Danubian confederation.

Italy's past fear of Austria now seemed to be replaced by her fear of the Slavs to the north and east. The Slavs might force the German Austrians into a Slav-dominated Danubian confederation, as harmful to Italy as the old Austrian Dual Monarchy had been. On January 24, *Corriere della Sera* wrote as follows:

> The political axis of the old Austria ran from northwest to southeast along the flow of the Danube and had a tendency toward Balkan expansionism. In the new Austria, which only for euphemism's sake calls itself the Danubian confederation, but could well call itself "Czecho-Yugoslavia," the political axis would run from northeast to southwest, from Prague to Zagreb, and the joint goal would consist in descent toward the Adriatic . . . the Czech-Yugoslav corridor is as much justified from the point of view of geography and nationality as would be an Italo-Rumanian corridor across the living body of Serbia.[9]

---

[7]*Ibid.*, May 15.
[8]*Ibid.*, May 17.
[9]*Ibid.*, Jan. 24.

The destruction of the Habsburg monarchy, "the principal fruit of Italy's sacrifices," was considered to have been the main objective of Italy's foreign policy; the liberation of the subjugated Italians of Austria and the acquisition of all the territory south of the Brenner Pass were mere by-products, though not unwelcome ones, of Austria's disintegration. It was the Dual Empire which had been the "mortal enemy" of Italy, and French attempts in Vienna and Paris to resurrect this state under a new label were bitterly attacked. *Corriere della Sera* was opposed to a *paix française* in Central Europe, a Franco-Slav alliance in which Prague and its dependency in Zagreb would take the place of fallen Petrograd. Czechs and Yugoslavs would form a bloc of 20 million, and other people like the German Austrians would be forced into a state system which would make Pan-Slavic policy.[10] Italy feared not only Pan-Slavic but also French domination of the revived colossus to the north. Italy insisted upon German Austria's right to the Anschluss, "because Italy, an enemy of German hegemony, cannot be a friend to another hegemony: because she would be suffocated if from west to north as well as to the east she bordered on France and French zones of influence."

The revived Austria would be Slav and anti-German, a state "in which the oppressed peoples of yesterday will have their turn as oppressors"; this state would pursue a "provocative and greedy foreign policy."

> The Yugoslavs, forced to participate in a system from which they actually wanted to flee in order to live as masters in their own Balkan houses . . . , will receive sympathy for their Adriatic grievances; German Austria, gagged, will be consoled for her decline with fraternal tears for Tyrolese irredentism. This state system, extending from the Vardar to the heart of Europe, . . . will necessarily have a defensive front toward Germany, an expansive front toward the Aegean Sea, and an immediate and potentially offensive front toward Italy. In short, five years after the assassination at Serajevo, here we have the grand Austria of the assassinated Francis Ferdinand![11]

---

[10]*Ibid.*, May 15, "St. Germain-en-Laye."
[11]*Ibid.*, May 11 "L'Austria e Italia nel Trattato di Parigi."

At times Italy's mistrust of France reached a crescendo. *Corriere della Sera* was suspicious of the alleged cordial reception of the Austrian delegation in Paris and of rumored Austro-Yugoslav negotiations and resentful of continued disregard of Italy's interests and sensitivities. But to establish a common anti-German position with Paris the paper took pains to impress the French with the likelihood of the Danubian confederation's perhaps falling once again under German Austrian and Magyar control, and to assure them of Italy's determined opposition to the "German octopus," from whose aggressiveness France had suffered in the past as had Italy from that of Austria. Both Prussia and Austria merely represented different "tentacles" of the same German monster.[12]

In the end, the French obtained the prohibition of the Anschluss, but were unable to set up a Danubian confederation, which was considered a long-range guarantee against the union with Germany. Yet the Danubian confederation failed to materialize not so much because of Italian opposition to the project, but rather because of the opposition of the heirs to the Dual Monarchy, the new Slavic states of Central and Southeastern Europe. An independent Austria, relying on her own resources and strength, not in combination with other Central European states or with Germany, was an alternative considered neither likely nor desirable by Italy, France, and the Austrians themselves. Yet it was this alternative which emerged triumphant! It was one which had not attracted the Italians, since they feared that an independent Austria would prove to be a mere stepping stone to the disliked Danubian confederation. Nor did it please France who feared that an independent and isolated existence would quickly lead Austria to the Anschluss with Germany.

In 1918-1919 the Italian and French press carried on an extensive dialogue on the future of German Austria, one marked by sharp exchanges. French diplomacy and the French press expressed concern over the threat to Italy's security from the north, warned Italy against the Anschluss, against seeking Germany as a neighbor and about German

---

[12]*Ibid.*, May 11.

ambitions in the Mediterranean—the *Drang nach dem Süden.*
They insisted that French and Italian interests were
somewhat identical on these crucial issues. The French press
seemed to fear that Germany might exploit the differences
between Italy and her allies over Yugoslavia and the Adriatic
coast by expanding into Austria. It overwhelmingly supported Italy's demand for the Brenner Pass. On March 16, *Le
Temps* observed: "The task is to fix along the crest of the Alps
a frontier which will finally protect the plains of Lombardy
against Germanic invasion: a protection which—as the wars
of four centuries testify—will be useful to France as well as to
Italy." [13]

On May 24, *Le Temps* came out into the open admitting
recent differences between France and Italy over several
questions, including that of Austrian independence, and en-
deavored to win Italy over to the French point of view. *Le
Temps,* battling against any aggrandizement of Germany, including the Anschluss, even implied that the independence
of Austria was, or should be, of greater importance to Italy
and Switzerland than to France herself, since it would
prevent a German encirclement of the former and a German
attack upon the latter. *Le Temps* wrote:

> Maintaining Austrian independence can be the basis of a
> durable link between France and Italy. Considered as a whole,
> the peace conceived by the Allies establishes two important
> precautionary strategic measures against a resurgence of Ger-
> man imperialism. One prohibits any kind of military
> preparation on the left bank of the Rhine and on a strip of the
> right bank; the other prevents the annexation of Austria by the
> German Reich. The first of these precautions is designed to
> prevent an invasion of Belgium and an attack on France; the
> second, while fully respecting Austrian freedom, aims at
> preventing an encirclement of Switzerland and an attack on
> Italy. [14]

As far as the first precautionary measure was concerned,
Great Britain and the United States would support France if
Germany should violate the treaty stipulations. "Why could

---

[13]*Le Temps,* March 16.
[14]*Ibid.,* May 24.

not the second precaution"—the prevention of the Anschluss—be strengthened by an "analogous guarantee?"

> [France and Italy] could pledge to consult each other for the defense of their common rights in the event that Germany attempted to change to her advantage the status which the treaty created in Austria and . . . in other territories that were part of the Austro-Hungarian monarchy.

Le Matin too underlined the necessity of an Italo-French alliance, but not like *Le Temps* solely for the purpose of preventing the Anschluss. "Why should we," wrote *Le Matin*,

> for Fiume's sake, lose the proffered opportunity to establish *vis-à-vis* the menacing alliance of Berlin and Vienna the intimate and definitive "Entente" of Paris and Rome, which alone will make it possible to set 80 million Latins against 80 million Germans who are preparing to create a bloc against us?[15]

France, fearful that Italy would lean to the Entente's vanquished enemies, her prewar allies, Germany and Austria-Hungary, attempted thus to play upon Italy's sympathies and her fears of the colossus across the Alps.

Though in the end no Latin alliance materialized, the Great Powers, including Italy, finally agreed on the prohibition of the Anschluss. Ultimately, the forces in Italy which were opposed to the union of Austria with Germany were to gain the upper hand.

In late 1918 and 1919 the Italian press sharply reflected the growth of the Franco-Italian rivalry in Central Europe. But at the end of the war it had appeared as if Austria would not become a diplomatic battleground between Rome and Paris: Italy's influence in Austria seemed to be paramount. The armistice at Padua on November 3, 1918, had terminated hostilities between the Allies and the Austro-Hungarian monarchy; it was the last document which bore the latter's name. While the armistice was presented to Austria-Hungary in the name of the Allied and Associated Powers, it actually came from the hands of the Italian High Command. The armistice took Italian claims and demands fully into consideration. Italy would occupy points even

---

[15]*Le Matin*, May 4.

beyond the line assured to her in the secret wartime Treaty of London. And officers of the Italian Armistice Commission were in charge of implementing the armistice terms.[16] After November 24, 1918, about 1,500 Italian troops were stationed in and close to Innsbruck.

An Italian mission arrived in Vienna on December 28, 1918. It was led by General Roberto Segre and attained its greatest strength in August, 1919, when it comprised 125 military and civilian officials and 400 soldiers.[17] General Segre was given specific instructions to insure that the Austro-Hungarian Supreme Command and its respective successors in Austria and Hungary complied with the armistice terms in regard to demobilization of the Austro-Hungarian army, cession of war materials, enforcement of naval clauses, and repatriation of Italian prisoners of war (of whom there were thousands in German Austria and the succession states), and that data on the maltreatment of people, which might be of possible interest to the Peace Conference, be gathered.[18]

In his book *Die Österreichische Revolution* Dr. Bauer sharply criticized General Segre's policies, but admitted that some groups in Austria—the "Austrian bourgeoisie"—had urged the general to occupy Vienna with Italian troops.[19] According to Bauer, General Segre sent an ultimatum to the Austrian government, demanding war materials, paintings, and even sums of money, under threat of stopping food shipments. "The threat of occupation by Italian troops hung constantly over our heads."

In spite of these differences, relations between the Italian mission and the Austrian government were not marked by unmitigated hostility. Though Italian public opinion was adamantly opposed to the reestablishment of the Austro-Hungarian empire in any form, it was not hostile to the German Austrian people as such: it looked favorably upon the Anschluss, at least for a time, and collaborated with German Austria against the new Yugoslav rival, especially resisting Yugoslavia's claims on the Klagenfurt Basin. Being in control

---

[16]For a detailed account in English, see Strong, 1939: pp. 214-240, "The Armistice Commission."

[17]Segre, 1929: p. 24.

[18]*Ibid.*, p. 4.

[19]Bauer, 1923: p. 83.

of the railway from Trieste, Italy—apart from the Tyrol— had a foothold in Austria proper and was interested in making her influence felt. According to Dr. Bauer, Italy was less hostile and more kindly disposed toward German Austria than were all the other Great Powers, including even the United States, and he hoped to be able to gain her support on the Anschluss issue at the Paris Peace Conference. He also thought it possible to reach an understanding with Italy on German South Tyrol.

Like his French counterpart, the envoy Henri Allizé, General Roberto Segre later wrote a book about his Austrian experiences. While the Anschluss was the focus of Allizé's account of Austrian developments in the immediate postwar period, General Segre made only scattered remarks on the union. He appears to have pursued his own course on the Anschluss.[20] As Colonel Cunninghame's views on German Austria did not always coincide with those of the British Foreign Office, so General Segre's opinion was his own and not always identical with that of his government. He did not share Rome's aversion to the Danubian confederation; that is, he was not against some kind of economic arrangement between the former members of the Dual Monarchy and German Austria, though he was critical of the idea of a political confederation. Segre suspected that Dr. Bauer's goal was to create a *fait accompli* in the form of an immediate union of Austria with Germany, but only for bargaining purposes, in order to win South Tyrol and the German-inhabited districts of Czechoslovakia.

During the months when the Peace Conference was writing the German and Austrian peace treaty, Italy, because of her proximity and military presence in parts of Austria, continued to wield influence in Vienna. In Paris, however, her position was precarious, entangled as it was in disputes with the West over her Adriatic claims. For Italy it was vitally important to have an early settlement of the Austrian question, of her frontier with Austria and of the disposition of the former Austrian possessions in the Adriatic, which were coveted by both Italy and Yugoslavia. As Sonnino pointed out in a meeting of the Council of Ten on February 22, 1919, the Austrian question contained more "dangerous"

---

[20]Segre, 1929: p. 296.

elements than the German one and was "a delicate and awkward one to settle."[21] When the French foreign minister Pichon insisted that the conference first of all consider the German question which he judged, as Tardieu had put it, the "principal and essential question," Sonnino revealingly interjected: "For you." For Italy, which for centuries had suffered from invasions from the north, the Austrian Empire had been the main foe, and the settlement with Vienna took precedence over the one with Berlin.

The wrangle over the relative significance of the German and Austrian issues was a natural outgrowth of the difference in the geopolitical situation and the primary interests of France and Italy. It focused attention on Italy's territorial demands on Austria, the Trentino and South Tyrol, as well as on the new Yugoslav state. In regard to these objectives Italy's interests were clearly separate from, if not contrary to, those of France and also Great Britain.

In order to understand Italy's position on the Anschluss in the immediate postwar period it is necessary to relate more fully the history of her claims to South Tyrol and to the Brenner Pass as a boundary, and to outline Allied wartime diplomacy.

In demanding the Brenner Pass after the war's end, Italy advanced strategic reasons and also pointed to the Allied wartime pledge, the secret Treaty of London of 1915. The great figures of the Risorgimento, Mazzini and Garibaldi, were quoted as having demanded the "Brenner-Quarnero" border, "though nothing beyond it."[22] Pointed references were also made to a remark by Dante in the *Divine Comedy* about how the Alps shut Germany out of the Italian peninsula, and to one of Petrarch's *Canzoni* according to which nature had taken good care of Italy when it placed the "protection of the Alps between us [Italians] and German wrath."[23]

---

[21]*F.R.U.S., P.P.C.* **4:** p. 87.

[22]*Corriere della Sera,* Jan. 13, 1919.

[23]Quoted by Herre, 1927: pp. 30-31. In 1926 Benito Mussolini in connection with an alleged intervention of Germany in South Tyrol remarked similarly: "The Italian frontier has been drawn by the Lord's infallible hand" (Feb. 6, 1926). As editor of *Il Popolo d'Italia* in 1921, however, he had gone farther north than the great Italian writers Dante and Petrarch by presenting historic and ethnological claims also to the people of the Inn valley itself (Herre, 1927: pp. 31-32).

The claims to the Brenner Pass and the crest of the Alps as the northern frontier between Italy and the Habsburg monarchy were definitely laid in the prewar period. Their history is tied up with the personality of Ettore Tolomei, an alpinist, geographer and ethnologist, and editor of the *Archivio per L'Alto Adige*. Originally aiming only at the incorporation of the Italian-inhabited "Little Trentino" (Piccolo Trentino), his horizon widened just prior to and after the outbreak of war and came to include German South Tyrol also. This objective, a "Greater Italy," became Italy's war goal when Sidney Sonnino, a former supporter of the alliance with the Central Powers, became the new head of Italy's foreign ministry.

Under the leadership of interventionists like Gabriele d'Annunzio and Benito Mussolini the original slogan "Trentino a Trieste" was replaced by the demand "Brennero a Trieste." The most significant work in presenting this claim was once again written by Tolomei, *L'Alto Adige*. He proposed therein that the German provinces of Austria be reunited with Germany. "A Germany defeated, but not humiliated, should be permitted to compensate herself with the annexation of the German provinces of Austria."[24] Perhaps his notion was that both Germany and German Austria would thus acquiesce to the cession of German South Tyrol. In the immediate postwar period these views were still fairly widespread.

Yet to other Italians it was a distasteful and fearsome thought that, after the breakup of the Habsburg empire, Germany would incorporate German Austria, thus reaching down to the Brenner Pass and establishing a common boundary with Italy either at the pass or farther south.[25]

Since the beginning of the First World War the German Foreign Office had strongly advised Vienna to purchase not only Italy's neutrality but also her military cooperation by making territorial concessions to her. Early in May of 1915, Austria finally declared that she was ready to make extensive territorial sacrifices, including the cession of the Trentino to Italy.[26] But Italy, wooed by both the Entente and the Central

[24]*Ibid.*, p. 115.
[25]Bainville, 1915: p. 245.
[26]Herre, 1927: p. 140.

Powers, was determined to strike the best possible bargain. In late April, Sidney Sonnino and Antonio Salandra had already concluded the Treaty of London with the Western Powers which offered more to Italy than Austria had done. After Italy's entry into the war on the side of the Allies, the leading irredentist Salvatore Barzilai became cabinet minister. In mid-July he proclaimed in the Chamber of Deputies that the Brenner Pass was a war goal which must be attained against "the egoism of Teutonic hegemony."

When the war ended, Italian public opinion was not fully united in regard to the Brenner claim. Italy's Socialists too were divided. The Reform Socialist minister Leonida Bissolati warned that the inclusion of the German Tyrolese would contradict the liberal and democratic spirit of Italy and insisted that peace should be made on the basis of the Wilsonian program.[27] Therefore, Italy's position on this issue at the Peace Conference could not be anticipated with absolute certainty.

The same held true of Italy's probable attitude on the Anschluss. This issue of course was to some degree linked with the demand for the Brenner Pass. In the event of Austria's union with Germany, Italy would become Germany's neighbor. In the eyes of some Italians, this would constitute a real danger to Italy. As Baron de Vaux wrote from Berne to Dr. Bauer on February 12, 1919, Italy considered the Brenner frontier "absolutely necessary" because of the possibility of Austria's Anschluss. "The Italians would then face a unified nation of 80 million people *vis-à-vis* which a strategic frontier was more necessary than ever."[28] Thus when Italy asked for the Brenner Pass, she had, according to de Vaux, Germany rather than Austria in mind. Italy might fear a strong German neighbor, but might also hope that a vanquished Germany in return for the absorption of German Austria and Italy's diplomatic support in this matter would gladly renounce German South Tyrol. Many Italians must also have been influenced by the circumstance that German Austria

---

[27]*Ibid.*, p. 83. Bissolati, 1923: pp. 406-407: The Brenner pass, the author admitted, would be "the best defensive line" for Italy. At the same time, however, he was convinced that German South Tyrol culturally would "remain German." About the position of other Italian Socialists to the Brenner Pass as a boundary, see *O.S.*, K. 682, de Vaux to F.O., Feb. 12, 1919, p. 331.

[28]*O.S.*, de Vaux to F.O., Feb. 12, 1919, p. 331.

spoke out loudly as champion of German South Tyrol, while Germany, facing numerous territorial problems all along her borders, remained on the whole strikingly silent. The Anschluss would not only remove an active and obstreperous claimant to German South Tyrol but also the country which for centuries was the very core of the hated Habsburg empire. Its incorporation into Germany would forever doom all chances of a restoration of that empire either under its old Habsburg form or under a new form, a Danubian confederation.

On the other hand, Italy had no guarantee that the old Pan-German and Prussian militarism was dead, that it would not reassert itself and, disregarding past services, not reclaim German South Tyrol. Germany might also present her claims in the Balkan and the Adriatic Sea and become a more menacing neighbor and rival than the old disintegrating multinational Habsburg empire had ever been.

The Italian press, though not unfriendly toward defeated Germany, sharply castigated Pan-Germanism and German nationalism. A declaration of the National Assembly in Innsbruck in behalf of continued links with South Tyrol was found by *Corriere della Sera* "not surprising." It was Tyrolese tradition, "particularly the mission of Innsbruck, which insists on playing the avant-garde of Pan-Germanism." While previously the southern boundaries of the German world were sketched by the Germans on the Po river, today they ran as far north as the Salurno Gap. "This is an improvement." The Tyrolese intelligentsia was entrusted with keeping "the door open" at Salurno. It was suspected of wishing to "resume the German march toward the Po in better times."[29] On May 8 *La Stampa* of Torino noted that the Viennese campaign regarding South Tyrol was beginning to have repercussions in Berlin also. Many German journals were showing increasing interest in South Tyrol, though displaying a "certain reserve" and acting "without excessive passion."[30]

When immediate Italian interests seemed at stake, not only Tyrol and Austria, but even Germany herself felt the whiplash of Italian criticism. On February 12, referring to the waves of chauvinist sentiment which had swept the Weimar

[29]*Corriere della Sera*, Jan. 21, 1919.
[30]*La Stampa*, May 8.

National Assembly, *Corriere della Sera* spoke ironically of the "new German mentality" and "the strange illusions" regarding the new borders which were being nurtured in the new Germany.[31] On March 26, the newspaper printed an article on "The German Machination" by Luigi Barzini, according to whom the "most secure barrier" against German resurgence would be a diplomatic alignment between Italy and France.[32]

The truth of the matter was that in questions of foreign policy, whether they related to Austria, Tyrol, the Anschluss, Pan-Germanism or other problems, Italy was confused and divided. Still gripped by the perils of yesterday and concerned about new dangers that had arisen, she seemed unable to overcome her internal differences and chart a new straight course which would be clear to herself and others.

As mentioned, in the London agreement of April 26, 1915, in return for entering the war on the side of the Western Powers, Italy had been promised the Brenner Pass as her northern boundary. After the war, the Austrian government, counting on the circumstance that the United States had not been a party to the secret London agreement, thought it possible that the Treaty of London might be re-examined and that Austria might obtain American support for her claim to the compactly German South Tyrol, in accordance with President Wilson's pledge of national self-determination. Yet, as it turned out, German Austria's attempts were doomed. President Wilson refused Italy not only Fiume, but also areas in Dalmatia and Istria which the wartime treaty had promised her. Since Wilson thereby clashed with the Italian government, he was in no position to make further objections to Italy's claims to German South Tyrol and the Brenner Pass. Thus Austrian hopes, which had rested on the United States and its president, evaporated.

Under Dr. Bauer's leadership the target of Austrian diplomacy was not only the United States but also Italy herself. The efforts to reverse Italian opinion in regard to South Tyrol failed, though at times its prospects were by no means dim. For several months during the spring of 1919 both the

---

[31]*Corriere della Sera*, Feb. 12.
[32]*Ibid.*, March 26, L. Barzini, "German Machination."

MAP 3. The problem of the South Tyrol.

Austrian and Italian governments initiated moves to enter into mutual negotiations in regard to South Tyrol.

On February 12, in a telegram labeled "secret" and addressed to Baron Haupt, the Austrian envoy in Berne, Otto Bauer disclosed that the "Italian government has sent a diplomatic representative to Vienna . . . in order to negotiate about German South Tyrol." On February 21 in a letter to the State Councillor Dr. Ämilian Schöpfer, Dr. Bauer similarly referred to recent direct negotiations with a plenipotentiary of the Italian Foreign Office. One of the main topics of the diplomatic talks had of course been Tyrol. "I presented the following propositions: German Tyrol up to the Salurno Gap remains German Austrian," but would be militarily neutralized: German Austria would have neither fortresses nor garrisons in the regions south of the Brenner; the only troops there would be recruited from the local inhabitants. In the event of war, both the German Reich and Italy would have the right to demand that Switzerland occupy the area. "This way the region would enjoy international protection just like Switzerland."[33] The northern frontier of Italy would thus be guaranteed. If Italy gave her consent to these plans, German Austria, according to Bauer, would be prepared to fulfill Italy's wishes in other respects, especially in the economic field. Austria would be ready to surrender her properties in the Balkans to Italy. Though Dr. Bauer's proposals made an impression on his counterpart, the Italian plenipotentiary disclosed that the Italian chief of staff was opposed to the attempt to neutralize any part of Tyrol.

Italy's policies in regard to South Tyrol and the Anschluss were far from clear-cut. As a close student of the South Tyrolean question, Paul Herre, observed, Italy's policy toward Austria vacillated between "friendly encouragement and cold rejection" and concluded, "Italy did not know what she wanted."[34] In any case, Italian policy was couched in vague generalities. On March 1, Vittorio Emanuele Orlando declared in the Italian Chamber of Deputies that Italy believed in the justice of her national claims, but was contemplating a just compromise between her own needs and those of other nations. Similarly, the political representative with the Italian Armistice Commission in Vienna, Machioro, spoke repeatedly of the need to establish good relations with Germany and Austria. Under these circumstances it was hardly surprising that German Austrian and German politicians remained hopeful that the recurrent negotiations between Rome and Vienna might still produce favorable results.

But when on April 19, 1919, the Council of Four turned to the question of the frontier between Italy and Austria, Orlando presented Italy's claim to German South Tyrol:

---

[33]O.S., Fasz. 262, Präsidialakte, Bauer to Haupt, Feb. 12; Bauer to Embassy, The Hague, March 19, espec. Promemoria, p. 236.
[34]Herre, 1927: p. 88.

[He] said that Italy's first claim related to her desire for union with the territory on the Italian side of the natural frontiers; the boundaries were clearly defined by nature; there was a geographic unity for Italy, bounded by the sea and by the mountains encircling her northern limits; Italy claimed the watershed of the mountains as her natural frontier.[35]

Orlando admitted that Italy would thus include non-Italian peoples. He insisted, however, that even granting all of Italy's territorial claims would bring in only a small foreign element, a mere 600,000 out of a total of 40 million.[36] President Wilson then found "no great difficulty" in accepting the Italian view, since "within certain limits . . . natural boundaries must be taken into consideration." Lloyd George, however, expressed the opinion that it was "a very serious matter for Italy to antagonize two of the most powerful races in Europe, the Germans in Tyrol and the Slavs in Austria." In the words of Lloyd George, Baron Sonnino had "taken upon himself a heavy responsibility" in rejecting Austria's terms for the neutralization of German South Tyrol. While the United States acquiesced to Italy's demands regarding that region, Great Britain through Lloyd George uttered a final word of warning.

As Lloyd George conceded, France and Great Britain were bound by the Treaty of London to support Italy in her claim to German South Tyrol. However, they would have been pleased if Italy had relinquished her claim. Both Western Powers believed that, if German Austria were able to retain German South Tyrol, she would be less eager for the Anschluss with the German Reich. Only a militarily exposed and vulnerable German Austria would throw herself into Germany's arms. Yet Italy was in no mood to make territorial concessions in favor of Yugoslavia or Austria for the purpose of retaining the good will of her wartime allies. The Italian delegation had quarreled with them over Adriatic problems and had demonstratively left Paris. When it returned to the Peace Conference on the fifth of May, the Western Powers

[35]Miller, 1926f.: **19**: pp. 512-515, Annotations on the Supreme Council's Discussions on the Austro-Italian Frontier.
[36]*Ibid.*, p. 335.

were unable to wring from it any concession in regard to German South Tyrol.

In early June, in a speech to the Austrian National Assembly, Dr. Bauer revealed in detail Austria's earlier proposals to Italy and made known more freely than before the basic assumptions of his Italian policy. It had been clear to the Austrian government from the first "that [it] could not save German South Tyrol unless [it] could reach agreement with Italy to renounce the German territory."[37] Because of the Italian irredentist movement it had not been possible to develop a durable friendship with Italy under the old Austro-Hungarian monarchy. Now, however, the Austrian people would no longer dominate a single Italian village. It would be a misfortune for the two peoples if German South Tyrol became "the obstacle to a friendship which would now be feasible." It was possible, Bauer still held, to find a solution to the question of South Tyrol which would give "satisfaction to the strategic needs of Italy and would not do violence to German South Tyrol."

Even at this late hour, after the presentation of the peace terms in St. Germain, Dr. Bauer did not abandon all hope. During the months of June and July of 1919 he continued his efforts in behalf of South Tyrol. Many Austrians believed it was still possible to divide the Allies, especially to drive a wedge between Paris and Rome.[38]

When it became clear, however, that Italy would insist on her pound of flesh, Dr. Bauer in a last-minute effort turned to America and Great Britain. Having failed both in his Anschluss policy and in his attempt to retain German South Tyrol, Dr. Bauer had already sent a letter of resignation to Chancellor Renner on July 13. Nonetheless, as late as July 16, the Austrian under-secretary of foreign affairs, Pflügl, called on the American representative Halstead to discuss with him the boundary between Tyrol and Italy. The following day the latter learned from Colonel Cunninghame, the English representative in Vienna, that Dr. Bauer through one of his under-secretaries had likewise made to him a "last appeal for a rectification of the Tyrolese border."[39]

---

[37] *Arbeiter-Zeitung*, June 11.
[38] *F.R.U.S., P.P.C.* **12:** p. 530. Bauer attempted to enlist France against Italy's claims to the Brenner pass, *O.S.*, K 110, Bauer to Embassy, The Hague, March 19; *ibid.*, see also Memorandum signed by Pauli, pp. 595-598.
[39] *F.R.U.S., P.P.C.* **12:** pp. 541-543.

The Orlando-Sonnino Cabinet had appeared not disinclined to reaching an agreement with Austria on German South Tyrol, but it had suffered humiliation and defeat in Paris at the hands of the Western Powers over issues relating to the Adriatic and Yugoslavia. On June 20, 1919, it encountered a hostile Italian parliament, and was replaced by the Cabinet of Francesco Nitti and Tommaso Tittoni. Prime Minister Nitti was a man of democratic and pacifist views. But in Tittoni he had a strong foreign minster. Furthermore, the dispatch of Vittorio Scialoja as a member of the Italian peace delegation foreshadowed a determined stand in Paris. When the Supreme Council in Paris resumed its work, it came face to face with an Italian delegation which insisted on the strict fulfillment of the Allied promises made in the secret wartime Treaty of London. The Italian government, whose far-reaching ambitions in the Adriatic—going even beyond this treaty—were to remain unfulfilled, was in no position to renounce German South Tyrol, which was among the territories pledged to her in 1915.[40]

Dr. Bauer's policy had been to gain the support "of at least one of the Great Powers at the Paris Peace Conference."[41] He had hoped that Austria, in her drive toward the Anschluss and her opposition to the idea of a Danubian confederation, would be able to count on Italy's assistance and to exploit the difference between the two Latin countries. While Italy was at no time definitely and irrevocably in favor of the Anschluss, she was, in Bauer's words, "not so hostile to our union policy as was France." Italy was entangled in a serious boundary dispute with Yugoslavia. The latter in turn also claimed Austrian Carinthia, Marburg, and Radkersburg. Rome sided with Vienna against Belgrade, preferring a long border with Austria to a shorter one with Yugoslavia. Dependent on grain imports from abroad, Italy also wanted free access to the Hungarian plain. Should Italy and Yugoslavia come to cross swords, Italy's best chance for access to

[40]Bauer, 1923; pp. 154-155. The new Italian Cabinet was quite satisfied with its country's territorial gains. In a speech in the Senate in late June Nitti boasted: "No European nation, not even France, has today such security of frontiers as Italy. Let us not forget . . . that after many centuries Italy has gained the boundary that renders her secure from German invasions" (see also Nitti's speeches in the Chamber on July 9, July 14 and Aug. 5; *The New Europe*, 12, July 17, 1919-Oct. 9, 1919, pp. 92-94).
[41]Bauer, 1923: p. 153.

Hungarian grain was over the Austrian railroad Villach-Marburg. While Yugoslavia was France's prótegé, Italy reached out to her former enemies, German Austria and Hungary. Yet all those who had placed high hopes on Italy as the new friend of German Austria were to be disappointed. Italy was unwilling to relinquish her claims to German South Tyrol.

Italy's policy of favoring Austria's Anschluss with Germany on national grounds, but insisting on incorporating German-Southern Tyrol, was of course contradictory. This was perceived by many a German who, while appreciating Italy's efforts in behalf of the union, was bitter about the loss of this purely German region. Thus wrote the *Frankfurter Zeitung* on January 31, 1919:

> Neither we nor our Austrian friends are permitted to deceive ourselves that the Italians are so zealously promoting this protection of German Austria [against Slavic excesses] and the Anschluss of this state to our Reich only to secure as large a counterweight as possible against the South Slavic people. . . . To accomplish that it would be easier to take [*einstecken*] the desired German districts of South Tyrol.[42]

The Socialist *Vorwärts* similarly called Italy's policy "openly imperialistic."[43] However contradictory Italy's position, many people, aside from Dr. Bauer, long thought that an Italo-Austrian agreement on South Tyrol was "by no means beyond the realm of possibility."[44]

In the end Italy not only insisted on incorporating the promised South Tyrol, but also switched to the side of the Western Powers in the, from the Austrian point of view, even more vital question of the Anschluss with Germany.

Italy's flirtation with Germany and willingness to accede to the Anschluss was closely connected with the growth of hostility to France and the West. On January 18, 1919, Dr. Viktor Naumann had written the German foreign secretary Brockdorff-Rantzau from Munich: "Recently news has reached me from Italy that public opinion has become in-

---

[42]*Frankfurter Zeitung*, Jan. 31, 1919.
[43]*Vorwärts*, Apr. 5, 1919.
[44]Herkner, 1919: p. 66.

creasingly Germanophile and Francophobe. I have been confidentially informed that the Italians would very much like German Austria to join us, so that they would become Germany's direct neighbors."[45] Dr. Bauer also thought for a while that Italy wanted Germany as a neighbor. Even as late as June 1 the German ambassador von Wedel sent the following telegram from Vienna: "Secretary of State Dr. Bauer has the impression that the Italians, in order to obtain a direct border with Germany, are working toward the Anschluss of North Tyrol with Bavaria." And another time Bauer remarked in a letter to Hartmann: "The Italians feel a rather strong need to keep the road to Germany open."[46]

While France opposed the Anschluss of Austria, Italy for a time inclined toward it; a few Italian newspapers favored at least the union of Tyrol with Bavaria, which also would have made Italy Germany's neighbor. French and Italian diplomats were thus pulling in opposite directions and were keenly aware of their contrary objectives.[47]

Whatever the differences between Italy and the Western Allies — especially France — on the question of the Anschluss and the Danubian confederation, they were all equally opposed to the extension of Hungarian Bolshevism into neighboring Austria. Nonetheless, Italy's suggestion that the Allies occupy German Austria to prevent the expansion of Soviet Hungary into the adjoining Austrian republic met with rejection in London and Paris.

On April 4 the Italian government, in view of the apparent spread of social revolution in Austria, emphasized to the

---

[45]*A.A.*, Nachlass Br.-R.'s . . . 7/1, Presseangelegenheiten, V. Naumann to Br.-R. Jan. 18, 1919; several months later, virtually the same view was expressed in *Vorwärts,* June 25, even. ed.

[46]*O.S.*, K 261, Bauer to Hartmann, IIc, "Stellungnahme Deutschland's zum Frieden"; see also Bauer to Haupt, Jan. 9, 1919. — On May 24 Hartmann wrote to Dr. Bauer: "As you told me, the Italians have for some time been seeking *Anschluss* !] with Germany through us . . . Not a single Italian paper upholds Entente policy now and all of them support Germany, especially our *Anschluss*." (*Ibid.,* Inoffizielle Fühlungsnahme mit der Entente).

[47]According to Allizé, however, Italian diplomacy was divided (*A.E.,* Europe 1918-1929, Autriche Z 88I, Doss. Gén. II, Sept. 20, 1919, p. 627). It always showed some disquiet over the prospect of a common frontier with Germany. Sonnino opposed such a boundary (*Ibid.,* A Paix, A 1056, June 2, 1919, p. 259). Members of the Italian Mission in Vienna, however, did not share the Italian Premier's doubts about the union, but, according to Allizé, rather followed the inspirations of *Corriere della Sera* (*Ibid.,* Doss. Gén. II, p. 628).

Peace Conference the "urgent necessity" of an inter-Allied occupation of Vienna and other Austrian cities. This was two weeks after Count Michael Károlyi, faced with an Allied ultimatum, had stepped down from the premiership, and after the Hungarian Bolsheviks, led by Béla Kun, had seized power in Hungary. Budapest then cast covetous eyes toward neighboring Vienna. Italy, already the occupying power in both South Tyrol and Tyrol proper, wanted to stem the surge of Bolshevism into neighboring Austria, but also wished to gain an additional foothold there. Marquis Imperiali warned Minister Balfour that there would be the "gravest consequences" if the Western Powers failed to act.[48] However, the British Foreign Office's comment on Marquis Imperiali's suggestion was negative.

Actually, the Italian government was not alone in calling for an inter-Allied occupation of Austria. Many Austrians would have welcomed it. Moreover, Allizé, General Haller, and Colonel Cunninghame at that time considered Allied military occupation of German Austria "indispensable." Yet the Western Powers seemed hopeful that Austria, menaced as she was by an expansionist Bolshevik Hungary in the East and an Anschluss-minded Germany in the West, would be able to weather the threats from her neighbors and resist her own urges to unite with either.

Whatever the reasons the Italian government advanced in behalf of the foregoing proposal, the actual effect of an inter-Allied occupation of Austria would have been to bury any Anschluss project which either country or both entertained or promoted. Designed to "save" Austria from Hungarian Bolshevism, it would also have prevented the implementation of the Anschluss. Whatever its previous position on the union, the occupation project of the Italian government actually went much farther than any French proposition toward bolstering Austria's independence and countering the movement for union.

There had been indications of a change of Italian policy regarding Austria and the Anschluss as early as March, 1919. On March 17, the Vienna *Neue Freie Presse* reported "rumors" about a change of heart in Italy.[49] By mid-April it also appeared to the Germans that Italy, which previously had sharply

---

[48]*P.R.*, F.O. 608, v. 16, Marchese Imperiali, note, Apr. 7.
[49]*Neue Freie Presse*, March 17.

opposed the French anti-Anschluss policy, was vacillating. As the German delegation in Paris summed it up, the policy of the Italian government was no longer "very clear at the present time." And on the twenty-fourth of April Baron de Vaux reported a talk between Professor Lammasch and Paulucci, the Italian ambassador in Switzerland, during which the latter declared that "Italian interest in Austria's Anschluss with Germany has substantially declined since the project of the Danubian confederation could be considered as definitely abandoned." [50] Thus it was Italy's opposition to the Danubian confederation and, with it, to a restoration of the Habsburg monarchy, which made her opt for the Anschluss with Germany in the first place. Many Italians may have judged the union not as desirable as such, but rather as a lesser evil. With the project of the Danubian confederation seemingly buried, Italy was now faced with another alternative. Between an independent Austria which was supported by the Western Powers, and the Anschluss, with its obvious threats to Italy, Rome decided for the former.

These threats were apparent to many Italians even at the height of the differences with the Entente over Adriatic questions when the Italian Cabinet, for tactical reasons, may have found it advisable to exaggerate the dispute also over Central Europe. According to Barrère, French ambassador in Rome, Sonnino had confided to him that a common frontier with Germany had never appeared to him a cause for rejoicing for Italy. Sonnino had always expressed himself along these lines even while the Austrian empire still existed.[51]

It was on May 18 that the Italian Cabinet, with Sonnino presiding, officially accepted the majority decision of the Allied and Associated Powers to oppose the Anschluss, provided the Entente would honor Italy's claims to South Tyrol and Fiume.[52] Thus the priority of Italy's border demand to the north and east over the question of the Anschluss was clearly established. The Brenner Pass was of greater importance to Italy than her stake in Austria's right to join Germany. And Austria's independence, Italy may finally

[50]Luckau, 1941: p. 182f.; *O.S.*, K 262, de Vaux, Apr. 24.
[51]*A.E.*, A Paix, A 1056, Duval, June 2, 1919, p. 259.
[52]Paller, "Entstehung d. Anschlussfrage," Kleinwaechter-Paller, 1930: p. 57; Herre, 1927: p. 100.

have reasoned, need not necessarily lead Austria into a French-sponsored Danubian confederation—a position which Italian papers had widely held earlier.

Thus Italy's decision to oppose the Anschluss was tied up with the wish to gain German South Tyrol.[53] Yet it was not until July 8 that Dr. Bauer was notified that the Italian government was no longer interested in continuing negotiations concerning German South Tyrol. Though Rome moved on the union issue to the point of view of her Western allies, it was unwilling to make territorial concessions to Austria in the matter of German South Tyrol, as the West had suggested. On the contrary, in return for her consent to Austria's independence, Italy asked of the Entente a *quid pro quo*. This included reconfirmation of the London Treaty in regard to the Brenner Pass.

In early June the Austrian treaty was presented to Austria's delegation in St. Germain. In September, 1919, the Austrian National Assembly finally ratified it. Though the peace treaty prohibited the Anschluss, Franco-Italian differences in regard to Austria continued, with some objectives different, some unaltered.[54] An independent Austria could still link up with other states in a Danubian federation. While France

---

[53]*Herre* held that with the crystallization of the Italian point of view in regard to South Tyrol went hand in hand a change in regard to the position on the *Anschluss*. He likewise stated, without, however, offering any evidence, that the irredentist leader and author Ettore Tolomei had been influential also in regard to this change.

[54]The following letter to Dr. Bauer dated July 3 and marked "confidential" came most likely from the pen of the chief of the Vienna police, Johann Schober. It dealt with the arrival of Prince Borghese as Italy's representative in Vienna: "Vienna may become the scene of a diplomatic struggle between Allizé and Borghese, which would not be without danger to us. Allizé has taken decisive steps in favor of the reestablishment of a Dual Monarchy, which is a red flag to Italy." To upset these plans and to lure Austria into an alliance with Germany and Italy against France was allegedly the main task of Prince Borghese. One was intensely curious in Vienna's diplomatic circles "how the diplomatic and political Allizé-Borghese duel will develop" (*O.S.*, Fasz. 262, Präsidialakte, Tschechoslowakei, Z 1938). About a week later Schober followed up his earlier letter with another confidential communication to Dr. Bauer, repeating some of his charges. Schober pointed to the continuing differences between France and Italy in Central Europe. This clash of interests was indeed to shape the history of Europe between the wars. The anticipated alliance between Berlin, Vienna, Rome, and Budapest was ultimately forged, but in a manner and form which could not yet be foreseen. In 1919 there were already forces operating to create such an alliance, but the differences between Rome and Berlin over Austria's future and the question of South Tyrol produced then only a stillbirth.

encouraged the latter as a means of strengthening Austria politically and economically against the continuing threat of the Anschluss, Italy continued to fear the resurrection of the Austrian empire.

As far as the Anschluss movement of 1919 was concerned, Italy's final switch of policy toward opposing it was first motivated by the realization that she would fare much better with weak little Austria as a neighbor than with a strong, potentially threatening power like Germany. A German irredenta in South Tyrol would be a much greater threat to Italy if she had a common boundary with Germany than if she had one with Austria. Germany, having absorbed all of Austria, would come menacingly close to the Adriatic Sea and challenge Italy's domination over it. Italy would lose any potential influence in Hungary and even Rumania. And Germany would gain entrance to the Balkans and become a rival to Italy in southeastern Europe. On the other hand, by opposing the Anschluss, Italy would join the Western Powers in their opposition to German expansionism into Central Europe and ingratiate herself with the Entente.

4. THE UNITED STATES ON THE ANSCHLUSS. PRESIDENT WILSON AND SECRETARY OF STATE LANSING

> "Our territorial experts are in substantial agreement with the British and French respecting the boundaries of Germany." Colonel House to President Wilson, 1919

IN the course of the year 1918 the United States and her allies had reached the conclusion that the Austro-Hungarian monarchy, in Secretary of State Lansing's words, should be "blotted out as an Empire." All its nationalities were to satisfy their national aspirations, in accordance with their wishes. For a brief moment in September, 1918, the American secretary of state—perhaps driven by the inner logic of the situation and the seemingly general validity of the principle of national self-determination—had toyed with the idea of endorsing the Anschluss, but quickly retreated. The United States seemed to have no policy on the union until early 1919. Then her leaders gave support to the prohibition of the Anschluss and never wavered subsequently.

While Secretary of State Lansing's brief endorsement of the Anschluss in the autumn of 1918 did not become a matter of public knowledge, the republican senator Henry Cabot Lodge in the Foreign Affairs Committee of the Senate in December, 1918, came out openly for the inclusion of German Austria into the German federation, advocating the union of Tyrol with Bavaria.[1] The American Peace Delegation, the State Department, and President Wilson himself, however, largely ignored Senator Lodge's views.

---

[1] Paller, Kleinwaechter and Paller, 1930: p. 51. Strangely enough, during the summer of 1918 Senator H. C. Lodge had struck a rabidly anti-German note when he asked for the "unconditional surrender" of Germany, for a "dictated peace" and had said: "No peace that satisfies Germany in any degree can ever satisfy us" (*Congressional Record*, Aug. 23, 1918, cols. 9394f.).

In October, 1918, a so-called official American commentary on the Fourteen Points was prepared by Frank Cobb and Walter Lippmann. It interpreted point 10 thus: "German Austria. This territory should of right be permitted to join Germany, but there is strong objection in France because of increase in population involved."[2] The document was presented by Colonel House to Clémenceau and Lloyd George and in the foregoing ambiguous wording was likely to strengthen French objections to the union. As the historian Hajo Holborn wrote, "It was clear that in all cases the United States would take as benevolent a view of the interests of her wartime allies" as possible.[3] Neither the American experts of the Inquiry at the Peace Conference nor the higher American policy-makers felt themselves bound by the "official" American commentary which asserted Austria's right to the Anschluss. The commentary was written for self-clarification and for the information of the Allies, but not proclaimed as the authoritative interpretation of American war goals.

On December 31 the *Daily Bulletin*, which had a wide circulation among American delegates in Paris, stated that it might be well for the American Commission to Negotiate Peace to consider whether the United States was "interested in preventing the Union" and, if so, what steps should be taken to implement this policy.[4] On January 29 A. W. Dulles asserted that there was "apparently no clear majority" for the union of German Austria with Germany and also that it was "in the interests of the Allies that it should not come about." It was his opinion that it was "desirable to take such steps as are consistent with the President's principles to prevent such a union. The most effective way of doing this would be to adopt the position that the present unsettled world situation is not a time when the future of German Austria should be prejudiced by decisive action."[5] This was the view that came to prevail in American and Entente circles and it was not openly challenged by any American expert. In a dispatch to

---

[2]Quoted by Seymour, 1928: **4:** pp. 192-200.
[3]Holborn. Craig and Gilbert, *Diplomats*, p. 135.
[4]*N.A.*, American Commission to Negotiate Peace, box 8, R 6265, *Daily Bulletin*, Dec. 31, 1918.
[5]*Ibid.*, Jan. 29, 1919, A. W. Dulles.

the *New York World* James Tuohy wrote on March 12: "America agrees with the other powers that a union between Germany and Austria is undesirable."[6] On March 20, 1919, Wallace Notestein in a study sponsored by the Inquiry, "The Future of German Austria, Economic and Political Considerations," asserted, as A. W. Dulles had done earlier, that "at present" it was "far from clear" that the people of German Austria wanted union with Germany.[7] This opinion was then strongly advanced in the French press.

The move of the American experts toward the French position on the Anschluss was accelerated by the need to take France's interests into consideration. This becomes clear in a communication of William C. Bullitt to Secretary Lansing on February 12: "In opposing the union, a welcome opportunity is afforded to the U.S. of supporting a vital point of French policy at a time when American prestige in France is suffering because of divergence of views on other important subjects."[8] Although the resolute French opposition to the union weighed heavily with the Americans in reaching a final position on the Anschluss issue, it was by no means the only determining factor. In no case did the United States simply surrender to a differing French point of view.

When President Wilson sailed for Paris, he apparently had no definite plan for German Austria. While en route to Europe, he revealed to Professor Charles Seymour that he saw Austria's desire for the union with Germany as a mere temporary phenomenon growing out of the postwar economic dislocation and likely to disappear once the results of the war had been overcome.[9] His apparent lack of determined opposition to the Anschluss at that moment was taken by H. von Paller and other pro-Anschluss-minded German and Austrian historians as proof that France later used guile to win the president over to her point of view.[10] The utterance to Seymour should be differently interpreted. Just

---

[6]*Ibid.*, Press Clippings . . . , R.C. 256, box 92, "Austria," *New York World*, March 2, 1919, J. Tuohy.

[7]*N.A.*, Inquiry Nr. 998, W. Notestein, "The Future of German Austria, Economic and Political Considerations," March 29, 1919.

[8]*Ibid.*, American Commission . . . , v. 303, 185.1136/1, Nr. 10, Wm. Bullitt to Lansing, Feb. 12, 1919.

[9]Kleinwaechter and Paller, 1930: p. 51.

[10]*Ibid.*

because the Austrians, in the president's opinion, were in favor of the Anschluss because of the temporary economic dislocation of their country, a temporary prohibition of the union, such as Wilson came to favor, would help the Allies over the hump; with the general recovery of Europe Austria's drive for the Anschluss would lose its force. Wilson's change of view was thus a gradual one, developing logically from his former position; he was not worsted by clever French stratagems.

In any case, when the New Year was rung in and the Peace Conference had opened its doors, the United States had not yet come to grips with what was undoubtedly the most decisive problem of Central Europe, the union between Austria and Germany. Like France and Great Britain, the United States had rather turned her attention to the insistent territorial claims of the Czechs, Yugoslavs, Rumanians, Poles, and Italians in regard to former Austro-Hungarian territory than to demands of the German Austrians. Under these circumstances individual American experts and advisers, pulling in opposite directions, offered different solutions to the Austrian problem.

On December 30, 1918, James Brown Scott and David Hunter Miller, the American Technical Advisers to the Commission to Negotiate Peace, submitted to the secretary of state a "Skeleton Draft of the Peace Treaty." They suggested that of the defeated Central Powers not only Austria and Germany but also Bavaria be made a signatory of the peace treaty.[11] Although separatism in Germany might not proceed so far as to lead to Bavaria's "complete independence" from the rest of the empire, the independent role recently assumed by the Bavarian government, coupled with its historic position in the empire, justified in their opinion the inclusion of Bavaria among the signatories. The chief difficulty in dealing with the Central Powers and in relying on their execution of the Treaty of Peace arose out of the extreme uncertainty as to the relative strength of political groups in Germany and what was formerly Austria-Hungary. The possibility even of the "complete disappearance of Austria as an independent state" was mentioned by the Technical Ad-

---

[11]*F.R.U.S., P.P.C.* **1:** p. 308.

visers. They also considered the possibility that the Peace Conference might recognize the annexation of German Austria by Germany, in which case Austria would no longer appear as a signatory.[12] While James Brown Scott and David Hunter Miller contemplated the possibility of the Anschluss, irrespective of its being approved or not by the United States and the Peace Conference, on January 21, 1919, the Inquiry recommended borders for an independent German Austria.

In the event that Austria should choose the path of independence the Black Book or "Outline of Tentative Report and Recommendations" of the Inquiry recommended that historic boundaries be preserved between German Austria on the one hand and Bavaria, Bohemia, Moravia, and Hungary on the other. The authors estimated that this would leave about 250,000 Germans in Western Hungary and an equal number of Germans in Bohemia and Moravia. The American experts held that the latter Germans seemed to prefer union with the Czechoslovakian state, though their sentiments had "not yet been clearly enough expressed to form the basis of a positive conclusion." The authors of the Black Book were convinced that it was "decidedly disadvantageous" to disturb such historic entities as Bohemia and Moravia.[13] In regard to Austria's frontiers with Italy and Yugoslavia, they recommended deviating from the principle of ethnic frontiers on account of overriding economic and military considerations. In every recommendation, German Austria was the loser.

Like the French and most of the English experts, the American experts clearly favored Czechoslovakia at the expense of German Austria and Germany. The American advisers, though not subscribing to the secret Treaty of London of 1915 concluded between Italy and the Entente, were nonetheless willing to leave as many as 160,000 Germans of South Tyrol with Italy, since this gave Italy a defensible frontier. The task of the League of Nations in maintaining peace

---

[12]*Ibid.*, p. 309.

[13]*N.A.*, Records of the Amer. Delegation to Negotiate Peace, v. 297, 185.112/1, Black Book or "Outline of Tentative Report. . . ." Perman, 1962, holds that in regard to drawing the Czechoslovak-Austrian border in particular the American delegation was "greatly confused" about the principle of national self-determination, "this fundamental part of President Wilson's policy" (p. 205, also p. 212). Wilson himself had "no clear idea" what type of settlement he was seeking in Central Europe.

and that of Italy in defending herself against possible "armed aggression by a powerful German state" would thus be greatly facilitated. Fear of Germany's military resurgence motivated not only French and English experts, but also the American authors of the Black Book.

In the late winter months and in the spring of 1919 the French, English and Italian press took the problem of German Austria and the various solutions suggested, such as the Danubian confederation, Anschluss, neutralization, and independence, increasingly into account; occasional articles in the American press also tried to come to grips with these issues.

The *New York Times* voiced doubts that the union of Germany and Austria was really a threat to France.[14] In view of the territorial losses Germany was likely to suffer, the new Germany, even including German Austria, would not surpass imperial Germany in territory and population. Austria would exercise a moderating influence in Germany and weaken Prussia's role. On the other hand, Austria could not stand alone. And the concept of a Danubian confederation would merely help to preserve the dying Habsburg imperialism. What the *New York Times* did not take into account was the Entente's patent desire to weaken Germany rather than to restore her strength to what it had been prior to 1914.

During the month of May, the *New York Times* apparently had some change of heart and mind. Its Austrian correspondent not only admitted that an independent German Austria would need foreign assistance but also said that many Austrians themselves opposed the union.[15] Yet after the publication of the Austrian peace terms and the prohibition of the union project, the *New York Times* reverted once more to a position critical of the Allies. If German Austria should want union in the future, the Allies would be ill-advised to "maintain by force an artificial division." The *New York Times* believed that in any case the West would have the power to "restrain" Germany.[16]

The Nation was in an even more critical mood and scoffed at the claim that the Treaty of St. Germain was "a peace of ab-

---

[14]*New York Times*, Feb. 20.
[15]*Ibid.*, May 16.
[16]*Ibid.*, June 6, 1919.

solute justice." One wondered, the journal added sar-
castically, "what a treaty of vengeance would look like."[17] It
contrasted the actual peace treaty with Wilson's promise at
the time of the declaration of war on the Austrian empire in
December, 1917, that it was "not American intention to dictate to them [the people of Austria] in any way."

When the last touches were added to the Austrian peace
treaty and the Austrian National Assembly finally accepted
the document, *The Nation* and *The New Republic* were more or
less reconciled to the treaty, though the latter magazine
especially found it difficult to believe that Austria was not
only denied the right to self-determination, but that the
French had also deprived her inhabitants of the right "even
to agitate for it."[18] Both these influential magazines were opposed to the peace settlement on many other grounds than
the denial of self-determination to German Austria.

There were perhaps a few more critical voices in the
American press than in the British press, and in the latter
in turn more criticism was leveled at the prohibition of the
Anschluss than in the French newspapers. Objectivity,
appreciation of the general validity of the right to national
self-determination, indifference toward the implications of
the growth of Germany's resources, and plain lack of understanding of the realities of power, seemed to increase in
direct ratio to the distance from Central Europe.[19]

Irrespective of occasional American criticism of the Entente's emerging Anschluss policy, American experts and
policy-makers continued to move closer to the Entente and
especially to the French point of view on the union.

One of the most significant expressions of American policy
toward Austria and the Anschluss came on February 21 at a
meeting of the British and American delegates to which
reference has already been made. It was then agreed that no
union between German Austria and Germany would be
recognized until the peace treaty had been signed.[20]

---

[17]*The Nation,* June 7, 1919, p. 2814.

[18]*Ibid.,* Sept. 13, pp. 357f. and the *New Republic,* Sept. 17, p. 184, and Sept. 10.

[19]Slosson, "America and the Anschluss Question," in Kleinwaechter and Paller,
1930: pp. 191-194, pointed to a perhaps greater "impartiality" of Americans in
regard to the *Anschluss* than that of any European people, but added that this was
"partly the product of distance and ignorance" (p. 191).

[20]*P.R.,* F.O. 608, v. 16, minute by W. Tyrrell, Feb. 21, 1919, Attitude of Allies
towards proposals for union of German Austria to Germany.

Of all the Allied and American diplomatic moves relating to the Anschluss, this was so far the most definite and far-reaching one. While it postponed ultimate decisions to a later day, it set clear limits on Austria's freedom of action. A similar move in the direction of Berlin was not considered necessary, since Germany was tied by the armistice terms and anxiously awaiting the peace terms. The Anglo-American agreement of February 21 on the Anschluss signified a turning point in Allied policy toward Austria and the question of her union with Germany. Having so far drifted along, the two powers now steered onto a major highway. The specific ultimate goal was not yet indicated and perhaps not yet quite clear, but the over-all direction for the immediate future was no longer in question. But from the point of view of a firm Allied policy, there was still the serious shortcoming that the agreement was not publicized. It thus failed to produce a restraining effect on German and Austrian public opinion.

No wonder therefore that at the same time the French urged the Americans to "intimate" to Vienna that the Anschluss was contrary to Allied wishes. Clémenceau, reported Colonel House to President Wilson on February 23, 1919, insisted that the Allies warn the German Austrians. And the following day Colonel House informed the president: "Our territorial experts are in substantial agreement with the British and French respecting the boundaries of Germany."[21] It was obvious that Colonel House himself wanted President Wilson to heed Clémenceau's suggestion.

The American position had clearly hardened during the months of February and March. The high momentum the Anschluss movement then gained in Central Europe was countered by a rallying of the Western Powers, including the United States, to stave off immediate danger. Early in March E. L. Dresel of the United States Peace Commission suggested in a memorandum that the Council of Ten publicly declare that it considered the Anschluss "under present abnormal conditions . . . premature and precipitate."

But American policy was still far from being clear even to American spokesmen. On March 1, at a meeting of the commissioners plenipotentiary in Paris, in which President

---

[21]*F.R.U.S., P.P.C.* **11:** pp. 512-513.

Wilson, Secretary of State Lansing, White, and General Bliss participated, the latter mentioned that E. L. Dresel had discussed with him the question of the union of German Austria with Germany and had left a memorandum with him. Lansing then made the startling statement, mentioned before, that he did not know what the American position on the Anschluss was; he added that in his view any idea of preventing an eventual union of the German peoples was a dream. He expressed an interest in the project of the union between Bavaria and German Austria.[22]

Two days later, on March 3, another meeting of the commissioners took place. In addition to Lansing, General Bliss, White, and Allen Dulles took part. The commissioners discussed a memorandum, no doubt the one previously left by Dresel, which outlined the objections to the Anschluss. Dulles listed the arguments against a *laissez faire* policy on this question. Lansing remarked that, if the question of opposing the union was brought up by one of the Allied powers, it might well be considered, but that he could not approve of America's taking the initiative on an issue affecting the territorial settlement of Europe, especially in view of the fact that such initiative might appear to be in contradiction to the president's principles.[23]

In general the American experts were opposed to the Anschluss in particular, but no final decision had yet been reached at the highest level of American government. While Secretary of State Lansing considered a link-up inevitable in the long run, at the moment he was only interested in a union between German Austria and Bavaria. The American secretary of state's position reveals him to be less a friend of the Anschluss than fearful of the resurgence of German power and therefore interested in splitting Germany along religious and regional lines, that is to say, between the Catholic South and West and the Protestant North and East. Lansing's suggestion early in March, 1919, of linking Austria and Bavaria also indicates how far he had traveled since September, 1918, when he had recommended a union between Austria and the entire Reich.

---

[22]*Ibid.*, pp. 87-88.
[23]*Ibid.*, pp. 88-89.

In the above conferences of the American commissioners Lansing, though plagued by doubts about the reconcilability of President Wilson's "principles" with the prohibition of the union, opposed America's taking the initiative in forbidding the Anschluss. The implication, however, was clear: if either France or Great Britain were prepared to shoulder the responsibility for taking the first step, the United States might under some circumstances follow, irrespective of the president's principles. During the month of March it became increasingly clear that the United States was moving toward relinquishing the *laissez faire* policy in regard to the Anschluss and becoming resolved to prohibit the union at least for the immediate future.

On March 5, the Council of Ten discussed the problem of furnishing food to Austria. Clémenceau revealed that he had placed this matter on the agenda after a previous conversation with Balfour and Colonel House. "They all agreed that the matter was urgent and that it was incumbent on the Allied Powers to show goodwill to the German Austrians, in particular with a view to preventing them from throwing themselves into the arms of the Bavarians and Germans of Germany." The governments of Great Britain, France, and Italy agreed to advance credits to finance food supplies to Austria.[24]

In the ensuing discussion Colonel House pointed out that all reports indicated that the sending of food to German Austria "will weigh heavily in the scale when the German Austrians come to decide whether or not they will throw in their lot with Germany. This is the political aspect of the case." Pichon remarked that he wished to support Balfour and Colonel House and also send food to Austria: "German Austria is about to make a decision regarding its adhesion to Germany. There is a possibility of influencing the decision. This is a question of general policy and of great interest to the entire Alliance."[25]

Later in the month the Allies lifted the blockade against Austria, but they continued it against Hungary which had just gone Bolshevik and against Germany which seemed

---

[24]*Ibid.*, p. 94.
[25]*Ibid.*, p. 98.

unrepentant and had put forth extreme territorial and other demands. Colonel House and the French statesmen Clémenceau and Pichon all openly admitted that they hoped to influence Austria's decision on the Anschluss adversely.

But at the same time the Allies also attempted to make Germany renounce the concept of union with Austria. Late in February the American and French delegations to the Central Committee on Territorial Questions of the Peace Conference aimed at making Germany refrain from any political or economic move which might threaten the independence of Austria.[26] While this understanding did not prevent German Austria from making a move toward the Anschluss, it clearly prohibited Germany from encouraging the Anschluss movement. The American agreement with the French, determined opponents of the Anschluss movement, was, of course, revealing in itself.

The following month the United States moved even closer to the French point of view by hitting upon a formula which would make German unification with Austria impossible without the consent of the Council of the League of Nations, France of course included. This was to prevent the Anschluss not only before the signing of the peace treaty, but also thereafter, by placing the ultimate power in this matter into the hands of the government in Paris.

In the session of the Council of Four on April 24, 1919, Clémenceau suggested the inclusion of a clause in the peace treaty with Germany which would require Berlin to recognize the independence of Austria as "inalienable."[27] Thereupon President Wilson raised the question of the meaning of this word. Clémenceau countered: "I know quite well that we can't hinder this union permanently, if it is desired by the peoples concerned. But this formula will greatly aid the Austrian party which desires Austria to remain independent." President Wilson replied: "I think, as you do, that it is desirable to prevent the immediate link-up of Austria with Germany. But I would withdraw the word

[26]*P.R.,* F.O. 608, v. 16, Report of the Central Committee on Territorial Questions to the Supreme Allied Council. Communication by Secretary General, March 16, 1919; see also Woodward and Butler, 1946: **1:** pp. 183-184.

[27]Mantoux, 1955: **1:** pp. 461-462; the French version appears fuller than the American one, *F.R.U.S., P.P.C.* **5:** p. 114, 118, 425, Appendix IV to IC-179C.

'inalienable.'" Clémenceau thereupon made this rejoinder: "If I withdrew it, Austria would take advantage of it by proclaiming its union with Germany tomorrow."

President Wilson continued:

In regard to Austria, I am afraid to infringe upon the right of peoples to self-determination. It is not Germany in which I am interested in this context, but German Austria. We can prohibit an annexation, but we cannot deny a country the right to link up with another; we cannot refuse a country the right to join another, if she wishes it. One cannot forbid Luxemburg to link up with Belgium or France.

Whereupon Lloyd George asked the vital question: "Let us assume that there were an independent Rhenish state and that we judged its permanent separation from Germany indispensable to the security of Europe; why could we not impose it?" Wilson countered: "I cannot accept this principle. I believe in maintaining the right of people to self-determination." When Clémenceau interjected, "Even if it does not mean linking up with our allies and associates . . . ?" Wilson countered that his attitude to Austria was friendly. Upon Clémenceau's rejoinder that his was too, Wilson developed his position as follows:

I do not wish to impose on Austria a permanent obligation; yet on the other hand, to fix a time limit would be equivalent to inviting Austria to link up with Germany at the expiration of the provided time limit. *Lloyd George*: A text presented by our experts forces the German government to abstain from manoeuvres which have as a goal the union of Austria to the German state. *Clémenceau*: Germany will sign an article of this kind, will act to the contrary, and then deny it. *Lloyd George*: I realize that this text is not worth a great deal. *Wilson*: Can't we write that Germany recognizes the independence of Austria and will respect it and that it will remain inalienable except by a contrary decision rendered by the League of Nations. *Clémenceau*: Very good. *Lloyd George*: I would willingly accept such a text.

This session of the Council of Four determined the final Allied policy on the Anschluss which was incorporated into the peace treaties with German Austria and Germany. The session clearly revealed President Wilson's thinking on the Anschluss problem. In principle the president asserted the right of all, even the vanquished peoples, to self-determination, and rejected by implication Lloyd George's weighty theoretical consideration concerning the security of all of Europe. President Wilson was still unwilling to consider the possibility of a theoretical and practical irreconcilability between self-determination for all peoples, including the vanquished Germans, and the security of her smaller neighbors. But the president's actual formula for the solution of the German Austrian problem was heartily embraced by Lloyd George and enthusiastically accepted by Clémenceau.

As the session revealed, the final formula for prohibiting the Anschluss but permitting the hope that the League of Nations might some day give its approval to the link-up was President Wilson's own. It was, of course, a compromise. Wilson's formula, by holding out the hope for a later consent to the union, was based on recognition of the right to national self-determination. By prohibiting it for an indefinite time, however, it acknowledged the realities of power and also the latent fear in Europe of the vanquished foe. Even Clémenceau realized that the two German states could not be kept apart forever if they really desired the union. But he was determined to keep them separate as long as possible. When President Wilson finally offered a formula which tied the Anschluss to the approval of the Council of the League of Nations, Clémenceau quickly gave his approval. He understood that France would thus exercise a permanent veto over the Anschluss. Lloyd George was likewise won over to the French point of view and promptly gave his consent. President Wilson himself, and no other American, took thus the leading role in shaping Allied Anschluss policy.

Some German and Austrian historians, embittered about the peace treaties of Versailles and St. Germain, including the prohibition of the Anschluss, have vacillated between accusing President Wilson of having "betrayed" his own ideals and violated his pledges and belittling the president's knowledge and grasp of Europe, especially Central European affairs, history and geography.[28] Yet President Wilson had

---

[28]Paller, 1928: p. 48.

surely never promised the Anschluss as such, though many Germans, interpreting his program quite liberally, claimed that he did. As far as the president's alleged lack of knowledge is concerned, the American historian A. J. May, a leading expert on Austrian history and a close student of American policy toward Austria, has discarded the "myth" that President Wilson was not familiar with the conditions and problems of the Dual Monarchy. According to May, Wilson in his treatise on comparative government, *The State*, had written with "clarity and penetration" on the Austro-Hungarian empire.[29]

President Wilson also had a direct voice in the decision of the Council of Four to change the name of German Austria (Deutsch-Österreich) to Austria. This decision was reached at President Wilson's residence on May 29, 1919. The Yugoslav and Czech delegations had voiced their concern that the designation German Austria would encourage the belief that there existed a non-German Austria. They disliked this implication and the inherent claim to some or all of their territories. In their view, the name "Deutsch-Österreich" would strengthen the ties between German Austria and the Germans in Czechoslovakia and might also give encouragement to the Anschluss movement. Thus Lloyd George, Cambon, and President Wilson approved that the designation "Ger-

---

[29]May, "W. Wilson and Austria-Hungary to the end of 1917," *Festschrift* ... 1957. About Wilson, see also May, 1966: **2**: pp. 559, 563, and 570-572. Later on a casual, unfortunate statement about the "new immigration" from Austria-Hungary which Wilson compared unfavorably with Chinese immigration to the United States, was to plague the politician Wilson for years to come, but does not detract from his rightful claim to solid knowledge of the affairs of Central Europe. President Wilson has been especially criticized for the prohibition of the Anschluss. Charles Seymour, chief of the Austro-Hungarian Division of the American Peace Commission, has conveyed the impression that the president's decision to prohibit the union came about only by disregarding the opinions of the majority of American experts. A reading of the available record disposes of Seymour's claim that permitting Austria's *Anschluss* with Germany "was, on the whole, approved by the American delegates" ("End of an Empire. Remnants of Austria-Hungary," E. M. House and Chs. Seymour, 1921: pp. 87-111, p. 108).

Seymour held in 1921 that the Peace Conference "made a mistake the economic consequences of which may prove disastrous, in not permitting the union of lesser [sic] Austria with Germany." This view reflected no doubt the immediate postwar American disappointments and disenchantment over the peace treaty, but seems to ignore the harmful political and military consequences of a union which became quite apparent in later years. In the opinion of the

man" be dropped and that the new state be known as the "Republic of Austria."[30]

After his return to the United States, the president never touched on the question of the Anschluss again, neither when addressing the Senate in the summer of 1919 nor in his speeches throughout the country, though he discussed many details of the peace treaties. While he was anxious to explain to the American people the territorial settlement which had been arrived at in Paris, he never took up the prohibition of the Anschluss or the question of German South Tyrol. He obviously wanted to avoid explaining such negative provisions and assuming a defensive and apologetic position.

President Wilson played a key role not only in making the final decision on the Anschluss, but also on the political future of German South Tyrol, an issue which was closely linked with the Anschluss question.

On April 14, 1919, President Wilson sent a memorandum to the Italian Delegation at the Peace Conference. While disputing Italy's claims to the Adriatic, he accepted her claim to the Brenner Pass as her northern frontier, and also the incorporation of German South Tyrol. He wrote: "Personally, I am quite willing that Italy be accorded the whole length of her northern frontier and, wherever she comes into contact with Austrian territory, all that was accorded her in the so-

---

peacemakers, and also of a majority of the American experts, these evil consequences would have by far surpassed the regrettable and partly avoidable economic disadvantages of the treaty of St. Germain. Following the war's end there was apparently a strong temptation to shift the blame for an unpopular peace treaty, and for the prohibition of the Anschluss in particular, on the American president and on France's alleged intransigence.

It was on Seymour's testimony alone that von Paller in Kleinwaechter and Paller, 1930, long a major reference work on the Anschluss problem, "concluded" that the American and even British delegates had been for the union (p. 54). This work, however, is quite uneven and frequently lacks the evidence which even then was available.

About the tendency of some American writers to acquit the United States and place the blame for the decisions on Austria and the Anschluss on France, see also the letter by Leygues, Embassy in Paris, to Ambassador Francais Washington, December 21, 1920 (A.E., Europe 1918-1929, Autriche Z 881, Doss. Gén. III, L'Amérique et l'Autriche, pp. 52-53) where he criticized the American undersecretary of state who "tends to decline the responsibility of the United States for tracing the boundaries of the Austrian republic." According to Leygues, contemporary Austria was essentially the product of the nationality principles to which President Wilson had attached at least as much value as any of the other allied governments.

[30]Wilson, 1927: 1: p. 461.

called Pact of London." But he added that he was of the opinion that the Pact of London could no longer apply to the settlement of her eastern boundaries. The line drawn in the Pact of London was established for the purpose of furnishing "an absolutely adequate frontier of safety for Italy against any possible hostility or aggression on the part of Austria-Hungary. But Austria-Hungary no longer exists." Wilson thus suggested that Italy renounce her excessive claims in the Adriatic. But he had no such objective in mind in regard to the northern boundary; quite the contrary.[31] On April 23, President Wilson reaffirmed his assent to the Italian demands for the Brenner Pass as the northern boundary, and on April 30 the foregoing note of April 14 was made public.

When the Austro-Italian frontier was being discussed in the Supreme Council, Orlando, as stated, claimed the mountains encircling her northern limits, in particular "the watershed," as the country's natural frontier. President Wilson promptly agreed that "within certain limits natural boundaries must be taken into consideration. . . . Nature has swung a great boundary round the north of Italy; it included Trieste and most of the Istrian peninsula. He had no great difficulties there in meeting the Italian views."[32] This was the same point of view which he had expressed in his memorandum to the Italian Peace Delegation on April 14.

About six weeks later, on May 29, President Wilson disclosed that the Heads of Governments had reached a decision concerning the southern frontier of German Austria. It was basically the frontier which had been laid down in the Pact of London on April 26, 1915, the only ex-

---

[31]This position of President Wilson differed from that of the American authors of the *Black Book* of the Inquiry in being more favorable toward Italy than to Austria. The *Black Book* had earlier recommended a boundary line to the south of the Brenner Pass, a line not identical with the linguistic boundary, but running somewhat north of it. This boundary would have left 161,000 German Tyrolese in Italy! The *Black Book* recommendation fell short of what had been promised to Italy in the secret Treaty of London of 1915, but would have given her a boundary which would have rendered her "peaceful existence reasonably sure." The American experts assumed that their recommended frontier would leave no "rational" basis for future irredentist agitation. However, they saw clearly that Italy's desire for South Tyrol in combination with her approval of Austria's union with Germany would lead to "confrontation by a united and potentially powerful German state on the north" and that her policy therefore was likely to be self-defeating.

[32]Miller, 1926: **19:** pp. 512-515, p. 335.

ception being that the Sexten Valley and Tarvis should be Italian and the junction of Villach Austrian.

These provisions in favor of Italy represented a further concession by the Big Three to Italy. As Paul Herre put it from the Austrian and German point of view: "Instead of retreating from the waterless frontier to the linguistic boundary, they went even beyond it." [33] Even Ettore Tolomei, the irredentist leader and passionate champion of the theory of national boundaries, opposed this ruling, but submitted to Italian military demands.

Colonel House has shed light on why President Wilson decided to support the cession of German South Tyrol to Italy. According to his account, in turn based upon an account by Frazier, when Orlando pleaded for Fiume, President Wilson replied: "I cannot consent that Fiume go to Italy, but you may count upon me for the Brenner line." [34] Though Orlando was not satisfied, according to Frazier, he "held Wilson to his promise." And Colonel House added: "I have often wondered why Wilson consented to this line. Clémenceau, Lloyd George and I discussed it during the Armistice proceedings and the three of us came to the conclusion that the Tyrol should not be taken from Austria. They were committed by the Secret Treaty, but thought the United States could protest."

During the month of May, 1919, President Wilson began to have second thoughts about the decision on German South Tyrol. He conceded at that time to Charles Seymour that his own approval of the Brenner frontier had been based on insufficient study. Ray Stannard Baker, though completely devoted to President Wilson, inserted a critical remark in his *Wilson and the World Settlement*, not unlike Colonel House's quoted reservations: "Already, the President had, unfortunately, promised the Brenner pass boundary to Orlando. . . . Perhaps he also thought that a concession in the

---

[33] Herre, 1927: p. 102.

[34] Seymour, 1928: **4:** p. 435. Actually, in the session of the Supreme War Council of November 4, 1918, Colonel House made no point or reservations when Orlando asked for a limitation of point nine of Wilson's fourteen points. In that same period he expressed himself toward the Italian ambassador in the United States, Conte Macchi di Cellere, to the effect that Italy would not experience any difficulties in regard to South Tyrol. In view of this position Colonel House's own consistency appears more than questionable.

Alps might mitigate Italian claims in the Adriatic; but the Italians wanted both!"[35]

The American position both on the prohibition of the Anschluss and on German South Tyrol took definite form at virtually the same time. While the former decision was especially pleasing to France and also to Great Britain, the latter was favorable to Italy. Yet Italy was hardly pacified by it and remained resentful of the American stand on Adriatic questions. Though the United States had thus contributed to thwarting German Austria both in the matter of the Anschluss and in German South Tyrol, she managed to earn and retain the good will of the great majority of Austria's population partly by various forms of economic assistance and partly by speaking softly and tending to shift the burden of unpleasant decisions onto France's shoulders.

After the peace treaty of St. Germain had been signed, Renner voiced Austria's gratitude to Great Britain and the United States for their impartiality during the peace negotiations, as contrasted with the attitude of France and Italy. Although the treaty had been harsh, he said, it had been mitigated by England and America to whom the new Austria now looked for friendship and assistance.[36] Even Otto Bauer expressed himself similarly in appreciation of the American and British attitude immediately after his resignation in July 1919.

---

[35]Stannard Baker, 1927: **2:** p. 146. The question arises whether Italy would ever have voluntarily abandoned the region south of the Brenner Pass. Most likely, an American protest would have produced no tangible results except the exacerbation of already tense Italo-American relations.

[36]*F.R.U.S., P.P.C.* **12:** 570-573, Halstead to Lansing, Sept. 15, 1919.

V. Austria's Neighbors on the Anschluss. The Position of the Second and Third Internationals

1. AUSTRIA'S SMALLER NEIGHBORS AND THE ANSCHLUSS

"Renner was an adherent of Mitteleuropa too long for me to trust him." Th. G. Masaryk

NOT only the Great Powers, but also Austria's smaller neighbors, such as Czechoslovakia, Hungary, Yugoslavia, and Switzerland, were much concerned about the Anschluss movement. Their present and future would be decisively affected by its success or failure. Their economic, political, cultural, and military situation would depend largely on whether little Austria or the formidable German colossus would be rubbing shoulders with them. The hopes and fears of their peoples found expression in the speeches of their political leaders, the editorials of their press, and the communications of their diplomats; all contributed in turn to influencing and shaping the policy of the Great Powers.

The strong pro-Anschluss sentiments uttered in the Weimar Constituent Assembly in early February, 1919, quickly reverberated throughout Europe. The first reaction was rather feeble. On the eve of the mid-February elections in Austria, *Le Matin* considered the battle against the Anschluss as good as lost. So did the president of Czechoslovakia, Th. G. Masaryk.[1] The only thing he felt the Peace Conference had still the power to do, and should do, was to balance the Anschluss of German Austria "with territorial compensations" along other frontiers. However, the Czechoslovaks soon grew more confident that the union between Austria and Germany might still be prevented.

The Czechs' immediate concern was to retain the occupied regions of German Bohemia and Moravia and have them confirmed in the peace treaty. They had also occupied Slovakia. Militarily challenged by Soviet Hungary, they became engaged in a bitter conflict with her in the course of which the Entente gave them diplomatic support. In the light

---

[1] *Prager Tagblatt*, morng. ed., Feb. 15, 1919.

of past historical ties and the circumstances under which their state was born, Czechs and Slovaks still considered Austria and Hungary their main enemies. They were resolved to defend the integrity of their new state, including the occupied regions, against Austrian and Hungarian claims and military moves. But in the long run, in President Masaryk's opinion, it was Germany which would be the real danger. In an interview with *Le Temps*, Masaryk warned: "France and Czechoslovakia are both threatened by Germanism which is once more raising its head. The Germans don't change; they don't consider themselves beaten."[2] And if Germany absorbed German Austria—which in turn continued loudly to demand the return of German Bohemia—Czechoslovakia's existence would be doubly threatened; with the lengthening of an already over-long frontier her geopolitical and strategic situation would become hopeless.

For some time during the war prominent Polish as well as Czechoslovak leaders had favored the Anschluss of the German provinces of Austria with the Reich. They had worked toward the dissolution of the Habsburg monarchy, since they considered that to be the *sine qua non* of the liberation of its numerous nationalities. To make the breakup alluring to all ethnic groups of the Dual Monarchy, including the German Austrians, they felt the need to hold out to them also the promise of "national liberation." But the Anschluss would be a consolation not only to the German Austrians but also to Germany herself since it would compensate her for anticipated territorial losses at the end of the war. Permitting the Anschluss of Inner German Austria to Germany thus seemed to some Polish and Czechoslovak leaders the key to the solution of the problems affecting Austria and Central Europe.

Early in 1917, Roman Dmowski, a leader of the Polish émigrés, circulated a memorandum concerning Poland's future to influential statesmen and political leaders of the Allies, in which he claimed East and West Prussia as well as Danzig. To compensate Germany for these losses he was prepared to let her take over the German provinces of Austria. This plan was designed primarily to further Polish national objectives, but also to destroy Prussian hegemony

---

[2]*Ibid.*, quote from *Le Temps*.

over Germany—a major objective of the Allies—by shifting the balance within the Reich to the South, to Catholicism, and to create a less warlike and less expansionist Germany. Similarly, shortly before the breakup of the Habsburg monarchy the Polish deputy Ignacy Daszyinski of Krakow told his German colleagues in the lower house of the Austrian Reichsrat that the time had come for the Germans of Austria as well as the other peoples to establish themselves on a national basis.[3]

During the war the Czechoslovak leaders also were by no means dead set against the Anschluss but, curiously, even assumed that it might be in the Czechoslovak interest. In a letter to William Martin, Beneš wrote:"In regard to German Austria we believe that it would be best for everybody if Austria became German immediately; for us, because the irredentism would be much less strong among our Germans versus Germany than versus Austria."[4] Obviously, these reasonings were dubious, and represented wishful thinking. But until 1917 Masaryk too was rather favorably disposed toward the Anschluss.[5]

During the war years Masaryk came out in favor of the dissolution of the Austro-Hungarian monarchy, frequently picturing the Habsburg empire as a tool, "a mere instrument" in the hands of Germany.[6] Another time, in his inaugural lecture at the School of Slavonic Studies of the University of London, he referred to Austria-Hungary deprecatingly as the "baggage-porter" of Germany.[7] Bismarck's policy toward Austria, according to Masaryk, had been shaped by Pan-German considerations. By "colonizing" Austria, following Lagarde's precept, Germany aspired to colonize the Balkans and to reach Constantinople and Baghdad.[8] Appealing to the anti-German sentiments of the warring Western Powers, Masaryk was intent on persuading them that the disintegration of the Habsburg empire would be a devastating

[3]*Sten. Protokoll d. Sitzungen d. Hauses d. Abgeordneten d.Öst. Reichsrates,* 1918: **4:** 12th sess.

[4]Beneš, "Notes de Guerre," Mss. Hoover War Library, Strong, 1939: pp. 169-170.

[5]Seton-Watson, 1943: p. 195; Macdonald, 1946: p. 83.

[6]Seton-Watson, 1943: p. 195.

[7]*Ibid.,* p. 152.

[8]*Ibid.,* pp. 120-121.

blow to Germany. "The lasting defeat of Germany will be the defeat of Austria-Hungary and the dismemberment of this artificial state. Every weakening of Austria is a weakening of Germany."[9] A year later he still insisted on the dismemberment of Austria-Hungary. "Any scheme for the preservation of Austria-Hungary is a direct form of 'travail pour le roi de Prusse.' "[10] Yet while Masaryk wished to weaken Prussia and Germany, he did not object to the Anschluss of the German Austrian territories. He tended to minimize the incorporation of even "10 million [sic] Germans." "Today Germany is disposing of 50 million of Austria's population," but after the liberation of the non-German and non-Magyar nations only 10 million would be left. Yet immediately thereafter he expressed the "wish and hope" that Bohemia's "Russian brethren will soon succeed in occupying the Bohemian and Slovak districts. This would be the best solution not merely for Bohemia, but also for the Austrian, German, and other questions at issue."

While promising constant "loyalty" to the Entente, Masaryk wanted Russia's military presence in Central Europe, at least temporarily, as a counterweight to Germany. Under such circumstances he apparently did not fear the Anschluss, Germany's projection into Austria, and Bohemia's further envelopment. Focusing his eyes upon the liberation of "Bohemia," Masaryk found it difficult to deny to German Austria the principle of self-determination which he claimed

---

[9]*Ibid.*, pp. 134 and 195.

[10]This position had not been that of eminent Czech leaders before 1914. The Czech historian and political leader Frantisek Palacký, in his famous letter to the Frankfurt National Assembly of April 11, 1848, spoke out against the union of the German areas of Austria with any emerging German state, since it would mean the destruction of the Austrian realm. Without this state construction, Slavs, Rumanians, Magyars and Germans would be unable to resist the "overpowering neighbor in the East." He concluded that if Austria did not exist, "one would have to hurry to create it in the interest of Europe and in the interest of humanity" (Palacký, 1866: p. 27). And Karel Kramař, leading spokesman of the Czechs, remarked in 1906 that under existing conditions the "preservation of Austria," admittedly of a "domestically better Austria," is the "vital interest of our people." Similarly, before 1914, Th. Masaryk himself criticized in the Austrian parliament the "dreams about the disintegration of Austria" as unrealistic and promised his cooperation in the reconstruction of the realm. This position was in line with that of other past and contemporary Czech leaders who merely wanted to reform Austria to gain equality, but did not aim at the breakup of the Monarchy. In accordance with this view, they also opposed the Anschluss of German Austria, which would have led to Austria's disintegration.

for his own people. Perhaps he was unable fully to envisage the postwar geopolitical situation of Central Europe and its full meaning for the newly liberated "Bohemian" state.

A year later in a "Memorandum on the Military Situation," which was circulated in London in April, 1916, Masaryk again contemplated the possibility of German Austria's becoming "in one way or another a member of the German empire" after the war. "In that case Germany would have at her disposal only 10 extra millions, whereas Austria, if only reduced but not dismembered, would strengthen Germany by two or three times as much." It would be naive to assume that postwar Austria would be inclined to go against Germany. Yet, "Catholic Austria, if included in Germany, would naturally weaken Prussia." It was apparently these considerations that seemed to reconcile Masaryk to the thought of a postwar Anschluss; also the thought that such a union would at least be better than the preservation of the Austro-Hungarian empire with its continued dependence on its German neighbor.[11] Beneš and Masaryk may also have hoped that a union of German Austria proper with Germany would force the remaining smaller nations of Central Europe to form a closer political and economic alliance. Propaganda maps used by the Czechs during the war showed the German provinces of Austria within the boundaries of a proposed postwar Germany.[12]

Later on, however, Beneš gave in to what apparently were Italian and French pressures. Italy opposed any sort of Danubian confederation as a mere camouflage for the restoration of the hated Austrian empire, and France opposed the Anschluss which would only add to Germany's strength. Czechoslovakia followed suit, thus pleasing both Italy and France. As Beneš put it: Czechoslovakia, having been "completely loyal to our friends in the war . . . , accepted their standpoint in this matter." It may of course be debated to what extent Czechoslovakia's apparent pro-

---

[11]Seton-Watson, 1943: pp. 197-198, also p. 202.
[12]O.S., Fasz. 5a, Apr. 17, 412. E. Beneš, 1934: pp. 28-30. Beneš was fully cognizant that the position of the Czech leaders in 1918-1919 was contradictory. He revealed as much in the Czechoslovak parliament in 1934 when he conceded that it might still cause "astonishment." According to him, however, the Czechoslovak leadership was "then already, just as today, aware of all the unfavorable consequences of the Anschluss."

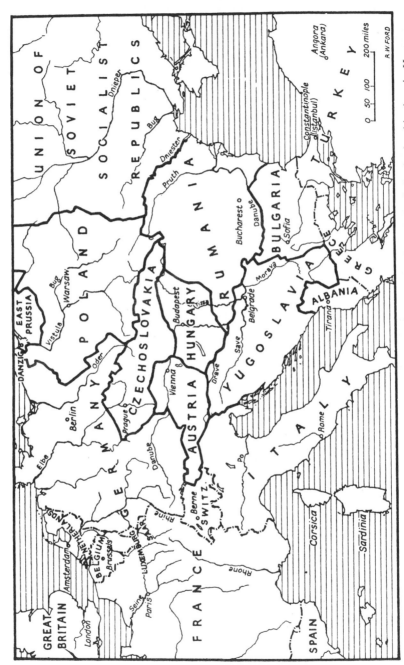

MAP 4. Central and eastern Europe after World War I, showing the succession states—Poland, Czechoslovakia, Austria, Hungary, Rumania, Yugoslavia—and their new frontiers.

Anschluss policy during the war was a matter of genuine conviction on Prague's part. It is more likely that the Anschluss was looked upon as an unavoidable evil accompanying the glorious birth of Czechoslovakia's national independence.

Late in December, 1918, just after his triumphal return to Prague, President Masaryk in a speech in the Hradčin laid down Czechoslovakia's program in regard to German Bohemia and her relations to German Austria and Germany.

> The territory inhabited by the Germans [of Bohemia] is our territory and remains ours. . . . We shall regulate our relations with Germany in accordance with whatever policy Germany pursues toward us. We shall behave correctly, and we want the defeat of Prussian militarism to become a victory for the German people; we want the German people to get accustomed to limiting itself to its own nationality, to renounce its desire for conquest and dedicate its strength and its capacities to the international organization of peoples and to humanity. There are nobler goals than Pan-Germanism.[13]

Masaryk made also a strong bid for a corridor linking Czechoslovakia and Yugoslavia, which was bound to separate Austria from Hungary, a project which was later shelved in Paris. He also pointed to the possible creation of a huge East Central European confederation. He agreed with Rumania and Yugoslavia on the desirability of an "intimate union." The Greeks also approved of this project. Once the Yugoslav-Italian dispute had been settled, "then the Pan-German Central Europe will be replaced by a *rapprochement* of the states from the Baltic to the Adriatic, a formation extending to Switzerland and France. It will form a strong barrier against imperialist Germany and at the same time be a defense for Russia." This confederation in East Central Europe was also to remain only a dream.

Masaryk admitted that the Germans of Bohemia and Moravia were in a "difficult position." "Unfortunately," in the past they had been too ready to support the Pan-German attacks on the Czechs, and even recently had been "intoxicated by illusory victories." The new Czechoslovakia was unwilling to "sacrifice our important Czech population to the

---

[13]*The New Europe*, Dec. 18, 1918.

so-called 'German' Bohemia." All national minorities were going to enjoy full rights, but Czechoslovakia would not permit any secession, just as during the Civil War the United States had not allowed the secession of the South.[14]

Turning then to German Austria, he averred that it was not his business to give advice to the German Austrians. But he reminded them that, "[as] a natural result of our long union, we have numerous economic relations with them." Masaryk made the improvement of relations clearly contingent on their renunciation of the restoration in any form of the Habsburg monarchy—"the German Austrians must abandon their desire for domination"—on their recognition of the *status quo,* meaning acknowledgment of the historic boundaries of Bohemia—"they must not meddle in our affairs"—and this time also on their renunciation of the *Anschluss*—they must "renounce their Pan-German plans."[15] Under these conditions, he declared, normal relations were possible, and Austria might maintain her "independence"

What Masaryk apparently meant by "normal relations" was the resumption of full economic exchange between the two countries, and particularly the export of coal, on which Austria was heavily dependent for her economic restoration. These closer economic relations, probably held out as bait for renunciation of the claims to German Bohemia, Moravia and the Anschluss, may still have been linked in Masaryk's mind, as they were in the mind of French policy-makers, with closer economic relations within the entire Danubian area, with the establishment of some sort of Danubian confederation. In the end the latter failed to come about, partly on account of Czech suspicion and resistance.

The huge East Central European and Danubian federation, at which President Masaryk hinted and of which German Austria might have been a part, never emerged. While France and Great Britain were prepared to sponsor it, Italy vehemently opposed it. The Austrian government and

[14]*Prager Tagblatt,* morng ed., Dec. 22, 1918. In an interview with a journalist from the *Corriere della Sera* Masaryk admitted the existence of a German majority in the occupied areas. He justified, however, the Czech claims with the statement that the government in Prague could not possibly tolerate German domination even over a fraction of the Czech people. (Also Kramar, Nov. 13, 1918, *Pester Lloyd,* ev. ed., Nov. 14, 1918).
[15]*The New Europe,* Dec. 18, 1918.

Dr. Bauer, in spite of occasional lip-service, wanted it to fail, to be carried *ad absurdum*. During the year 1919 the Czechs fought the concept of a confederation, but in the words of Beneš, "not a possible economic tie or any other modest link-up."[16] A similar plan was evolved by the Czechoslovak secretary for defense Klofáč in a talk with the Austrian plenipotentiary in Prague in December, 1919, a scheme which the latter found "most interesting." While Klofáč called it "United States of Central Europe," he stressed the full political independence and sovereignty of all member states. "The future of this league of states lies in the economic realm." Thus, even after the signing of the treaty of St. Germain, Czechoslovak policy was to steer German Austria away from Germany by establishing close economic ties with her. Masaryk at the same time assured the Austrian representative that it was "high time for us to come finally to an understanding of each other."[17]

The contradictions which characterized Czechoslovak policy in regard to the project of a Danubian or even the larger East Central European confederation were apparent: the Czechs realized the advantages of a larger economic realm in Central Europe and desired to play an important role in it. They wished to induce German Austria to become part of it and thus to prevent the potentially dangerous, if not immediately threatening Anschluss. On the other hand, they hesitated to surrender any bit of their prized sovereignty to a larger economic, not to mention political, unit.

French diplomats therefore, like the envoy Henri Allizé in Vienna, felt the need for making Prague understand her own interests. Once Czechoslovakia realized, Allizé wrote, that the Anschluss was not in her interest, she will be anxious to regulate amicably outstanding major questions between herself and the new Austria. Czechoslovakia must prevent the union which would result in the aggrandizement of Germany, encircling her on three sides.

It was perhaps strange that Prague showed greater hostility against Vienna than against Berlin, though historically it was

---

[16]Seton-Watson, 1943: p. 27, Aide Memoire on talk with Beneš, Oct. 30, 1919: "Beneš rejected completely the concept of a confederation."

[17]*O.S.*, K 821, Liasse Tschechoslowakei, I/II, 1919-1924, Dec. 13, 1919, 1: p. 7282.

understandable. The French envoy in Prague, Clément-Simon, wrote thus to Premier Millerand in the early postwar period,

> Blinded by the memory of the past, the Czechs continue to look upon Vienna as their principal enemy. They do not understand that present-day Austria is no longer dangerous, that it can't become so unless it joins the German Reich. In this case, the little Czechoslovak republic would be caught, as it were, in a vice.

According to him, the same vice gripped also Italy: "At this moment Italy, hypnotized by an imaginary peril — the Slav gnat — neglects to see the German eagle, a peril more distant perhaps, but unquestionably more real."[18] The knowledge of the source of past perils dulled their perception of the direction from which future danger might approach them. It led both countries, Czechoslovakia and Italy, to underestimate the peril from the Reich, at least for a certain period.

Utterances of leading Czechoslovak politicians early in 1919 about the Anschluss contained thus ambiguities and contradictions. Partly they seemed to believe that the union was inevitable and could no longer be halted. Partly they entertained the illusory hope that German Austria and Germany, in the event of their reunion and newly found happiness, might be more disposed to renounce German Bohemia. Masaryk was also quoted by L'Echo de Paris as saying that it was "preferable to see 9 million Germans enter into German unity than to see 25 million Slavs placed under the yoke of the Germans and Magyars."[19] Yet the Slavs were already free. Apparently Masaryk still assumed that Austrian independence was not feasible, and that the only real alternative to the Anschluss was the restoration of the Habsburg empire and with it German Austrian and German dominion over the Slavs of Central and Southeastern Europe.

The view seems to have persisted that German Austria was not capable of living by herself and that, without firmly leaning on Germany, she would become "the victim of every intrigue of the Old Austria." The Czechs were as opposed to a restoration of the Habsburg empire as was Italy, and

---

[18]*Ibid.*
[19]*L'Écho de Paris*, Feb. 17, 1919.

perhaps for more convincing reasons. They were deeply suspicious both of the black and yellow circles[20] and of the Reich. Thus there were times when Czechoslovak feelings about the Anschluss were rather mixed. But just as in Italy, fear of the specter of the Habsburg empire and its possible resurrection overshadowed Prague's fear of the new Germany and her territorial ambitions.

In conversation with Ackermann, the Bavarian envoy, Tusar, Czechoslovakia's envoy in Vienna, feigned indifference about the Anschluss of inner German Austria to Germany, but perhaps revealed his inner thoughts when he voiced his conviction that German Austria's economy could not be reconstructed without Czechoslovakia's help.[21] What he seemed to suggest was an economic *rapprochement* between Vienna and Prague which, incidentally, Dr. Bauer and Brockdorff-Rantzau had likewise favored in their Berlin meeting early in March, 1919. On February 18 *Corriere della Sera* reported a statement of Masaryk which pointed in the same direction and which the newspaper promptly interpreted as a "Czech proposal for federation," adding that the Anschluss would wedge in Czechoslovakia, and thus create for her an "uncomfortable and dangerous situation."[22]

On the whole, there is little doubt that the possibility of Austria's Anschluss caused increasing concern in Prague. But in 1919 the Czechoslovakian government was primarily engaged in keeping the recently occupied regions of German Bohemia and Slovakia under her control and warding off all foreign and domestic attempts to weaken Czech domination of the new state. Facing numerous dangers all along her frontiers, it found confidence in having recently surmounted all obstacles and in having trustworthy friends and allies in the Western Powers. Czechoslovakia thus tended at times to slight the danger that the Anschluss posed to her. In any case, relying on her own resources, she could not have prevented the union.

Czechoslovakia's fear of a plot directed against her newly won independence and integrity reached its apex in early

---

[20]*Voss. Zeitung,* June 29, 1919, K. Lahn, "Der Staat Masaryk's."
[21]*G.A.,* MA 103024, Öst. Friedensangebote und Umwälzung in Öst.-Ungarn, Tusar to Ackermann, Jan. 21, 1919.
[22]*Corriere della Sera,* Feb. 18, 1919.

March, 1919, after the return of Dr. Bauer from his journey to Weimar and Berlin. Czechoslovakia raised rather far-reaching accusations against German Austria as well as against Germany and Hungary, citing a vast conspiracy which was allegedly aimed at the forcible military occupation of the German regions of Bohemia and Moravia by German Austria and Germany and of Pressburg by the Magyars.[23] On March 10, *Ceske Slovo* repeated these accusations.[24] The persistence of German Austria in her claims to German Bohemia, Brockdorff-Rantzau's recent criticism of Czechoslovakia's policies toward her German minority in the Weimar Assembly, and the dispute with Hungary over Slovakia may well have made the Czechoslovaks jittery. On March 13, in an eleven-page *Note Verbale* the Austrian government countered these "grave accusations," and denied the charges completely. It actually reversed them, accusing Czechoslovak policy of being responsible for the rising dissatisfaction of the Germans in Czechoslovakia.[25]

The charges of actual military preparations by Germany and German Austria seemed to have lacked any substantive basis, but the activities of Karl Schwarz, German Vice Consul in Prague, were apparently highly improper. That the Czechs had a solid case against Schwarz is clearly indicated by Brockdorff-Rantzau's remark in his *Nachlass*.[26] But in the background loomed also the Anschluss issue. When in an interview with the correspondent of the *Vossische Zeitung* on March 16 Bauer was asked point-blank whether the "difficulties" which had arisen with Czechoslovakia were connected with the Anschluss, he denied it.[27] Nevertheless, this seemed to be a widespread view.

After centuries of subjugation the Czechs were resolved to establish an independent and economically and militarily viable state. On the winning side, they were to liberate all Czechs, though this meant including a substantial German minority with all its attendant risks. After initial hesitation

[23]*Ochrana*, Prague, quoted in *Ö.S.*, K826, Tschechosl., March 6, 1919.

[24]*Česke Slovo*, quoted in *Voss. Zeitung*, March 11, 1919.

[25]*O.S.*, K826, Note Verbale, Departement des Affaires Étrangères de l'Autriche Allemande, March 13, 1919, I-2151/1. See also *Le Temps*, March 11, 1919. Its correspondent took the Czech accusations at face value. Colonel Cunninghame in Vienna thought the charges baseless and concocted.

[26]*A.A.*, Nachlass Br.-R.'s, Öst. Anschlussfrage, H 234605; see als *Arbeiter-Zeitung*, "Deutschösterreich u.d. Tschechoslowakei," March 11.

[27]*Voss. Zeitung*, March 17.

and vacillations, they came to feel hostile toward the Anschluss of Inner German Austria with Germany. In view of German Austria's claims to her former co-citizens now living in Czechoslovak-occupied territory as well as Czechoslovakia's precarious geopolitical and military situation, the Anschluss was looked upon as a potential danger to the new state.

All of Austria's neighbors, whether a new state like Czechoslovakia, an old one like Switzerland, or a substantially enlarged one like Yugoslavia, were bound to be concerned about the possible projection into the heart of Central Europe of the still powerful German Reich with its huge industrial potential, its skilled population, and its far-reaching aspirations and ambitions.

On November 23 *La Tribune de Génève* published an article by Marcel Rouff in which he pointed to the recent correspondence between Dr. Bauer and the German people's commissar Hugo Haase, and suggested that the Entente counter the attempt to unify German Austria with either Germany or Bavaria by insisting on the surrender of certain German border regions to neighboring states.[28] The correspondence, in Rouff's view, proved "the persistence of imperialist tendencies in the new German government," and recalled the phrase often cited and pronounced in Rome in September, 1914, by a leading German diplomat: "We shall win the war, even if we do not win it; we shall gain in any case, since we shall annex the 9 million Germans of Austria!"[29] *La Nation* of Geneva printed the same story the following day.[30] There could be little doubt about the hostility of these papers to the concept of the union between German Austria and the Reich.

Early in February of 1919 the Swiss press devoted a number of articles to the Anschluss; according to Haupt, Austria's envoy in Switzerland, they all emanated from Paris or were inspired by the Austrian opponents of the union.[31] Both the *Gazette de Lausanne* and *La Tribune de Génève* came out against the Anschluss with dire warnings.[32] The latter journal expressed the opinion that, however the question of the An-

---

[28]*La Tribune de Génève,* Nov. 23, 1918.

[29]*Ibid.*

[30]*La Nation,* Nov. 24, 1918.

[31]*O.S.,* K 109, Anschluss, Z I-1488, Haupt, Feb. 5.

[32]*Gazette de Lausanne, La Tribune de Génève,* both Feb. 1, 1919; also *Journal de Génève,* Feb. 18, 1919.

schluss was decided, the right to self-determination of the peoples should not be permitted to become a tool in the hands of Germany for the purpose of resuming her ambitious plans of conquest. It must not happen that Germany, in the name of this great ideal of national freedom, be enabled to resume domination over her liberated slaves within the next twenty years. *Journal de Génève* warned that the union of Austria with Germany "will be an event of major concern for Europe." That Germany was on her way of achieving the unification of the German race was a matter "which must alarm us Swiss." Germany then will "perhaps not halt at our frontier." One day German claims "may menace even the equilibrium of our domestic life." It was perhaps still time to hinder the union.

In view of her multinational character and especially her large German element, Switzerland feared that her very existence was threatened by the same linguistic and cultural arguments which were advanced by German Austria in behalf of the Anschluss and approved by Germany. In the event of Anschluss, Switzerland would have a longer boundary with Germany and would be more exposed and vulnerable. In addition, the German unification movement next to her borders, growing by leaps and bounds and gaining an irresistible momentum, was bound to have a disturbing impact upon segments of its own German-speaking population and might give rise to fears among its non-German elements and regions.

On February 16 the British ambassador in Berne, Sir H. Rumbold, recorded "Swiss anxiety" on the subject of the Anschluss, as expressed to him by the Swiss minister for foreign affairs himself. If the union became a reality, both Switzerland and Czechoslovakia would have an extended boundary line with Germany and would be "almost surrounded" by her.[32a] Sir Eyre Crowe of the British Foreign Office interpreted Swiss "anxiety" as an indication of their desire to participate in the peace settlement.[33] In view of Switzerland's neutrality during the war, he opposed its participation, though others in the British Foreign Office took a broader view: "The point for us,"[34] Sir Headlam Morley

---

[32a]*P.R.*, F.O. 608, v. 27, Rumbold, Feb. 16.
[33]*Ibid.*, Eyre Crowe.
[34]*Ibid.*, H. Morley.

wrote, "is to consider not merely what the Swiss want, but what is in the general interests of Europe." If it were agreed that a neutral Switzerland, comprising three nationalities, was desirable, it was then "surely necessary to give serious considerations to warnings which may come from Switzerland that certain changes contemplated on the map of Europe would in their opinion seriously compromise their future."[35]

Swiss opposition to the Anschluss remained steadfast. On March 21, 1919, the British Embassy in Berne reported to the Foreign Office that members of the Swiss government "are losing no opportunity to emphasize how undesirable" the Anschluss of German Austria with Germany would be for their country. In a situation in some respects comparable to the new Czechoslovak state, Switzerland was especially interested in extending recognition to the new Czech government and in establishing relations with it, provided Prague would take the initiative. The English favored direct contact between the two states and seemed to encourage their joint opposition to the Anschluss. On April 15, Lord Acton sent a telegram to the British Foreign Office to the effect that no formal diplomatic conversations regarding the union of German Austria with Germany had yet taken place between Berne and Prague, though the Swiss government "felt strongly on the question [of Anschluss], if only for the reason that they do not desire extension of the German line of frontier."[36] More than a year later, in October, 1920, a known member of the Nationalrat in Zürich assured Zeidler of the Austrian Embassy in Berne that the Swiss leaned toward the French point of view of prohibiting the Anschluss, a point of view "which we, in a manner, really have appropriated, for under no condition do we wish to be encircled by Grossdeutschland."[37]

When the Austrian Anschluss project failed to materialize in November of 1918, German Austria faced not only threats along her borders from Yugoslavia, Czechoslovakia, and Italy, but also the internal threat of simple disintegration. The pitiful German residue of the once powerful Austro-Hungarian empire was itself on the point of breaking up under the pressure of strong separatist movements in Salzburg,

---

[35]*Ibid.*

[36]*Ibid.*, Lord Acton, Berne, to F.O., Apr. 15.

[37]*O.S.*, K 110, Zeidler to F.O., Oct. 7, 1920. p. 723.

Tyrol, and Vorarlberg and Slovene claims in Styria and Carinthia. Vorarlberg gravitated toward Switzerland. A plebiscite about the future of this former imperial crown land was held in Vorarlberg on the first Sunday of May, 1919. An overwhelming majority, almost 81 percent, voted for the union of Vorarlberg with the Swiss confederation. On their part, however, the Swiss had made no binding promises.

On April 14, Lord Acton reported to the British Foreign Office that the Swiss government, according to information furnished him by the Swiss minister for foreign affairs, would first consult the Peace Conference before deliberating on the desirability of admitting Vorarlberg to the Confederation. Personally, the Swiss foreign minister "would prefer an independent German Austria, but it may be necessary to assent to the wish of Vorarlberg as an alternative to the latter's union with Germany." Some people in Vorarlberg had suggested an incorporation into Württemberg or Bavaria,[38] if entrance into the German federation as a unit was not feasible. As far as Switzerland was concerned, she only considered Vorarlberg's Anschluss with herself, because the alternative, an Anschluss with Germany, seemed to constitute a clear threat to her.

Not only was the Swiss government opposed to the Anschluss of German Austria in her entirety with Germany, but also to the union of some of the individual Austrian crown lands with the German Reich. This applied not only to Vorarlberg, but also to Tyrol. On May 8 Lord Acton reported that the Swiss foreign minister had informed the French representative in Berne that the federal government "would view with dismay the union of North Tyrol with Germany."[39] Any strengthening of Germany was likely to add to Swiss discomfort and deepen the concern for their security. "There is no doubt," wrote Akers Douglas in a memorandum for the British government on April 25, 1919, that the Swiss "view with anxiety the union [of Vorarlberg] with Germany and the consequent extension of the embrace of the German frontier."[40]

---

[38]*P.R.,* F.O. 608, v. 27, Lord Acton, Apr. 14; also *Frankfurter Zeitung,* first morning ed., April 13.

[39]*P.R.,* F.O. 608, v. 27, Acton to F.O., May 8.

[40]*Ibid.,* Douglas, Apr. 25.

Swiss opinion was actually divided about the possibility of the union of Vorarlberg with Switzerland, which, in combination with extraneous factors, including Allied wishes, accounts for Vorarlberg's ultimately remaining with Austria. Many people in Switzerland had hoped that the link-up of rural and conservative Vorarlberg would, under the political circumstances existing in 1919, "form a counterpoise to the Bolshevik element in Switzerland."[41] On the other hand, the Swiss government was wary of opposition in the French cantons of Switzerland to the addition of a German-speaking province.[42] It also feared that Italy might raise the question of compensation, claiming Italian-inhabited cantons of Switzerland.[43] While the Swiss foreign minister was in favor of the "annexation" of Vorarlberg, the president of the Swiss Republic opposed it.[44]

Apart from Vorarlberg, in the immediate postwar period Switzerland and German Austria had no territorial differences, as they had had none before. If the union of Vorarlberg with Switzerland had taken place, it would have had all the earmarks of a voluntary change of sovereignty: one in accordance with the principles of self-determination. Nor could Austria have objected to it on the ground that a segment of the German Austrian population was passing under control of an alien nationality.

However, Austria's situation in regard to Czechoslovakia and Yugoslavia was entirely different. Austro-Yugoslav diplomatic quarrels over Carinthia and parts of Styria and military clashes were the order of the day in 1918 and 1919, and the threat of war hung continuously over the area. For a time the project of a Czech-Yugoslav corridor added to the hostility of both German Austria and Hungary toward Czechoslovakia and Yugoslavia. German Austria and Hungary, and Italy too, feared Slavic preponderance in Central Europe, which would be increased by the joining of the Slavs of Central Europe with the Slavs of the Adriatic.

Yugoslavia, in turn, became most concerned about the possibility of the absorption of Austria by Germany and of a Ger-

[41]*Ibid.*, Acton to F.O., May 14.
[42]*Ibid.*, Acton to F.O., June 15.
[43]*Ibid.*, Douglas, Apr. 25.
[44]*Ibid.*, June 15.

man projection into Central Europe—which would make Germany her neighbor. While Italy for a time seemed to be strangely indifferent and even favorably disposed to the Anschluss, Yugoslavia, following her own national self-interests as well as French policy, was opposed to Austria's union with Germany.

On May 5, Lord Acton notified the Foreign Office of Yugoslavia's new policy. His Serbian colleague had informed him that he had received instructions to collaborate with the Swiss government.[45] Both governments were equally interested in a rapprochement with German Austria and in resistance to the project of the latter's union with Germany. The Serbian minister had also informed him that "the newly accredited Serbian representative in Vienna has been authorized to make propaganda for the purpose of opposing the scheme of union." The Anschluss of German Austria would make Germany a direct neighbor and permit her to approach dangerously close to the Adriatic and the new Yugoslav outlets onto it. Preoccupied with the threat which Italy posed to her, Yugoslavia did not wish to face, in addition, the potential threat of Germany. From the Yugoslav point of view, German Austria, in spite of the Austro-Yugoslav clashes over Carinthia and Styria, was preferable as a neighbor to a great power such as Germany, which would bear down heavily upon the enlarged but not yet integrated South Slavic state.

Switzerland was, as mentioned, interested in establishing diplomatic ties with Czechoslovakia, largely for the reason of making their common opposition to the Anschluss more effective. The Yugoslavs may have learned of these endeavors via Prague and wished to turn the bilateral understanding into a "Triple Alliance." These diplomatic maneuverings highlight the anxieties which the Anschluss movement produced among Germany's and German Austria's neighbors.

Both France and Great Britain were keenly aware of the concern of her Central and Southeastern European friends over the union of Austria with Germany. The Earl of Curzon believed that the Anschluss would "have a direct and unfor-

[45]*Ibid.*, Acton, May 5. Pehler, "Schweiz und die Anschlussfrage," Kleinwaechter u. Paller, 1930: p. 183f., has very little to offer and nothing on the situation in 1918-1919.

tunate effect upon the position of the new states of Czechoslovakia and Yugoslavia, whom His Majesty's Government are morally bound to support."[46]

Yugoslavia's negative attitude toward the Anschluss continued in the postwar period for largely the same political, ethnic and geopolitical reasons which had determined her position in 1918-1919. The Slovenian newspaper *Slovenski Narod* insisted that the Anschluss would be equivalent to "a flood of 80 million Germans inundating the Karawanken" and that via Yugoslavia a German road would be hewn toward the Middle East and even beyond it. Thus "the retreat for a millennium before the Germans would end tragically."[47] Yugoslavia should never consent to the borders of Grossdeutschland reaching so far south.[48] The newspaper *Jutro*, also of Laibach, warned similarly that it was

> quite enough for us [Yugoslavs] to have one Great Power as neighbor, Italy. Austria in the north forms a protective wall against Germany and is for us much more reassuring than Grossdeutschland alone . . . Germany would not only strive across Slovenia to the Adriatic Sea but also would support the Hungarian aspirations aiming at Belgrade. This would be a restored Austria-Hungary with all its evil consequences. Our *ceterum censeo* is therefore not to permit Germany to enter Austria.[49]

Since the Compromise of 1867, the Magyars had been co-rulers with the German Austrians in the Dual Monarchy. But in 1918 they had cut loose from the Habsburg monarchy. Entrusting their ship of state to the waves from the West, they entertained the vain hope of being therefore spared national humiliation and territorial losses. But their harsh treatment by the Entente in combination with their unrealistic expectations had catapulted radicalism, nourished by defeat and disintegration, into the seat of power.

On the eve of the Bolshevik seizure of power in Hungary the Austrian ambassador in Budapest, Cnobloch, reported at length about an interview with Count Csáky, the "most im-

[46]Woodward and Butler, 1946: **1,** F.O. to Treasury, July 9, 1919.
[47]*O.S., Slovenski Narod,* Nov. 1924, pp. 607-608.
[48]*Ibid., Slovenski Narod,* Jan. 25, 1925, pp. 646-647.
[49]*Ibid., Jutro* (also Laibach), Jan. 30, 1925, p. 644.

portant personality in the [Hungarian] Foreign Office," who made far-reaching propositions to Vienna to create a Berlin-Vienna-Budapest alliance against Prague for the avowed purpose of wresting Slovakia from Czechoslovakia; he claimed Entente approval, at least lack of opposition to any military move by Budapest. To Austria he held out the chance of "liberating the German areas of Bohemia and Moravia," but he did not conceal that Austria's endeavors aiming at the Anschluss "disturbed" his concept in a most important point. Count Csáky held that Austria in her own interest should presently not insist on the Anschluss, since this would only worsen Austria's and Germany's situation at the Peace Conference.[50]

The emergence of a Soviet Hungarian republic radically altered the political situation of Central Europe. The push of Communism into Central Europe not only threatened countries in East Central Europe such as Rumania, Czechoslovakia, and Poland, but also posed the question of the extent of the westward expansion of Bolshevism. During the spring and summer of 1919 Soviet Hungary made desperate efforts to broaden her base not only by waging war against Czechoslovakia and Rumania over Slovakia and Transylvania respectively, but also by linking forces with the radical Austrian labor movement. Communist followers in Austria opposed the Anschluss with the Germany of Noske and Scheidemann and propagated union with Soviet Hungary.[51] The voices for union with Hungary among a small Austrian minority were not muted until the Soviet Hungarian regime collapsed on August 1; it did so because of its own contradictions and the military blows of the Rumanians who occupied the Hungarian capital. During the 133 days of its existence the Soviet Hungarian regime had vainly attempted to woo Vienna. It had run into firm opposition of the democratic leadership of Austrian socialism.

Thus failed the attempt to create a Danubian confederation under Soviet Hungarian and Russian auspices. Of the various plans competing with the Anschluss project it was, given the power relations in the area, the one which held out the least prospects for success.

[50]O.S., K 880, Cnobloch, Budapest, to Bauer, Feb. 24, 1919, pp. 11-14.
[51]Ibid., May 11, 1919, p. 129.

While Red Budapest had worked toward an Anschluss with Vienna, Vienna had been anxious for an Anschluss with Berlin.[52] But Berlin had never lavished its attentions on Vienna, since it was always fearful of the Entente's angry reaction. The Western Powers, of course, were as much opposed to Austria's union with the "East" as with the "West," Budapest or Berlin.

Thus neither under Count Károly's democratic leadership, which lasted until March, 1919, nor under the Soviet regime thereafter was Hungary in favor of the Anschluss of Austria with Germany. Beset on all boundaries by hostile neighbors who had wrested from her territories inhabited by Slovaks, Rumanians, South Slavs, and Hungarian minorities, Soviet Hungary had set her eyes upon extending the communist base into Austria. Thus she considered the Austrian Anschluss movement a rival. Some in Hungary may have looked upon Germany, a potentially revisionist power, as a future ally. Others feared Germany's embrace and Hungary's subsequent dependence. Count Bethlen voiced later the fear that the loss of West Hungary (Burgenland) in the Treaty of Trianon would become permanent in the event of the Anschluss, that it would "merely serve to aggrandize the future Germany with a portion of Hungary."[53] Also, the German minority in Hungary, scattered as it was, would likely cause Budapest anxiety in case the Anschluss became reality.

Hungary's opposition to the Anschluss and the following anti-union arguments, which an Austrian ambassador and a leading Hungarian newspaper listed in 1922, were equally valid in the immediate post-war period 1918-1919. The ambassador wrote: "Hungary, in my opinion — excepting certain revanchists — is by no means sympathetic toward the Anschluss." "Emotionally it appears to me that the great majority in Hungary looks upon the concept of fusion of the two German states with uneasiness and a certain anxiety. The notion of being a direct neighbor to a highly developed state produces understandably a nightmarish impression upon a completely landlocked seven-million people."[54] At about the same time the newspaper *Magyarsag*, though anticipating that

---

[52]Low, 1970: p. 62.
[53]*O.S.*, K 110, p. 329.
[54]*Ibid.*, p. 305.

France would lose her predominance and Germany regain a Great Power position, seemed assured as long as Austria stood "between us and Germany."

> What will happen if we border an ethnically completely homogeneous, powerful Germany of 70 million? And what will happen if Germany—spurning past lessons—enters again the road of ruthless imperialism crushing everything beneath it? The Anschluss of Austria with Germany conceals dangers for all nations in the Danubian valley and therefore also for the Magyars.[55]

Not a direct neighbor of German Austria, Rumania's interests in the Anschluss were much more limited than those of the states which had a common boundary with Austria. But as a beneficiary of the peace treaties and linked with France and later her partners in the Little Entente, Rumania already in 1918 could be expected to align herself with France on the Anschluss issue. Other considerations pointed in the same direction. Rumania had a large German minority in Transylvania which might become uneasy by Germany's thrust into German Austria and the growing proximity of the Reich to this new Rumanian province. Rumania's Magyar neighbor was likely to draw strength from an adjacent Germany in his revisionist demands. As an article in the Rumanian journal *Adevarul* several years later put it, the Anschluss would produce a "counter-effect . . . upon Hungary since she would be drawn into Germany's orbit and would rise more menacingly" against Rumania.[56]

After the November Revolution in Central Europe some Rumanians were fearful of a Habsburg restoration in Austria which would threaten the integrity of all the new succession states, including Rumania. As the Austrian envoy in 1921 wrote from Bukharest: "Then in 1918-1919, of course, one was *feu et flamme* for our Anschluss." But when the danger of restoration receded, Rumanians rather preferred that Germany, recent enemy during World War I, remain at a safe distance from Rumania's borders and liked to have German Austria as a buffer between Germany and Hungary, Rumania's direct neighbor. Then one preferred that Austria was, as a pro-union Austrian envoy put it, a "res nullius, a

---

[55]*Ibid.*, p. 318 (*Magyarsag,* June 27, 1922).
[56]*Ibid.*, 848-849 (*Adevarul,* Bucharest, July 16, 1925).

no-man's land where everybody may do what he pleases."[57] The writer went on denouncing Rumania's anti-Anschluss position and criticized demarches lodged at the Ballhausplatz against the Anschluss as "chauvinistic."

While Rumania was neither the neighbor of German Austria nor of Germany, the newly restored Poland had of course a common boundary with Germany. Of all her neighbors, Poland's territorial ambitions in the west clashed most with Germany's interests and were most deeply resented by all parties in Weimar Germany. Concerned with the defense of her new borders and with preserving her integrity, Poland was in league with France and the West and opposed any strengthening of the German neighbor, such as would have resulted from the Anschluss. In the mid-twenties Roman Dmovsky, the National Democratic party chief, was admittedly to repeat his wartime proposal that, in exchange for the Anschluss of Austria, Germany surrender East Prussia to Poland.[58] But the suggestion was as unrealistic as German nationalistic claims for a far-reaching revision of the Versailles Treaty in regard to the German-Polish frontier. Like France, Poland in 1918-1919 was determined on the reduction of the German power potential, not on strenghtening it in any way.

The account of the Austrian ambassador from Warsaw in February, 1925, was thus also true for the immediate postwar period. He reported that in the eyes of Polish politicians, an Anschluss of Austria with Germany would only underline "German danger, increase the fear of the threat to Poland's western boundaries, and prompt Poland to ask for compensation at Germany's expense." The Anschluss furthermore would cut off Poland's connection with the South and the Mediterranean. Poland, however, would favor an economic Danubian confederation provided the dominance of Czechoslovakia could be avoided, and then would even consider joining the confederation. Leaning on a "powerful" economic structure such as the Danubian confederation would offer Poland a "valuable protection against Germany and Russia, and would contribute to a lasting pacification and stabilization" of the situation in Central Europe.[59]

---

[57]*Ibid.*, p. 329, Storck, Budapest, May 26, 1921.

[58]*Ibid.*, p. 682.

[59]*Ibid.*, pp. 681-682, Austrian Embassy, Warsaw, to F.O., Feb. 25, 1925.

2. THE SECOND INTERNATIONAL AND THE CONGRESS AT BERNE

"The Socialism of Marx and the diplomacy of Bismarck work together for the Pan-Germanization of Europe." Bakunin

THOUGH internationalism and the fraternal community of European Socialism had been early war victims, the hope was rising among Socialists that the end of the war would see a rebirth of the Socialist International and of the old prewar comradeship, together with a retreat of nationalism. This hope was especially strong among the defeated Germans whose national interests demanded the political victory of Socialist, radical, and anti-nationalist parties in the countries of the Entente. The Socialist parties of the West were likely to have a decisive influence on the writing of the peace treaties and the future of vanquished Central Europe, and with it on the development of German and Austrian Socialism. The thoughts of Western Socialist leaders on a just peace treaty with Germany and Austria and on the Anschluss in particular were therefore of far-reaching importance.

During the last days of the war German and Austrian Social-Democratic leaders were already appealing for help to the leaders of the great Socialist parties of Western Europe. In its editorial of October 29, the Berlin *Vorwärts* urged that an "immediate call" be issued "for a congress of the International."[1] On November 2 Philip Scheideman, prominent wartime leader of the dominant patriotic wing of the Social Democrats, wrote a first-page editorial in *Vorwärts*, "Friede und die Internationale," in which he proclaimed that "Germany and the German Social Democrats are now agreed

---

[1]*Vorwärts*, Oct. 29, 1918.

about the self-determination of our border nationalities."[2]
The fate of the world now depended on the action of the Entente Socialists, since "a new world war" would be inevitable if the future peace were not based on democratic justice, but represented instead a victory for imperialism. On December 22 *Vorwärts*, referring to the impending gathering of the International Socialist Conference in Lausanne on January 6, warned: "To save Germany from the ruin which threatens her through a peace based on force means to save the entire world, to save Socialism."

From the Austrian side Dr. Bauer, secretary for foreign affairs of the new German Austrian republic, pressed for a just peace and the Anschluss. Wary of the opposition which he might encouter in the West, he tried to prepare the ground for the Anschluss by influencing the prominent Socialist leaders and liberal public opinion in the countries of the victorious Entente. The Austrian republic was only eight days old and Dr. Bauer himself had functioned as foreign secretary for the same length of time, when he appealed to the noted English labor leader Arthur Henderson on November 20, 1918, with an urgent request for food, coal, and raw materials. At the same time he expounded his views on the future Central Europe, trying to make converts:

> I beg you first to use your influence to see that the old Austro-Hungarian monarchy does not reemerge in any form and that the Habsburg dynasty is not forced upon German Austria again under any pretext. We have proof that certain circles of the Entente, especially in France, are thinking of such a restoration. Here in Roman Catholic reactionary circles there is still a strong following, which is held down today by the might of the working class but which is holding itself ready. A further danger exists in the intentions of the Czechoslovak state to annex German Bohemia. . . . I also beg you to influence our brotherly parties in America, France, and Italy to the effect that the resistance against the union of German Austria with the German Reich be broken down.[3]

---

[2]*Ibid.*, Nov. 2, Scheidemann, "Friede u.d. Internationale."

[3]*O.S.*, K261, Nachlass Bauer, I Deutschland (Anschl.), Bauer to Henderson, Nov. 20, 1918, 95f.-Henderson had entered the war cabinet of Lloyd George late in 1916, but resigned from it in August, 1917, when he developed a new labor policy on war aims.

Bauer continued by saying that German Austria had always been a part of the German Reich. The fear that the power of Germany might be unduly strengthened was unjustified. Aside from the circumstance that imperialist Germany was "dead today" and would never rise again, the union of both countries would strengthen not Prussia, but rather the democratic forces of southern Germany.

Several weeks later, on January 9, Bauer penned two similar letters to two leading French socialists, Albert Thomas and Jean Longuet. In each case the letter was carefully and diplomatically adapted to its recipient. In the letter to Thomas, Bauer reminded the right-wing Social Democrat that Austrian Socialism and Bauer himself had succeeded in reversing the party's course from a policy which, at the beginning of the war, had strongly supported German imperialism, to one sharply opposing all plans of conquest. "We have thus come so close to the political conceptions of our comrades in France that I may perhaps voice the hope that the old friendly relations between the French and German Austrian parties can soon be resumed."[4]

Toward Longuet, who belonged to the then dominant Left in the French party, Bauer felt that he had to defend the existence of a coalition regime in Austria, "dangerous" as this might be, "especially in revolutionary times," Then he turned to the theme of "union with Germany." Longuet, the grandson of Karl Marx, was reminded that "German Social Democracy, as far back as Marx and Engels, has always supported" this idea.

> The concept of the Danubian federation, which is juxtaposed to the program of German unity, today fully serves imperialist purposes. In the past German imperialism considered the existence of Austria essential to its survival—that is to say, the 10 million Germans in Austria enabled it to subject 40 million Slavs and Magyars to German command. Today French imperialism sees the restoration of Austria, under the title "Danubian Confederation," as a means not only of preventing

---

[4]*Ibid.* Bauer to A. Thomas, Jan. 9, 1919, pp. 90-93. During the war, Thomas became minister of munitions, thus binding the Socialist party closely to the war policy of the French government. But in 1917 the Socialists rejoined the opposition.

the Anschluss of 10 million Germans, but also of forcing these 10 million Germans into a Slavic coalition against Germany.

Apparently wishing to assure Longuet of his "leftist" orientation and his opposition to any kind of imperialism or expansionism, Bauer mentioned his "most intimate understanding with Fritz Adler"; Friedrich Adler was the son of the noted Socialist leader Victor Adler and since the assassination of the Austrian minister — President Stürkgh, and his trial, a hero to revolutionaries at home and abroad. Bauer also reminded Longuet that after his return from Russian imprisonment he had played a not unimportant role "in pushing the party to the left."[5] These propagandistic efforts in behalf of the Austrian Social Democratic Party and the Anschluss fell on fertile soil as far as Longuet was conerned. In several articles in the French Socialist press, Longuet's was one of the few voices raised loudly in behalf of the cause of union with the Reich.

On February 3, 1919, the Congress of the Second or Socialist International opened in Berne. While at the outbreak of war in 1914 the waves of nationalism had virtually swept away international Socialism, at the war's end its future appeared bright. In most European countries the Socialist position was stronger than ever; it was hoped that it would outweigh the chauvinistic and vengeful tendencies of the victors. The English labor leader Arthur Henderson voiced his belief in Berne that the conference would exercise "a decisive influence" upon the course of the Peace Conference. Yet in order to succeed, there would have to be agreement among the proletariat. "Mr. Clémenceau is not all-powerful. Wilson and Lloyd George thought differently from him." Lloyd George had pledged Henderson that a delegation of the Socialist Congress in Berne would in due time be heard by the Peace Conference.[6]

Altogether, about eighty delegates from twenty-one countries converged upon Berne.[7] Arthur Henderson and the German Austrian Socialist leader Karl Seitz were elected

---

[5]*Ibid.*, Bauer to Longuet, Jan. 9, 1919, pp. 91-92.
    [6]*Ibid.*, correspondence between Bauer and Henderson, pp. 95f.; see also *ibid.*, K 762, Haupt to Bauer, Feb. 19, 1919, pp. 461-469, and Feb. 20, pp. 496-503.
    [7]*Vorwärts*, Feb. 1, 1919.

chairman of the conference and the Swedish Social Democrat Hjalmar Branting became its president. In his opening speech Branting came out against annexationism and demanded the right to national self-determination both for the victors and the vanquished. Yet the convention was actually only a rump conference; important detachments of the international army of Socialism stayed away from Berne.[8] Belgian, American, and Swiss Socialists refused to take part, the first two from patriotic motives, the last because they charged that the Berne Conference was a meeting of "Social-Patriots" only and not in accord with the radical class-war concepts of the earlier Zimmerwald Conference. The war had stirred up hostilities and passions, and even now many a bitter exchange of words took place. Karl Kautsky and Kurt Eisner freely stressed the guilt of German militarism, and insisted that the comrades of the majority Social Democratic party admit that they had been deceived by the German government; mistrust against the German people would then vanish.[9] French and German delegates clashed with each other, and so did Czechs and German Austrians.[10] Many who were disposed to be friendly to their German comrades seemed to doubt their own influence upon the Paris Peace Conference and warned them to "prepare themselves for the worst."[11]

On the twenty-first of February the Austrian ambassador in Switzerland, Baron von Haupt, reported to Dr. Bauer on "utterances of Entente Socialists about our Anschluss with Germany." Haupt had obtained the following detailed information from a confidential source. The English labor leader Ramsey MacDonald had come out for the Anschluss "without qualification," declaring that French resistance would be overcome. Mrs. Snowden took the same position. Norman Angell, the well-known English pacifist, "explained to me public opinion in England concerning the Anschluss which resulted from the tremendous propaganda waged against the old Danubian monarchy during the war." "Their dislike of an aggrandizement of Germany was incomparably smaller than their repugnance against ethnic mixture."

---

[8]*Arbeiter-Zeitung,* Feb. 5, 1919.
[9]*Ibid.,* Feb. 6.
[10]*Frankfurter Zeitung,* first morning ed., Feb. 15.
[11]*Ibid.*

The French Socialists were seemingly torn between recogition of the principle of the right to national self-determination and the fear of an aggrandized, potentially more powerful Germany. Albert Thomas—to whom Dr. Bauer had vainly, as it turned out, appealed early in January—came out paying his respects to the popular will, but he regretted unreservedly German Austria's desire to link up with the Great German republic. German Austria should not be surprised if she is treated the same way as Germany." Renaudel, another right-wing French Socialist, expressed similar thoughts. His fellow-countryman Jean Longuet, however, spoke out "incomparably clearer for the Anschluss." But the writer Marc Henry, an opponent of the union, sharply condemned the passivity of the French Cabinet in the Anschluss question and voiced the hope that perhaps "at the last minute they will decide to influence public opinion against it." [12]

Not only Dr. Bauer but also Brockdorff-Rantzau paid close attention to the proceedings of the congress of the Second International in Berne, Bauer largely in the context of the Anschluss issue, Brockdorff-Rantzau more on other grounds.

Henderson, according to Professor Schücking who at Berlin's suggestion attended the conference, pointed out that the Entente still did not know whether the new Germany was repudiating the old imperial policies. He referred to his queries to Ebert of last October when the majority Socialists had refused to admit that Germany bore a heavy guilt in violating Belgian neutrality. Even Bethmann-Hollweg had from the very beginning conceded that Germany was at fault.

Why could this not be dealt with now . . . one would have to know whether the German people had yielded only grudgingly, since it could not do anything else, or whether it has genuinely renounced the policy of violence. Only in the latter case will the English working class bring about a rap-

---

[12]*O.S.*, K 261, Baupt to Bauer, Feb. 21. Not only Dr. Bauer but also Brockdorff-Rantzau paid close attention to the proceedings of the congress of the Second International in Berne (*A.A.*, Nachlass Br.-R.'s, Presseangelegenheiten 7/1, Dr. Guttmann to Br.-R. H 233897), Bauer largely in the context of the Anschluss issue, Brockdorff-Rantzau more on other grounds. The German foreign minister was kept informed of the proceedings by a Dr. Guttmann and the noted Professor Schücking.

prochement toward the German proletariat and be able to make its influence felt. . . .

Henderson made the point that it was "not enough for Ger-many to have the Independent leader Hugo Haase make an admission of guilt for the outbreak of the war (the violation of Belgium); the German government itself ought to come forward with such a declaration. The German declaration need not be at all servile; on the contrary, this would only harm it in the eyes of the English." [13]

But the leadership of the German majority Socialists in Berne did not concede any error and, according to Professor Schücking's report to Brockdorff-Rantzau, had an "antagonizing effect" on the delegates. The general mood against David, one of the leaders of the delegation, "came forth strongly." [14] Mistrust of some German Socialist leaders was widespread and was caused by the unstinted support they had given to the war, the Kaiser, and German war goals. In the neutral Hague the appointment of Scheidemann as chancellor had been looked upon with "suspicion"; he was considered a "Kaiser-Socialist, handicapped by his support of the old regime." [15] At the Conference in Berne the French socialist Albert Thomas finally voted for President Branting's resolution expressing belief in the revolutionary spirit of the new Germany and in her complete abandonment of the old system which was held responsible for the war, but privately he expressed his doubts about the dedication of his German comrades to international ideals. [16]

Though the clouds of war and continuing mistrust were thus by no means entirely dispelled, the resolutions of the conference pleased the German and Austrian socialists. On February 11 the *Arbeiter-Zeitung,* commenting on "The International Socialist Conference," pointed out that the resolution adopted on the territorial question was a "victory for self-determination" and was of the "greatest importance" for German Austria, German Bohemia, and German South Tyrol. [17] On the other hand, the London *Times* criticized not

[13]*Ibid.*

[14]*A.A.,* Nachlass B.-R.'s, Presse 6/4, H 234065.

[15]*Ibid.,* Presseangelegenheiten 7/1, Embassy The Hague, Jan. 18, 1919.

[16]*Arbeiter-Zeitung,* Feb. 7.

[17]*Ibid.,* Feb. 11, "Die internationale Sozialistenkonferenz."

only the "frankly unrepentant attitude of Herr Hermann Müller," but also what it judged the "sanctimoniousness of the Herren Kurt Eisner and Kautsky."[18] And *The New Europe* found the resolutions on the whole favorable to Germany, adding that they demanded "denial of nationalism for all countries, except Germany," and accused the conference of carrying out "propaganda for a revived International under German domination."[19] The *New Europe's* article on "The Significance of the Berne Conference" began with a motto from Bakunin: "The socialism of Marx and the diplomacy of Bismarck work together for the Pan-Germanization of Europe."[20]

However true or exaggerated the charges in many a French and British journal leveled against the nationalism of Germany's Social Democracy may have been, international Socialism remained divided on the Anschluss problem. The concepts of national self-determination and democracy and the repudiation of chauvinism appealed to democratic Socialists everywhere. Socialist internationalism, the desire to rebuild the new Europe on progressive, democratic, and possibly Socialist principles, and perhaps the lack of full appreciation of national power, worked in favor of a lenient treatment of Germany. However much these sentiments and principles aroused sympathy for the plight of Socialist-controlled Austria and the Anschluss movement, doubts persisted as to the real change of heart and mind of the German people, including the German working class and its leaders. It was one of the factors which prevented the Socialist Congress in Switzerland from exercising a real and decisive influence upon the "other" conference, the Peace Conference in Paris.

---

[18]*Times,* Feb. 13.

[19]*The New Europe,* Nr. 10 (Jan. 16-Apr. 10, 1919), pp. 138-139. The report by Baron Haupt to Dr. Bauer on February 20, 1919, pointed to the incongruity "that the socialists of the vanquished countries appeared domestically as the victors, while the socialists of the Entente countries came as losers to the congress. Germany and German Austria are today socialist countries par excellence and this circumstance will be the foundation for a new and better prestige of Germandom" (*O.S.,* K 261, 503). If the final resolutions in Berne were relatively favorable to the principle of national self-determination, the reason was not only the victory of moderate over more nationalist and chauvinist elements at the congress, but also the new prestige of Central European Social Democratic parties who seemed to be in the driver's seat in their countries.

[20]*The New Europe,* p. 136.

3. SOVIET RUSSIA AND INTERNATIONAL COMMUNISM ON CENTRAL EUROPE AND THE ANSCHLUSS

"[The Allies] wish to prevent the unification of Austria with Germany.... They are carrying out ... political robbery and coercion in Austria."
Pravda, March 27, 1919

"This act of violence [the annexation of Austria in 1938] was committed in the center of Europe, and has no doubt created a danger not only for the eleven states which border the aggressor state, but also for all European states, and even for those outside of Europe." Maxim Litvinov, 1938

WHILE the leading statesmen of the Great Powers, France, Great Britain, the Unites States, and Italy were writing the peace treaty in Paris, the Soviet Russian regime was fighting a civil war for its very survival. It was a war against opponents who were receiving a moderate measure of support from the West and from Western troops on Russian soil. An outcast among nations and uninvited by the Peace Conference, Soviet Russia did not participate in the territorial and political settlement in 1919 and played no role in shaping Allied policy in the matter of the prohibition of the Anschluss. Yet in spite of, indeed because of, immediate and urgent military pressures, Soviet Russia and international Communism were keenly interested in European territorial problems, especially those of German Central Europe; they clearly perceived the close interrelationship between social revolution and territorial-national problems.

In the spring of 1919 brisk confidence prevailed in Moscow concerning the future of Communism in Europe and in German Central Europe especially. An *Izvestiia* editorial of March 12, "Russia and Europe, 1917-1919," predicted victory for the German proletariat "in the very near future." An "alliance" with Germany, a country with "colossal technological possibilties," would then become feasible. "This alliance will be invincible."[1] The spread of revolution was anticipated first to Germany, Austria, Hungary[2] and thereafter to neutrals like Switzerland and Sweden, and even to victorious states like France. Clearly, Soviet Russia was bent on spreading the Communist Revolution into Central Europe as a step toward the communization of all Europe rather than on any particular move to link Germany and Austria in the Anschluss movement. *Pravda* displayed a lively interest in link-up between the newly established Soviet Hungarian republic in Central Europe, which had come into existence on March 21, 1919 (the second Soviet republic in Europe and the world) and the new Soviet republic in Munich, born about two weeks later. Yet the missing link in the chain was German Austria. Budapest and Munich could overcome their precarious isolation only if the new Austrian republic which lay between them followed their example.[3]

The Soviet press pointed to Allied diplomatic blunders which had inadvertently contributed to the rise of the Soviet Hungarian republic. The West had indeed imposed such severe armistice terms upon Hungary as to leave her no other way out but revolution. The Soviet journals confidently expected the Entente to repeat its errors by decreeing a vengeful peace treaty for Germany and Austria. The Western Powers had resumed "the very same policy of disintegration and plunder in regard to Germany."

[They wished] to prevent the unification of Austria with Germany, to take a number of German districts for Czechoslovakia, and to cut off some German territory from Poland . . . and separate East Prussia. All their attempts will strongly arouse the people of Germany and push it on the road leading to the proletarian revolution . . . which alone can save Germany from spoliation. They are also carrying on the very same political robbery and coercion in Austria. As a consequence, revolution is developing in that country also.[4]

---

[1]*Izvestiia,* March 12, 1919, "Russia and Europe, 1917-1919."
[2]*Pravda,* March 16.
[3]Low, 1958: see Conclusions.
[4]*Pravda,* March 27, 1919.

On May 16, *Izvestiia* likewise criticized the prohibition of the Anschluss in the peace treaty with Germany; Versailles would thus become a "symbol of enslavement" not only for Germany, but also for the Austrian proletariat.[5] Following the Russian model, the Austrian Communist organ *Die Soziale Revolution* attacked the Western Powers which were writing the peace treaty and criticized the leaders of the Austrian Social Democracy for their "betráyal" of the working class and their failure to chart a revolutionary course in Mitteleuropa.[6] And the Austrian Communist leader Toman likewise denounced the Social Democratic policy which aimed at the Anschluss with a German republic "personified by Noske," the German Social Democratic minister of the interior, who was primarily responsible for the bloody repression of the German Spartacist revolt.[7] Clearly, Soviet Russia and the Communist movement favored an Anschluss only with a revolutionary and proletarian, if not outright communist Germany, or an "Anschluss" with the Soviet Hungarian republic. Such a bloc, in due time, might join with newly emerging Soviet republics in Europe, and perhaps soon with Soviet Russia herself.

The Soviet press had castigated Entente policy toward Germany and Austria, including the prohibition of the Anschluss, but it was clearly more interested in exploiting national sensitivities and national frustration and diverting them into revolutionary channels. Its goal was not merely to spur the development of a new unified Soviet Grossdeutschland, but to spread revolution over all of Europe. As the leading theoretician Bukharin wrote in *Pravda*, Soviet Russia must gain "powerful external support" in Hungary, Bavaria, Austria, and all of Germany: thereafter it would attain an infectious influence upon France and Great Britain also.[8] While Entente imperialism wished to turn Central Europe into a "continuous anti-Bolshevik fighting front," a victory of

---

[5] *Izvestiia*, May 16.

[6] *Soziale Revolution*, June 28.

[7] *Ibid.* The Austrian Communists, a negligible force, were in 1918-1919 quite disinterested in the Anschluss issue. In the second number of the journal *Der Weckruf* on November 9, 1918, they put forth numerous demands, but the Anschluss was not among them! Similarly, their first party congress remained silent on this problem (Hautmann, 1971; p. 121). It is in the thirties, under the influence of a changing Soviet policy, that they came to oppose the Anschluss.

[8] *Pravda*, Apr. 11, Bukharin; also *Izvestiia*, Apr. 9.

Communism in the area might "quickly" result in a "continuous Communist Central European front which faces the countries of Western Europe." Central Europe would then become a potential base for the Soviet advance against the countries of the West. Only then would the Russian question, which figured so large at the Paris Peace Conference, cease to exist.

Throughout the months of April and May, 1919, German Central Europe was a focal point of interest for *Izvestiia* and *Pravda.* A special daily column was set aside for news from Germany. Russia's interest in Germany and German revolution transcended her interest in revolution in any other country, and the importance of a Communist victory in Germany was held to be immeasurably greater than victory in Hungary, Austria, Poland, or any Balkan country. Even the possibility of a revolution in Turkey was judged in terms of its favorable effects upon Central Europe.[9] Both a German and an Austrian Soviet republic already appeared "on the horizon."

The founding Congress of the Communist International in Moscow in March of 1919 had adopted a number of important theses, "On the International Situation and the Policy of the Entente." The resolutions expressed the opinion both of the Congress and of the Russian Communist party, which dominated the gathering, on the Russian situation and the revolutionary potentialities of Europe and Central Europe in particular. The so-called peace policy of the Entente imperialists had been "unmasked." Instead of "a democratic foreign policy," secret diplomacy had triumphed in Paris. National self-determination, previously proclaimed by the Entente, was publicly repudiated. Yugoslavia and Czechoslovakia had been set up by means of armed force. The vanquished nations had been plundered, and prisoners of war made slaves of the victors. "A continuous compaign of hate against the defeated nations by the Entente press and the occupation authorities, as well as the hunger blockade imposed by the Allies, condemned the people of Germany and Austria to death. This policy leads to pogroms against the Germans."[10] These acts of violence were committed by the

[9]*Isvestiia,* Apr. 13.

[10]*Kommunisticheskii Internatsional,* Nr. 1, May 1, 1919, p. 113.

"agents of the Entente," and "Czech and Polish Chauvinists."
The " 'democratic' " Entente had embraced a "policy of extreme reaction."

The foregoing Theses on Western Imperialism contained
sharp criticism of annexations and reparations and of the
denial of self-determination of nations, and condemned the
Entente and its East European and Central European
"agents," Poland, Rumania, Czechoslovakia, and others.
They also showed distinct sympathy for Germans and
Austrians. All this left little doubt that German-speaking
Central Europe and Hungary, the chief losers of the war,
were in the spring of 1919 judged to be the most fertile field
for Communist propaganda and the most promising target
of Soviet expansionism.

The Soviets were resolved to exploit the national resentment caused by the prohibition of the Anschluss in German
Austria and the Reich. The prohibition was one of several
weapons in the Communist arsenal to be used to further the
spread of social revolution in German Central Europe.

The armies of the vanquished Central European nations
and their economies had been shattered and the hold of the
ruling classes on their population weakened, if not entirely
lost, as a consequence of the military debacle. Thus a
revolutionary spirit was sweeping their lands. Communism in
Russia had only a narrow base. A union with German Central
Europe held out the promise of crushing the nascent
bourgeois states of Eastern Europe; the latter, outposts of
hostile Western imperialism and heirs to territories formerly
included in the Russian empire, constituted an immediate
and long-range threat to Russia.[11]

---

[11]Also, Soviet Russia looked with little sympathy on the large number of new
"small states," which had arisen on the ruins of the former Austro-Hungarian
monarchy (Kundgebungen des Exek. Komm. der Kommunistischen Internationale, June 18, 1919, *Die Kommunistische Internationale*, v. 3) and on the strong
national movements which had given birth to them. "Only the proletarian
revolution can assure the small nations a free existence" (*ibid.*). It was not the first
nor the last time that international Communism discriminated openly between
nations, as also Marx and Engels had occasionally done, siding with "progressive"
against "reactionary" ones, big ones against small ones. The then triumphant
nationalism of the Czechs, Poles, and Rumanians and many others doomed for the
moment any chances of social revolution in these new countries. For Soviet Russia
the national movements of these smaller, frequently neighboring nations had to be
enemies, both for "revolutionary" reasons and for plainly nationalist considerations. Yet the Soviet "sacro egoismo" was well wrapped in acceptable Communist
verbiage, saturated with "revolutionary" and "internationalist" phraseology.

The publication of the terms of the Versailles peace treaty was taken by the Soviet press as an occasion for denouncing this ultimatum.[12] It prophesied that the Allies would only succeed in arousing popular resentment in Germany and would thus increase the chances for the German proletarian revolution. The Comintern too violently denounced the terms of the Versailles treaty.[13] *Pravda* on May 9 asserted that both the German bourgeoisie and the German Socialists were agreed that Versailles and its stipulations were "deadly" for Germany, which, under these circumstances, could "not get upon her feet."[14] The Russian press continued to display special sympathy for the defeated nations, Germany, Austria, and of course Soviet Hungary. And *Izvestiia* revealed the reasons for its special concern about Versailles. The Allies wanted peace with Germany in order to wage war against Russia more effectively, "in order to throw themselves with all their might against Bolshevism."[15] An *Izvestiia* editorial of June 30 bore the characteristic title "Peace is signed, War continues."[16] *Izvestiia* would have preferred to see Germany waging a "revolutionary war" against the Allies and against the peace terms, instead of meekly submitting to them.

The Austrian Communist organ *Die Rote Fahne* similarly denounced the peace treaty of St. Germain. The treaty "hit the proletariat of German Austria in a terrible manner."[17] "The murderous peace of St. Germain" was "unacceptable" and aimed merely at the "strangling of the Soviet Russian and Soviet Hungarian republics and the enslavement and colonization"[18] of German Austria. And on the victor's side,

---

[12]*Izvestiia*, May 11.
[13]*Komm. Internatsional*, Nr. 2, June 1919, pp. 150-163.
[14]*Pravda*, May 9.
[15]*Izvestiia*, May 21.
[16]*Ibid.*, June 30, "Peace is signed. War continues."
[17]*Die Rote Fahne*, July 7.
[18]*Ibid.*, July 31, "Annehmen oder ablehnen?" Soviet historiography on the Anschluss has been hardly more sophisticated than the Soviet press or the Vienna *Rote Fahne* were in 1918-1919 (See Tyrok, 1955: pp. 223-232, especially "Preparation of the peace treaty with Austria. The peace treaty of St. Germain"). Tyrok managed virtually to ignore the Anschluss movement which, admittedly, cannot be placed easily and neatly into the Marxist, respectively Bolshevik, framework. The Soviet historian rather concentrated on revolutionary developments in 1918-1919, completely overlooking the close, indissoluble ties between these events and the foreign policy course of the Austrian government. But he discerned an alleged "anti-Soviet tendency" (p. 229) in the treaty of St. Germain. See also Stein, 1953: p. 366 (the Russian original was not accessible).

the radical Socialist newspaper *L'Humanité* had earlier warned against the "Balkanization" of Central Europe, stressing that Austria had no choice but the Anschluss, and had gone on to denounce France's "integral nationalism."[19]

None of the Austrian or German leaders of the 1918-1919 Anschluss movement took Soviet Russia and her policies into closer calculation. Her domestic turmoil, distance from Central Europe, and absence from the Paris Peace Conference were not likely to make her a decisive influence either in Vienna and Berlin or at the Paris peace table. But in the early postwar period Ludo Hartmann, still Austrian envoy in Berlin, writing then to the Austrian foreign minister Karl Renner, counted not only on the English and Italians parting company with French Anschluss policy, but also hoped that the Russians would "throw their weight on the scales in our behalf."[20]

While non-German Social Democrats were, as pointed out earlier, divided on the Anschluss question, Communists, following the lead of Soviet Russia, vehemently criticized the peace treaties of Versailles and St. Germain, including the prohibition of the Anschluss. The Soviets were resolved to exploit to the full the national disappointments and frustrations of the vanquished Germans and German Austrians against the Western Powers, their enemy in the Russian Civil war and bulwark of international capitalism. By riding the crest of the waves of German nationalism, they hoped to sweep far west and to extend effectively the base of Communism into Central Europe. But they actually cared little about the Anschluss as such. And the rather small and not too significant Austrian Communist party made its consent to the Anschluss contingent on the particular political and social complexion of the German Reich, opposing the union with a Germany dominated by right-wing Social Democrats à la Noske and Scheidemann.

---

[19]*L'Humanité*, March 5, "The Socialists and the Austrian Problem."
[20]*O.S.*, K 110, Hartmann to Renner, Aug. 9, 1920, pp. 670-671.

VI. Toward the Prohibition of the Anschluss

1. GERMANY AND THE PEACE CONFERENCE

> "[There was] the deeply immoral . . . stipulation
> which obligated Germany not to . . . take her Austrian
> brethren in as long as it pleased the Council of the
> League of Nations to oppose the union." Ulrich von
> Brockdorff-Rantzau

G ERMAN preparations for the coming Peace Conference
began at the order of the chancellor Count Georg von
Hertling as early as December, 1917.[1] After November, 1918,
when Germany was forced to sign the armistice terms, German preparations for the Peace Conference took on a more
definite character. A special committee, named Paxkonferenz, was created and placed under the direction of Count
Johann Heinrich von Bernstorff, former German ambassador to the United States.[2] The Paxkonferenz published a
total of 51 documents under the title *Drucksache, Geschäftsstelle
für die Friedensverhandlungen, 1919*. The author of one paper
estimated the war costs for German Austria and Austria-
Hungary, and another dealt with the continuation of the
blockade after the armistice. No document, however, came to
grips with the problem of German Austria and the Anschluss.[3] The same held true for another German governmental organ, charged with preparing for the expected peace
negotiations with the Allies, the Committee for Peace
Negotiations of the Constituent National Assembly. This
Committee, too, hardly touched on the problem of German
Austria and the Anschluss.[4]

As far as the German Foreign Office was concerned, it
became more assertive on the subject of Austria and the Anschluss after Brockdorff-Rantzau assumed its leadership. In a

---

[1]Luckau, 1941: Introduction.
[2]*Ibid.*, p. 38f.
[3]*Drucksache*, Geschäftsstelle für d. Friedensverhandlungen (51 v., 1919) (some
of these volumes are in the Hoover Libr.); see also Luckau, 1941: p. 49f.
[4]*Ibid.*, p. 44 (Akten über d. Verhandlungen d. Ausschusses f.d.
Friedensverhandlungen, Reichstagsarchiv, Berlin, 1919).

document designed for internal use, "Aufzeichnung über die Vorschläge des Auswärtigen Amtes für die Friedensverhandlungen," drafted in March or April of 1919, the Auswärtige Amt recommended that the question of the future frontier of Italy should "first of all be agreed upon by the future neighbors of Italy." Though Germany was thus to have a voice in this matter only in the event that the Anschluss materialized, the document seemed to take the latter for granted when it declared:

> Germany must insist that the Germans in South Tyrol shall not, without their own consent, be brought under the sway of those who speak a foreign tongue. . . . These Austro-Hungarian areas which adjoin Germany and are German in population are considered by Germany to constitute part of the new German republic that is in the process of formation.[5]

In these notes the Foreign Office made clear its interest in supporting German Austria not only in regard to the German-inhabited border regions of Hungary and in her defense of German South Tyrol, but also in her rejection of the Danubian confederation (a position which the Reich refrained from adopting publicly) and in the matter of the Anschluss itself.

Support for the Anschluss, though, in accordance with the Austro-German protocol of March 2, 1919, less vigorously applied, found expression in the instructions drafted by the German government for the use of its delegates to the Paris Peace Conference. The "Richtlinien für die deutschen Friedensunterhändler," probably drawn up in the month of April, 1919, dealt with numerous territorial questions such as Alsace-Lorraine, the Saar, the Rhineland, the Rhenish Palatinate and Rhenish Hessen, the boundaries with Poland, the claims of Czechoslovakia and Lithuania, with North Schleswig and other problems of an economic, financial, or legal character: it treated disarmament, colonies, the League of Nations, the question of war guilt, and other matters. But the "Richtlinien" did not deal specifically with Austria. In the preamble to the instructions, however, the German Foreign Office stressed that the general basis for the evaluation of the

---

[5]Luckau, 1941: pp. 197-198, "Aufzeichnungen über d. Vorschläge d. Auswärt Amtes f.d. Friedensverhandlungen."

Allied terms would be the Wilson program "which is binding upon both Germany and her opponents"; questions not explicitly mentioned in that program should be solved in its "spirit."

To this category belonged among other questions that of the Anschluss of German Austria. "The latter question is to be discussed only if the Allies explicitly put their ban on the Anschluss of German Austria."[6] The very same recommendation—hardly accidental—was made in the instructions drawn up by Otto Bauer for the Austrian delegation. The Richtlinien, because of their intended use by German experts only, were free to admit that President Wilson had never explicitly promised the Anschluss. German and Austrian proponents of the union, however, frequently made it appear as if such a specific pledge had in fact been given by the American president.

At this stage German policy aimed at keeping the road toward the Anschluss open until after the conclusion of the peace. In view of the numerous territorial disputes the Reich was involved in and the obvious hostility of the West toward an immediate Anschluss, the German delegation did not place the issue of the union on the agenda. But it was prepared to counter any move the Entente might make to prohibit it, since this would defeat future German hopes of working toward an early Anschluss.

During the critical months of 1919 German foreign policy was largely in Brockdorff-Rantzau's hands, and he was also responsible for the Reich's policy toward the Anchluss. It is therefore necessary to focus attention upon Brockdorff-Rantzau, the strong-willed and determined head of the Foreign Office.

In his first programmatic speech as foreign minister on January 2, 1919, soon after taking office, Brockdorff-Rantzau had come out strongly for the right of national self-determination. He denounced as hostile the view that the revolution was Germany's attempt to escape the obligations incurred in her acceptance of the Wilsonian program.[7] In a later address to the representatives of the foreign press in Berlin on January 24 he took statesmen like Clémenceau and

[6]*Ibid.*, "Richtlinien für d. Friedensunterhändler."
[7]Brockdorff-Rantzau, 1925: p. 37f.

Poincaré sharply to task, for making critical remarks about Germany, and deprecated the concept of the European balance of power. This concept was advanced as an argument against Germany's retaining prewar territories and regaining others like German Austria. Rantzau blamed it in large measure for the outbreak of the recent war.[8]

Finally, in his address to the Constituent Assembly on February 14, 1919, Brockdorff-Rantzau had warned the Allies not to treat the German people like a "second-class people" and also gave notice that without colonies and a merchant fleet Germany could not enter the League of Nations. (Little did he realize that Germany was to lose her colonies and was also to be precluded from entering the League, at least for the immediate future.) It was not his aim, he expounded, to "revive world history backwards and to preach Pan-German goals," nor was it his intention to claim Switzerland and the Netherlands. But he presented a definite claim to German Austria and also criticized Czechoslovakia for its forcible incorporation of the Germans of Bohemia and Moravia.[9]

On March 2, 1919, Brockdorff-Rantzau had placed his signature under the Austro-German protocol.[10] In accordance with this agreement, joint Austro-German commissions had begun working to prepare the Anschluss. But Brockdorff-Rantzau refrained from pressing the issue before the peace treaty was signed, accommodating himself for the moment to Allied policy in this matter. In his report to the National Assembly of April 10, he assured the Constituent Assembly:

> Undercurrents which run against the merger do not disconcert me. We are face to face with a historic movement which is taking its course, driven by inner necessity. Therefore, I would warn you not to rush this development. It is not necessary and could do only harm. It suffices if we continue our work calmly and in a matter-of-fact manner.[11]

Brockdorff-Rantzau and Bauer, steering the German and Austrian ships of state, seemed to be in agreement as to the

[8]*Ibid.*, p. 40, Jan. 24, 1919.
[9]*Ibid.*, p. 44f., Feb. 14.
[10]*O.S.*, K 261, Berlin Protokoll v. 2. März, 1919 über Anschlussfrage.
[11]Heilfron, 1919: **3:** p. 2281.

direction and by this time even the speed to be pursued in the Anschluss question. Though the German foreign secretary was an intransigent nationalist on virtually all of Germany's numerous border problems, he was a "moderate" on the issue of the Anschluss.

The "moderation" was unquestionably of a tactical nature. Since German diplomacy would have to fight in Paris on many fronts, it had to refrain from pressing the Anschluss issue at this particular time. Still, before a definite invitation was extended to the German delegation to attend the Paris Conference, Brockdorff-Rantzau tested once again the probable resistance of the West to the idea of the union. His immediate predecessor Dr. Wilhelm Solf had done so late in 1918 when he requested the German envoys in the neutral capitals to ascertain the position of the enemy powers and the neutral states on the Anschluss question.

On the eighteenth of April, Neurath, the German representative in Copenhagen, reported that the English government supported the French endeavors to prevent the Anschluss; he had been unable to ascertain "whether and to what degree an agreement had been reached between the English and Americans in Paris."[12] From The Hague the German envoy Rosen reported that so far England had been favorably disposed toward the federation of the former parts of the Austro-Hungarian monarchy.[13] The American envoy at The Hague had expressed no hesitation concerning American support of the Anschluss. An equally favorable position on the part of Schmedemann, American envoy to Norway, was reported by Hoesch, German ambassador to Christiania (Oslo). Hoesch assumed that Schmedemann, who was considered a strong adherent of Wilson and in general a cautious man, would not likely voice positive opinions on the Anschluss at the risk of contradicting the position of his own government.

From Berne the envoy Adolf Müller reported on April 25 that according to all information available there the English government was taking a negative stand on the Anschluss. Apart from her regard for France, who was attempting to defeat the Anschluss by all possible means, England appar-

---

[12]*N.A.*, T 136-25, Akten . . . , Neurath, Apr. 18.
[13]*Ibid.*, Rosen Tel. Apr. 16, Hösch, Apr. 19.

ently wanted to further the project of a Danubian confederation and desired a restoration of the Habsburgs, particularly because she wished to preserve her own monarchy and did not want to be the only monarchy left in Europe.[14] On the basis of reports received, Müller also expected the American government to show a negative attitude on the Anschluss question.

On the whole, reports on the Anschluss reaching the Foreign Office in April were not promising and could not change but only confirm the wisdom of the already projected cautious German Anschluss policy.

Brockdorff-Rantzau entertained few illusions about the kind of peace treaty the Allies would write for Germany. Apparently he entertained none at all in regard to the Anschluss. In late March of 1919 he warned his colleagues in the Cabinet that the treaty would diverge from the Wilsonian program and would not be subject to modification by negotiation. While projecting the course the German delegation was to take in regard to numerous territorial questions, Austria and the Anschluss were simply ignored in this session. As Brockdorff-Rantzau then conceded, the Anschluss was even "outside the Wilsonian program."[15]

Privately Brockdorff-Rantzau rejected the idea that, in dealing with the Allies, Germany should out of mere spite throw herself into "the arms of Bolshevism."[16] But in accord with numerous other German contemporaries he threatened publicly that Germany would have no choice but to join Bolshevik Russia if she were harshly treated by the Entente. This was the policy to which he, an "Easterner" in the Wilhelmstrasse, was tenaciously to cling later in the twenties, against Stresemann and the "Westerners" in the Foreign Office.

This policy also found expression in his encounter with the American E. L. Dresel on April 19, 1919. Dresel was co-author of a memorandum on the Anschluss, widely circulated among the peace delegations in Paris, which revealed him as an opponent of it. It is doubtful, however, that Brockdorff-Rantzau was acquainted with this fact. At the sug-

---

[14]*Ibid.*, Müller, Apr. 25.
[15]*B.A.*, Reichskanzlei, cabinet minutes, March 21-22, R 43/1348, v. 1.
[16]Brockdorff-Rantzau, 1925: pp. 65-67.

gestion of Colonel House, Dresel had sought an interview with Brockdorff-Rantzau in the course of which he expressed to him "America's warmest sympathies for Germany." He assured him that the United States "would attempt everything to further the reconstruction in Germany and her economic recovery." Yet when the talk turned to Alsace-Lorraine, the Saar, and the German-Danish border, Brockdorff-Rantzau began to denounce the scheme of "amputating" Germany and of first "raping" and then "castrating" the Reich, and left Dresel "ostensibly impressed," apparently less by his arguments than by his fanatical and intemperate outburst. He warned Dresel that under certain circumstances he would not sign the treaty. In conclusion, he threatened that the peace treaty would make Bolshevism in Germany "inevitable."[17] The Entente would have to shoulder the responsibility for the world revolution. In this way Brockdorff-Rantzau tried to exploit the revolutionary tempest in Germany to obtain better peace terms. On the other hand, he feared the impact of continued domestic disturbance and the threat of social revolution upon both the Peace Conference and upon the German Austrian people.[18]

That Brockdorff-Rantzau thought continually of union with Austria and the effect of German domestic developments on the chances of Austria's union with the Reich is also evidenced by a remark made to Count Harry Kessler. Brockdorff-Rantzau voiced fear that dropping the deputies of the Catholic Center party from the Weimar coalition would alienate the Catholic Christian Social party and thus "endanger" the Anschluss movement in Austria.[19]

On national and political grounds Brockdorff-Rantzau was deeply committed to the idea of the Anschluss. But the diplomat in him seemed to be fully aware of the hopelessness of achieving union at the conference table.

On April 28 the members of the German delegation left for Versailles. They had been appointed by the party leaders of the German republic, were headed by Brockdorff-Rantzau, and accompanied by numerous experts and assistants. Special trains carrying the German delegates and

[17]*A.A.*, Br.-R. Nachlass, Geh. Aufzeichnung, H 234068-193.
[18]*Ibid.*, Presse 6/4, H234068.
[19]Kessler, 1961: p. 145, March 4, 1919.

other personnel, 180 persons in all, arrived in Paris the following day. It was not until May 5 that the leader of the German delegation was informed that the peace terms would be
presented to him in the afternoon of May 7 at the Trianon
Palace Hotel in Versailles.

There followed in dramatic succession the presentation of
the treaty, Clémenceau's address, and Brockdorff-Rantzau's
rejoinder which was considered offensive in both content and
delivery by most of the gathering. Count Brockdorff-
Rantzau accused therein the Western Powers also of continuing ruthless policies against Germany by not lifting the
blockade and thus allegedly causing the death of tens of
thousands in the Reich. He remained seated while reading
his answer to the Assembly. When he was subsequently
criticized for this, it was claimed that he had been too weak
and nervous to stand up. But his friends in the Foreign Office quickly disavowed this excuse, stressing that during the
entire session his "calm, dignity and composure" had stood
out clearly.[20]

The liberal *Manchester Guardian,* generally not unkindly
disposed toward Germany, sharply criticized Count Brockdorff-Rantzau's "discourtesy."[21] According to Tardieu, the
speech was "cold, harsh, and insolent,"[22] and Lloyd George's
opinion was much the same: "It is hard to have won the war
and to have to listen to that."[23] The historian Hajo Holborn,
while rightly criticizing the humiliating position in which the
Germans were placed at Versailles, judged Brockdorff-
Rantzau's speech "undiplomatic" and his language "aggressive," and thought that several remarks showed a "rather
demagogic attitude."[24]

In Germany, however, there was little tendency to accuse
Brockdorff-Rantzau of having committed a tactical error.
The treaty generated only waves of impassioned indignation
and fury. While criticism was leveled at most of the treaty
provisions, the prohibitive clauses relating to Austria and the
Anschluss figured prominently in its denunciation.

---

[20]*A.A.,* Nachlass Br.-R., Versailles 8/2, May 7: Überreichung d. Friedensvertrages, H 235619-f.
[21]*Manchester Guardian,* evng ed., May 8.
[22]Tardieu, 1921: p. 119.
[23]*Ibid.,* p. 120.
[24]Holborn, Craig and Gilbert, *Diplomats:* pp. 137-138.

Georg Bernhard of the *Vossische Zeitung* pilloried the Versailles treaty as "a document of political shamelessness . . . out of which grins the English wish to annihilate Germany."[25] At the same time he declared that the Anschluss had not been directly prohibited. He recommended that Germany insist in her counter-proposals that the Entente carry on negotiations jointly with the Reich and German Austria. "German Austria belongs to the German people. It is not feasible to negotiate with one part of its people in Versailles and with another part in St. Germain."[26]

When the treaty was submitted to the German delegation, *Vorwärts* denounced it as a "peace of annihilation." The so-called peace was "nothing but a latent war of destruction, an attempt to exterminate a people . . . by means of the most brutal economic slavery."[27] On May 24 it sharply criticized the French Socialists for their lukewarmness toward German Socialism and Austria.[28] France was accused of trying to prevent the development of Grossdeutschland.[29]

Many Germans had long indulged in excessively optimistic expectations and were bitterly disappointed when they had to surrender on the Austrian issue as well. Their hopes that German losses might be compensated by the Anschluss of German Austria evaporated. And many people in Germany as well as Austria cried out aloud against what they considered another injustice meted out to the German people.

The last session of the Constituent Assembly before the Peace Delegation departed for Paris had been held on April 15. Barely a week after the conditions of peace had been received by that delegation in Paris, the Constituent Assembly met again, this time not in Weimar but in Berlin, and in the new aula of the University of Berlin. The Peace Treaty was sharply attacked by representatives of virtually all parties.

This 39th session of the German National Assembly also turned out to be a resolute demonstration against the prohibition of the Anschluss. Appreciation was expressed for the "warm words" which had been voiced by many Austrian

---

[25]*Voss. Zeitung*, May 8.
[26]*Ibid.*, May 12, Bernhard, "Illusion, Illusion. . . ."
[27]*Vorwärts*, May 8.
[28]*Ibid.*, May 20; see also May 13 and 25.
[29]*Ibid.*, May 26, "Frankreich und Österreich."

leaders.[30] Haussmann quoted the Austrian chancellor Karl
Renner: "The *grossdeutsch* idea remains, and we shall not surrender our German souls."[31] Müller, the Social Democratic
representative from Breslau, pledged: "We are united with
our Austrian brethren heart and soul. . . . Only force can stop
us now."[32] Hirsch, President of the German Secretariat of
State, disclosed to the audience that it was Germany's mission
to place herself at the head of a world-wide movement of all
socially and nationally "oppressed" peoples against the victorious Entente![33]

Gustav Stresemann, who was to strike a more moderate
tone in years to come, blurted out that the peace treaty, the
"greatest fraud" which history had ever witnessed, did not
"dishonor the vanquished, it dishonored the victor," and
Count von Posadowsky-Wehner likewise denounced the
peace as a work of "French vengeance and English brutality."
The pacifist Dr. Quidde joined these men in "condemning"
in an equally unrestrained manner the "rape of Germany,"
declaring the prohibition of the Anschluss "unacceptable,"
and predicted the rise of a German irredenta. In a major address Chancellor Scheidemann, leader of the Majority
Socialists, thanked the Austrians for the eternal "devotion"
and "pledge of loyalty" to Germany which at this very
moment was being expressed in Vienna: "Brethren in German Austria, who even in the darkest hour do not forget the
road to the *Gesamtvolk* [totally integrated nation], we salute
you, and we support you. (Stormy consent and applause.)"
Dr. Kahl of the German People's party rejected the peace
treaty on several grounds—one of which was that "we do not
wish to abandon German Austria"[34]—and Hugo Haase of
the Independents, who during the war had been one of the
few courageous spokesmen for peace and international conciliation, accused the Entente of violating the right to self-
determination "in an almost despicable manner," to the
disadvantage of the German nation. Though he claimed that
Germany recognized Austria's independence as
"inalienable," at the same time he insisted on the "inalienable

---

[30]Heilfron, 1919: **5:** 2652, 39th sess.
[31]*Ibid.*, 2668.
[32]*Ibid.*, 2652.
[33]*Ibid.*, p. 2650.
[34]*Ibid.*, p. 2762.

right of German Austria to join the German people in accordance with her wish."

Thus even the radical and least nationalistic Left felt that Germany would sooner or later obtain German Austria to which she was entitled; but she would acquire the desired prize only through the back door, by way of Austria's right to national self-determination. The interests of the other European states in peace and general European security—both potentially threatened by an over-sized, traditionally militaristic Germany—were disregarded or minimized, or balanced against German claims and found wanting.

Feelings in the German National Assembly thus ran feverishly high over the Anschluss issue, and the passion of nationalism engulfed men of the most different political persuasions, ranging from the Right to the democratic Center, to Majority Socialists and even Independents, from north German Protestants to German Catholics in the region of the Rhine and southern Germany, from militarists and military-minded Germans to pacifists.

On May 18, giant demonstrations were staged in Berlin against the peace treaty. One of these was a march of German Austrian residents of the Reich from the Wilhelmplatz to the Reich's Chancellery where Scheidemann addressed the demonstrators thus: "In the long run the voices of nature cannot be suppressed. And the voice of common blood shouts: 'Germans belong to Germans.'" The following day President Ebert denounced the peace of "strangulation" and pledged: "The German government will never accept these terms."[35]

German reaction to the Versailles peace treaty was, of course, a matter of greatest concern to the Austrian ambassador in Berlin, Ludo Hartmann. Though Chancellor Scheidemann enunciated the slogan "*unannehmbar*" (unacceptable), on May 12 a deep chasm opened up in the National Assembly between Scheidemann, whose heroic posture Hartmann admired, Brockdorff-Rantzau, and the German delegation in Versailles on one side and the bulk of the German people on the other. "The entire work of the peace delegation in Versailles which made such a dignified

---

[35]*Vorwärts*, May 20.

impression . . . was apparently quite distinct from the mood in the hinterland,"[36] wrote Hartmann. Scheidemann assured him that the entire Cabinet was "completely agreed" that this treaty could not be signed, and he prophesied that none would sign it[37] — which proved to be incorrect. According to Scheidemann, the worst which could befall Germany would be for the French army to move from Frankfurt and Mannheim along the Main up to Eger, in order to separate the North from the South.[38] Scheidemann was thus prepared to pursue a policy of brinkmanship with all its attendant risks.

But war-weariness was deep and widespread, and Germany was in no position to challenge the victorious powers. Many a German politician who joined in the denunciation of the treaty as part of an expected patriotic ritual may have considered the terms not as unbearable as he publicly professed them to be.

On May 29 Germany finally submitted her counterproposals and a covering letter to the Allies.[39] In the covering letter Brockdorff-Rantzau warned that the demands of the treaty were beyond the strength of the German people and that a whole nation was being "asked to sign her own proscription, more than that, her death sentence."[40] He asked for a free plebiscite in Alsace-Lorraine and Schleswig and took exception to other territorial cessions along the western and eastern borders. A brief reference to Austria followed. "Germany requests that the right to self-determination also be respected in the case of the Germans of Austria and Bohemia."[41]

The comprehensive German counterproposals submitted to the Allies at the same time criticized the violation of the right to self-determination in the treaty provisions affecting Germany's boundaries also with Poland and Czechoslovakia. The principle of self-determination was also declared to have been flagrantly disregarded in regard to millions of Germans in German Austria who were denied the union with Germany which they desire.[42]

---

[36]*O.S.*, K 261, Hartmann to Bauer, May 20.
[37]*Ibid.*, Hartmann to Bauer, May 22.
[38]*Ibid.*
[39]Luckau, 1941.
[40]*Ibid.*, Doc. 39, pp. 244-247.
[41]*Ibid.*, covering letter, Doc. 56, p. 304, pp. 302-306.
[42]*Ibid.*, Doc. 57, pp. 306-307 and 318-319.

Number 6 of the German proposals referred to article 80 of the treaty which demanded "the permanent recognition of the independence of Austria within the frontiers established by the treaty of peace of the Allied and Associated Governments." It asserted that

> Germany has never had, and never will have, any intention of shifting the Austro-German frontier by force. However, should the population of Austria, whose history and culture have been most intimately connected with its mother country Germany for more than a thousand years, desire to restore the national connection with Germany which was but recently severed by war, Germany cannot pledge herself to oppose that desire of her German brothers in Austria, as the right to self-determination should apply universally and not only to the disadvantage of Germany.

Of all the formal exchanges between Paris and Berlin so far, this was the Germans' boldest challenge on the Austrian subject. Without even an attempt at diplomatic disguise, it revealed the clear intention of bringing about the union in the near future.

Three weeks later, on June 16, the Allies sent their reply to the German delegation. Though there seemed to have been some hesitancy in the British delegation and among some American delegates, very few concessions were actually made. No change whatsoever was made concerning German Austria.

Thereafter, the German peace delegation left for Weimar to consult with the government as to whether the Reich should accept the revised treaty. The delegation's report to the Assembly stressed that the peace conditions were "unbearable."[43] There was no indication that the provisions in regard to Austria had any appreciable bearing on the recommendations of the delegation.

The rigid attitude of the German peace delegation reflected the unbending position of its leader, Foreign Secretary Brockdorff-Rantzau. In late December, 1918, before he had assumed office, he had sought assurances that he would be released from his duties if presented with an unacceptable

---

[43]*Ibid.*, p. 91.

treaty.[44] Before leaving for Paris in late April, he had reminded President Ebert of his earlier sharply defined position.[45] On the very same day he jotted down the following: "I am not going to Paris in a pessimistic frame of mind, but a very skeptical one."[46] Clearly, Brockdorff-Rantzau, who had hesitated to accept the post of foreign minister in the last days of imperial Germany and who had laid down "conditions" prior to his final acceptance of this post in December, 1918, did not wish his name to be linked with the anticipated harsh peace treaty. He had gone to Paris, but he was prepared to leave the sinking ship.

The stern Allied reply to the German notes, taking the character of an ultimatum, had been made public on June 16, and the German delegation was given just seven days to answer it! Brockdorff-Rantzau and most members of the delegation left Paris and returned to Weimar on June 18. The German foreign minister then recommended a wavering German Cabinet to reject the Versailles treaty.[47] After Chancellor Scheidemann, a bitter opponent of the treaty, resigned, on June 22 a new cabinet headed by Gustav Bauer presented itself to the Constituent Assembly. In the end the Assembly came out in favor of signing the Peace Treaty.[48]

On June 24 a bitterly disappointed Hartmann reported in a detailed, twenty-one page letter that the German signature had been affixed to the treaty: "The German people apparently is so exhausted that it is not capable of heroic decisions."[49] Although he perceived the depth of Germany's misery, Hartmann could not forgive her political leaders for spurning "radicalism"—a radicalism which, in his view, the hour seemed to demand.[50]

---

[44]Brockdorff-Rantzau made a point of frequently posing "conditions." When he was appointed German ambassador in Moscow in 1922 — a post he continued to occupy until his death in 1928 — he made the "curious" demand (Holborn, Craig and Gilbert eds., *The Diplomats*, p. 149) to be allowed to report directly to the president of the Weimar Republic instead of to the Foreign Office — a practice which represented a "departure from the constitution."

[45]*A.A.*, Nachlass Br.-R., 7/7, Gespräch mit Ebert, Apr. 27.

[46]*Ibid.*

[47]Brockdorff-Rantzau, 1925: pp. 21-22. In the Nazi period, Peter Lankhard, 1935: p. 8, held that the German foreign secretary was entitled to be considered "the first protagonist against Versailles."

[48]Luckau, 1941: p. 314 f.

[49]*O.S.*, K 261, Hartmann to Bauer, June 24.

[50]*A.A.*, Gutachten in Kabinettssitzung, June 18, H 235486-493.

On June 17, two days before his resignation, Brockdorff-Rantzau had jotted down the following notes, entitled "Thoughts about a speech of the Reich Minister for Foreign Affairs in the Cabinet," in which he developed the idea that the goal of the Versailles treaty was "the political and economic ruin" of Germany. His thoughts ran as follows: the intention of both France and England to weaken Germany revealed "very long-standing and deeply rooted needs and traditions of English and French policy." The peace terms could not be accepted. There was also "the deeply immoral stipulation which obligated Germany not to take her Austrian brethren in as long as it pleased the Council of the League of Nations to oppose the union."[51] Though the prohibition of the Anschluss was merely one feature of the treaty which aroused Brockdorff-Rantzau's bitterness, it was one which rankled deep and contributed to his decision to resign.

In Brockdorff-Rantzau's interview with Ebert, the latter assured him that he had "surpassed [his] expectations"; what he had performed would be fully appreciated only by history. Brockdorff-Rantzau himself had a similarly exaggerated view of his own role, including his role in the Anschluss affair. Long after he had relinquished the position of foreign secretary he disclosed to Ludo Hartmann, when the latter left office, that he had the satisfaction of having worked with him to lay the foundation of the work "which nobody can prevent." Yet friend and foe of the Anschluss movement must conclude that Brockdorff-Rantzau's contribution to laying the "foundation" for the later temporary "union" of Austria with Germany was a limited one. Aggressive in every respect, as he appeared to the Entente, he actually played on the Anschluss issue *vis-à-vis* the dynamic Austrian leadership a rather restrained and defensive part, hoping to slow down the movement.

A genuine nationalist, Brockdorff-Rantzau impressed Germans and foreigners as being a hard-liner. Yet in spite of the dramatic gesture of his resignation and the personal and national protest which it signified, his policy on German Austria and the Anschluss was a relatively moderate one. Though a dedicated partisan of the Anschluss movement, he

---

[51]*Ibid.*, Versailles I 8/7, H 235444, June 17, "Gedanken über eine Rede."

at least in this area was able realistically to assess insuperable obstacles once he came face to face with them. While insisting on national self-determination and striking an unyielding pose against the West's refusal to grant it to German Austria, he went contrary to Austrian, and even German activists by carefully refraining from moving on the Anschluss issue to an irreversible and explosive *fait accompli.*

German Austria and the Anschluss question may have continued to stir German public opinion, but they were rather subordinate problems as far as the German peace delegation was concerned. The delegation's primary concern was the diplomatic defense of Germany's prewar territories. The military as well as diplomatic defense of German Austria during the troublesome postwar period had to be left to the government and people of German Austria themselves. Little German Austria also had to fend for herself at the Peace Conference. Still, the diplomatic record shows clearly that, while unable to offer any definite help during this entire period, Germany was indeed concerned about German Austria and her borders.

Germany did not claim the three and a half million Sudeten Germans who were included in Czechoslovakia and on the whole avoided any intervention in their behalf. Nor was she in the geographic, military, or diplomatic position to assist German Austria in the struggle to retain disputed regions in Styria and Carinthia, or to help her gain West Hungary. She showed hardly greater interest in German South Tyrol. Some German circles, admittedly, toyed with the idea of an Anschluss of Vorarlberg and Tyrol with adjacent German states or with the Reich. But the German Foreign Office, with its eyes on the union of Austria at a later date, finally perceived the dangers of a piecemeal Anschluss. During the critical year 1918-1919 Germany did not rush to defend Austria against intruders, but she showed a lively interest in the borders of German Austria which, after all, would be hers when the union was consummated.

German foreign policy files reveal some German encouragement of the Anschluss movement in Vorarlberg and Tyrol and considerable maneuvering during the spring and summer of 1919, in spite of the clearly implied prohibitions of these tactics in the Austro-German agreement of March 2,

1919, and notwithstanding the peace treaty the Allies submitted to Berlin. These German endeavors and interests were of course not touched upon by the Foreign Office in its exchange of notes with the Peace Conference. Yet without reference to these backstage developments and events which affected the participants of the Peace Conference, the decisions of the Conference in regard to Austria and the Anschluss tell a rather incomplete story.

Toward the end of the war one of the strongest separatist movements in Austria burst forth in little Vorarlberg. Its goal was a union with Switzerland. That country, perturbed about the Austrian Anschluss movement and the longer and more vulnerable border which would result from a union of Austria with the Reich, at first did not discourage the movement in Vorarlberg, while the Austrian government stood helplessly aside. In the end Vorarlberg's union with Switzerland was prohibited by the Entente who feared that the German remnant of the Habsburg monarchy would disintegrate if Vorarlberg were permitted to set such a dangerous precedent.

Some German groups were working against the Anschluss of Vorarlberg with Switzerland and for its union with the Reich. The German minister in Berne warned the German Foreign Office that any deliberate campaign to promote the union of Vorarlberg with Germany would produce adverse results in Switzerland and France. During the month of May the Foreign Office was disturbed by the progress of the movement for Vorarlberg's union with Switzerland and alarmed by Ludo Hartmann's disclosure that Vienna was "more or less disinterested" in the fate of Vorarlberg.[52] Erzberger, prominent member of the German Cabinet, pledged financial support to one Locher, member of the Württemberg Assembly, who was prepared to thwart the link-up of Vorarlberg with Switzerland. And the German Foreign Office actually paid one Dr. Bergen 20,000 marks to journey to Vorarlberg and Tyrol to establish unofficial contact with pro-German circles there and disseminate propaganda. After a plebiscite in Vorarlberg revealed that more than eighty percent of its inhabitants favored Anschluss with Switzerland,

---

[52]*Ibid.*, Öst. 112, v. 1, Grünau, May 25.

the German consul in Bregenz, Padel, warned the Foreign Office against flooding the little province with German marks in the hope of reversing the situation. But as late as July 7 Grünau of the German Foreign Ofice drew attention to the "lively interest" which broad segments of the German population adjacent to Switzerland and Vorarlberg took in the latter's fate and emphasized that "German interests demand that a last-minute effort be made not to let Vorarlberg be lost to Switzerland."[53]

On the whole Germany was not greatly stirred by the fate of German South Tyrol. The Italians criticized certain Munich circles for their concern about the future of German South Tyrol, but refrained from accusing Berlin itself. The geographic remoteness of South Tyrol from the German capital, the circumstance that South Tyrol was clearly of greater concern to Vienna than to Berlin, and Italy's determination to hold on to the Brenner Pass, all these accounted for Germany's restrained attitude; last but not least, so did the desire to widen the split between Rome and the Allies and restore the traditional friendly relations between Germany and Italy.

In regard to Tyrol proper (where Italian interests did not weigh as heavily) the German Foreign Office acted in a bolder manner, though in view of the special relationship with German Austria, hardly a loyal one. The purpose of Dr. Bergen's journey to Tyrol was to establish contact with supporters of the Anschluss, such as Gilbert In der Maur, and to help found a *grossdeutsch* daily newspaper, which the German government was prepared to finance with as many as 700,000 marks.[54] This tactic hardly differed from similar attempts made in Vienna itself, where the German Foreign Office tried to purchase Austrian newspapers to further the cause of the Anschluss.

The Austrian government had worked steadfastly toward the Anschluss of the entire German Austrian republic. But when the peace terms offered by the Entente seemed to have

---

[53]*Ibid.*, v. 2, Grünau to Prittwitz, July 7.

[54]*A.A.*, Öst. 112, v. 1, undersecretary of state to Padel, May 27, Memorandum, May 31. *Ibid.*, v. 2, Padel to F.O., Report 24, June 4. *Ibid.*, Weimar II, Grünau to Prittwitz, Tel. 97, July 7. *Ibid.* Öst. 113, v. 1, Wedel to F.O., Report 57, May 10, Memorandum by Grünau, June 18. *Ibid.*, Öst. 74, v. 2, Grünau to Wedel, Tel. 404, June 26.

blocked the Anschluss movement, the German Foreign Office toyed with the idea of encouraging Tyrol's secession from Austria, confident that an independent Tyrol would soon cast its lot with the Reich.

On July 25 a Tyrolese delegation, with the blessing of the government in Innsbruck, journeyed to Berlin to confer with the German government about a possible future Anschluss with the Reich. The delegation included members of the Christian Social and German Liberal parties, business representatives, and Gilbert In der Maur and the German consul Külmer.[55] The people of Tyrol were bitterly disappointed with Vienna and Rome, despairing of regaining German South Tyrol, and fearful of the emergence of a Danubian confederation. In this mood they turned to Germany, as they had done in the early November days of 1918 when they appealed for German military help.

In Berlin the Tyrolese delegation explored the possibilities of a customs union with Germany, since a political Anschluss was out of the question. Though the visit occurred a few days after the reins of power had passed into the hands of a more moderate and compliant German government, Foreign Office officials were strangely assertive and in a mood to challenge the Western Powers. Apart from disregarding the interests and attitude of the Entente, these exploratory talks in the German capital violated, of course, both the spirit and the letter of the Austro-German agreement of March 2, 1919.

Nevertheless, several German diplomatic officials such as Riepenhausen and Grünau in Berlin supported the so-called "artichoke theory."[56] In accordance with it the Austrian *Länder* had to be broken off from German Austria separately, one leaf at a time, before being united with Germany. Grünau, however, questioned whether Germany could support Tyrol in this event, in view of the provisions of the Treaty of Versailles. Stolberg, chargé d'affaires of the German Embassy in Vienna, warned Germany outright not to follow a course which would make matters only "more difficult" for the German Austrian government.[57]

[55]*Ibid.*, Öst. 113, v. 2, Külmer to F. O., Tel. 68, July 28; Tschurtschentaler to Grünau, July 25.

[56]*Ibid.*, Riepenhausen to Grünau, July 29; *ibid.*, Öst. 70, v. 1, Riepenhausen to Grünau, Aug. 9.

[57]*Ibid.*, Öst. 113, v. 2, Stolberg to Grünau, Tel 727, July 30.

In early September, when there was no longer any doubt about the final provisions of the Treaty of St. Germain, the German Foreign Office advised the Tyrolese leaders through Consul Külmer in Innsbruck to desist from any further move toward union.[58] Otherwise the Entente would take counter-measures against the Anschluss.

---

[58]*Ibid.*, Müller to Külmer, Tel. 49, Sept. 4, 1919.

2. AUSTRIA AND THE PEACE CONFERENCE

> "The right which Europe and America conceded to the Poles, Italians and South Slavs cannot be refused to the German people." Austrian Memorandum to the Peace Conference *

W HEN the new year was rung in, it was clear to the German Austrian government that the struggle for the Anschluss would have to be waged also in Paris where the Peace Conference was soon to open its doors. In the early stages of the Conference Austria was not invited to send a delegation to Paris, yet the Austrian government had the opportunity to clarify its position in a number of notes and declarations addressed to the Great Powers in Paris.

In one such note, probably written in January, 1919, the Austrian government voiced the hope that an early conclusion of world peace would be possible and urgently pleaded that consultations and "preliminary negotiations" be initiated for this purpose in the very near future. To maintain peace and order in Europe the German Austrian republic should be offered an opportunity to participate in these negotiations through her representatives.[1]

German Austria's case had previously been elaborated upon in speeches, diplomatic notes, and editorials in the Austrian press, and the document finally presented to the Peace Conference contained few new arguments. It stressed the right to national self-determination of all peoples, insisted on its application to all German Austrians, including the German population of North Bohemia, and strongly criticized the recent actions of the Czechoslovak government.[2] It denied the possibility of an independent existence for German Austria. It declared a Danubian confederation to be theoretically feasible but questioned its practicability in

---

*Probably written in January, 1919.

[1] *O.S.*, K 261, Memorandum n.d. 4202/1 ad 4245/I.
[2] *Ibid.*

view of the hostility of the new succession states toward German Austria; it therefore insisted on the right of German Austria to unite with Germany.[3]

Taking account of the fear of Germany which haunted the West, especially France, the Austrian government attempted to discard the balance of power factor as a weighty argument against the Anschluss. Yet the argument that a Germany with ten or even only seven million more Germans would not change the political and military equilibrium in Europe lacked persuasive power.

The period between January and May of 1919 was critical for the fate of the Anschluss movement, registering little actual progress but many setbacks and mounting opposition. All this affected the last instructions of the Austrian government and the Foreign Secretariat to the Austrian Delegation ready to depart for Paris.

The Instructions given to the Austrian delegation to the Paris Peace Conference were neither signed nor dated, but were probably written some time in April, or at the latest in early May.[4] From their authoritative tone it would appear that Dr. Bauer, minister of foreign affairs, wrote them himself. There had been considerable talk that the noted jurist Dr. Franz Klein, minister of justice under the monarchy, would head the delegation. But finally Chancellor Karl Renner took the assignment himself. The Instructions may well have been drawn up in the expectation that Dr. Klein rather than the chancellor would head the Austrian delegation.

The Instructions warned "that the representatives of the Austrian *Länder* must be prevented from making policy of their own." Under some circumstances, however, a special representation for German Bohemia and the Sudeten region might be permissible. The same concession might be extended to Tyrol if it should wish to negotiate independently of German Austria, and to Vorarlberg if its representatives should express a desire for Anschluss with Switzerland. The Instructions to the Austrian peace delegation thus clearly reflected the already well-advanced threat of German Austria's disintegration.

---

[3]*Ibid.*
[4]*O.S.*, K 261, IIa: Allg. Instruktionen f.d. Delegation z. Pariser Friedenskongress, pp. 466-493.

The Instructions stated that it would not be suitable for German Austria to emulate the assertive attitude of the German delegation.

We are by far the weaker state and our relationship toward the Entente is quite different from Germany's; we shall therefore have to be careful not to strike a note similar to that of the Germans of the Reich. I believe that it will be useful for our attitude toward the representatives of the opposing powers if on every possible occasion we stress with emphasis that we very well know that we are vanquished and powerless and that the Entente is in a position to dictate peace to us.

The Instructions focused on the right to self-determination, but warned the delegation not to refer to it too frequently or too loudly. The Entente should rather be reminded that it was in their own interest to maintain peace and order in Central Europe and to create none but politically and economically viable realms. At no time should the delegation threaten to break up the negotiations, or even to interrupt them. The Austrian government was aware of its weakness, and was in no mood to challenge the peacemakers.

In case a question should be raised about the relationship between the Austrian *Länder* and any foreign powers, the delegation was to defer to Vienna for a decision. In regard to specific territorial questions the delegation was to strive for "full self-determination" for German Bohemia and the Sudeten region. "Mere autonomy" was to be rejected; the main emphasis should be on creating "an independent state" out of these separate regions. If, however, they should be made a part of the Czechoslovakian republic, the full equality of the three or four different languages was to be demanded, and the model of Switzerland followed. The president of Czechoslovakia should be chosen consecutively from each of the major nations composing the state and neutralization should be insisted upon, since otherwise the Czechoslovakian republic would become anti-German.

South Tyrol should be militarily neutralized, but should legally and economically remain with Austria. If Tyrolean independence, however, was the only way of retaining South Tyrol and preserving the integrity of the province, then it should be supported.

After next touching on the problem of Carinthia, Lower Styria, and West Hungary, and pleading that the entire Banat go to Rumania [it was actually divided between Rumania and Yugoslavia], the Instructions tackled the Anschluss question: "We have no interest at all in initiating a discussion of the Anschluss issue at the Conference. It is only to be taken up if its opponents begin talking about it or if they wish to impose upon us peace terms which make the Anschluss impossible or substantially more difficult." It was desirable to start discussion of the Anschluss, if at all, only after the territorial question had finally been decided and the most important economic problems settled, particularly the liquidation of the long-standing public debt. In the event that the problem of the Anschluss was brought up by the other side, the right to national self-determination, generally recognized in regard to all other peoples, should be asserted. It should be stressed with great decisiveness that a pan-German plan was not at issue and that the Anschluss project was basically different from the plan for the Central European customs union and economic federation, as it was debated during the war. The economic difficulties of an independent existence and the danger of a Balkanization of Central Europe should be emphasized.

The delegation was to demand a plebiscite for German Austria to be held under control of the League of Nations. If an immediate plebiscite were not feasible, "it is to be proposed that one be held after the concessions made by the Allied Powers, in return for renunciation of the Anschluss, have been made public." In this event the plebiscite could take place "after a longer period, perhaps one year." The Austrian government, curiously enough, assumed that it would gain concessions for renouncing the Anschluss even for as short a period as one year.

Should the Anschluss be flatly rejected, it might next be proposed that German Austria remain militarily separate from the German Reich, also that Germany not retain troops on Austrian soil, and that in the event of war Austria must remain neutral; otherwise, however, German Austria should be permitted to link up with Germany if both sides can agree about it. If both the military and the political Anschluss is prohibited, then Austria's freedom must at least be preserved, so that she can fully and independently regulate legal and economic relations with the German Reich. . . . The military neutralization could be accepted in the event of the legal and economic Anschluss with the German Reich, but not without it.

The delegation was to point out that the opposition to a Danubian federation on the part of Poles, Rumanians, and probably South Slavs, doomed any chances for its establishment.

In regard to the war guilt question the Instructions made these points:

> The responsibility of the Austro-Hungarian monarchy for the war is not to be denied. . . . It is to be strongly emphasized that we are well aware that Austria-Hungary, through its ultimatum to Serbia, conjured up the immediate danger of the world war. . . . It should, however, be made clear that it was not an Austrian regime that was responsible for this war, but the regime of the old Austro-Hungarian monarchy whose foreign policy was then dominated by a Magyar clique . . . Of course, we should not start such a discussion. . . . The notion that Germany had shoved Austria-Hungary into the foreground is false. . . . However, it cannot be the task of the peace delegation, and it would aggravate or weaken its own position, to pose as the defender of Germany.

It is instructive in several respects to compare the Austrian documents submitted to the Peace Conference in January of 1919 and the foregoing Instructions to the Austrian delegation, written most likely in April of 1919. True, the recipients were not the same; in the first case, they were the victorious powers, in the second, the members of the Austrian peace delegation. Nevertheless, the difference in tone and content of the two documents is striking and conclusive. The assertive, strident, and warning tone of the earlier statement is missing in the second. While the earlier paper attempted to persuade the Western Powers that the Anschluss contained little danger for them, at the later stage no attempts of this kind were made, and the earlier demand for the "Anschluss" of German North Bohemia and the Sudeten region was simply dropped in favor of a project of a multinational Czechoslovak state, based on true national equality. National self-determination and the Anschluss of Austria proper, the Instructions suggested, should be taken up only in response to Allied queries, and then with caution. The instructions were marked by a shrewd sense of what was tactically advisable and politically attainable.

A sense of realism had taken hold of the Austrian government, and the hopes and expectations along territorial lines which at first had been placed on the Peace Conference had become rather modest. The Austrian government now squarely faced the possibility of a flat rejection of the Anschluss.

It was not until May 1, 1919, that Paris dispatched a rather circuitous invitation to Vienna. It asked the Austrian government to send a delegation to St. Germain-en-Laye, and specified that it should arrive there in the afternoon of May 12! Clémenceau imperiously suggested in his code telegram to the Chief of the French Military Mission at Vienna that the Austrian government strictly confine its mission to persons especially qualified for their peacemaking task. The invitation, which sounded more like a summons, was bound to freeze any hopes which the Austrian delegation might have entertained. It was calmly acknowledged by Dr. Bauer. He gave assurance that the delegation would be composed only of properly qualified persons and that the "hospitality" of the French republic would not be abused. Still, the Austrian Foreign Office, not deterred by Clémenceau's curt suggestions, decided to send a rather sizable delegation.[5] As Dr. Bauer explained, the federal character of the German Austrian republic made it necessary to provide a broad representation for the various *Länder*. The Austrian delegation was headed by Chancellor Karl Renner and included the deputies Dr. Gürtler and Dr. Schönbauer who represented the Christian Social and German National parties respectively; in addition, there were about thirty experts, eight journalists, and fifteen members of the staff.

In the midst of the preparations for the delegation's departure for Paris came the publication of the German peace terms, which had the effect of a bombshell. The harsh terms

---

[5]About the criticism of the Austrian delegation by Czechoslovaks and also Baron S. Sonnino, see Stadler. 1966: p. 39 and the chapter "The Austrians and St. Germain," espec. pp. 39-43.

portended little hope for Austria and a wave of indignation swept the country. The *Arbeiter-Zeitung* called the peace one of "annihilation" and the Catholic *Reichspost* a "robber's peace."[6] On May 10 the *Arbeiter-Zeitung*, exaggerating as it often did, spoke of "Germany's dismemberment."[7] And the *Neue Freie Presse*, alluding to the prohibiton of the Anschluss in the treaty, declared that if the Great Powers "force upon us an independence which we do not want, then they will have to bear the responsibility for our life."[8] "Never has anyone dared committing such a crime before the civilized world." In its defiant tone the Austrian press merely followed the example of many prominent German and Austrian political leaders.

The Austrian chancellor Karl Renner commiserated with the Germans as "the most unfortunate people."[9] In a similar vein Ludo Hartmann declared that the German peace terms gave cause for a "day of mourning."[10] On May 12 he again pleaded energetically for Austria's right to self-determination and her right to fuse with Germany,[11] though in his view the Allies had condemned the latter to misery and poverty.

As if anticipating objections to Austria's protest against Germany's peace terms, Dr. Bauer asserted that Austria had a right to protest against the peace terms "not only because the German people is our people," but also in the interest of all the peoples of the entire world. Just because the Austrian Socialists were "enthusiastic adherents of the League of Nations, we cannot consent that the League of Nations be made an instrument of exploitation of people." He reminded the Austrians once more that German Austria was too small to exist by herself and that Socialism too would have to be postponed:

If we cannot enter Great Germany, neither shall we remain German Austrians. We shall disintegrate into Tyrolese, Carinthians, Salzburger, Upper Austrians, and Lower Austrians — in other words, into small bits of states. Out of such a structure

<hr>

[6]*Arbeiter-Zeitung,* May 8; *Reichspost,* May 9.
[7]*Arbeiter-Zeitung,* May 10.
[8]*Neue Freie Presse,* morng ed., May 8, "Friedensbestrebungen f. Deutschland."
[9]*Arbeiter-Zeitung,* May 12.
[10]*Ibid.,* May 11.
[11]Quoted in the *Neue Freie Presse,* May 14.

nothing great can develop. The fate of socialization is very closely tied up with this great political question.[12]

Ludo Hartmann then raised in the pages of the *Arbeiter-Zeitung* the question "What now?" Referring to the treaty clause which demanded of Germany to recognize Austria's independence, Hartmann did not interpret it as prohibiting the Anschluss, but merely as prohibiting German "interference in our free decision." And in his incorrigibly optimistic view, he held that nothing is lost yet, though "perhaps Germany's hands are tied for today and tomorrow."[13] On May 10 he pointed out that in the event German Austria should be denied the right to self-determination, she would have to turn to the League of Nations and to ask for a plebiscite. The League would then have to be reminded "to fulfill its duty."[14] Expecting the prohibition of the union, Hartmann in his untiringly persistent way had already mapped out a detailed strategy and tactics by means of which little Austria was to manipulate the League of Nations and the Great Powers and tactically overwhelm them!

The Austrian press campaign against the German peace treaty and the prohibition of the Anschluss was closely followed by numerous demonstrations in Austria in behalf of union with Germany. Among some of the organizations which staged these demonstrations and participated in them were the German Nationalists, the German Peasants League, the German People's Council for Austria, and the League for Protection of German soldiers. A major purpose behind these manifold activities seems to have been to impress the Paris Conference with the depth of German sentiment in the Austrian population and to strengthen the backbone of the Austrian delegation which was ready to leave for Paris.

The harsh German peace treaty, however, had produced a sobering effect on many Austrians and had strengthened the opposition of many to the Anschluss. Also, a fierce agitation had flared up among the Austrian Christian Socials against Dr. Otto Bauer and Dr. Franz Klein, former minister of justice, who for a while had been considered the likely leader of the Austrian peace delegation. The Austrian government

---

[12]*Arbeiter-Zeitung,* May 11.
[13]*Ibid.,* May 9, Hartmann, "Was nun?"
[14]*Ibid.,* May 10, Hartmann, "Der Weg zum Anschluss."

thus decided to appoint the more pliable and conciliatory chancellor Dr. Renner as head of the delegation rather than the firmly pro-Anschluss oriented Dr. Klein. Apparently French influence was also thrown into the scales against the latter. On May 8 Allizé, French ambassador in Vienna, called upon members of the Austrian government and indicated France's readiness to deal gently with Austria. The *Vossische Zeitung* interpreted the appointment of Renner as head of the Austrian peace delegation and his speech on that occasion as lowering the flag.[15]

Dr. Renner's greater flexibility reflected a realistic turn of mind. The Austrian chancellor seemed to be preparing his people for the inevitable defeat of their expectations.[16] On May 12, the day before his departure from Vienna, Renner addressed well-wishers from the balcony of the Austrian Chancellory and pledged that "however bitter the cup of misery, we shall not sacrifice . . . our German soul and our German character. The life of peoples and the life of the nation is not the life of a day nor of a year." The message was clear beyond any doubt. Renner left for Paris with few hopes and the expectations of the Austrian government which remained behind were not much higher. Bauer himself was far from confident.[17]

The reception of the Austrian delegation by the French and English press was rather mixed, ranging from hostile to moderately friendly. The Austrian delegation made every effort to be ingratiating, and Professor Lammasch and Renner received favorable comments, Renner especially after delivering his address to the Peace Conference in early June. To Clémenceau, Renner appeared a "simple and well-meaning man," a judgment which hardly took account of the

[15]*Voss. Zeitung*, May 9.

[16]*Ibid.*; here also quote from Renner's speech. On May 12, a giant demonstration in support of self-determination and the Anschluss was organized in front of the Rathaus in Vienna. Ludo Hartmann, then in Vienna, still exuded confidence: "Do not be intimidated by the pessimists who say: 'Everything is in vain, because it is the Entente which decides and whatever she decides we have to do!'" (Almond-Lutz, 1935: pp. 44f., May 26). Friedrich Adler spoke then too, as follows "Now the war is at an end, the main enemy is no longer in one's own country. The main foe is the imperialist victor (roaring and continually recurring applause)." And in the same vein Dr. Bauer ended his address with the call: "Down with imperialist capitalism!" Thus Austrian Socialist leaders were pouring oil on the still raging fires of German nationalism, hoping no doubt to harness it for the higher purposes of socialism.

[17]*Ibid.*, May 12.

Austrian's considerable intellectual achievements and political and diplomatic talents.[18]

The Austrian delegation soon complained about its seclusion from the press and the Conference, its being virtually placed "behind barbed wire," and last, but not least, its inability to make its observations and replies directly and orally, instead of having to submit them in writing. Yet years later, in 1946, when Dr. Renner was once again Chancellor, he considered the reception of the Austrian delegation in St. Germain in 1919 as not having been an unfavorable one. Unlike the German delegation, he observed then, the Austrian delegation had been received as "guests of the French republic," and "with friendliness." Through a famous Austrian, Freiherr von Slatin—who as Slatin Pasha had served as governor of a district in the Sudan under Gordon—Renner had been in touch with Lord Balfour, von Slatin's "personal friend."[19]

But there could be no doubt about the mounting tension in St. Germain. Some French papers had shown definite animosity. *Le Matin* introduced Renner rather inaccurately, as a partisan of union "at any price."[20] On May 16 it accused Renner of pursuing the same tactics as the German foreign secretary Brockdorff-Rantzau.

There were reasons for the growing mutual suspicion between Vienna and Paris. Paris may have feared that Renner would be tempted to imitate Brockdorff-Rantzau's undiplomatic performance of May 7 when the German foreign secretary, presented with the treaty, had resorted to a sharp and bitter attack against the Allies. Vienna, on the other hand, shocked already at the severity of the German peace terms and uncertain whether it would receive any better treatment, anticipated with some trepidation the economic and territorial provisions of the peace with which it would be saddled. While it expected that the Peace Conference would prohibit an immediate union, it hoped that it would not place insuperable obstacles on the road toward Anschluss in the future.

---

[18]Almond-Lutz, 1935: pp. 329-330.
[19]Stadler, 1966: pp. 41-42.
[20]*Le Matin*, May 14, "St. Germain awaits the Austrians."

FIG. 4. Dr. Karl Renner, 1870-1950. Austria's chancellor, 1918-1919.

In Versailles, the Austrian delegation waited even longer than the German delegation had done before receiving an official communication from the Peace Conference. Chancellor Renner became irritated and vented sentiments of annoyance and impatience. On May 24 Renner wrote to Georges Clémenceau, the president of the Peace Conference, to complain that since its arrival ten days before, no communication on the opening of the negotiations had reached the German Austrian delegation. The long delay in the making of the peace raised in the mind of the German Austrian people "an uneasiness all the more serious as its prolongation seems incomprehensible to the masses and must necessarily provoke all sorts of rumors and fears." The Austrian government entertained serious apprehensions about the possibility of maintaining peace and order in Austria, notably in the great industrial centers "as well as in the contested districts, whether occupied by a neighboring state or exposed to military invasion. This condition of uncertainty may offer favorable ground for an irritation of the masses among whom unhealthy ideas may ferment." In conclusion, the delegation pointed to the expenses entailed by their long stay in St. Germain, expenses which were out of proportion to the precarious economic situation of German Austria.[21]

Soon thereafter Dr. Renner received a note from the office of the president of the Peace Conference, indicating that the Peace Treaty would be presented to the Austrian delegation on May 30.[22] When that day approached the presentation was postponed for three more days. Thereupon, in a new note to the Conference dated May 30, Renner mentioned his earlier letter of the twenty-fourth and three verbal communications of the twenty-second, twenty-sixth, and twenty-ninth. He had then, he reminded the Conference, drawn attention to the circumstances that a postponement of the peace treaty would have "the most dangerous social consequences and cause bloody uprisings in the contested territories," and he repeated his warnings.[23] The threat of social radicalism, particularly Bolshevism, real though it was in the critical postwar era, was repeatedly used as a bargaining point; for this very reason it lost some of its effectiveness.

The following day Clémenceau informed Dr. Renner that according to the rules set by the Conference an exchange of views could take place only in writing; he promised to keep all memoranda which the Austrian delegation cared to forward strictly confidential.[24] Finally, on June 2, Clémenceau handed the preliminary treaty over to the Austrian delegation, informing it that the treaty could be modified only within certain limits.

In reply, Dr. Renner delivered his address to the Assembly, speaking in French. He stressed that the Danubian monarchy, against which the Allied and Associated Powers had

---

[21]Almond-Lutz, 1935; pp. 43-44, Renner to Clémenceau, May 24.
[22]*Ibid.*, May 26.
[23]*Ibid.*, May 30, Renner.
[24]*Ibid.*, May 31, Clémenceau to Renner.

waged war and with which they had concluded an armistice, was dead. The twelfth of November, the day the Austrian republic was proclaimed, should be considered the day of its demise. The new German Austrian state could no more be considered a successor of the late monarchy than the other national states which had sprung up on its ruins, but was just "one part of the vanquished and fallen empire." He also voiced thanks for the generous relief action that had saved the Austrian people from "downright starvation." The delegation was well aware of the fact that Austria's fate rested in the hands of the Allied Powers, but appealed to the conscience of the world not to deny or curtail "[the Austrians'] inalienable right of self-determination . . . a right realized by our neighbors with our ready consent," and one which the Austrian people had adopted as a fundamental basis of its constitution.

Dr. Renner pointed to the orderly revolution in Austria which had become a "mainstay of peaceful and organized social development in Central Europe," thus reminding the Allies of the contrast with Bolshevik Hungary and the civil-war conditions which prevailed in Germany. He promised that the new republic would continue to develop along orderly lines, "provided that a just and democratic peace renders economic existence possible to our country."[25]

The contents of Chancellor Renner's speech and his firm but unassuming personality made a favorable impression upon the Conference and the French press. Though Renner was not a professional diplomat, his reply was considered by *Le Temps* "much more skillful" than the declarations made earlier on Germany's behalf by Foreign Secretary Brockdorff-Rantzau.[26]

The Austrian peace terms should have caused no great surprise in Vienna; the prohibition of the Anschluss and the loss of German Bohemia and South Tyrol were not unexpected. Nevertheless, the publication of the Austrian peace treaty caused general cries of protest and expressions of bitterness and anguish. "Unacceptable," wrote the *Neue Freie Presse* on June 4.[27] Renner denounced the "hypocrisy of the right to

[25]*Ibid.*, June 2, Renner.
[26]*Le Temps,* June 4, "La Paix avec Autriche."
[27]*Neue Freie Presse,* morning ed., June 4.

self-determination," and referred to German Austria as a country which "is left over," "a mountainous country which cannot live and which cannot die."[28] On June 3 the *Arbeiter-Zeitung* complained: "They have taken everything from us." Its editorial on June 4 bore the title: "No peace, but death for German Austria." "One would search in vain throughout history for a peace treaty which in malice, cruelty, and brutal violation of every right, is equal to the one which is being forced upon us." It put to shame even the base peace dictated to Germany. The paper denounced the "cruel sacrifice of three and a half million Germans in Bohemia, Moravia, and Silesia to the most oppressive and violent[!] people in Europe, the Czechs." The peace treaty was "without exaggeration the greatest infamy of recent history."

Yet, after all the harsh words, the *Arbeiter-Zeitung*, unlike the *Vorwärts* after the publication of the German peace terms a month earlier, came out not against signing the treaty, but rather for improving it.[29] Earlier Karl Kautsky had urged the Germans to look at the peace terms calmly and had warned them that "passions" were "bad advisers."[30] Now Otto Bauer spoke similarly to the Austrian National Assembly about the "understandable eruption of passion," but warned that it was unwise to be guided by the "tone of passion" in pursuing negotiations with the Associated Powers.

Sharp opposition to the Austrian peace treaty, but composure and the desire for modification of the peace terms also characterized the attitude of Dr. Otto Bauer in his address to the Austrian National Assembly on June 7. He protested the forcible separation of four million Germans from the republic as well as the prohibition of the Anschluss of German Austria. He warned the Assembly of the rise of a new German—and also Magyar—irredentism. German Austria's peace terms were even harsher than Germany's and had thus "refuted" the "sad illusions of those who sought salvation in separation from the German Reich." It was "not the degree of hatred but the estimated strength still left to the vanquished which determined the nature of the peace terms." The line of policy which Dr. Bauer intended to pur-

---

[28]*Ibid.*, June 11.
[29]*Arbeiter-Zeitung*, June 8, "Überzeugen!"
[30]*Vorwärts*, May 16.

sue in order to improve the peace treaty was indicated by his analysis of it. He found particularly bad those provisions which the Western Powers had imposed upon German Austria in behalf of the succession states, while he considered other terms stipulated in favor of the Entente "perhaps tolerable."[31] The Vienna government concentrated its efforts on modifying Austria's peace terms affecting her relation to the succession states.

The entire German press, bourgeois and Socialist, did not lag behind the Austrian press in its bitterness about and denunciation of the Austrian peace terms. Four weeks earlier Austrian Social Democracy had come to the help of the German comrades by condemning the German peace treaty. Now German Socialism was equally critical of the Austrian peace terms. On June 3 *Vorwärts* denounced the treaty of St. Germain with Austria as marked by a "petty spirit of vengefulness" and prophesied that Allied policy would surely be defeated.[32] At the convention of the German Social Democratic party on June 11, Hermann Müller, its presiding officer, curiously enough, still exuded confidence that "perhaps now Great Germany will become a reality" and extended greetings to "our Austrian brethren" who had experienced "the same misery." Once again he reassured the German nation that it could "rely" on its working class.[33]

But such demonstrations and professions could obviously not alter the harsh realities already determined at Versailles and St. Germain.

---

[31]*Stenogr. Protokolle über d. Sitzungen d. Konstit. Nationalvers.*, 1919, Bauer, June 7 and 8.

[32]*Vorwärts,* June 3.

[33]*Ibid.,* evng. ed., June 12.

3. GERMAN AND AUSTRIAN DIPLOMACY
AND ANSCHLUSS PROPAGANDA

"A propaganda agency should be created." Subcommittee of the German National Assembly

THOSE reports on the position of France and Great Britain on the Anschluss question which reached Berlin during April of 1919 had sounded rather unfavorable. Equally disheartening was the news about the mood in Austria, especially Vienna, which Wedel forwarded at this time from Vienna.

On the second of May, Wedel had written: "The pro-Anschluss mood [in Austria] has slackened considerably during the last two weeks." The revolution in Bavaria and the threatened severity of the peace terms for Germany were both responsible for this change. "Yet the main reason lies in the much more intensive and skillful counteragitation of the Entente."[1]

As he had done before and was to do again, Wedel burst out in a flurry of anti-Viennese and anti-Austrian utterances, revealing a dislike of Austria which was not quite uncommon among contemporary Germans, through strangely inconsistent for a convinced partisan of the Anschluss and of national unification.

Almost the entire Viennese press supports his [Colonel Cunninghame's] endeavors. It has always been venal like a hussy, and in the manner of hussies loves the strange and the novel. . . . Journals which lay claim to quality and political sophistication are writing against the Anschluss. Whoever does not participate therein is adventurous and lacking in political acumen and understanding of tactics. The Entente has made it clear that if they [the Austrians] behave nicely, the borders of German Austria will be drawn in a favorable manner.[2]

---

[1]*N.A.*, T 120-3270, Wedel to F.O., May 2.
[2]*Ibid.*

Wedel's reports to Berlin apparently confirmed the wisdom of the cautious policy Germany had adopted regarding the union.

As Berlin was critical of Vienna, so Vienna had doubts about Berlin. Dr. Bauer was afraid that the German government "would be forced to yield under pressure."[3] These fears were well grounded. On the ninth of May, Brockdorff-Rantzau sent the following telegram to the Paxkonferenz in Berlin:

> Urgent please: wire immediately the following to the ambassador in Vienna: "Request you inform Dr. Bauer at once that in the peace treaty submitted to us the Entente demands that we strictly recognize the independence of Austria within the limits provided in the treaty and respect it as unchangeable, unless the consent of the Council of the League of Nations to another solution is obtained. Please assure Dr. Bauer that I shall hold unconditionally to the agreements reached by him and myself in Berlin as long as I am responsible for Germany's foreign affairs. The rumor spread especially by the Viennese press that I would like to take advantage of the peace negotiations to treat the German Austrian question as a barter trade is nothing but a slanderous suspicion about the tendency and origin of which there can hardly be any doubt."[4]

Dr. Bauer thought it necessary promptly to inform the Austrian Peace Delegation in St. Germain of the German foreign secretary's disclaimer.

In view of the expected Allied resistance to the union and the threat of territorial losses along Germany's borders, a political deal between Germany and the Allies could never be entirely discarded. In return for renouncing the Anschluss, disputed border regions might be left with Germany. Wedel himself had earlier made such suggestions. On April 24, 1919, Prince Karl Lichnowsky, former ambassador to the Court of St. James, wrote similarly to Brockdorff-Rantzau: "German Austria would be for us only a questionable present; it would be a burden, politically and economically speaking."[5] "North Bohemia, formerly Austrian territory,

---

[3]*Ibid.*, Wedel to F.O., May 5.
[4]*N.A.*, T 136-25, Akten . . . , Br. R. to Paxkonferenz, May 9.
[5]*A.A.*, Nachlass Br.-R., 7/8, Lichnowsky, Apr. 24.

should be left to Czechoslovakia. I still hope, however, that we might keep our remaining borders in exchange for renouncing German Austria."[6] On another occasion, in an updated letter from Upper Silesia, Lichnowsky advised Brockdorff-Rantzau that in order to save "the mixed Eastern territories (West Prussia, Upper Silesia, etc.)," Germany had better "renounce the German Austrians." For many Germans their own threatened Eastern home territories assumed unquestioned primacy over distant Austrian lands. Lichnowsky continued: "That Austria wishes to come to us does no harm; on the contrary, it strengthens our position."[7] In the same sense and at about the same time the Bavarian minister for foreign affairs, Ritter von Dandl, corresponding with the Bavarian ambassador in Berlin, Hugo von Lerchenfeld, observed with great interest the developments in neighboring Austria and suggested that the "inclination which the German Austrians show to link up with us" was quite "valuable" and "could be skillfully used by us."[8]

By early May when the prohibition of the Anschluss became public knowledge, a mood of disillusionment seized even the most loyal partisans of the movement for union. Active participation on the part of the Austrian leaders in the work of the German National Assembly seemed no longer purposeful. Bauer wrote thus: "The German Constitution will have to be written without us, since the Anschluss is unattainable."[9]

This decision of Dr. Bauer encountered some criticism in German official circles, as for instance by von Körner who reminded Hartmann that yielding led nowhere and that any hopes for consideration by the Entente were in vain. Hugo Preuss, on the other hand, pointed out " 'that he had never placed great value upon the participation of the National Assembly in framing the constitution' and that it had only symbolic significance."[10]

When the peace terms were submitted to the Austrian delegation in St. Germain, Dr. Bauer immediately appealed to the German Foreign Office in Berlin for diplomatic as-

[6]*Ibid.*, 7/5, n.d.; also *Le Temps* about Lichnowsky, Apr. 18.
[7]*O.S.*, K 109, Wedel to F.O., May 15.
[8]*G.A.*, MA 103024, Das öst. Friedensangebot u.d. Umwälzung, Von Dandl to Lerchenfeld, Apr. 17.
[9]*Ibid.*, K 261, I, Deutschland (Anschl.), Bauer, May 24.
[10]*Ibid.*, Hartmann to Bauer, May 26.

sistance in behalf of German Bohemia. (It was not the Anschluss of Inner German Austria which was the issue at this time.) He wanted the German government to dispatch a note to the Entente in support of German Bohemia's cause. Bauer voiced the hope that this would "very favorably influence the mood here [Vienna]."[11] The German Foreign Office promptly passed Bauer's plea on to Brockdorff-Rantzau. Three days later the German foreign minister in a letter to his cousin, State Secretary Freiherr von Langwerth, rejected Bauer's suggestion:

> Please reply to Secretary Bauer that the German government agrees with the Austrian government in condemning the peace terms through which our joint opponents wish to bring millions of German Austrians under alien domination. However, a protest of the German government on this ground appears inopportune. The opponents have declined to accept further notes until a reply has been made to the German counterproposals.[12]

Support of the German Austrians by Berlin would at present only aggravate their situation. However, the German government considered a "parallel procedure" by the German and Austrian delegations in negotiating with the Peace Conference as urgently needed.

Bauer could hardly have entertained any illusions about the effectiveness of a diplomatic note by the German government. Yet he apparently thought of the psychological impact of such a move upon the flagging Austrian Anschluss movement, a movement which always suffered from uncertainty as to the genuine dedication of the German government and nation to the German Austrian cause and the Anschluss.

By turning Dr. Bauer down, Brockdorff-Rantzau must have further disillusioned the Austrian supporters of the Anschluss movement. Bauer, realizing the futility of all his appeals, instead of continuing to communicate directly with Brockdorff-Rantzau, simply requested Hartmann to "inform" the German secretary about developments in Austria.[13]

---

[11]*Ibid.*, Bauer, June 2; F.O. to Br.-R., June 4.
[12]*Ibid.*, Br.-R. to Langwerth, June 7.
[13]*Ibid.*, Hartmann to Br.-R., June 9.

Germany might be defeated and have to accept the peace terms, including the prohibition of the Anschluss, but she did long not hesitate before laying the groundwork for a future union. On June 7 Dr. Hartmann participated in a meeting which was attended by Constantin Fehrenbach, president of the Weimar National Assembly, two ministers, Mathias Erzberger and von Brentano, and eleven deputies, representing altogether a broad spectrum of German political parties. Fehrenbach presided and opened the discussion by pointing out that the German Austrian mood in regard to the Anschluss seemed to have improved. He claimed to know that Italy was prepared to renounce Southern Tyrol if German Austria joined Germany. "The time has now arrived" to do everything to bring about the Anschluss soon. "The peace treaty did not represent an absolute obstacle. The parties in the Austrian parliament are ready for the Anschluss. Some problems (currency, etc.) of course need to be solved." He suggested the formation of an executive committee from among members of the German National Assembly to speed the union.

The very boldness of Fehrenbach's utterances at this moment apparently pleased Austria's ambassador Ludo Hartmann, through it also stunned him. Now it was his turn to play a restraining role. He assured the distinguished gathering that the Anschluss concept remained as ever the basis for German Austria's policy. However, it was not practical to come out into the open with demonstrations during the next few weeks while peace was still debated. "In about six weeks will be the best psychological moment to resume action."[14]

Actually, Fehrenbach had not suggested challenging the prohibition of the Anschluss within the next few days or weeks. And Hartmann pleaded for caution and restraint only for the next few weeks, until the peace treaty had been signed. "After conclusion of the peace treaty will be the moment to start moving rapidly." Then a plebiscite would be in order. And with his usual propensity to exaggerate, he assured the meeting that "already 90% of the population" were for the Anschluss. Agreement would easily be reached on the currency question.

---

[14]*Ibid.*, Hartmann to Bauer, June 7.

Minister Erzberger then assured the meeting that the German government extended "a hearty welcome to the Anschluss," and that the National Assembly should prepare it. "The German government would do anything for the Anschluss, but at the moment it cannot come out openly in its favor." Von Delbrück declared that the union could be talked about in the National Assembly, but the delegate Dr. Trinborn favored restraint in the Assembly and recommended proceeding "as quietly as possible in order not to draw the attention of the Entente toward it." Erzberger likewise came out in support of an open discussion of the Anschluss question only after the signing of the peace treaty. Finally, Dr. Preuss, Minister von Brentano, and Dr. Hartmann agreed on setting up an executive committee. According to Brentano, "after Ludo Hartmann's and our declarations our success cannot be doubted." While preparations for the union were in order on both sides, the public should for the moment not be taken into their confidence. It was then decided to set up two committees, one of seven members which was to establish contact with the German government through Rittmeister von Brentano, and a smaller one for the purpose of making plans for preparatory work for the Anschluss with the assistance of Dr. Pfeiffer and Dr. Hartmann.[15]

If the publication of the peace terms had had a depressing and even shattering effect upon the German people and some of its leaders, this joint session of Cabinet members and parliamentarians showed little of it. These men were busily and boldly engaged in planning Germany's expansion and moving toward the Anschluss promptly "after the signing of the peace treaty." German "revisionism" was beginning clandestinely to assert itself even before the treaty was signed! And it was to test the Entente in what was considered to be its weakest link, Austria.

The new buoyant, self-confident, and defiant mood in Germany was also clearly noticeable in the debates of the German Constituent Assembly in early July. While considering the question of the flag, the Assembly touched again on Austria and the Anschluss. The Social Democratic minister of the interior Dr. David spoke of the past struggle

_____
[15]*Ibid.*

between the *grossdeutsch* ideal and the Great Prussian idea. The colors black, white and red had been the symbol of the hegemony and predominance of Prussia in Germany. With the dissolution of the Habsburg dynasty "the *grossdeutsch* ideal of unity has once more become the goal of our longing [Bravo! from the Left] and the black, red and gold banner shall be a symbol of this grossdeutsch goal and its visible expression. It will win adherents for the reunion of the Germans who live beyond the borders of the Reich." He expressed "wrath" over the prohibition of the Anschluss with the mother country. "Where dynastic Germany has failed, there democracy must succeed: namely, in making moral conquests beyond the border and especially with all those who belong to us by blood and language [Bravo! from the Left]." *Grossdeutsch* unity should be won not through war and violence, but through the strength of the political and social culture of the new republican Germany.[16]

Laverrenz of the German National People's party held that the Anschluss was much too important a matter to be seriously tied up with the flag question. But he left no doubt that he wanted Germany to stand guard on the Danube, whatever flag Austria accepted. Dr. Petersen of the German Democratic party likewise disputed the need for a new flag, the black, red, gold banner of 1848-1849. As far as the *grossdeutsch* idea was concerned, there was no one in the Assembly who did not share this concept. The Social Democrat Molkenbuhr, however, stressed that the new flag should display the "colors of the *Grossdeutschen*"; the Austrian ambassador himself had come out for it. He was seconded by the pacifist leader Dr. Quidde of the German Domocratic party, who said that foreign countries wanted to prevent "the unification of the entire[!] German nation," but Germans wanted "union with our German Austrian brethren." Black, red, and gold was a flag which pointed "to the future, to the future of freedom and of Grossdeutschland."[17]

Exactly a week later Hermann Müller, the new minister of foreign affairs voiced regret in the Constituent Assembly that Germany did not have the power to prevent the "misfortune" that territories German in language and custom were being

---

[16]Heilfron, 1919: **5:** pp. 2994-2995, 44th sess., July 2, 1919.
[17]*Ibid.,* pp. 3001-3019.

torn from the Reich. But the Social Democrat Krätzig gave expression to the hope that all Germans would soon be joined together in a unitary state, and his party colleague Traub likewise promised that the day of "German liberation" would come.[18]

The endeavors of the Constituent Assembly during the month of July were no doubt aimed at bringing that day closer. A subcommittee of the National Assembly devoted a large number of sessions exclusively to the subject of the Anschluss. Particularly important discussions were held on July 7, daily between the ninth and twelfth of July, and on July 17. Present were Dr. Pfeiffer, Dr. Hartmann, and Rittmeister von Brentano. "It is the opinion of the subcommittee that a grandiose propaganda scheme must be organized in Germany as well as in Austria" on behalf of the union. It must be promoted not from the party-political point of view, only

> from patriotic and general German considerations. The following propositions are considered useful: A propaganda agency should be created to furnish materials to both German and German Austrian newspapers. In this agency attention is to be given to historic, political, economic, financial, and general cultural points of view . . . It should do impartial justice to all political parties.[19]

The subcommittee also recommended ascertaining whether financial assistance could be arranged by the German or the German Austrian government, or both. The subcommittee itself was of the opinion that it would be better to pay for this propaganda from the resources of the German government alone.

"Propaganda of the spoken word" was soon to be initiated. It was to be conducted, like that of the written word, in Germany as well as in German Austria. Political speeches were to be presented by adherents of all parties. The dispatch of propagandists into Austrian towns was to be arranged by the individual parties, but it appeared more useful to the subcommittee if the General Executive Committee which was composed of the different parties would choose the speakers.

[18]*Ibid.*, pp. 3436-3446, 51st sess., July 9.
[19]*O.S.*, K 261, pp. 425-426.

The subcommittee was also of the opinion that nothing should be done until peace was signed with German Austria. "Real harm" would be caused if activist propaganda in behalf of the union were started immediately; it would only produce "counter-pressure by the Entente."

In accordance with Fehrenbach's earlier suggestion, the subcommittee recommended that existing organizations of a private nature, such as the Deutsch-Österreichischer Alpenverein, the Historikertagung, and the Verein für Sozialpolitik, be drawn into the propaganda work for the union.

The subcommittee then examined the possible risks of a policy aimed at the annexation of Austria. It also raised the question of whether a parallel steering committee might be established in German Austria.[20] It concluded that such a committee was urgently needed in Austria, but as Ambassador Hartmann had already pointed out, it could only be formed after the conclusion of the peace.

At late as July, 1919, the subcommittee of the German National Assembly continued its activities in preparation for the Anschluss in spite of the fact that such a union had already been prohibited in the peace treaty. The subcommittee emphasized the need for silence and secrecy. For the time being, it kept its rather detailed plans from the plenary assemblies. It operated as clandestinely as did the participants in the joint gathering of members of the German Cabinet and leading German parliamentarians about which Ludo Hartmann had earlier reported. But across the Inn River the German Austrian Anschluss movement, in closest association with German propaganda originating in Berlin and the Weimar Assembly, operated in full daylight, reaching a crescendo during the summer months of 1919.

Allizé, French envoy in Vienna, was quick to notice it. He warned that public opinion in Austria was subjected to German "propaganda of a scope which exceeds anything we have seen during the war in neutral countries," referring to his diplomatic service in the Netherlands. For several weeks, since the Treaty of Versailles had been signed, German propaganda had "redoubled its activities." Germany held that the prohibition of the Anschluss had not been clearly

---

[20]*Ibid.*

enunciated in the treaty; therefore, "the question remained open and could still be resolved in a manner favorable to [Germany's] interests." "She tries at this moment to arouse by all means Pan-German sentiments among Austrians and German irredentism among the German inhabitants of the new states." In his communication to Pichon, dated as late as September 1, Allizé pointed therefore to the need for inserting clauses in the peace treaty which were aimed at curtailing German propaganda in Austria.[21]

The very soul of this propaganda, according to Allizé, was the Deutscher Schulverein, the oldest national league founded in Vienna in 1880. In 1917 it had a membership of a quarter of a million people and had a huge budget at its disposal. The society was linked with the Pan-German Union. Vienna had numerous other political leagues such as the Verein Südmark, Bund der Deutschen in Bôhmen, Bund der Deutschen in Mähren, Bund der Deutschen in Niederösterreich, Verein der Deutschen in Sprachinseln, Deutscher Volksbund, Deutsch-nationale Partei, National Demokratische Partei, and Deutscher Volksrat.

> Whatever may be the particularities and nuances of all these parties, they all are united in the idea of a Greater Germany of the incorporation of Alemannic Austria into the Reich. The Anschluss is the goal of this entire propaganda, whether avowed or not. This is the leitmotif of all the tracts and posters which are distributed.

In this context he mentioned the "Flugblätter für das deutsch-österreichische Recht." The fifth pamphlet in this series was entitled *Anschluss und Deutschland* (February, 1919). Another brochure contained the appeal of the German National party, dated January, 1919, still another one was a

---

[21]*A.E.*, Allizé, pp. 288-297. There were published in Vienna, Allizé continued, a multitude of illustrated postal cards on controversial subjects. One showed two soldiers, one a German, the other an Austrian, shaking hands in front of what is to become the foundation stone of the structure of Greater Germany, bearing the inscription "union." Other cards evoked the Middle Ages, and the legend of the sleeping Emperor Barbarossa who is soon to rise to save Germany. Stamps and vignettes were also used as instruments of German propaganda. One stamp carried the slogan "from the Adige to the Baltic." The numerous vignettes focused on the idea of German unity. Even match boxes and cigaret boxes displayed more or less subtle propaganda in behalf of the Anschluss.

catechism of the National-Democratic party which was already known for its support of the Anschluss. All these brochures attempted to demonstrate that Austria had not only a sentimental but also an economic interest in the union with Germany.

Allizé reported further that a new periodical entitled *Deutsch-österreichische Nachrichten* had been founded in Berlin. It was supposed to be the organ of German Austrians in the Reich. "Whether one considers this question from the point of view of Berlin or that of Vienna, we find the same organization, the same method, the same principles or rather the same secret thoughts." In view of these developments the French mission, Allizé reported, had mounted a vigorous counteroffensive.

4. AUSTRIA'S PLEAS AND
THE NEW GERMAN CABINET.
DR. OTTO BAUER'S RESIGNATION

> "Regrettable as the conditions are, they should not prevent us from going on secretly spinning threads and there are enough areas in which work could be continued to prepare the political Anschluss at a later time. . . . It is this very thing that Dr. Bauer has in mind." Stolberg, German Embassy in Vienna, 1919

NOT only Foreign Secretary Brockdorff-Rantzau, but also Chancellor Scheidemann was unwilling to sign the Peace Treaty of Versailles. Thus on June 22, 1919, a new German government was formed, headed by the Majority Socialist Gustav Bauer and with Hermann Müller as minister of foreign affairs. Resolved as it was to accept the Treaty of Versailles, it nevertheless continued the moderate and cautious pro-Anschluss policy of its predecessor. While unable to give more encouragement to the union concept than Brockdorff-Rantzau had rendered, the new government felt it to be a matter of national duty and honor to be no less committed to it than its forerunner had been.

The Austrian ambassador Ludo Hartmann, sensing his new opportunity, lost no time. While the Austrian government and its foreign secretary Dr. Bauer remained convinced that the union would have to be postponed, Ludo Hartmann still believed that a successful coup might be pulled off within the next few weeks, and continued his various activities toward that end. According to him, many German political leaders were still agreed "about the necessity of an early and strong agitation" to bring about the Anschluss. He therefore suggested that delegates of the German Constituent Assembly visit German Austria. "One evening recently," he reported to Vienna, "I saw many Herren, Minister-President Bauer, Minister of Foreign Affairs Müller, Minister of the Interior David, Fehrenbach, Preuss, Schiffer, Under

Secretary of State Albert, Erzberger"—he singled out the latter as having displayed the "greatest willingness to help"—and others.

The talks, interspersed with wine, sandwiches, and cigars, were drawn out until 1 A.M., and climaxed in the following concrete matters: (1) the setting up of a secretariat of German-Austrian affairs (probably to be attached to the Foreign Office), (2) the establishment of an inter-party committee, parliamentary in character.[1]

Again, writing to Hartmann on July 8, Dr. Bauer seemed alarmed at these new developments at the highest governmental level—and after the presentation of the peace treaties—and sounded a note of caution: "Until the conclusion of the peace treaty in St. Germain, the Anschluss should not be talked about at all." Yet, as before, Bauer did not close the door to the Anschluss for the future, after the peace treaty had been signed.

How matters will develop after the signing of the peace treaty depends of course on the political situation and economic conditions, yet I hope we shall be able to resume negotiations very soon [!] after the conclusion of the peace. Should the Anschluss not be immediately feasible, then I conceive it possible to create for the time being a transitory state, say a German *Bund* between the German republic and German Austria, and to establish so many common bonds between them as the international situation permits. In this form, one to which the Entente could probably make few objections at first, one could also create so many common interests that complete legal unity would develop on its own within a few years. However, this would pre-suppose that Germany took care of (1) furnishing our food, (2) providing us with raw materials, and (3) extending credit to us and restoring our currency, since under

---

[1]*O.S.*, K 261, Hartmann to Bauer, July 5, pp. 390-392. This suggestion, apparently, was not identical with that made in an earlier meeting, on June 7, attended by distinguished members of the German cabinet and parliamentarians, reported previously. About the lively interest of German political leaders in the Anschluss movement in July 1919, see also Protokoll über d. Sitzg. am 7. Juli, pp. 399-402; Hartmann to Bauer, July 12, pp. 407-408; Hartmann to Bauer, July 14, pp. 409-410.

these circumstances we would not receive credit from the Entente.[2]

Dr. Bauer's activist course after the signing of the peace treaty thus clearly depended on Germany's rendering substantial assistance to help German Austria ward off any retaliatory strikes by the Entente.

In accordance with Bauer's line of thought, Hartmann submitted suggestions for strengthening the economic ties between German Austria and Germany. These ideas had been developed partly by the Centrist leader Erzberger, who thus emerged as one of the foremost protagonists of the German Anschluss movement. But even Hartmann confided to Bauer that these economic proposals "will constitute a burden for Germany which must not be underestimated—a matter which we probably see clearer than Erzberger."[3]

On July 15 Hartmann was received by Hermann Müller. Hartmann impressed upon the foreign secretary that he considered it of the greatest importance that "within the next few days" a Cabinet decision be reached pledging that Germany would assume the foregoing obligations *vis-à-vis* Austria.[4] Once again he appeared to have the German government cornered. Bauer's letter to Hartmann had made no mention of any time limit, but Hartmann, exceeding his instructions as usual, had added one. Hartmann's request had all the earmarks of an ultimatum.

On the very same day Bauer again warned his envoy to proceed more cautiously in the Anschluss question and, as far as Austria's friends in Germany were concerned, in a more forthright and open manner. Perhaps it was the sharpest rebuke that Bauer had administered to the Austrian envoy in Germany. "The protocol of the June 7 session of the Commission on the Anschluss to Germany," he wrote, compelled him to make several remarks:

First of all, if the protocol is correct, you have informed the German parliamentarians inaccurately; nobody here who knows the conditions well can assert that all three parties of the German Austrian parliament are united in the question of the

---

[2]*Ibid.*, Bauer to Hartmann, July 8, p. 394.
[3]*Ibid.*, Hartmann to Bauer, July 12, p. 407.
[4]*Ibid.*, Hartmann to Bauer, July 15.

Anschluss, or even that 90 per cent of the population are for the Anschluss. I consider such embellishments among friends utterly inappropriate. Likewise, I consider it quite wrong to assert today that action could begin in six weeks. In six weeks we shall probably have to negotiate with the Entente about credit for food and raw materials. . . . "Action" will only be possible if the Entente breaks up and their armies are demobilized. . . . There is admittedly a possibility that the Anschluss could perhaps be undertaken earlier; namely in the event of rapid revolutionary development either in Germany or in the countries of the Entente. At the moment, however, one cannot count on it. . . . Therefore, I urgently plead with you to proceed somewhat more cautiously so that we do not make promises which later turn out to be impossible to keep.[5]

Yet Bauer's diplomatic caution and his rejection of the dubious means employed by his German envoy did not mean that he was willing to shelve the Anschluss question permanently or even for a long time, but merely until after the conclusion of the peace of St. Germain. Thereafter he thought that German Austria would move again, and might within a few years achieve her objectives. In the meantime, as he had previously explained to Hartmann, a "transitory" stage might be reached, "a German *Bund*," if Germany would only lend a helping hand against possible counter-measures by the Entente. Bauer did not propose that German Austria lie still. On the contrary, he had laid down "Principles for our further procedure in the Anschluss question." On July 14 Hartmann informed Bauer that he had communicated the contents of those "Principles" to President Friedrich Ebert and Foreign Secretary Hermann Müller and that both were in agreement with the Austrian government.[6]

In suggesting that Dr. Hartmann contact the German government, Dr. Bauer was laying the groundwork for a policy to be sustained during the next year or the next few years. But Hartmann, with his characteristic impatience and drive, interpreted his directions very liberally indeed, and approached the German Foreign Office with the idea of extracting immediate advantages. Even at this late stage he hoped at least to secure pledges to strengthen the backbone

---

[5]*Ibid.*, Bauer to Hartmann, July 15, pp. 421-424.
[6]*Ibid.*, Hartmann to Bauer, July 14, pp. 409-410.

of the discouraged Austrian Peace Delegation in St. Germain[7] — a task which Dr. Bauer had not assigned to him. Thus on various occasions Dr. Hartmann attempted to seize diplomatic initiative not only from Berlin, but also from Vienna.

As if Bauer had a premonition of what Hartmann was promoting, on July 18 he admonished his envoy again "not to exceed the framework of your instructions."

> As long as peace has not been concluded in St. Germain and our relations have not been clarified, I consider it quite wrong to take any steps in the direction of the Anschluss. Any news about negotiations relating to the Anschluss or to matters which are evidently directed toward the Anschluss would at this point weaken our position in St. Germain and burden the government with responsibility for it.

Any disclosure, or even the suspicion of a double-play on Austria's part, was likely to undermine rather than strengthen Austria's case before the Peace Conference.[8]

On July 8 Bauer had voiced the hope that he would be able to proceed in the matter of the Anschluss "soon" after the signing of the peace treaties. A week later he made it clear that "soon" did not mean "six weeks." The domestic opposition displayed by the Christian Socials against the Anschluss, combined with the foreign opposition by the Entente — especially France — had weakened the pro-Anschluss forces. According to Bauer, the Christian Socials had mounted a steady counter-propaganda against the union with Germany; the Austrian bourgeoisie had placed its entire hope upon the Entente. Among the working class too enthusiasm for the Anschluss had undeniably declined, since the Communist agitation against the "Anschluss an [with] Noske" had not been without effect. The Austrian Communists continued to denounce the German labor bureaucracy which had "betrayed" the interests of the German proletariat. And Bauer concluded: "We shall still need a great deal of patience. I therefore consider it appropriate for us not to deceive ourselves and

---

[7]*Ibid.*, Hartmann to Bauer, July 17.
[8]*Ibid.*, Bauer to Hartmann, July 18.

our German friends and thus create only disappointment for them and for us."

Actually, while Bauer was corresponding with his ambassador in Berlin during the month of July, admonishing, scolding, and warning him on occasion, in thought he was already removing himself from the direction of Austrian foreign affairs. On July 13 he had sent his letter of resignation to Chancellor Karl Renner who then headed the Austrian peace delegation in St. Germain. At home and abroad Bauer was known to be the driving force behind the Austrian Anschluss movement which he had served with great talent and dedication, but in vain. The ship of the Anschluss had been wrecked on the rock of France's determination. Bauer had also failed in what was perhaps an equally hopeless attempt to retain South Tyrol for Austria. The time had come to draw the consequences from these defeats. Suspected abroad on account of his alleged radical leanings — especially his support for the Soviet Hungarian regime — Dr. Bauer was fully aware that he could never obtain the confidence of the Entente which the new Austria, dependent as it was on Allied resources and good will, would urgently need. Nor was he the type to modify or reverse his convictions on the Anschluss merely in order to retain his post.

Thus Bauer's exposition of "further procedure" in the Anschluss question was not an indication of Austria's future course under his own stewardship, but rather his policy recommendation to his successor.

Dr. Otto Bauer's last-minute program of July 8 to secure German Austria's Anschluss at the first opportune moment came to naught. Dr. Hartmann, who had approached Foreign Minister Müller with these suggestions on July 15 and requested a rather hurried reply, received one dated July 17. Müller informed Hartmann that the cabinet thought that an agreement was possible in the currency question, though "at the moment" it could not be "definitely" decided, since its solution presupposed a settlement with the succession states. "Incidentally," he continued, "the Reich's economy is incapable at present of provisioning Austria with raw materials and food. Perhaps a way out could be found by the formation of a joint purchasing company." However, the minister for economic affairs had stated that the Reich was unable, as Müller put it, "to commit itself at the present time" in this respect.[9] The German Cabinet thus clearly rejected Dr. Bauer's plan for economic assistance in the event that Austria, soon after the peace treaty was signed, moved toward the Anschluss. On the other hand, only a week later, Minister for Defense Noske voiced no objection to the fulfillment of Dr. Hartmann's wish that a plenipotentiary of the German Austrian Department of the Army participate in the consultations about the future organization of the armed forces of the Reich. Such participation, of course, required hardly any sacrifice on the part of Germany; on the contrary it held out tangible benefits for her in the future.[10]

Whatever theoretical common ground there was between the German and Austrian partisans of the Anschluss, the tactical disagreements and differences as to timing were substantial. While Otto Bauer did not share Ludo Hartmann's opinion that union would be possible within the next few weeks, he was prepared to have Austria begin to move toward it after the conclusion of the peace treaty. Only recently had the German Cabinet defiantly laid the groundwork for the future realization of the union. But now it held that such an early move as Dr. Bauer had in mind was premature and flatly turned his suggestion down. The new German Cabinet was more moderate and conciliatory than its predecessor in matters of foreign policy, especially about the signing of the peace treaty. It could hardly be expected to proceed in the Anschluss question more boldly and in a more challenging manner than Scheidemann and Brockdorff-Rantzau.

The view that an Anschluss would be more opportune at a considerably later period was also voiced by Stolberg of the German Embassy in Vienna. He expected Austria to remain a "colony" of the Entente "for the next few years." He advised Berlin to renounce the union at once and let the Anschluss movement in Austria run its own "natural course." This need not prevent Germany "from going on secretly spinning threads." On July 23 Stolberg in a report to the German Foreign Office questioned whether it would have been desirable for Germany which was now in the grip of an economic crisis.

[9]*Ibid.*, Chancellor Müller to Hartmann, July 19, p. 436.
[10]*Ibid.*

to annex a more or less bankrupt country and thus shoulder quite incalculable burdens. . . . The Entente has relieved us for the moment of this decision. Yet better times will surely come again, and the Anschluss of German Austria must after all remain the goal worth striving for for every national-thinking German. The thought of it must not be allowed to die, neither at home nor in this country, though for tactical reasons extreme restraint toward the rest of Europe is imperative for both sides.[11]

Restraint in the Anschluss question was apparently also impressed upon Stolberg when he was received by the Austrian president Karl Seitz, though the latter assured him that the basic guidelines of Austria's foreign policy would remain unchanged.

Only a few days before Stolberg saw the Austrian president Karl Seitz, the latter had received the following letter of resignation, dated July 25, from Dr. Otto Bauer:

Since I assumed the direction of the Foreign Office, one of the leading principles of my policy was to gain the friendship of Italy, the most powerful of our neighbors. I hoped to secure Italy's support for the union of German Austria with the German Reich and her protection against the claims of our Slavic neighbors to German regions, and to find in friendly discussion a mutually acceptable solution to the question of German South Tyrol.[12]

Bauer had concentrated his endeavors on South Tyrol, as he had already explained to the Austrian National Assembly on June 7. Unfortunately, these endeavors had failed. With it his policy had "suffered bankruptcy because of the intransigence of Italian imperialism."

Italian imperialism forces us to turn to new roads. But I do not believe myself to be the right leader on this new path. I cannot hope to acquire the confidence of the French powerholders who, as Marx has scoffed, still consider the state of disunity which tore the German people apart a right of the French nation.

---

[11]*Ibid.*, Stolberg to F.O., July 23.
[12]*Arbeiter-Zeitung*, July 26; also *ibid.*, "Bauer's Rücktritt."

But my inability to obtain the confidence of the present French government stems not only from my struggle for the union of German Austria with the *grossdeutsch* republic, but also from my wartime position in regard to differences of opinion in international Social Democracy. True, it was just my closer friends and I who most determinedly battled German and German-Austrian imperialism during the war; we fought for the historic right of the bourgeois democracies of the West against the military monarchies of Central Europe. But current French policy judges us not on our relationship to France, but on our attitude to social revolution.

The same day that the *Arbeiter-Zeitung* published Bauer's letter of resignation, it commented on it editorially as follows: "The causes were exclusively of a foreign policy character. . . . Bauer, whose very character signifies principles, does not wish to be the obstacle to a new policy. However, he cannot serve it." It was evident that France was in a very powerful position at the Peace Conference. Although her suspicions of Austria were unfounded, Austria was "compelled to take note of and dissolve even unjustified prejudices." Bauer had aroused fears among certain French circles, though it was "quite unjustified" to consider his course anti-French. "A loyal advocate of the interests of our republic," "the most energetic representative of the Anschluss concept," Bauer had once again with his resignation demonstrated his loyalty and dedication.

One could only hope that Bauer's sacrifice would not be in vain, since he had given character and emphasis to the republic's foreign policy.

Bauer has steered the ship with a sure hand, and knowing him to be in this thankless and difficult office has filled us with confidence in our worst moments. In this comrade, who has proven himself in the most diverse areas, is something firm, straightforward, and reliable which assures steadiness and radiates confidence. Even our opponents have not been able to escape this impression, and the entire National Assembly — in complete contrast with the tactics of a venal press whose motives cannot remain concealed from anybody — was agreed in its appreciation and recognition of his conduct of foreign policy which . . . was dedicated to the cause.[13]

[13]*Ibid.*, July 23.

In the main committee of the Austrian National Assembly President Hauser had indeed voiced his regret at Bauer's resignation and thanked him for the loyalty which he had always demonstrated. Members of all major Austrian parties thus joined in expressing their appreciation for Dr. Bauer's stewardship during the difficult previous eight months.

On July 28 Chancellor Renner, having returned from St. Germain, called together the officials and members of the Foreign Secretariat who had been delegates at St. Germain. Then he turned to praising his predecessor with whom actually he had not always seen eye to eye: "In personal contact you have experienced what an extraordinarily keen intellect, what an unusual capacity for work and what an honest creative will was embodied in Otto Bauer. . . . Our fatherland is making a heavy sacrifice by permitting Otto Bauer to leave office."[14]

It was then Dr. Franz Klein's turn to reply to the new chief's address:

> You can be convinced that a similar picture of Dr. Bauer will always be in our memory. We have learned to esteem the clarity of his vision, the breadth of his intellect, the keenness of his understanding, and sharp decisiveness which sparkled forth every moment and carried along anybody who tended to doubt or hesitate. In everyone who saw him in his office he instilled confidence that the foreign relations of German Austria were conducted in a sure and sovereign manner, just as at the time Dr. Victor Adler stood at the helm.

Dr. Bauer, only thirty-seven years old, brilliant and persuasive, had been defeated in his immediate purposes. Yet he

---

[14]*Ibid.*, July 29. About the considerable impression Bauer made upon Brockdorff-Rantzau, see chap. III, 3 of this study. See also the favorable remarks in Lloyd George's *Memoirs* . . . , 1939: **2:** p. 362, about a "remarkable" speech of Bauer and his evaluation of Bauer: "He was an able and eloquent leader of the Socialist party in Austria" (pp. 612-613). The German Social Democrats had hardly men of a stature equal to that of Bauer and Renner. Harold Butler, first director of the International Labor Office, expressed this view in *Lost Peace* (pp. 127-128, quoted by Stadler, 1966: p. 79), "No one could fail to respect Bauer's brilliant intellect or Renner's strong character, which expressed itself with a typical Austrian charm of manner. Both were convinced democrats who fought Communism and Fascism alike sternly and consistently. In vigor and vision they were superior to the German socialist leaders and might have breathed the spirit of democracy into the German revolution . . . which led by men like Bauer and Renner might possibly have become a reality."

had made an impact upon his Austrian party colleagues, upon many non-Socialist compatriots, and upon numerous German leaders and politicians. He had also focused upon himself much of France's and the Entente's hostility toward the Anschluss project, and—less deservedly—had incurred the dislike of the Entente for his social radicalism, and French opposition for his seemingly pro-Italian policy.

On July 29 Bauer presented a concluding account to members of the Social Democratic party in the Landstrasse district of Vienna. Disputing the charges that the propagation of the Anschluss concept since November, 1918, had been harmful to German Austria, Bauer pointed out that on the contrary the resolution of November 12 had forced the entire world to face the question of whether German Austria was viable on her own.

> Whenever a voice is raised in a friendly country in support of the improvement of our lot, we may justly point out that, if we do not link up with Germany, we ought at least to be better treated if we are to continue to exist. And for the future it still remains the greatest achievement of these eight months that through the policy of the Anschluss we have compelled the entire people here to come to grips with the problem, that we have sunk deep roots, created the will to the Anschluss in this people. And I believe that it will grow and that the hour of the union will come.[15]

Bauer disavowed the rumors that the Entente had demanded his resignation. Departing from the criticism of the

---

[15]*Arbeiter-Zeitung,* July 30. At the session of the Executive Committee of the Austrian Social Democratic party on July 25 Bauer had declared that he wanted to relinquish the Foreign Office, since he could no longer "do anything in the matter of the Anschluss and the mood toward him in Paris was unfavorable" (Sitzungsprotokolle, Parteivorstand, July 27, 1916-Nov. 15, 1921, Verein für Geschichte der Arbeiterbewegung, p. 708). It is of considerable interest that Otto Bauer who in 1918-1919 championed the *Anschluss* and minimized the danger of the resurgence of German militarism and imperialism and feared only Western imperialism, in the thirties had come to sharply alter his views. In 1927 already he was prepared to abandon the *Anschluss* position, since he had reached the conclusion that it was utopian to expect its realization by peaceful means ("Wandlungen und Probleme der Anschlusspolitik," *Der Kampf,* 1927). On May 13, 1933 the Party leadership and the socialist club of deputies proclaimed jointly that in view of the Nazi dictatorship in Germany the Anschluss movement was dead. Austrian Social Democrats had wanted the Anschluss with the German democratic republic, but not with Hitler's "prison house" (Zuchthaus; Bauer's speech at the

Anglo-Saxon powers he had expressed while in office, he acknowledged now that he took with him "the most grateful memory" of his relations with the representatives of the United States and England. These two powers were "relatively little interested in our affairs. They are big and we are very small. During the entire period they were extremely just toward us." Though Austria was weak, they had never done anything "to injure our self-esteem, our dignity. And economically they made it possible for us to live." In regard to Italy Bauer acknowledged Austria's past sins for which the country now had to "atone."

With the above three Great Powers he had always been able to maintain relations "which brought many an aid to our people and prevented many a hardship." Yet it had been difficult for him to establish similar relations with France. The French had opposed him, mistakenly assuming that the Anschluss policy was "primarily his affair." Furthermore, the French saw in him "a most dangerous Bolshevik," sent by Lenin and Trotsky in order to bring about the Anschluss, "and for this reason the social order in Central Europe was especially threatened by me (lively amusement)." As was known, he had been in Russian captivity, and had been permitted to return from Petrograd in September, 1917. That was what the French offered as "proof." The truth of the matter was that revolution in Austria had of course been desired by France as long as the war lasted. At the time he returned as an exchange prisoner Trotsky himself was in prison and Lenin was in Finland whither he had fled from the Provisional Government. Yet, Bauer added, the bourgeois press, having until recently shown little interest in

Social Democratic party Congress, Oct. 14-16, 1933, reprinted in *Archiv, Mitteilungsblatt d. Vereins f. Gesch. d. Arbeiterbewegung,* 3. Jahrgg, 1963, pp. 45-67). After the annexation of Austria in 1938 Bauer also changed radically his views on the Sudeten German problem. He now clearly realized that at issue was not just conditions of the Sudeten Germans — a "disadvantaged," but "never a repressed" minority! What was really at stake, he now clearly perceived, was "supremacy over Europe." And he warned against "the pacifist sentimentality" which falls into Hitler's trap, especially against English and French pacifism. National self-determination should no longer be the battle-cry, since Hitler merely pointed to the injustice of Versailles and St. Germain to justify his road of conquest. Bauer called in this article, "Das Setbstbestimmungsrecht der Sudetendeutschen" (*Der sozialistische Kampf,* 1938), written on the eve of his sudden death, to a struggle against "fascist imperialism and, quite differently from 1918-1919, looked upon the German nation in 1938 as a "counterrevolutionary" one.

affairs of Socialism, had a difficult time keeping matters straight.

Though Austria had suffered defeat on the issues of the Anschluss and South Tyrol, there was no ground for despair. The history of a people was not measured by weeks and months. "The important seed has been planted. The great idea of the self-determination of peoples cannot be defeated; it is unconquerable."

The resignation of the Austrian foreign secretary was also considered a blow to the Anschluss movement in Germany. *Vorwärts* judged the resignation of Dr. Bauer, "the fiery fighter" for the concept of the Anschluss with the great sister republic of Germany "the greatest victory of the Paris powerholders."[16] No question was raised, however, as to whether Germany might have prevented Austria's surrender by pursuing a more vigorous policy. "German Austria's hour of true freedom still lies some distance away. When brutality has lost its strength and capitulates before justice, then the voice of blood will make possible the union of all brethren of the German race." In spite of the current setback, *Vorwärts* predicted the final victory of the Anschluss movement, but ominously, laid less stress on its significance for the democratic and socialist development of the German nation, and more on that of its ethnic and racial union.

Yet it was German democracy and German socialism, Austria's pressing economic need, and the desirability of cultural and political unity of Germany, rather than the voice of "blood" and "race," which made Bauer champion and lead the Anschluss movement. On the other hand, it was the emphasis on, or occasional but revealing glimpses of, the latter ideology (which was to reach its apogee in the frantic thirties) with its apparent Europe-wide implications, including the domination of non-German nationalities by Germans, which made France, the Entente in general, and the neighbors of Germany and German Austria hesitate and finally oppose the movement for union in Central Europe.

---

[16]*Vorwärts*, July 30.

5. THE LAST ACT IN VIENNA, BERLIN, AND PARIS

"In regard to Austria I had a 'de mortuis' feeling. My antiquarian interests regretted her disappearance. My modernist tendencies rejoiced at the new vitality which would now spring forth from that exhausted soil. My attitude towards Austria was a rather saddened reflection as to what would remain of her when the new Europe had once been created. I did not regard her as a living entity: I thought of her only as a pathetic relic." Harold Nicolson

On July 20, the "Final Text of the Peace Terms" was presented to the Austrian delegation at the Paris Peace Conference. The delegation was given ten days for a reply and thereafter seven more days. In its answer of August 6, the Austrian delegation stressed that in the present state of negotiations it would request only those changes in the treaty which were necessary for its country's very existence and for the prevention of anarchy and misery. Realistically enough, Anschluss was no longer mentioned. Foremost among the peace terms criticized was the subjection of vast German-inhabited territories, partly to Czechoslovakia and partly to Yugoslav and Italian rule (portions of Styria and Carinthia, and Tyrol beyond the Brenner Pass respectively). "It is not for us to make reproaches," the Austrian note read ambiguously, "we can only make use of the right to protest, decline the responsibility, and leave the consequences to history."[1]

So far the Allied Powers had refrained from engaging in a dispute with the Austrian delegation. But when they presented the delegation with the final peace terms on September 2, they sent Dr. Renner, as president of the Austrian delegation, an accompanying letter in which they finally came to grips with the arguments earlier advanced by

---

[1] Almond-Lutz, 1935: final text of the treaty.

the Austrian delegates. The letter began with the assurance that the Allied and Associated Powers had examined with the greatest attention the Austrian delegation's observations in regard to the peace treaty. They underlined what they considered the "fundamentally erroneous conception of the responsibilities of the [German] Austrian people." The latter shared with the Hungarian nation "responsibility" for the ills which Europe had suffered in the course of the last five years. The Austrian ultimatum in 1914 was only a "hypocritical pretext to begin a war which the old autocratic government of Vienna, in close accord with the rulers of Germany, had prepared long ago." The Austrian delegation attributed responsibility solely to the Habsburg dynasty and its satellites. "To believe them, the Austrian people, by reason of the collapse of that monarchy under the onslaught of the victorious allies, escapes responsibility for the acts committed by a government which was its own and had its seat in its capital."[2]

The Allied note charged that before the war the Austrian people had made no effort to combat the spirit of militarism and domination which had been rife in the country. It had not effectively protested against the war and had not refused to aid and support its rulers.

> The war was acclaimed from the moment of its declaration in Vienna. From beginning to end the German Austrians were its ardent partisans. . . . The policy of the old Habsburgs had become in its essence a policy designed to maintain the supremacy of the German and Magyar peoples over the majority of the inhabitants of the Austro-Hungarian monarchy. . . . It is this system of domination and aggression, setting the races against one another—a policy to which the Austrian people has given its constant support—that was one of the most profound causes of the war.[3]

The policy of Austria-Hungary, the note continued, had not been one of generosity and justice toward all its subjects. On the contrary, it had been one of the most cruel tragedies of the recent war that millions of men of the subject peoples

---

[2]*Ibid.*, p. 636f., Sept. 2, 1919.
[3]*Ibid.*

of Austria-Hungary were "forced, under penalty of death, to fight against their will in the ranks of an army which served at the same time to perpetuate their own servitude and to accomplish the destruction of the liberty of Europe." This policy of German Austrian and Magyar supremacy had produced its inevitable result: dismemberment. And it was this dismemberment which was the origin of all the real difficulties of Austria. The dislocation of Austria and the disintegration of its economic network could not fail to deal serious blows to the Austrian state and its capital.

The Allied and Associated Powers had no desire to aggravate Austria's unfortunate situation; on the contrary, they wished to do everything possible to help Austria regain prosperity.

As to the territorial frontiers which had been fixed for the Republic of Austria, no essential modification could be admitted. The decisions had been made after months of profound study. The Allied Powers had, however, taken note of the Austrian protest concerning the city of Radkersburg. The Allies had adopted for Czechoslovakia the "historic frontiers" of the Crown of Bohemia; "where these frontiers are in common with those of Austria they have not deviated therefrom, except in two cases of secondary importance where the economic interests of the new states appeared, and still appear, to prevail over the claims of the Austrian republic."

As to the Tyrol, the Allied and Associated Powers recalled that for a long time the Italian people had been exposed to the menace resulting from Austria-Hungary's possessing advanced military positions commanding the Italian plains. The best solution "therefore seemed to be to grant to Italy the natural boundary of the Alps which she has been claiming for so long."[4] Finally, the Allies offered the hope that Austria might be admitted into the League of Nations at an early date.

Making it clear that the modifications made in the treaty were final, the Allies declared that they expected the Austrian government to inform them within five days that it was ready to sign the treaty in its present form. In default of such a declaration the armistice of November 3, 1918, would

----
[4]*Ibid.*

be considered at an end. The Allied threat of an occupation of Austria, in the event that her government should balk at signing the treaty, was unmistakable.

In a personal appeal to Clémenceau, Dr. Renner explained that the Austrian National Assembly would have to be convened to express its opinion on the peace treaty. These circumstances demanded his return to Vienna, and therefore he again requested an extension of the time limit. Clémenceau thereupon granted two more days, extending the time limit to September 9.[5] However, as early as September 6, Jean-André Eichhoff of the Austrian delegation informed Clémenceau that the German Austrian National Assembly had voted that very same day to authorize Chancellor Renner to sign the peace treaty. At the same time he attached to this communication the text of the declaration voted on this matter by the Austrian National Assembly, as well as a protest resolution passed by the representatives of the assemblies of German Bohemia, Carinthia, Lower Austria, Upper Austria, Styria, the Sudeten region, Tyrol, and German Southern Moravia, against the subjection of three and one-half million German Austrians to foreign domination.[6]

At the very beginning of the foregoing declaration the Austrian National Assembly solemnly protested before the entire world the provisions of the peace treaty which, "under the pretext of protecting the independence of German Austria, has deprived the Austrian population of its right to self-determination and denied it the right to realize its ardent desire for union with the German mother country." The Assembly simultaneously expressed the hope that, as soon as peace had dispelled the spirit of "animosity and national rancor provoked by the war," the Powers would, thanks to the intervention of the League of Nations, cease to deny the German people its right to unity and national liberty. The Allied rejection of the right to union was thus simply attributed to "animosity"—not to any consideration of the European balance of power, Allied national interests, and plain fear of a Germany strengthened by the attachment of Austria.

In spite of the dim prospects for the immediate future, the Austrian National Assembly expressed its faith that the union

[5]*Ibid.*, pp. 73-75.
[6]*Ibid.*, pp. 76-79.

with Germany would come about at a later, more opportune moment. It warned however that the settlement concerning Czechoslovakia, based on the violent separation of three and a half million Germans, would perhaps be "irrevocable." Their subjection to foreign domination by a "hostile" nation was protested "with the utmost profound bitterness." The German Austrian government had made itself the spokesman of the Sudeten Germans since the very birth of the new Austrian Republic. This swansong seemed to be only a fitting climax.

On the whole, the declaration by the German Austrian Assembly was more for the historic record and for self-justification on the home front than an actual threat to the future. The Austrian government merely wished "to spare Europe the troubles that will inevitably result from this offense against the most sacred rights of a nation." Evil would also befall Europe for the violation of national rights in South Tyrol, the loss of which was likewise lamented by the Assembly. This region, unlike the German Sudeten region, was of course contiguous to Tyrol proper and to Austria. The Germans of South Tyrol were "torn from their one and only country, the Tyrol."

The National Assembly also voiced its hope that the League of Nations, aside from rescinding the Anschluss prohibition, would repair "as soon as possible the incomprehensible injustice" committed against the Germans of the Sudeten region and the Germans of South Tyrol and important parts of Carinthia, Styria, and Lower Austria. It noted, however, with satisfaction that the Allied Powers had taken account of the ethnic and economic situation in German west Hungary by recognizing the right of the latter territory to join the Germans of the Alpine *Länder*.[7]

Everything considered, the foregoing resolution of the National Assembly of Austria, a defeated country, was a rather striking document. In the annals of diplomatic history few countries can be found who dared to strike such a defiant tone toward their all-powerful victors. The Austrian National Assembly probably thought that it had little to lose and, in terms of the domestic appeal of a defiant posture, much to gain. It wanted to place the responsibility for the anticipated

---

[7]*Ibid.*

evil consequences of the peace treaty squarely on the shoulders of the Great Powers. Austria herself had no choice but to accept the treaty. "Our country depends on the Great Powers for its food, coal and raw materials, as well as for the reestablishment of its credit and the value of its currency." The National Assembly of Austria must, "unfortunately, take this constraint into account," although it considered the Peace of St. Germain "nationally unjust, politically fatal, and economically inexcusable." While at the mercy of the Great Powers, the government of the Austrian republic, in order to appease a socially, politically, and nationally aroused and frustrated population, dared to raise its little finger threateningly, while fully aware of the utter futility of the gesture.

In a letter to President Clémenceau a few days later—dated September 10 from St. Germain—Chancellor Renner, realist that he was, struck another chord. He suggested that immediately after the signing of the treaty Austria resume official diplomatic relations with the Powers that had been assembled at Paris. A special plenipotentiary could be placed at the disposition of the Supreme Council, namely Jean-André Eichhoff, former general commissioner of the Austrian peace delegation and director of the Department of Foreign Affairs. Dr. Renner inquired whether Eichhoff would be *persona grata* as far as the High Conference and particularly the government of the French republic were concerned. On September 30, Clémenceau indicated that Eichhoff would be acceptable to the French republic as envoy extraordinary and minister plenipotentiary, but avoided the question of whether he would also be acceptable to the High Conference. He may have thought that after the ratification of the peace treaty Austria would no longer need any close contact with the Paris Conference. The formal ratification of the peace treaty of St. Germain was finally accomplished by a vote of the Austrian National Assembly on October 17.[8]

The prohibition of the Anschluss was not a bilateral affair (involving only the Peace Conference and German Austria), but by its very nature triangular in character; it was aimed at Germany just as much as at Austria. Little German Austria, for so long the driving force in the Anschluss movement, had

[8]*Ibid.*, p. 84.

lost much of its impetus as the summer approached. In the following months it was rather Germany which became the "villain" of the piece.

It was Article 80 of the Treaty of Versailles which dealt with the prohibition of the union. The article had been definitely decided upon in late April, and the entire treaty presented to the German delegation on May 7. It read as follows: "Germany acknowledges and will strictly respect the independence of Austria within the frontiers to be fixed in a treaty between that state and the principal Allied and Associated Powers; she agrees that this independence shall be inalienable except with the consent of the Council of the League of Nations."[9] Article 434 of the same treaty further provided that Germany would fully recognize the treaties concluded by the victorious powers with her former allies, "whatever disposition may be made of the territories of the former Austro-Hungarian Monarchy," and also of Bulgaria and the Ottoman empire; Germany would also recognize the new states carved out from these former states and empires.

In presenting its "Observations" on the treaty on May 29, 1919, the German delegation in Paris denied that Germany had ever had or ever would have "any intention of shifting the Austro-German frontier by force. However, should the population of Austria, whose history and culture have been most intimately connected with its mother country, Germany, for more than a thousand years, desire to restore the national connection with Germany which was but recently severed by war [the war of 1866], Germany cannot pledge herself to oppose that desire of the German brothers in Austria."[10]

In their reply of June 16 the Western Powers limited themselves to "taking note" of Germany's declaration that she had no intention of violating the Austro-German frontier.[11] The final treaty signed by Germany on June 28, 1919, contained the foregoing declaration.

But the German challenge to the peacemakers on the issue of the Anschluss, on the eve of signing the peace treaty, was unmistakable. Though the Western Powers refrained at the

---

[9]*Great Britain, Treaty Series*, Nr. 4, Cmd. 153: Treaty of Peace. Pt. III, sect. 6, p. 95.

[10]*F.R.U.S., P.P.C.* **6:** p. 832.

[11]*Ibid.*, p. 945.

moment from what probably seemed to them dragging out a purposeless discussion with little immediate and practical results, they were soon to learn the error of their ways. Their unwillingness to take immediate issue with the untiring German insistence on self-determination and Austria's — not Germany's — right to union was soon to involve them in a new serious dispute with Germany in the course of which they resorted to blunt threats to make her yield.

By the summer of 1919 the German Constituent Assembly had finally completed its work on the German constitution. On July 2, four days after the Versailles peace treaty had been signed, the draft of the German constitution was given a second reading in the German National Assembly. Article 61, Paragraph 2 of the proposed constitution provided that German Austria, "after its union with the German Reich," shall receive "the right of participation in the Reichsrat" with a number of votes in proportion to its population. Until that time the representatives of German Austria would participate in an advisory capacity only. Chairman Haussmann of the Constituent Committee, had made a special appeal to leave the clause as "a rallying-cry . . . and a pledge for future fulfilment." [12] Little attempt was made to hide the purpose of this move. On the other hand, by inserting Article 178 of the Constitution — which was to assure the Western Powers that "provisions" of the peace treaty would not be affected by the Weimar Constitution — it was believed that the Allied and Associated Powers would find no cause to protest Article 61.

It might, of course, have been expected that the Western Powers would not accept this German interpretation and would see Article 61 for what it was, a thinly disguised attempt to circumvent the just-proclaimed prohibition of the union. The matter was first brought up in Paris in the Council of the Heads of Delegations on August 29 and preoccupied the Council for several days. On September 2 the Allies sent a letter to the German government to the effect that they had taken note of the articles of the German Consitution of August 11, 1919. They declared that the provisions in the second paragraph of Article 61 constituted a formal violation of Article 80 of the treaty of peace signed at Versailles. The

---

[12]Heilfron, 1919: **5:** p. 3275.

article was said to be "incompatible" with, and "in absolute opposition" to, Austria's independence. The Western Powers reminded the German government that Article 178 of the Weimar Constitution declared that the provisions of the Versailles treaty could not be affected by the Constitution and invited the German government to take all necessary measures to remove this violation without delay by declaring the second paragraph of Article 61 null and void. There followed the clear warning that Germany's violation of her pledges on an essential point would constrain the Allies immediately to order "an extension of their occupation of the right bank of the Rhine,"[13] if their just demand was not complied with within 15 days from the present date.

The German government replied with a letter from the president of the German delegation, Von Lersner, to the president of the Peace Conference, Clémenceau. It restated its declaration of May 29 to the effect that it "had never had and would never have any intention of changing the German Austrian border by force," but that it could not oppose a possible desire of the population of Austria "to reconstruct the unity of the state with the lands of the old German stock." It referred once again to Article 178 of the German Constitution, which stipulated that the conditions of the peace treaty could not be affected by the Constitution. They then declared that the provisions of Article 61, Paragraph 2 of their constitution were "null and void" and that, specifically, the admission of German Austrian representatives to the Reichsrat could not be carried out until the Council of the League of Nations consented to it. The German government concluded by peremptorily declaring that "the affair in question [is] settled by the preceding declaration"[14] and not without regretting the Allied threat of a territorial extension of the occupation.

In the discussion of the German reply by the Heads of the Delegations Clemenceau stressed the need for enforcing the provisions of the Peace Treaty by the proposed extension of the military occupation on the right bank of the Rhine. He went so far as to "threaten" that he would rather resign his post than consent to France's being left unassisted by the

[13]*F.R.U.S., P.P.C.,* **8:** pp. 62-63.
[14]*Ibid.,* pp. 138-140.

American and British governments to enforce the provisions of the peace treaty. Balfour, though perhaps considering the issue debatable from a strictly legal point of view, nevertheless seemed to side with Clémenceau by declaring the issue confronting the Peace Conference "one of utmost gravity and importance." It was "clear to [him] that the persons who had framed the German Constitution had deliberately attempted to draw it up in such a way as openly to challenge and possibly to violate the Treaty of Versailles."[15]

The reply to the German note was agreed upon by the Allies on September 11. The note referred with biting irony to the German commentary on the Weimar Constitution, according to which the treaty superseded anything the Constitution said to the contrary. "By this ingenuous device" the German Constitution could eventually be so amended as formally to contradict every provision which the treaty contained. No one could believe that when the framers of the German Constitution inserted Article 61 and settled the terms of Article 112 they were not aware that their wording was irreconcilable with the engagements which Germany had solemnly entered upon only a few weeks before. "This condition of things cannot be allowed to endure. The German government itself admits and declares that if the Constitution and the Treaty clash the Constitution must give way."[16]

The Allied and Associated Powers called upon the German government to sign "forthwith" the enclosed draft declaration, in accordance with which the German government was to declare that Article 61 of the Constitution was null and void and that in particular Austrian representatives could not be admitted to the Reichsrat unless the Council of the League of Nations, in agreement with Article 80 of the peace treaty, should consent to such a change in Austria's international status. The German government had to pledge that this Declaration would be signed at Versailles by an authorized representative of the German government; it would also have to be duly approved by the competent German legislative authority within fifteen days![17] Allied patience was running low.

---

[15]*Ibid.*, pp. 155-163, Sept. 9, espec. pp. 158-159.
[16]*Ibid.*, p. 183f., espec. pp. 192-193.
[17]*Ibid.*, pp. 193-194.

The protocol described above was indeed signed in Versailles on September 22, 1919, by Baron von Lersner in the presence of representatives of the Western Powers, just as they had demanded. It was subsequently approved by the Reichsrat and the National Assembly on November 17 and December 15 respectively. Thereafter, Clémenceau as president of the Peace Conference was duly notified of the German acceptance of the Allied document.

The battle over the Anschluss had reached its apex, ironically enough, after the peace treaty of Versailles had been signed. Now it had come to its inevitable end. Faced with a virtual ultimatum which threatened Germany with the occupation of additional German territories on the right bank of the Rhine, the German government had faltered. The constitutional provisions, intended to open a breach in the wall through which in due time Austria could squeeze herself into the Reich, were annulled.

The defeat could have been foreseen, as could the circumstance that the German government and German representatives would make an attempt to circumvent the prohibition of the Anschluss. For months the written and unwritten policy of the German government as well as of the Allied Powers had been that the issue of Austria's union had to be postponed until the peace treaty was signed. The German motivation in all this had been more patent and understandable than the Allied rationale. The Allies had simply wanted to shelve a troublesome issue in the hope that it would miraculously dissolve in due time. The trends in German public opinion as well as the debates in the Weimar Constituent Assembly and the Cabinet during the spring and summer of 1919 had long foreshadowed German attempts to make legal and material preparation for Austria's Anschluss soon after the peace treaty was signed. The Austrian ambassador Ludo Hartmann, as his reports show, had continued his close and intimate contacts with the new Bauer-Müller Cabinet together with leading German administrators and legislators, including President Ebert himself. The new Social Democratic foreign secretary Hermann Müller apparently made a point of being no less dedicated to the union than his aristocratic predecessor Brockdorff-Rantzau had been. And in July a subcommittee of the National Assembly had begun to preoccupy itself with the Anschluss problem and especially with propaganda. The legal battle over the Anschluss between Berlin and the Peace Conference during the summer of 1919 was a fitting climax to these developments.

In the course of the year after the November Revolution of 1918 the roles of Berlin and Vienna in regard to the Anschluss had been almost reversed. First, Vienna had pursued Berlin; the latter became very gradually more responsive and toward the end even aggressive. Before the first year in the life of the two republics had come to an end, both foreign secretaries, Dr. Bauer and Brockdorff-Rantzau, had been forced to step aside. After Chancellor Karl Renner assumed also the duties of foreign minister, German Austria ceased to be the hub of the Anschluss movement. Under the new stewardship Austria entertained no illusion in regard to an early union with Germany.

Germany, however, quickly recovered from the series of blows in November, 1918—*Zusammenbruch*, defeat, and revolution—was seized by a mood of national challenge and defiance against the West and the Peace Conference in which she was unwilling to face the reality of her debacle. Brockdorff-Rantzau gave more encouragement to the Anschluss movement than his predecessor Dr. Solf. Yet he never lost sight of his primary goal, the defense of Germany's prewar boundaries. Compared with these interests, the Reich's stake in the Anschluss, in spite of its importance, was of only secondary significance. The final Anschluss crisis to rise on the horizon of the Peace Conference developed after Brockdorff-Rantzau's resignation, under his successor Hermann Müller. By that time the peace treaty had already been submitted to Berlin and could not be changed for the worse. Thus Germany had dared to throw down a challenge to the Allies over the Anschluss such as she had not done before. But the Western Powers had deliberately taken it up, and the German government came to realize that the time was not yet ripe for it.

VII. Conclusion.

"The fateful word of the right to self-determination of peoples has been enunciated. One day the statesmen of the Entente will be horrified by it. Meanwhile we shall pick up the word, give it, in German fashion, a deeper meaning, and make it a guiding star for our actions. They can only lose this way; but we shall win unreservedly." Werner Sombart, November 1918

In the course of the year 1918-1919 the Austrian people vacillated back and forth while pondering about the union with Germany. The uneasy course reflected the pressures from the Entente, Germany's cautious persuasions, and the fierce struggle of its own indigenous forces battling for and against the union. Many close observers have differed as to the strength of the Anschluss movement in Austria, but on the whole there appeared to have been a majority in its favor. Though some Christian Socials paid lip-service to the union, most opposed it in word and deed. In the last days of the dying monarchy the leadership of Austria's Social Democracy, destined soon to play a preeminent role in the new republic, had pushed an unwilling working class toward the concept of union. It was only after the November Revolution, which brought a purely Socialist government to power in Germany, that the Austrian workers began to show growing interest, though hardly ever enthusiasm, in the Anschluss. German Nationalists, traditionally supporters of the *grossdeutsch* movement, felt drawn to the Anschluss concept, but were repelled by the thought of a union with a revolutionary and Socialist German Reich. Under these circumstances it was not surprising that the Austrian Social Democratic Party, in the past a pillar of the *grossösterreichisch* point of view, reverted to the *grossdeutsch* tradition and became the flag-bearer of the Anschluss movement.

449

Neither the Socialists nor most members of the other Austrian political parties considered the German Austrian remnant of the Habsburg monarchy a viable state. They also held that the former suppressed nations of the Habsburg monarchy would be unwilling to join German Austria and renounce some of their newly won sovereignty. Thus Austria's entire future seemed to hinge on the issue of the Anschluss. Its champions in the Austrian Social Democracy and other circles hoped that Austria would be able to share in the future economic growth of the still great German Reich, which because of its central location and the technical skills and cultural level of its people was likely soon to regain its past position and leave its smaller and economically less developed neighbors behind. They longed to unite with a country in which democratic and Socialist forces were surging forward at that time, promising bold political, economic, and social changes, especially the development of Socialism. The latter seemed likely to be precluded in a Danubian confederation whose individual members would display strong national sentiments and among whom Socialist experimentation would be subordinate to, if not canceled by, bourgeois national reconstruction. The Anschluss seemed to Austria's Socialist leadership likely to be the fulfillment of their boldest dreams.

On the other hand, a separate and independent German Austria would have to depend on the Western Powers for support because of her economic weakness. For this very reason, as well as because of the agrarian and politically conservative-clerical character of most of the Austrian Länder, she would be unable to participate in the active construction of a new Socialist society. Instead of taking part in bold Socialist experimentation, Austria would be condemned to the dull, uninspired existence of provincial life, to being an insignificant hinterland to the Reich. She would be bypassed by history.

While the Anschluss issue was a central one for German Austria, it never acquired the same significance for Germany. True, to the Germans the Anschluss was like an unexpected ray of hope. But Germany's future did not seem to hinge on the union with Austria, however important the latter was in several respects; rather it would be shaped by the territorial and economic provisions of the Peace Treaty and by her remaining economic and human potential and her impressive powers of recuperation. The hope of a union with Austria was one which made the heart of many Germans beat faster. But should the Anschluss be denied and Germany unable to bring it about, her chances for a speedy recovery from the war still seemed most favorable.

Not all Germans were enthusiastic about the union with Austria and some even opposed it. Some preferred a strongly Protestant Germany and shuddered at the thought that the Anschluss would dangerously strengthen the Catholic influence in the Reich. The East Prussian Junkers, an arrogantly assertive class in the new Reich, were more concerned with carving out a favorable eastern border against the new Poland than with the Anschluss of German Austria; they seemed convinced that the Entente would never permit the union without penalizing Germany in the East. Others applied the same reasoning toward the Rhineland and the western borders in general. The *grossdeutsch* tradition had never been as strong in the North as in southern Germany and Austria; many North Germans had looked down upon the Habsburg empire in general and German Austria in particular, and were convinced of the superiority of everything Prussian. The Anschluss of Austria, in the view of these people, was likely to weaken the role of Prussia in the new Reich—an argument repeated by a few Western spokesmen who favored the union of German Austria with Germany.

Still, in the wake of defeat, German feelings of superiority were badly shaken and Germany needed reassurance. That German Austria in the midst of the debacle was willing to join forces with her seemed to many Germans a godsend, a vote of confidence and encouragement at a moment when their fortunes had reached low ebb. Numerous Germans, whatever their political persuasion, had come to doubt the significance of their national wartime labors and sacrifices. They were inclined to lament their national fate as "undeserved." Their heroism, their endurance, their courage deserved a better destiny than the unjust surrender of their border regions, inhabited though these were by many non-Germans. With the Anschluss becoming a distinct possibility, the war suddenly seemed to gain "meaning"; perhaps the privations had not been quite in vain. Germany would soon be back on the road to prosperity, recognition, and greatness. Especially the theme of "greatness" was widely discussed.

Apart from the psychological boost, the addition of six and a half million Austrians, of magnificent Vienna, of Austria's industrial and natural resources and her valuable strategic location, promised to ease Germany's *Drang nach dem Süden*, toward Italy and the Adriatic Sea, and toward the Southeast, the Balkans and its numerous German minorities. However painful and injurious territorial and economic losses at the peace table might turn out to be, they would surely be compensated for by the unexpected gains in Austria.

In the first days and weeks of the new German republic the specter of revolution overshadowed all concern for foreign affairs and foreign policy. Yet when the Constituent Assembly in Weimar opened its doors early in Febrary, 1919, the demand for the inclusion of German Austria was stridently put forth. Still, the governments in Berlin and Vienna realized that its implementation would have to be postponed until after the Peace Conference.

The very same tactical decision to postpone the Anschluss was reached by the Western Powers. They preferred to take a position on the union which, while actually prohibitive, gave the impression that a union would be feasible at some time in the future. These tactics were designed to minimize Austrian and German criticism and also to reconcile their policy in some manner with the Wilsonian principle of national self-determination. Thus the tactics adopted by the Western Powers in regard to the Anschluss represented in some way a compromise between President Wilson's idealism, as shown in his principles of democracy and self-determination, and Clémenceau's hardheaded realism; the latter, while not negating the validity of the Wilsonian principles in the abstract, placed against them the security of Germany's neighbors and the rest of Europe. The compromise attained was one definitely weighted toward Clémenceau's position. It should, however, be recalled that most American experts were in agreement with the French and English advisers as to the desirability, if not the necessity of preventing the Anschluss. Great Britain, which had turned against the union, in the end adopted a policy almost parallel to that of France, but wanted the latter to carry the odium for a decision which had aroused doubts and misgivings in some English minds.

The first task of the new German government in the field of foreign policy was to preserve as much as possible of the country's territorial possessions. Alluring as new territorial gains, especially the Anschluss, might be, the preservation of German territory took clear precedence over all other considerations. The German government had to expect that an early Anschluss, one proclaimed and carried out before the Peace Conference had finished writing the German peace treaty, would embitter the Allies and make them retaliate by imposing heavy territorial losses upon Germany, and in general showing little consideration for her.

Under these circumstances the German government was trying to avoid irritating the West and gave the Austrian Anschluss movement only unofficial encouragement. Only gradually, in response to public opinion and popular pressure, did the Berlin government grow more outspoken on the union with Austria. A few Germans only raised their voices in warning against the Anschluss. They were convinced that the mistrust accumulated over decades by Germany's *Drang nach dem Osten* and *Weltpolitik*, and deepened during the war when German annexationism had reached its apogee, would be increased by demand for the Anschluss. However appealing in principle, the Anschluss would mean Germany's aggrandizement. To ask for a territorial increase after an unprecedentedly fierce and bloody contest of arms which had caused staggering losses of life and property would be, as seen by the other side, an unheard-of effrontery; it would also reveal an utter lack of judgment of what was politically attainable. Years later the German historian Erich Eyck in his *Geschichte der Weimarer Republik* expressed this very opinion, which even then was not shared by most of his German colleagues:

The total losses of the German Reich in Europe would have been more than balanced if the German demand for the Anschluss of German Austria had met with the approval of the Allies. . . . Could one seriously expect that the Allies, after

454   THE ANSCHLUSS MOVEMENT

defeating Germany by an exertion of their last ounce of
strength, would stand by to watch the vanquished emerge even
stronger and mightier than before.?[1]

Germany's diplomatic course during the negotiations with
the Austrian delegation at the end of February and early in
March, 1919, and thereafter was marked by caution. Charges
of timidity were leveled against Berlin not only by Austrian
activists such as Ludo Hartmann, but also by a fair number of
other Austrian and German observers and participants in the
movement for union. Yet German policy was not dictated by
fear, but rather by a hard-headed realism and even a streak of
Machiavellianism. Von Wedel warned Brockdorff-Rantzau
not to become "the champion of an idea whose present
realization is in any case very uncertain." Under the stewardship of the generally intransigent foreign minister
Brockdorff-Rantzau it pursued not a vigorous, but on the
whole rather a cautious course in regard to the Anschluss.
Its language bordered on the intemperate at times, but in
substance German policy was restrained. Even traditionally
nationalist circles did not see a more resolute and aggressive
course as a feasible alternative, though during the first
postwar year the Anschluss sentiment in Germany reached
dizzy heights at times.

When the Austrian empire disintegrated in November of
1918 the German Austrian remnant of the Habsburg monarchy, left to its own devices, had turned to Germany for the
Anschluss. But for the just-vanquished Reich this Austrian
profession of love could not have come at a more inopportune moment. For Germany to acquire German Austria
would have meant to snatch diplomatic victory from the
catastrophe of military defeat. Though the Anschluss issue
appeared to move onto the front stage—vigorously
promoted by Austria, more moderately pursued by Germany, and toyed with by the Italian government—it was actually doomed before it was articulated. France could be expected to oppose the scheme with all her strength, and
British considerations relating to balance of power were likely
to place Great Britain ultimately on the side of France. After

---

[1]Eyck, 1954: 1: p. 151.

CONCLUSION 455

the war's end Britain might at times favor defeated Germany against her wartime French ally, but never to such a degree as entirely to upset the newly created balance of forces.

In view of the defeat of Germany and the spread of revolution in Russia, France was likely to be the most influential power on the continent. But if German Austria had opted for the Anschluss, France's military preponderance would have been immediately challenged by the formidable concentration of more than 70 million Germans in the Reich. Vanquished Germany would have been enlarged by six and a half million people; she would have commanded strategically vital territories and would have posed an additional threat to Czechoslovakia and even Switzerland. By becoming the neighbor of Italy, Germany would have exerted pressure upon her in regard to German South Tyrol or, if she ever decided to write off this territory, would have been able to establish with Italy the close relationship of the prewar period. The then much talked-about Rome-Berlin alliance, which was forged later in the thirties between National Socialist Germany and Fascist Italy, might have become a reality at an earlier time.

The Anschluss would have brought Germany to the doorstep of Yugoslavia and Hungary. The gates of the Balkans would have been quickly opened to Germany as a neighbor of Yugoslavia. The Hungarian desire for revisionism would have been supported by a Germany herself anxious for a revision of her eastern frontiers; thus threats to Hungary's neighbors, Czechoslovakia, Rumania, and Yugoslavia, would have rapidly mounted. It is such considerations as these which determined not only French but also English policy. British interests too, as the Foreign Office and other British departments soon concluded, were irreconcilably opposed to the Anschluss project.

Judging Germany's desires by the pronouncements of German political and military leaders late in 1918 and early in 1919, there is little indication that permission for the Anschluss would have satisfied Germany, that in exchange for the acquisition of Austria she would have willingly resigned herself to her territorial losses in the East and West and overseas, and that this unexpected gain would have strengthened

German democracy and constitutionalism.[2] It is more likely that such a windfall would have merely whetted Germany's appetite and convinced the Germans of the opponent's political naiveté rather than of his moral grandeur or consistency of principle. Far from puncturing the inflated imperialist wartime goals, it would have given them a new boost, justifying, instead of exposing, the extravagant aspirations of Imperial Germany.

Given the historic conditions in Central Europe, Germany's recent ambitions and postwar demands, and the expectations of the countries of the victorious Entente, Allied consent to the Anschluss was quite unlikely. None of the Western nations could have permitted any government to stay in power which, against every rule of reason and expected national behavior, presented to the obviously "unrepentant" and little changed German enemy an unprecedented gift — an entire country. If the chance of preserving Germany's prewar boundaries intact was virtually nil, the likelihood of obtaining German Austria and thus improving upon Germany's frontiers of 1914 was even smaller.

It is easy to speculate on the peaceful, democratic, and undisturbed development of a Germany to whom the Anschluss had been conceded, if one makes the rather unlikely assumption that the Allies had turned into either angels or fools, since the actual consequences of such an improbable turn of events can hardly be disproved. The argument that, if only the West had permitted Germany's incorporation of German Austria, postwar history would have taken an entirely different and pacific course, can of course be neither proven nor refuted. If the forces of democracy in Germany and Austria depended for their survival on the gratification of historically

---

[2]After having completed the writing of this work, the author was able to examine some recent German studies which were the first to have made limited use of the correspondence between Bauer and Hartmann and that of von Wedel with the German foreign office, namely V. Reimann, *Zu Gross für Österreich,* 1968, pp. 293-307, O. Leichter, *Otto Bauer,* 1970, and the dissertation at the University of Vienna by Theo Schäfer, "Die Genesis der Anschlussbewegung und die Anschlussdiplomatie 1918-1919." N. Leser in his recent study *Zwischen Reformismus und Bolschewismus. Der Austro-Marxismus als Theorie und Praxis,* 1968, rather neglects the Anschluss (pp. 323-328). Leichter treats the Anschluss issue in somewhat greater detail. He is not uncritical toward Bauer in general or toward the Social

unprecedented demands, made after a lengthy conflict, the most bloody in modern times, their strength rested on rather shaky foundations. The foregoing thesis merely represents a convenient alibi for the failure of the German democratic, republican, and socialist movements.

British policy toward German Austria was shaped by conflicting tendencies. It was torn between the appeal of the principle of national self-determination which would have permitted the union, and the fear of rewarding the Reich which had just lost the war; a Reich whose annexationist ambitions had been bared only recently when it dictated the peace treaties of Brest-Litovsk and Bucharest. British policy vacillated between the fear of leaving a festering sore in Europe to give rise to a new irredentism, and the even greater fear of endangering the national security of, and doing injustice to, the vital interests of her French ally and the Entente's friends among the peoples of Central and East Central Europe. The Allies were bound by their wartime promises to these nationalities. British national self-interest demanded their fulfillment as well as opposition to Germany's aggrandizement through the Anschluss. Such a union would doom the national independence of many of the smaller peoples in Europe at the very moment when they were hoping to begin their independent national life.

While the Western Powers opposed the Anschluss with Germany, they too endorsed the view that Central Europe needed a larger political or economic framework. At the same time that they effectively prevented the immediate union of Austria with Germany, they left the door open for Austria to

---

Democratic Anschluss policy. (The party continued to favor the union policy, affirming it in the Linzer program of 1926 and did not repudiate it until 1933, after Hitler had come to power in neighboring Germany.) Leichter speaks of Bauer's persistence in his support for the union as an "error" (139). However, as far as 1918-1919 is concerned, he supports Bauer's and the Austrian Social Democratic party's Anschluss policy.

While Leichter blames the "false decision" of the victors in 1919 (105)— — expressing the questionable view that permitting the union would have removed the German "inferiority complex" and thus National Socialist domination and the outbreak of the Second World War (106) — he also accuses the vanquished for the failure of the movement for union, among them the German government, von Wedel and the Social Democrats in particular, and acknowledges the "strong resistance" in Austria.

reconsider the issue, partly because they did not wish to deny national self-determination for ever, and partly because they were plagued by doubts about the country's viability. They hoped that Austria's economy might show unexpected strength and that, when the revolutionary turbulence and emotional upheaval of the immediate postwar period had abated, the Austrian people would relinquish their pro-Anschluss position in favor either of continued Austrian independence or of joining a Danubian confederation.

Both France and Great Britain favored the establishment of a Danubian confederation and began vigorously to promote it when the danger of a *fait accompli* by German Austria and Germany seemed to mount. The unwillingness of the succession states to abandon any portion of their precious, newly-won sovereignty, coupled with their distrust of the long-ruling German Austrians and Magyars, doomed the Entente projects for a Danubian confederation. The Entente's hopes that the project for Austria's Anschluss with Germany would be wrecked by her "Anschluss" with a new Central European Federation evaporated into thin air.

It cannot be said that the United States played the role of an innocent by-stander when the prohibition of the Anschluss was finally agreed upon and that she merely approved the decision of the Allies. Actually, the United States contributed substantially to the emerging Allied policy on Austria, though American historians have rather soft-pedaled her role, placing the major responsibility for it on the shoulders of the Allies, especially France.

Secretary of State Lansing and other American experts moved increasingly nearer the Allied position of prohibiting the Anschluss. President Wilson himself considered it also desirable to prevent an immediate union with Germany. He had never looked upon national self-determination as an unqualified principle and had always underlined the need for taking other criteria into account, such as considerations of security, geographic and economic factors, and the vital interests of other parties concerned. It was President Wilson who ultimately suggested the formula in accordance with which Germany was to recognize that Austria's independence would remain "inalienable," except by a unanimous vote to the contrary by the Council of the League of Nations. And it was this formula which Clémenceau enthusiastically and Lloyd George happily agreed to. On other issues, such as the Rhineland, France had to yield to the Anglo-Saxon point of view. On the Anschluss issue, however, the American president offered an escape along a line which was most satisfactory to France. She herself could hardly have chosen a better formula.

Though American policy was subjected to some sharp criticism in Germany and Austria, the United States generally remained in the good graces of the Austrian population, and even the Austrian champions of the Anschluss movement, Otto Bauer and Karl Renner, were not unappreciative of American moves in behalf of Austria's welfare. It was France which, not quite deservedly, was to become at times the sole target of Austria's and Germany's wrath and frustration because of her stand on the Anschluss issue. But by making Paris the sole or main culprit, Berlin and Vienna would be able to drive wedges between Paris on the one hand and London and Washington on the other, and thus prepare the road for a revision of the Treaty.

During the months of February and March, 1919, statesmen and experts of France, Great Britain, and the United States reached bilateral agreements on Austria and her future, yet their net result remained largely unknown. This lack of Allied clarity and firmness introduced elements of confusion at home and abroad. The Austrian and German foreign secretaries themselves groped in the darkness of probabilities and uncertainties. While they entertained no doubt about France's opposition to the Anschluss, the policy not only of Italy, but also of both Anglo-Saxon Powers long remained a question mark to them. A firm and unambiguous stand by the Entente would probably have defeated the Anschluss movement in Germany and Austria at an earlier time. A policy declaration leaving no doubt as to the Allied intention of prohibiting the union in the peace treaty might well have broken the backbone of the movement in Germany. Had the German government been bluntly warned, it might have ceased to give encouragement to the movement through fear of a harsher peace treaty. Had the warning come in time, before the opening of the Weimar Assembly, the latter might not have given free rein to its sentiments and not acted as if it lived in a dream world — as if the union were entirely dependent on the wishes and decision of the Reich and Austria, and not contingent on the consent of other states. The German press would have lowered the tone of its propaganda activities, and Dr. Bauer and the Austrian delegation might not have been invited to travel to Germany.

A determined and early Allied stand on the Anschluss question would also have made a deep impression upon the German Austrian government. Dr. Bauer admitted that the Austrian Anschluss agitation for much of the year was based to a high degree on the Allies' failure to clarify their position. The first authoritative French declaration against the Anschluss, that of French Foreign Minister Pichon on December 30, followed the Anschluss declaration of the Austrian National Assembly by seven weeks! And it represented French rather than Allied policy. In the meantime, the Anschluss movement, in spite of many ups and downs during even this interval, gained ground.

The weakness of the Allied policy on the Anschluss was tied up with the inability or unwillingness to dispatch troops to Central Europe. In the spring of 1919 the Allies reached the decision to withdraw gradually those troops still on Russian soil, and refused direct military intervention against the new Soviet Hungarian republic which was fighting against Czechoslovakia and Rumania. Similarly, the Allies were not disposed to resort to force to prevent the union of German Austria with Germany. They were convinced that such extreme measures would not be needed and they were resolved to limit risks. They never threatened direct military intervention, and also failed to make timely political moves against the Anschluss. British policy, as some in the Foreign Office warned, tended to procrastinate and "drift."

Even a limited military presence of the Allies in Austria during the critical months of 1918-1919 might have easily and definitely dampened the Anschluss hopes; many elements of the Austrian bourgeoisie and some leading Austrian politicians privately recommended such a course.

If not a policy of firmness, perhaps one of making far-reaching concessions, or an approach deftly combining both policies, could have nipped the Anschluss movement in the bud. Were the Western Powers really prepared to make concessions of an economic and territorial nature to the German Austrian government in return for a timely renunciation of the Anschluss? The German Austrian government, though determined to achieve the Anschluss, was prepared to listen to tempting offers from Paris, but no such offers came forth. Bauer, in a letter to Haupt on May 2, made it clear that, although there were rumors about the Allies' willingness to make concessions to Austria, there was "no positive news whatsoever" that the Entente was prepared to "offer proper guarantees" or that it "would offer overwhelming advantages for our European position" that had "not been made to us from any side." No *quid pro quo* had actually been offered. In view of wartime pledges and subsequent moves in November and December of 1918—when the Allies approved Czechoslovakia's occupation of German Bohemia and Moravia—the Entente could hardly have made German Austria any significant and attractive promises of a territorial nature, enough to persuade her to disavow her Anschluss goal. It remains uncertain whether Allied pledges of an economic nature alone could have lured the German Austrian government away from union with the Reich.

The war's end had brought liberation and fulfillment to Germany's neighbors. But to the Germans it meant the end of preeminence and domination and embitterment not only over the loss of power and status, but over the loss of their German kinsfolk as well. Many Germans and Austrians thought that such a spirited mood as gripped the non-German and non-Magyar peoples of Central Europe in their newly independent or enlarged states was needed in their own countries also, to sweep away the despondency hovering over the area as an aftermath of war and revolution. The revolution itself had caused no genuine enthusiasm in Berlin, Munich, or Vienna, since it was accompanied by general breakdown and military catastrophe, and since it got stalled in its own tracks.

These were the conditions which swept the Anschluss concept into the very center of the stage in German Central Europe. Its real force in 1918-1919 lay in that it seemed to be able to fuse the movements of socialism and nationalism, while still retaining its attraction for the bourgeois and even outright anti-socialist nationalist elements. The Anschluss concept, promising the fulfillment of the national idea of *Grossdeutschland,* looked both back to the past and forward to the future. At a truly historic moment it combined the wounded but strong German nationalism with a new political and social vision, the socialist movement which then burst upon the domestic scene. Social Democracy, being deeply divided and seeing the rapidly built socialist tower crumbling, hoped to be able to save it by giving it the underpinning of the Anschluss.

Many Germans and Austrians of the most varied political persuasions were elated about the prospects of union. It lifted their spirit and infused them with new confidence. The completion of the national revolution seemed the needed catalyst, materially and psychologically speaking, to transform German Central Europe and speed its rapid progress toward a preeminent, if not dominant, role on the continent. On the other hand the idea of the Anschluss raised once again the serious threat of domination by the just-vanquished German nation over her non-German neighbors, and the threat of her once again unsettling a precarious balance of power.

In view of the realities of power and geopolitics, the vain hopes of the Anschluss should not have been permitted to confuse and alarm Europe for any length of time. The Western Powers, in their own interests, those of their friends in Central and East Central Europe, and even those of the vanquished German foe, should have torpedoed the union project at the earliest possible moment. Soon after the Armistice, and certainly long before the Treaties of Versailles and St. Germain were submitted to the German and Austrian delegations, the Allies openly and unmistakably should have proclaimed their resolve to prohibit the union.

Such an Allied declaration might not have succeeded in persuading all Austrian and German adherents of the Anschluss. But it might have dispelled the political fog; it would have given crystal-clear expression to a policy which was in the Allied and over-all European interest in 1919, in 1938, and ever since.

Bibliography

I. PUBLISHED AND UNPUBLISHED DOCUMENTS NEWSPAPERS AND PERIODICALS (1918-1919)

A. UNPUBLISHED DOCUMENTS

Austria   Neues Politisches Archiv, 1918-1938, Österreichisches Staatsarchiv.
Präsidialakte 5a (Liassen Deutschland, Anschlussfrage); K 109, Anschlussfrage; K 110; K 212 (I Deutschland, Anschluss), Präsidialakte Bauer, 261: Fasz. 274, Liasse Österreich, Innere Lage 1918-1921; Fasz. 372, 374-379, Liasse Österreich; K 465, Geheimliassen Deutschland, K 626 Liasse Frankreich; Fasz. 678-682, Liasse Italien, Tirol; K 762; Fasz. 826 and 860-863, Liasse Tschechoslowakei; Fasz. 880, 882 and 887, Liasse Ungarn; K 881, Tschechoslowakei 9/1; K 913, Ungarn, Re: Ungarn und das deutschungarische Gebiet, Korrespondenz Bauer-Cnobloch. — Korrespondenz Friedrich Adler-Otto Bauer, Verein für Geschichte der Arbeiterbewegung, Vienna. Verwaltungsarchiv, Wien, Sozialdemokratie, Kart. 10, 12, 15, 18, 19, 24, 29. Sitzungsprotokolle, Parteivorstand, Sozialdemokratische Partei Deutschösterreichs, Juli 1916-November 1921, Verein f. Gesch. d. Arbeiterbewegung, Vienna.

Bavaria   Geheimes Staatsarchiv, Munich. Volksstaat Bayern, Akten d. Ministeriums des Äusseren. Der Anschluss Deutschösterreichs an das Deutsche Reich, 1919-1927.

Canada   Public Archives of Canada. Foster Papers, "Southeast Europe and the Balkans," 56, file 119.

Germany   Deutsches Staatsarchiv, Koblenz. Reichsministerium, Auswärtige Angelegenheiten, v. 1, Feb. 1919-Dez. 1919. National Archives, Washington, D.C. Microfilm of captured files of the German Foreign Ministry, 1918, 1919, including Brockdorff-Rantzau's Nachlass, serial 9101 H, rolls 3429-3446, ser. 3728 H, rolls 1764 and 1765 and ser. 6812, roll 3154. Ser. 1690 H, 1691 H, 1692 H, roll 1013 contain the unpublished biography of Brockdorff-Rantzau by the well known historian Erich Brandenburg. This work, actually a compilation of sources with connecting text, was submitted to the Auswärtiges Amt in 1932, but permission for publication was refused.
Politisches Archiv. Auswärtiges Amt, Bonn Nachlass Brockdorff-Rantzau's. Österreichische Anschlussfrage 1918-1919. The Bonn Archive contains some important materials which have not been microfilmed.
Brockdorff-Rantzau Nachlass 1899-1903, 1/1, Ungeordnete Korrespondenz, 11/1, 12/3 — Akten betreffend seiner Exzellenz des Grafen Brockdorff-Rantzau vom Februar 1919-Juli 1919. — Akten betreffend Beziehungen zwichen Österreich und Deutschland, vols. 2-3, 14-18.

France   Ministère des Affaires Étrangères. Archives. Quai d'Orsay, Paris Allemagne NS 73
Affaires Étrangères, Europe 1918-1922, Autriche, Z 88.7, Politique Étrangère I, II, III, Mai 1918-Août 1920
Affaires Étrangères, Europe 1918-1929, Autriche, Z 88.7, Politique Étrangère. Dossier General, IV, V, VI, Sept. 1920-Déc. 1926
Affaires Étrangères, A, Paix. Photos Allemandes, A 1056, Bureau de Mlle Duval
A, Paix. A 1056 1, 1920
Bibliothèque de Documentation Internationale Contemporaine, Paris, Louis Lucien Klotz Papers

Nachlass Prof. Louis Eisenmann, Paris 16, 31. Général Délestraint.

Great Britain Public Records Office, London. Foreign Office 608, especially volumes 6, 8, 9, 11, 13, 14, 16-23, 27, 126, 133, 134, 151

United States National Archives. American Commission to Negotiate Peace, especially volumes 135, 175, 185, 297, 303, 495. Inquiry Doc. 509, Charles Seymour: Austria-Hungary Federalized within Existing Boundaries. Inquiry Doc. 514, Epitome of Reports on just and practical boundaries within Austria-Hungary; American Delegation. Correspondence and Papers, 1918-1919. Special Collections. Columbia University Library. Tasker H. Bliss Papers, National Archives. Robert L. Lansing Papers, Library of Congress

The Netherlands International Institute of Social History, Amsterdam; Karl Kautsky Archives (about 80 letters of Dr. Otto Bauer, including some dated 1918 and 1919)

B. PUBLISHED DOCUMENTS

Allied and Associated Powers. *Treaty with Austria.* 1919 (in French, English, and Italian)
Amtliche Urkunden zur Vorgeschichte des Waffenstillstandes, 1918 (2. Aufl., 1919).
Austria (Allied Commission for Austria). Die wichtigsten Beschlüsse des alliierten Organes zur Kontrolle, in Österreichische Dokumente (Vienna, 1954).
————. *Bericht über die Tätigkeit der Österreichischen Friedensdelegation in St. Germain* (2 v. 1919).
————. *Bundesgesetzblatt* für die Republik Österreich (30. Juli, 1955).
————. *Österreich Frei.* Dokumente II, hrsggb. vom Bundesministerium für Unterricht (Vienna, 1956).
————. *Staatsgesetzblatt für die Republik Österreich,* Jahresgg. 1918 and 1919, (Vienna, 1918 and 1919).
————. *Stenographische Protokolle über die Sitzungen der Provisorischen Nationalversammlung für Deutschösterreich 1918 and 1919* (Vienna, 1919).
————. *Index, Stenographische Protokolle über die Sitzungen der Provisorischen Nationalversammlung für Deutschösterreich 1918 and 1919* (Vienna, 1919).
————. *Stenographische Protokolle über die Sitzungen der konstituierenden Nationalversammlung der Republik Österreich, 1919* (Vienna, 1919).
————. *Index, Stenographische Protokolle über die Sitzungen der konstituierenden Nationalversammlung der Republik Österreich, 1919* (Vienna, 1920).
————. *Beilagen zu den stenographischen Protokollen der Provisorischen Nationalversammlung für Deutschösterreich, 1918, 1919,* 1 (Vienna, 1919).

Austria-Hungary, 1918. *Stenographisches Protokoll über die Sitzungen des Hauses der Abgeordneten des österreichischen Reichsrates im Jahre 1918*, **4** (Vienna, 1918).

———. 1918. *Stenographisches Protokoll über die Sitzungen des Herrenhauses des österreichischen Reichsrates*, XXII. Sitzung (Vienna).

Almond N. and Lutz R., eds. 1935. *Treaty of St. Germain. A documentary history of its territorial and political clauses* (London).

Czechoslovakia. Les revendications territoriales de la république tchecoslovaque, *National Archives*, Inquiry, No. 108

France. 1918. *Comité d'Etudes, Travaux du Comité d'Etudes*, 2 v. (Paris).

———. 1922-1926. *Conférence de la Paix 1919-1920 Recueil des Actes de la Conférence* (Paris) (in Library of Congress or Hoover Institute).

———. 1918. *Débats Parlementaires. Annales de la Chambre des Députés*. 11me Legislature. Session ordinaire de 1918

———. 1919. *Débats Parlementaires. Annales de la Chambre des Députés*. Session ordinaire de 1919

———. 1921. *Débats Parlementaires. Annales de la Chambre des Députés*. Session ordinaire de 1921

———. 1929-1939. Lapradelle, A. G. de, ed. *La documentation internationale. La Paix de Versailles* (13 v., Paris).

———. 1920. *Sénat. Annales du Sénat*. Session ordinaire de 1919. Débats Parlementaires; Documents Parlementaires (Paris).

Germany.1918. *Allgemeiner Kongress Arbeiter-und Soldatenräte Deutschland's am 16. bis 21. Dez. 1918; Stenographische Berichte* (Berlin).

———. 1919. Heilfron, E., ed. *Die deutsche Nationalversammlung im Jahre 1919 in ihrer Arbeit für den Aufbau des neuen deutschen Volksstaates* (5 v., Berlin).

———. 1949-1957. *Documents on German Foreign Policy 1918-1945*, ed. R. J. Sontag and others (Washington).

———. 1959. *Ursachen und Folgen. Vom deutschen Zusammenbruch 1918 und 1945 bis zur staatlichen Neuordnung Deutschland's in der Gegenwart*, Micnaelis, H. and Schrapler E., eds., v. **3**: *Der Weg in die Weimarer Republik* (Berlin).

———. 1919-1920. *Verhandlungen in der verfassunggebenden deutschen Nationalversammlung*. Stenographische Berichte, Sitzungen 6. Febr. 1919-21. Mai, 1920 (Berlin).

———. 1919. *Schulthess' Europäischer Geschichtskalender*, Neue Folge vols. 33 and 34, 1919 (Munich).

———. Von Wippermann und Purlitz, eds., *Deutscher Geschichtskalender*

Great Britain. 1946-1957. *Documents of British Foreign Policy 1919-1939*, eds. Woodward E. W. and Butler, R. (London).

———. 1919. *Parliamentary Debates. Official Report. House of Commons*. Fifth Ser. Session 1918-1919, 110 (London).

Italy.*Atti del Parlamento Italiano, Camera dei Deputati*. Legislature xxiv, Discussioni, v. 16-20.

———. 1948. *Ciano's Diplomatic Papers*, ed. Malcolm Muggeridge (London).

———. 1959. *I Documenti Diplomatici Italiani 1921-1935* (Rome).

League of Nations. 1932. *Austrian Protocol* (Geneva, July 15).

———. 1926. *The Economic Situation of Austria*. Report presented to the Council of the League of Nations. 1926.

Switzerland. 1919. *Les Résolutions de la Conference Internationale Ouvrière et Socialiste de Berne, Feb. 3-10, 1919*.

———. 1919. International Labor and Socialist Conference, held in Berne. Press Committee, *Official Bulietin*. V. **1**, Nos. 1-8, Feb. 3-21, 1919.

United States. 1919. *Senate. Treaty of Peace with Germany*. Hearings before the Committee on Foreign Relations, 66th Congress. 1st session, Senate Doc., no. 106 (Washington).

———. 1918. *Papers Relating to Foreign Relations of the United States, 1917*.

———. 1933. *Papers Relating to the Foreign Relations of the United States, 1918, Supplement I, The World War* (2 v. Washington, D.C.).
———. 1942-1947. *Foreign Relations of the United States. The Paris Peace Conference, 1919* (13 v. Washington, D.C.).
———. 1939. *Lansing Papers 1914-1920* (2 v. Washington, D.C.).
———. 1927. *Public Papers of W. Wilson*, War and Peace, Public Papers (1917-   ), eds. R. Stannard Baker and W. E. Dodd (2 v., New York).

C. NEWSPAPERS, PERIODICALS, AND SPECIAL COLLECTIONS
(primarily 1918 and 1919)

(Some magazine articles of these and other years are listed separately under "Articles")

Austria:

Der Anschluss, Jahrgg. 1-7 (1927-Aug. 1933), *Arbeiter-Zeitung, Der Kampf, Neue Freie Presse, Neues Wiener Tagblatt, Der österreichische Volkswirt, Reichspost, Die Rote Fahne, Die Soziale Revolution, Staatsgesetzblatt, Wiener Journal*

Czechoslovakia:

Bohemia, Česke Slovo, Ochrana, Prager Tagblatt.

France:

L'Action Française, L'Écho, L'Europe Nouvelle, Le Figaro, Le Gaulois, L'Humanité, Journal Officiel. Débats Parlementaires, Le Matin, Le Petit Parisien, Le Populaire, Revue des Deux Mondes, Revue Politique et Parlementaire, Le Temps, New York Herald (Paris ed.)

Germany:

Allgemeine Zeitung, Bayerischer Kurier, Bayerische Staatszeitung, Deutsche Allgemeine Zeitung, Frankfurter Zeitung, Freiheit, Die Grenzboten, Die Neue Zeit, Preussische Jahrbücher, Die Rote Fahne, Sozialistische Monatshefte, Vorwärts, Vossische Zeitung, Die Zeit.

Great Britain:

Daily News, Manchester Guardian, Morning Post, The New Europe, The New Statesman, The Times.

Hungary:

Pester Lloyd

Italy:

Avanti, Corriere della Sera, Giornale d'Italia, Secolo, La Stampa

Soviet Russia:

Izvestiia, Kommunisticheskii Internatsional, Pravda

Switzerland:

Gazette de Lausanne, Journal de Génève, Nationalzeitung, La Tribune de Génève, Züricher Zeitung

U.S.A.:

Congressional Record, Herald Tribune, Nation, New York Times, Outlook, Republic, Yale Review

Special Collections:

Bulletin de la Presse Étrangère. Ministère des Affaires Étrangères et de la Guerre, Paris, 1918-1919.

Bulletin Quotidien de la Presse Étrangère

Bulletin Périodique de la Presse (Allemande, Americaine, Anglaise, Hongroise, Italienne)

Press Review. Issued by the Second Section, General Staff, G.II.Q.A.E.F.

Literary Digest (of the American Press), New York, 1918-1919.

Review of the Foreign Press. Issued by the General Staff of the British War Office, London, 1918-1919, vols. 5 and 6.

II. MEMOIRS, DIARIES, AND SECONDARY WORKS

(For an evaluation of those works dealing in a substantial manner with the main topic of this study, see footnotes)

ADLER, FRIEDRICH, ed. 1954. *Victor Adler. Briefwechsel mit August Bebel und Karl Kautsky* (Vienna).

ALBRECIIT-CARRIÉ, RÉNÉ. 1950. *Italy from Napoleon to Mussolini* (New York).

————. 1938. *Italy at the Paris Peace Conference* (New York).

ALLIZÉ, HENRI. 1933. *Ma Mission à Vienne* (Mars 1919-août 1920). Preface by Gabriel Hanotaux (Paris).

ANGELL, SIR NORMAN, 1951. *After All* (London).

Annuaire de la presse française et étrangère et du monde politique, 1919, (Paris), 1919.

ANDICS, HELLMUT. 1962. *Der Staat den keiner wollte, 1919-1938* (Vienna).

ANDREAS, WILLI. 1927. *Österreich und der Anschluss* (Berlin).

ANSCHLUSS. 1919. *Der Anschluss an Deutschland und die Sozialdemokratie* (Vienna).

ARZ, ARTUR. 1934. *Kampf und Sturz der Kaiserreiche* (Vienna).

AUERBACH, BERTRAND. 1927. *Le rattachement de L'Autriche à l'Allemagne* (Paris).

————. 1925. *L'Autriche et la Hongrie pendant la guerre* (Paris).

BAERNREITHER, J. M. 1939. *Der Verfall des Habsburgerreiches und die Deutschen* (Vienna).

BAHR, H. 1915. *Das österreichische Wunder* (Stuttgart).

————. 1917. *Schwarzgelb* (Berlin).

BAHR, R. 1930. *Österreich, wie es ist* (Berlin).

BAILEY, TH. A. 1944. *Woodrow Wilson and the Lost Peace* (New York).

BAINVILLE, J. 1920. *Conséquences politiques de la paix* (Paris).

BAKER, R. STANNARD. 1922. *Woodrow Wilson and the World Settlement* (New York).

BALFOUR, MICHAEL. n.d. *Four-Power Control in Germany and Austria, 1945-1946.* Survey of International Affairs, 1939-1946, ed. A. Toynbee.

BALL, M. MARGARET. 1937. *Post-War German-Austrian Relations. The Anschluss Movement, 1918-1936* (Stanford Univ.).

BARDOUX, JACQUES. 1921. *De Paris à Spa: La bataille diplomatique pour la paix française* (Paris).

BARNETT, CORRELLI. 1963. *The Sword-Bearers* (New York).

BARTH, EMIL. 1919. *Aus der Werkstatt der deutschen Revolution* (Berlin).

BASCH, A. 1944. *The Danube Basin and the German Economic Sphere* (London).

BASDEVANT, J. 1935. *La condition internationale de l'Autriche* (Paris).

BASTELLI, GUALTINI. 1915. *Trento a Trieste* (Milan).
BAUER, OTTO. 1907. *Die Nationalitätenfrage und die Sozialdemokratie* (Vienna; 2nd ed. 1924).
———. 1923. *Die Österreichische Revolution* (Vienna).
———. 1925. *The Austrian Revolution* (London). (Abbreviated translation of the foregoing work.)
———. 1919. *Acht Monate auswärtige Politik* (Vienna).
BAUER, STEFAN. 1926. "L. M. Hartmann." *Neue Österreichische Biographie* l. Abt., **3**: pp. 197-208.
BAUMONT, MAURICE. 1946. *La faillite de la paix (1918-1939)* (Paris).
BECKER, H. 1946. *Österreich's Freiheitskampf* (Vienna).
BENEŠ, EDUARD. 1928. *My War Memoirs* (London).
———. 1931. *The Austro-German Customs Union Project* (Prague).
———. 1934. *Das Problem Mitteleuropas und die Lösung der österreichischen Frage* (Prague), Tschechoslowakische Quellen und Dokumente, Nr. 9.
BERGER, M., AND P. ALLARD. 1933. *Les dessous du traité de Versailles* (Paris).
BERGSTRÄSSER, DR. L. 1932. *Geschichte der politischen Parteien in Deutschland* (Mannheim).
BERNSTORFF, GRAF J. H. 1936. *Erinnerungen und Briefe* (Zürich).
———. 1936. *The Memoirs of Count Bernstorff* (English translation) (London).
BERRA, LUCIANA. 1937. *Vinti e vincitori nell'Europa Danubiana* (Milan).
BETHMANN-HOLLWEG, TH. V. 1919-1922. *Betrachtungen zum Weltkriege* (2 v., Berlin).
BIBL, VIKTOR. 1922-1924. *Der Zerfall Österreichs* (2 v., Vienna).
———. n.d. *Geschichte Österreichs im zwanzigsten Jahrhundert* (Vienna).
Bibliographie zum deutsch-österreichischen Anschlussgedanken, Westkriegsbücherei (2nd ed., Stuttgart, 1929).
BIRDSALL, PAUL. 1941. *Versailles Twenty Years After* (New York).
BIRK, BERNHARD. 1932. *Dr. Ignaz Seipel* (Regensburg).
BISMARCK, FÜRST OTTO V. 1913. *Gedanken und Erinnerungen* (new ed., 2 v., Stuttgart-Berlin).
BISSOLATI, LEONIDA. 1923. *La politica estera della Italia dal 1897 al 1920* (Milan).
BITTERMAN, M. 1931. *Austria and the Customs Union* (Prague).
BLOCH, CAMILLE. 1919. *Répertoire Méthodique de la Presse Quotidienne Française.* (Paris).
BONNET, GEORGES. 1961. *Le Quai d'Orsay sous trois républiques* (Paris).
BONSAL, STEPHEN. 1944. *Unfinished Business* (New York).
BORKENAU, FRANZ. 1948. *Austria and After* (London).
BOURGEOIS, LÉON. 1919. *Le Traité de Paix de Versailles* (Paris).
BRANDWEINER, DR. H. 1954. *Die Anschlussgefahr* (Berlin).
BRAUNTHAL, JULIUS. 1948. *The Tragedy of Austria* (London).
———. 1961. *Otto Bauer* (Vienna).
———. 1967. *History of the International.* **2**: 1914-1943, translated by J. Clark (New York).
———. 1965. *Victor und Friedrich Adler* (Vienna).
BRIGGS, MITCHELL PIRIE. 1932. *George D. Herron and the European Settlement* (Stanford).
BROCKDORFF-RANTZAU, U. V. 1925. *Dokumente und Gedanken um Versailles* (3 Aufl., Berlin).
BROOK-SHEPHERD, GORDON. 1963. *Anschluss. The Rape of Austria* (London).
BRÜGEL, LUDWIG. 1925. *Geschichte der österreichischen Sozialdemokratie* (5 v., Vienna).
BRYCE, JAMES VISCOUNT. 1918. *Essais and Addresses in War Time* (London).
BUCHNER, EBERHARD. 1921. *Revolutionsdokumente: Die deutsche Revolution in der Darstellung der zeitgenössischen Presse* **1** (Berlin).

BULLOCK, M. 1939. *Austria 1918-1938* (London).

BURIÁN, STEPHAN. 1923. *Drei Jahre aus der Zeit meiner Amtsführung im Kriege* (Berlin).

BUTTINGER, JOSEPH. 1953. *Am Beispiel Österreichs* (Cologne).

CAHÉN, FRITZ MAX. 1963. *Der Weg nach Versailles. Erinnerungen 1912-1919.* (Boppard am Rhein).

CHARLES-ROUX, FR. 1947. *La paix des Empires centraux* (Paris).

CHARMATZ, RICHARD. n.d. "Der Theoretiker und Praktiker des Marxismus: Dr. Otto Bauer," *Lebensbilder aus der Geschichte Österreichs*, pp. 219f.

⸻. 1907. *Deutschösterreichische Politik* (Leipzig).

⸻. 1916. *Minister Freiherr von Bruck* (Leipzig).

⸻. n.d. *Österreichische Geschichte von 1848-1895*, Aus Natur und Geisteswelt, II, Der Kampf der Nationen (3rd ed., Heft 657).

CHÉRADAME, ANDRÉ. 1902. *L'Allemagne, la France et la Question d'Autriche* (Paris).

⸻. 1906. *L'Europe et la question d'Autriche au seuil du XXe siècle* (Paris).

⸻. 1916. *Le plan pangermaniste démasqué* (Paris).

CHIALA, LUIGI. 1893. *La Triplice Alleanza*, Pagine di Storia Contemporanea dal 1858 al 1892, **3** (Turin-Rome).

CHICHERIN, GEORGI V. 1919. *Der Friede von Versailles: Ein Brief an die deutschen Arbeiter* (Hamburg).

⸻. 1920. *Two Years of Foreign Policy, 1917-1919* (New York).

CHRIST, ALFRED, ed. 1919. *Deutschland, wir kommen! Stimmen aus dem geistigen Deutsch Österreich für den Anschluss an Deutschland* (Halle a.d. Saale).

CIANO, GALEAZZO CONTE. 1952. *Ciano's Diary, 1937-1938* (London).

CLASS, HEINRICH. 1932. *Wider den Strom* (Leipzig).

⸻, ed. 1910. *Zwanzig Jahre alldeutscher Arbeit und Kämpfe* (Leipzig).

CLÉMENCEAU, GEORGES. 1930. *Grandeur and Misery of Victory* (London).

CLOUGH, NATHANIEL P. 1933. *Beiträge zur Beurteilung der österreichischen Anschlussfrage in der öffentlichen Meinung der Vereinigten Staaten Nordamerikas* (Heidelberg).

COLE, G. D. R. 1958. *Communism and Social Democracy, 1914-1931* (2 v., London).

CORTI, E. C., AND H. SOKOL. 1955. *Der Alte Kaiser: Franz Joseph I. vom Berlin Kongress bis zu seinem Tode* (Graz).

CRAIG, G. A. 1964. *The Politics of the Prussian Army, 1648-1945* (New York, Galaxy).

CRAMON, A. VON. 1921. *Unser Österreichisch-Ungarischer Bundesgenosse im Weltkrieg* (Berlin).

CRAMON, A. VON, AND P. FLECK. 1932. *Deutschland's Schicksalsbund mit Österreich-Ungarn von Conrad von Hötzendorff zu Kaiser Karl* (Berlin).

CRANKSHAW, EDWARD. 1963. *The Fall of the House of Habsburg* (New York).

CURREY, MURIEL. 1932. *Italian Foreign Policy 1918-1932* (London).

CURTIUS, JULIUS. 1947. *Bemühung um Österreich* (Heidelberg).

⸻. 1948. *Sechs Jahre Minister der deutschen Republik* (Heidelberg).

CZERNIN, F. 1964. *Versailles, 1919: The Forces, Events, and Personalities that Shaped the Treaty* (New York).

CZERNIN, OTTOKAR. 1919. *Im Weltkriege* (Berlin and Vienna). Or: *In the World War* (London).

DAMI, ALDO. 1932. *L'Anschluss et la question danubienne* (Paris).

DARCY, PAUL. 1919. *La République Pangermaniste et l'Autriche* (Paris).

DÉAK, FRANCIS. 1942. *Hungary at the Paris Peace Conference* (New York).

DEUTSCH, JULIUS. 1960. *Ein weiter Weg. Lebenserinnerungen* (Zürich, Leipzig, Vienna).

DEUTSCHLAND. 1900. *Die deutsche Politik der Zukunft* (Odin, Göttingen).

⸻. 1915. *Deutschland und der Weltkrieg* (Berlin). (For the English version of this work, see *Modern Germany in Relation to the Great War*, by various German writers. Translated by W. W. Whitelock, New York, 1916.)

472   THE ANSCHLUSS MOVEMENT

DILLON, E. J. n.d. *The Peace Conference* (London).
DOPSCH, ALFONS. 1919. *Die historische Stellung der Deutschen in Böhmen,* Flugblätter für Deutschösterreich's Recht, No. 6, ed. Dr. A. R. von Wotawa.
DROZ, JACQUES. 1960. *L'Europe Centrale: Evolution Historique de l'Idée de "Mitteleuropa"* (Paris).
DUNAN, MARCEL. 1921. *L'Autriche* (Paris).
──────. 1922. *Österreich* (Vienna) (This is the translation of the foregoing work.)
EBERT, FRIEDRICH. 1920. *Kämpfe und Ziele* (Dresden).
──────. n.d. *Ebert and his Times* (Charlottenberg).
──────. 1926. *Schriften, Aufzeichnungen, Reden* (2 v., Dresden).
EICHSTÄDT, ULRICH. 1955. *Von Dollfuss zu Hitler. Geschichte des Anschlusses Österreich's 1933-1938,* Veröffentlichungen des Instituts für Europäische Geschichte, Mainz (Wiesbaden).
EISENMANN, E. LOUIS. 1923. *Les Problèmes de l'Europe Centrale* (Paris).
EISNER, KURT. 1919. *Die neue Zeit* (Munich).
──────. 1919. *Schuld und Sühne* (Berlin).
ELTBACHER, PAUL. 1919. *Die neuen Parteien und ihre Programme* (Berlin).
EPSTEIN, KLAUS. 1959. *Mathias Erzberger and the Dilemma of German Democracy* (Princeton).
ERDMANN, K. D. 1959. *Die Zeit der Weltkriege,* Bruno Gebhardt, Handbuch der deutschen Geschichte, 4 (Stuttgart).
ERMERS, MAX. 1932. *Victor Adler* (Vienna).
ERZBERGER, MATHIAS. 1920. *Erlebnisse im Weltkriege* (Stuttgart-Berlin).
EULER, HEINRICH. 1957. *Die Aussenpolitik der Weimarer Republik 1918-1923* (Aschaffenburg).
EYCK, ERICH. 1963. *A History of the Weimar Republic* (2 v., Cambridge).
FAINSOD, MERLE. 1935. *International Socialism and the World War* (Cambridge).
FELLNER, FRITZ, ed. 1953-1954. *Schicksalsjahre Österreichs, 1908-1919. Das politische Tagebuch Josef Redlichs* (2 v., Graz).
FELS, COMTE EDMOND DE. 1918. *L'Entente et le problème autrichien* (Paris).
FERBER, WALTER. 1954. *Die Vorgeschichte der NDSAP in Österreich* (Konstanz).
FISCHER, FRITZ. n.d. *Germany's Aims in the First World War* (Norton). (This is the shortened English version of the following original German work.)
──────. 1961. *Griff nach der Weltmacht. Die Kriegszielpolitik des kaiserlichen Deutschland 1914-1918* (Düsseldorf).
FISCHER, LOUIS. 1951. *The Soviets in World Affairs. A History of the Relations Between the Soviet Union and the Rest of the World, 1917-1929,* 1 (Princeton).
FOERSTER, F. W. 1916. *Das österreichische Problem vom ethischen und nationalpädagogischen Standpunkt* (Vienna).
──────. 1920. *Mein Kampf gegen das militaristische und nationalistische Deutschland* (Stuttgart).
──────. 1940. *Europe and the German Question* (New York).
FRANKE, KARL. 1919. *Deutschösterreich's Zukunft. Politische und wirtschaftliche Ausblicke* (Vienna).
FUCHS, ALBERT. 1949. *Geistige Strömungen in Österreich, 1867-1918* (Vienna).
FUNDER, FRIEDRICH. 1952. *Von Gestern ins Heute. Aus dem Kaiserreich in die Republik* (Vienna).
GATZKE, HANS. 1950. *Germany Drives to the West* (Baltimore).
GAWTHORNE-HARDY, G. M. 1940. *The Fourteen Points and the Treaty of Versailles,* Oxford Pamphlet on World Affairs, No. 6 (London).
GEHL, JÜRGEN. 1963. *Austria, Germany, and the Anschluss* (Oxford).
GELFAND, L. E. 1963. *The Inquiry. American Preparations for Peace 1917-1919* (New Haven, London).
GEORG, FRANZ. 1955. *Liberalismus: die deutsch-liberale Bewegung in der habsburgischen Monarchie* (Munich, Cologne).
GIOLITTI, G. 1923. *Memoirs of My Life* (London).

GLAISE-HORSTENAU, E. 1930. *The Collapse of the Austro-Hungarian Empire* (London). (Available also in the original German; *Die Katastrophe: die Zertrümmerung Österreich-Ungarns* (Vienna. 1929).

GOLDINGER, W. 1954. "Der geschichtliche Ablauf der Ereignisse in Österreich von 1918 bis 1945," In: H. Benedikt, ed., *Geschichte der Republik Österreich* (Vienna).

GORBACH, DR. ALFONS. 1962. *Gedanken zur Politik* (Vienna).

GRATZ, GUSTAV, AND RICHARD SCHÜLLER. 1925. *Die äussere Wirtschaftspolitik Österreich-Ungarns. Mittel-Europäische Pläne* (Vienna).

———. 1928. *The Economic Policy of Austria-Hungary in its External Relations* (New Haven). (English translation of the foregoing work.)

GRAUER, H. 1929. *Die geschichtlichen Grundlagen der Anschlussbewegung* (Stuttgart).

GRAY, LOUIS H. 1920. *A Commentary on the History of the Treaty with Austria.* (Mimeographed copy in the Hoover War Library.)

GRAYSON, CARY TRAVERS, JR., 1953. *Austria's internal position, 1938-1953* (Geneva).

GROSSDEUTSCHLAND 1900. *Grossdeutschland* (Odin, Munich, 1900).

GREAT BRITAIN. 1923. *Cambridge History of Foreign Policy* **3:** 1866-1919 (Cambridge).

GRÖNER, WILHELM. 1957. *Lebenserinnerungen* (Göttingen).

GULICK, CHARLES. 1948. *Austria from Habsburg to Hitler* (2 v., Berkeley).

HAASE, ERNST. 1929. *Hugo Haase: Sein Leben und Wirken* (Berlin).

HACKER, WALTER, ed. 1966. *Warnung an Österreich. Neonazismus: Die Vergangenheit bedroht die Zukunft* (Vienna).

HAINISCH, MICHAEL. 1919. *Wirtschaftliche Verhältnisse Deutsch-Österreichs.* Ed. im Auftrage d. Vereins f. Sozialpolitik. Mit Beiträgen (Munich and Leipzig).

HALPERIN, W. WILLIAM. 1946. *Germany tried Democracy. A Political History of the Reich from 1918 to 1933* (New York).

HANAK, HARRY. 1962. *Great Britain and Austria-Hungary during the First World War* (New York).

HANDBUCH. 1918. *Handbuch der Auslandpresse, 1918* (Berlin).

HANNAK, JACQUES. 1966. *Johann Schober. Mittelweg in die Katastrophe* (Vienna).

———. 1965. *Karl Renner und seine Zeit* (Vienna).

HANTSCH, HUGO. 1947. *Geschichte Österreich's* (Graz).

HARTENSTEIN, WOLFGANG. 1962. *Die Anfänge der deutschen Volkspartei, 1918-20* (Düsseldorf).

HARTMANN, LUDO M. 1921. *Grossdeutsch oder Kleindeutsch* (Gotha).

HASKINS, CH. H., AND R. H. LORD. 1920. *Some Problems of the Peace Conference* (Cambridge).

HASSE, ERNST. 1905. *Deutsche Politik* (Munich).

HAUSSMANN, CONRAD. 1930. *Schlaglichter: Reichstagsbriefe und Aufzeichnungen* (Frankfurt A.M.).

HAUTECOEUR, LOUIS. 1919. *L'Italie sous le Ministère Orlando* (Paris).

HAUTMANN, HANS. 1971. *Die verlorene Republik. Am Beispiel der Kommunistischen Partei Deutsch-Österreichs* (Vienna).

HAYES, B. B. 1966. "Bismarck on Austrian Parliamentarianism, 1867-1890," *Austrian History Yearbook,* pp. 55-89.

HEIDEN, KONRAD. 1935. *A History of National Socialism* (New York).

HELBIG, HERBERT. 1958. *Die Träger der Rapallopolitik,* Veröffentlichungen des Max Planck Institutes für Geschichte (Göttingen).

HELMER, OSCAR. 1949. *Österreich's Kampf um die Freiheit* (Vienna).

HERKNER, H., ed. 1916. *Die wirtschaftliche Annäherung zwischen dem deutschen Reiche und seinen Verbûndeten,* Schriften d. Vereins f. Sozialpolitik, CLV (3 v., Berlin).

HERRE, PAUL. 1927. *Die Südtiroler Frage* (Munich).

HERTZ, FRIEDRICH. 1925. *Zahlungsbilanz und Lebensfähigkeit Österreichs,* Schriften d. Vereins f. Sozialpolitik, **167** (2. v., Munich).

———. 1947. *The Economic Problems of the Danubian States* (London).

HEUSS, THEODOR. 1963. *Erinnerungen, 1905-1933* (Tübingen).
———. 1937. *Friedrich Naumann: Der Mann, das Werk, die Zeit* (Stuttgart).
———. 1959. *Friedrich Naumann's Erbe* (Tübingen).
HEVESY, ANDRÉ DE. 1923. *L'Agonie d'un Empire. L'Autriche-Hongrie* (Paris).
HINDELS, JOSEF. 1947. *Von der Ersten Republik bis zum Zweiten Weltkrieg* (Malmö).
HISCOCKS, R. 1957. *Democracy in West Germany* (New York).
HITLER, ADOLF. 1939. *Mein Kampf*, eds. J. Chamberlain and S. B. Fay (New York).
HODZA, M. 1942. *Federation in Central Europe* (London).
HOEPER, GERHARD. 1928. *Österreichs Weg zum Anschluss* (Berlin).
HOLBORN, HAJO. 1969. *A History of Modern Germany, 1840-1945* (New Haven).
HOOPER, G. 1928. *Österreichs Weg zum Anschluss.* Geleitwort vom Reichstagsprasident Löbe (Berlin).
HOOR, ERNST. 1966. *Österreich, 1918-1938* (Vienna and Munich).
HOOVER, HERBERT. 1951. *Memoirs 1* (New York).
———. 1958. *The Ordeal of Woodrow Wilson* (New York).
HÖTZENDORFF, CONRAD VON. 1921-1925. *Aus meiner Dienstzeit 1906-1918* (5 v., Vienna).
HUBATSCH, WALTHER. 1963. *Germany and the Central Powers in World War 1914-1918* (Lawrence, Kansas).
HUGELMANN, KARL G. n.d. *Der Anschluss Österreichs an Deutschland,* Flugblätter f. Deutsch-Österreich's Recht, 18, ed. Dr. von Wotawa.
———. 1930. "Die politischen Parteien und die Anschlussfrage." In Kleinwaechter F. G. and H. von Paller, eds, *Die Anschlussfrage in ihrer kulturellen, politischen und wirtschaftlichen Bedeutung* (Vienna, Leipzig).
HUNT, RICHARD N. 1963. *German Social Democracy 1918-1933* (New Haven).
HUTH, W. 1919. *Die wirtschaftlichen Kräfte Deutschösterreich's und sein Anschluss an das Deutsche Reich* (Berlin).
JÁSZI, OSCAR. 1929. *The Dissolution of the Habsburg Monarchy* (Univ. of Chicago Press, Phoenix Books).
JEDLICKA, LUDWIG. 1966. *Der zwanzigste Juli 1944 in Österreich.* Sammlung: Das einsame Gewissen 2 (2nd. ed., Vienna).
JEDLICKA, LUDWIG, and ANTON STAUDINGER. 1969. *Ende und Anfang. Österreich 1918-1919* (Salzburg).
JOHNSTON, WM. M. 1972. *The Austrian Mind. An intellectual and social history, 1848-1938* (Berkeley).
JOUET, A. 1922. *Le problème de l'Anschluss* (Paris).
JOUVENEL, RENAUD DE. 1947. *Vingt années d'erreurs politiques* (Paris).
KANN, ROBERT A. 1950. *The Multinational Empire. Nationalism and National Reform in the Habsburg Monarchy 1848-1918* (2 v., New York)
KASAMAS, ALFRED. 1948. *Das Programm Österreichs. Die Grundsätze and Ziele der Österreichischen Volkspartei* (Vienna).
KAUTSKY, KARL. 1918. *Habsburg's Glück und Ende* (Berlin).
———. 1915. *Die Vereinigten Staaten von Mitteleuropa* (Stuttgart).
KELSEN, HANS. 1923. *Österreichisches Staatsrecht: ein Grundriss entwicklungsgeschichtlich dargestellt* (Tübingen).
———. 1919. *Verfassungsgesetze der Republik Österreich* (2 v., Vienna, Leipzig).
KEREKES, LAJOS. 1966. *Abenddämmerung einer Demokratie.*
KESSLER, HARRY GRAF. 1961. *Tagebücher, 1918-1937* (Frankfurt a.M.).
KLEIN, FRANZ. 1915. *Die Kulturgemeinschaft der Völker nach dem Kriege* "Zwischen Krieg und Frieden," 27 (Leipzig).
———. 1916. *Der wirtschaftliche Nebenkrieg* (Tübingen).
———. 1920. *Die Revision des Friedensvertrages von St. Germain* (Vienna).
KLEINWAECHTER, F. F. G. 1926. *Der österreichische Mensch und der Anschluss* (Vienna).

————. 1929. *Selbstbestimmungsrecht für Österreich* (Stuttgart).

————. 1920. *Der Untergang der österreichischen Monarchie* (Leipzig).

————. 1964. *Von Schönnbrunn bis St. Germain. Die Entstehung der Republik Österreich* (Graz).

KLEINWAECHTER, F. F. G. and H. VON PALLER. 1930. *Die Anschlussfrage in ihrer kulturellen, politischen und wirtschaftlichen Bedeutung* (Vienna).

KLEMPERER, KLEMENS VON. 1972. *Ignaz Seipel. Christian Statesman in a Time of Crisis* (Princeton).

KLOTZ, LOUIS-LUCIEN. 1926. *De la Guerre à la Paix* (Paris).

KOCH, E. 1930. *Deutschland's Aussenpolitik in der Nachkriegszeit 1919-1929* (Berlin).

KOMMUNISTEN. 1955. *Die Kommunisten im Kampf für die Unabhängigkeit Österreich's* (Vienna).

KOPLENIG, J. 1939. *Die nationale Frage und der österreichische Kampf um die Unabhängigkeit* (Paris), Vorwort Koplenig.

KRAMOLD, H. n.d. *Der deutsch-österreichische Wirtschaftsbund als sozial-demokratische Aufgabe* (Berlin).

KRAUSS-WIEN, ALFRED. 1923. *Die Bedeutung Österreichs für die Zukunft des deutschen Volkes* (Hannover).

KROFTA, KAMIL. 1934. *A Short History of Czechoslovakia* (New York).

KRUCK, A. W. 1954. *Geschichte des Alldeutschen Verbandes, 1890-1939* (Wiesbaden).

KUNSCHAK, LEOPOLD. 1935. *Österreich 1918-1934* (Vienna).

LAGARDE, PAUL DE. 1899. *Deutsche Schriften* (Göttingen).

LANKHARD, PETER. 1935. *Brockdorff-Rantzau contre Versailles*.

LANSING, ROBERT. 1921. *The Big Four and Others at the Peace Conference* (Boston and New York).

————. 1921. *The Peace Negotiations* (Boston).

————. 1935. *War Memoirs* (Indianapolis).

LAUN, R. 1921. *Deutsch-Österreich im Friedensvertrag von Versailles* (Berlin; Serie: Kommentare z. Friedensvertrage, Schuecking W. ed.).

LAVISSE, ERNEST, ed. 1919. *Travaux du Comité d'Études* (2 v., Paris).

LEDERER, I. J. 1963. *Yugoslavia at the Paris Peace Conference* (New Haven).

LÉGER, LOUIS. 1915. *La liquidation de l'Autriche-Hongrie* (Paris).

LEICHTER, OTTO. 1938. *Ein Staat stirbt. Österreich 1934-38* (Paris).

————. 1963. *Österreich's freie Gewerkschaften im Untergrund* (Vienna).

————. 1970. *Otto Bauer. Tragödie oder Triumph* (Vienna).

LESER, NORBERT. 1968. *Zwischen Reformismus und Bolschewismus* (Vienna).

LITVINOV, M. 1939. *Against Aggression* (London).

LLOYD GEORGE, D. 1936. *War Memoirs* (London).

————. 1938. *The Truth about the Peace Treaties* (2 v., London).

LODGMANN VON AUEN, R. 1955. *Reden und Aufsätze* (Munich).

LÖBE, PAUL. 1954. *Der Weg war lang: Lebenserinnerungen* (2nd ed., Berlin).

LÖBE, PAUL and H. NEUBACHER. 1926. *Die österreichisch-deutsche Anschlussbewegung* (Leipzig).

LOISEAU, CHARLES. 1901. *L'Équilibre adriatique (L'Italie et la Question d'Orient)* (Paris).

LORENZ, R. 1940. *Der Staat wider Willen. Österreich 1918-1938* (Berlin).

————. 1959. *Kaiser Karl und der Untergang der Donaumonarchie* (Graz).

LOW, ALFRED D. 1963. "The Soviet Hungarian Republic and the Paris Peace Conference." *Trans. Amer. Philos. Soc.* (Philadelphia) **53,** 10.

————. 1956. "Austria Between Two Soviet Republics. In the Mirror of the Russian Press" (unpublished thesis, Columbia University).

LUCAS, G. A., and F. OBEREGGER. 1926. *Das Friedensangebot von St. Germain* (Graz).

LUCKAU, A. 1941. *The German Delegation at the Paris Peace Conference* (New York).

LUDENDORFF, E. 1922. *Urkunden der Obersten Heeresleitung über ihre Tätigkeit 1916-1918* (Berlin).
LUSCHIN, VON EBENGREUTH. 1896. *Die österreichische Reichsgeschichte.*
LUTZ, H. 1931. *Eyre Crowe, der böse Geist des Foreign Office* (Stuttgart).
LUX, P. T. n.d. *La leçon de l'Autriche 1919-1937* (Paris).
MACARTNEY, C. A. 1934. *Hungary and her Successors* (London).
————. 1926. *The Social Revolution in Austria* (London).
MACARTNEY, M. H. H., and P. CREMONA.ʳ 1938. *Italy's Foreign and Colonial Policy 1914-1937* (New York).
MCCALLUM, R. B. 1944. *Public Opinion and the Lost Peace* (Oxford).
MACDONALD, MARY. 1946. *The Republic of Austria 1918-1934* (Oxford).
MAMATEY, V. S. 1957. *The United States and East Central Europe, 1914-1918* (Princeton).
MANN, GOLO. 1958. *Deutsche Geschichte des neunzehnten und zwangzigsten Jahrhunderts* (Frankfurt).
MANTOUX, P. 1955. *Les délibérations du Conseil des Quatre* (Paris).
MARSTON, F. S. 1944. *The Peace Conference of 1919* (Oxford).
MASARYK, TH. G. 1927. *The Making of a State: Memoirs and Observations 1914-1918* (London).
MATHIAS, ERICH. 1954. *Die deutsche Sozialdemokratie und der Osten, 1914-1945* (Tübingen).
MATHIAS, ERICH, and RUDOLF MORSEY, eds. 1962. *Die Regierung des Prinzen Max von Baden* (Düsseldorf).
MAY, A. J. 1960. *The Habsburg Monarchy 1867-1914* (Cambridge).
————. 1966. *The Passing of the Habsburg Monarchy* (2 v., Philadelphia).
————. 1957. *"Woodrow Wilson and Austria-Hungary to the end of 1917,"* In: H. Hantsch and A. Novotny, ed., *Festschrift für Heinrich Benedikt* (Vienna).
MAYER, ARNO F. 1967. *Politics and Diplomacy of Peacemaking* (New York).
MAX, PRINZ OF BADEN. 1928. *Erinnerungen und Dokumente* (Berlin).
MEISSNER, OTTO. 1950. *Staatssekretär unter Ebert, Hindenburg, Hitler. Der Schicksalsweg von 1918-1945, wie ich ihn erlebte* (Hamburg).
MENDELSSOHN-BARTHOLDY, A. 1937. *War and German Society.*
MERKL, A. 1919. *Die Verfassung der Republik Österreich* (Vienna).
MERMEIX (pseud. of Terrail, Gabriel). 1922. *Le combat des trois* (Paris).
MEYER, H. C. 1955. *Mitteleuropa in German Thought and Action, 1815-1945* (The Hague).
MIKOLETZKY, H. L. 1964. *Österreichische Zeitgeschichte. Vom Ende der Monarchie bis zum Abschluss des Staatsvertrages 1955* (2nd ed., Vienna).
MIKSCHE, F. O. n.d. *Donauföderation.* Forschungsinstitut für Fragen des Donauraumes (Salzburg).
MILLER, DAVID HUNTER. 1926. *My Diary at the Conference of Paris,* with Documents (20 v., New York).
MISES, LUDWIG. 1919. "Der Eintritt Deutschösterreich's in das Deutsche Reich und die Währungsfrage." In: M. Hainisch, ed. *Wirtschaftliche Verhältnisse Deutschösterreich's.* (Munich).
MITCHELL, A. 1965. *Revolution in Bavaria 1918-1919* (Princeton).
MITTERÄCKER, HERMANN. n.d. *Kampf und Opfer für Österreich. Ein Beitrag zur Geschichte des österreichischen Widerstandes 1938-1945* (Vienna).
MOLDEN, E. 1953. *Das Wort hat Österreich. Beiträge zur Geschichte der Zweiten Republik* (Vienna).
MOLDEN, OTTO. 1958. *Der Ruf des Gewissens. Der österreichische Freiheitskampf 1938-1945* (Munich).
MOLISCH, PAUL. 1932. *Die sudetendeutsche Freiheitsbewegung in den Jahren 1918-1919* (Vienna).

————. 1926. *Geschichte der deutschnationalen Bewegung in Österreich von ihren Anfängen bis zum Zerfall der Monarchie* (Jena).

————. 1919. *Vom Kampf der Tschechen um ihren Staat* (Vienna).

MOMMSEN, HANS. 1963. *Die Sozialdemokratie und die Nationalitätenfrage im habsburgischen Vielvölkerstaat* **11** (1867-1907), Veröffentlichungen der Arbeitsgemeinschaft für Geschichte der Arbeiterbewegung in Österreich (Vienna).

MOMMSEN, WILHELM, ed. 1952. *Deutsche Parteiprogramme* (Munich).

MOMMSEN, WOLFGANG I. 1959. *Max Weber und die deutsche Politik 1890-1920* (Tübingen).

MORSEY, RUDOLF. 1966. *Die deutsche Zentrumspartei, 1917-1923* (Düsseldorf, Bonn).

MUIR, JOHN. 1956. *Austria*, **2**, Survey of International Affairs 1939-1946, ed. A. Toynbee (London).

MÜLLER, HERMANN. 1928. *Die November Revolution: Erinnerungen* (Berlin).

MÜNCH, H. 1949. *Böhmische Tragödie* (Berlin-Hamburg).

MUSACCHIA, GIUSEPPE. 1933. *La questione austriaca e la politica italiana* (Rome).

NAUMANN, FRIEDRICH. 1900. *Deutschland und Österreich* (Berlin).

————. 1915. *Mitteleuropa* (Berlin).

NAUMANN, VICTOR. 1928. *Dokumente und Argumente* (Berlin).

NELSON, HAROLD I. 1963. *Land and Power. British and Allied Policy on Germany's Frontiers* (London-Toronto).

NENNING, GÜNTHER. 1963. *Anschluss an die Zukunft* (Vienna).

NICOLSON, H. 1965. *Peacemaking in 1919* (Univ. Libr. ed., New York).

NITTI, F. O. 1922. *The Wreck of Europe* (Indianapolis).

NOBLE, G. BERNARD. 1935. *Policies and Opinions at Paris* (New York).

NOSKE, GUSTAV. 1920. *Von Kiel bis Kapp. Zur Geschichte der deutschen Revolution* (Berlin).

NOWAK, K. F. 1929. *Der Weg zur Katastrophe und der Sturz der Mittelmächte* (New York).

OBWURZER. 1924. *Deutschösterreich und die deutschen Schicksalsfragen* (Vienna).

ONCKEN, H. 1917. *Das alte und das neue Mitteleuropa*, Perthes Schriften zum Weltkriege, 15. Heft (Gotha).

OPOČENSKY, JAN. 1928. *The Collapse of the Austro-Hungarian Monarchy* (also available in a German version, Prague).

————. n.d. *The Rise of the Czechoslovak State* (Prague).

ORLANDO, V. E. 1919. *Discorsi per la Guerra* (Citta di Castello); (also translated into English and French).

ÖSTERREICH. 1916. *Österreich nach dem Kriege* (Jena).

————. 1965. *Österreich. Zehn Jahre neutraler Staat* (Vienna).

PALACKY, FRANTISEK. 1866. *Die österreichische Staatsidee* (Prague).

PALLER, H. VON. 1928. *Der grossdeutsche Gedanke* (Leipzig).

PALMER, FREDERICK. 1934. *Bliss, Peacemaker: The Life and Letters of General Tasker Howard Bliss* (New York).

PAPEN, FRANZ VON. 1952. *Memoirs* (London).

PASVOLSKY, LEO. 1928. *Economic Nationalism of the Danubian States* (New York).

PAYER, FRIEDRICH. 1923. *Von Bethmann-Hollweg bis Ebert: Erinnerungen und Bilder* (Frankfurt a.M.).

PERMAN, D. 1962. *The Shaping of the Czechoslovak State* (Leiden).

PFAUNDLER, RICHARD. 1919. *Die Ansprüche Italiens auf Deutsch-Südtirol* (Vienna, Flugblätter, ed. Dr. A. von Wotawa).

PICHL, EDUARD (pseud. Herwegh). 1909. *Georg Schönerer und die Entwicklung des Alldeutschtums in der Ostmark* (5 v., Vienna).

PIERI, P. 1960. *L'Italia nella prima guerra mondiale*, N. Valeri, ed. Storia d'Italia (4, Turin).

PINSON, K. 1954. *Modern Germany* (New York).
PITTERMANN, BRUNO. 1966. *Das Zeitalter der Zusammenarbeit* (Vienna).
PLASCHKA, R. G., and K. H. MACH, eds. 1970. *Die Auflösung des Habsburgerreiches* (**3**, Schriftenreihe d. österr. Ost-u. Südeuropa-Institutes, Munich).
POINCARÉ, RAYMOND. 1932-1933. *Au service de la France* (**10**, Victoire et armistice, Paris).
POLLOCK, G. 1917. *The House of Hohenzollern and the Habsburg Monarchy* (New York).
POPOVITCH, M. 1889. *Trieste a Trento innanzi alla diplomazia* (Rome).
PRILL, K. 1890. *Die Kämpfe der Deutschen in Österreich* (Berlin).
PROTHERO, SIR GEORGE WALTER, ed. 1920. *Peace Handbooks* (25 v., London).
PUAUX, BAGRIEL. 1966. *Mort et transfiguration de l'Autriche 1933-1955* (Paris).
PURLITZ, FRIEDRICH, ed. n.d. *Deutscher Geschichtskalender: Die deutsche Reichsverfassung vom 11. August 1919* (Leipzig).
RABENAU, FRIEDRICH v. 1940. *Seeckt. Aus seinem Leben, 1916-1936* (Leipzig).
REDLICH, J. 1929. *Francis Joseph of Austria* (New York).
———. 1929. *Austrian War Government* (New Haven).
REICHHOLD, LUDWIG, ed. 1965. *Zwanzig Jahre Zweite Republik* (Vienna).
REIMANN, VIKTOR. 1968. *Zu gross für Österreich. Seipel und Bauer im Kampf um die Erste Republik* (Vienna).
REINOLD, K. 1910. *Die österreichische Sozialdemokratie und der Nationalismus* (Vienna).
REISMANN-GRONE, TH. 1919. *Der Erdenkrieg und die Alldeutschen* (Vienna-Leipzig).
RENAUDEL, PIERRE. 1919. *L'Internationale à Berne: Faits et documents* (Paris).
RENNER, KARL. 1946. *An der Wende zweier Zeiten. Lebenserinnerungen* (Vienna).
———. 1945. *Denkschrift über die Geschichte der Unabhängigkeitserklärung Österreichs und die Einsetzung der provisorischen Regierung der Republik* (Vienna).
———. (pseud. Rudolf Springer). 1906. *Grundlagen und Entwicklungsziele der österreichisch-ungarischen Monarchie* (Vienna).
———. 1902. *Der Kampf der österreichischen Nationen um den Staat* (Vienna).
———. 1952. *Nachgelassene Werke*, 1, Mensch und Gesellschaft, Nachwort Jacques Hannak (Vienna).
———. 1916. *Österreich's Erneuerung* (Vienna).
RENOUVIN, PIERRE. 1957. *Les crises du 20ième siècle*, **7**, Histoire des Relations Internationales (Paris).
RIDDELL, G. A. 1934. *Lord Riddell's Intimate Diary of the Peace Conference and After, 1918-1923* (New York).
RIEDL, R. 1919. *Bemerkungen zu den deutsch-österreichischen Friedensbedingungen* (Vienna).
RIEMECK, RENATE. 1965. *Mitteleuropa, Bilanz eines Jahrhunderts* (Freiburg i.B.).
RINTELEN, ANTON. 1941. *Erinnerungen an Österreichs Weg* (Munich).
RIOTOR, LÉON. 1927. *La Nouvelle Autriche* (Paris).
RITTER, GERHARD. 1955. *Carl Goerdeler und die deutsche Widerstandsbewegung* (Stuttgart).
———. 1964-1968. *Staatskunst und Kriegshandwerk* **3** and **4** (Munich).
RITTER-WINTERSTETTIN, A. 1919. *Grossdeutschland und die Weltpolitik* (Graz).
RITSCHEL, K. H. 1966. *Diplomatie um Südtirol* (Stuttgart).
ROHAN, KARL ANTON PRINZ. 1930. "Die Grossmächte und die Anschlussfrage," In Kleinwaechter-Paller, eds., *Die Anschlussfrage . . .*, pp. 159-172.
ROSENBERG, ARTHUR. 1962. *Die Entstehung und Geschichte der Weimarer Republik* (Frankfurt A.M.).
ROSENFELD, H. 1919. *Wilson und Österreich* (Vienna).
ROSS, DIETER. 1966. *Hitler und Dollfuss* (Hamburg).
SAILER, KARL HANS, ed. 1959. *Geheimer Briefwechsel Mussolini-Dollfuss*. Mit einem Vorwort von Vizekanzler Dr. A. Schärf (Vienna).
SALANDRA, ANTONIO. 1932. *Italy and the Great War* (London).
———. 1928. *La neutralità italiana* (Milan).

SALOMON, FELIX. 1926. *Die deutschen Parteiprogramme* (3v., Berlin).
SALVEMINI, GAETANO. 1918. *Delenda Austria* (Paris) (transl. from Italian into French).
SAMMINIATELLI, DONATO. 1899. *In giro sui confini d'Italia* (Rome).
SCHAAFHAUSER, FR. W. 1940. *Der grossdeutsche Gedanke* (Cologne).
SCHACHT, HJALMAR. 1955. *My First Seventy-Six Years,* transl. by Diana Pyke (London).
SCHÄFER, DIETRICH. 1920. *Der Krieg 1914-1916, 1916-1918* (Leipzig).
SCHÄRF, ADOLF. 1955. *Österreich's Erneuerung* (Vienna).
SCHEIDEMANN, PHILIPP. 1921. *Der Zusammenbruch* (Berlin).
———. 1929. *The Making of New Germany; the Memoirs of Philipp Scheidemann* (2 v., New York).
———. 1928. *Memoiren eines Sozialdemokraten* (2 v., Dresden) (German original of the foregoing work).
SCHENK, JOSEPH. n.d. *Unser Friede,* **3,** *Der wirtschaftliche Vernichtungsfriede von St. Germain,* 37, Flugblätter, A. von Wotawa, ed.
SCHIFF, VICTOR. 1930. *The Germans at Versailles* (London).
SCHIFFER, EUGEN. 1951. *Ein Leben für den Liberalismus* (Berlin).
SCHLESINGER, R. 1945. *Federalism in Central and Eastern Europe* (London).
SCHORSKE, C. E. 1955. *German Social Democracy 1905-1917* (Cambridge).
SCHÜSSLER, W. 1925. *Österreich und das deutsche Schicksal* (Leipzig).
SCHUSSCHNIGG, KURT VON. 1946. *Austrian Requiem* (New York).
———. 1937. *Dreimal Österreich* (Vienna).
———. 1969. *Im Kampf gegen Hitler. Zur Überwindung der Anschlussidee* (Vienna).
SCHWEND, KARL. 1954. *Bayern Zwischen Monarchie und Diktatur. Beiträge zur bayerischen Frage in der Zeit von 1918 bis 1933* (Munich).
SCHWONER, A. 1919. *Sollen wir uns Deutschland anschliessen?* (Vienna).
SEGRE, GENERAL ROBERTO. 1928. *La Missione Militare Italiana per l'Armistizio* (Dicembre 1918-Gennaio 1920) (Bologna).
SEIPEL, IGNAZ. 1916. *Nation und Staat* (Vienna).
———. 1930. *Der Kampf um die österreichische Verfassung* (Vienna).
SETON-WATSON, CHRISTOPHER. 1967. *Italy from Liberalism to Fascism, 1870-1925* (London).
SETON-WATSON, R. W. 1943. *Masaryk in England* (New York).
——— (Scotus, Viator, pseud.). 1906. *The Future of Austria-Hungary and the Attitude of the Great Powers* (London).
SEYMOUR, CHARLES. 1934. *American Diplomacy during the War* (Baltimore).
———. 1928. *Intimate Papers of Colonel House* **4** (Cambridge).
SFORZA, CARLO. 1930. *Makers of Modern Europe* (London).
SHEPHERD, GORDON. 1963. *The Anschluss* (Philadelphia).
———. 1957. *The Austrian Odyssey* (New York).
SHOTWELL, J. T. 1937. *At the Paris Peace Conference* (New York).
SIEGHART, R. 1932. *Die letzten Jahrzehnte einer Grossmacht* (Berlin).
SIEGLER, FREIHERR V. H. 1964. *Austria. Problems and Achievements 1945-1963* (Bonn).
SILBERSTEIN, GERARD. 1970. *The Troubled Alliance. German-Austrian Relations, 1914-1917* (Lexington).
SMITH, ARTHUR D. HOWDEN. 1940. *Mr. House of Texas* (New York-London).
SMITH, DENIS MACK. 1959. *Italy. A Modern History* (Ann Arbor).
SLOSSON, P. W. 1930. "Amerika und die Anschlussfrage," In: Kleinwaechter und Paller, eds. *Die Anschlussfrage,* pp. 191-194.
SOKOLOVA, MARIE. 1953. *Les Congrès de l'Internationale Socialiste entre les deux guerres mondiales* (Paris).
SOLF, W. H. 1916. *Lehren des Weltkrieges für unsere Kolonialpolitik* (Berlin).
SONNINO, S. G. 1925. *Discorsi Parlamentari* **3** (Rome).
SOSNOSKY, THEODOR V. 1912. *Die Politik im Habsburgerreich* (Berlin).

SPAHN, MARTIN. n.d. *Mitteleuropa und das deutsche Volk* (Sonderdruck aus *Volk und Reich*).
SPECTOR, SHERMAN D. 1962. *Rumania at the Paris Peace Conference* (New York).
SPERL, HANS. 1923. "Heinrich Lammasch," *Neue österreichische Biographie* 1 (Vienna).
SPITZMÜLLER-HARMERSBACH, A. 1919. *Der Politische Zusammenbruch und die Anschlussfrage* (Vienna).
SRBIK, H. VON. 1936. *Österreich in der deutschen Geschichte* (Munich).
———. 1949. *Aus Österreich's Vergangenheit* (Salzburg).
STADLER, K. R. 1966. *The Birth of the Austrian Republic 1918-1921* (Leyden).
———. 1968. *Hypothek auf die Zukunft* (Vienna).
STAHL, WALTER, ed. 1963. *The Politics of Post-War Germany* (New York).
STAMPFER, FRIEDRICH. 1936. *Vierzehn Jahre der ersten deutschen Republik* (Karlsbad).
STARHEMBERG, R. 1942. *Between Hitler and Mussolini* (London).
STEED, HENRY WICKHAM. 1924. *Through Thirty Years, 1892-1922* (London). 2
———. 1913. *The Habsburg Monarchy* (London).
STEIN, BORIS E. 1953. *Die Russische Frage auf der Pariser Friedenskonferenz 1919-1920* (Leipzig).
STEINER, HERBERT. 1968. *Die kommunistische Partei Deutschösterreichs von 1918-1938* (Meisenheim am Glan).
STERN-RUBARTH, EDGAR. 1929 *Graf Brockdorff-Rantzau* (Berlin).
———. 1947. *Drei Männer suchen Europa* (London).
STIMSON, H. L., and MCGEORGE BUNDY. 1948. *On active Service in Peace and War* (New York).
STOLPER, GUSTAV. 1921. *Deutsch-Österreich als Sozial-und Wirtschaftsproblem* (Munich).
———. 1921. *Deutsch-Österreich. Neue Beitrage über seine wirtschaftlichen Verhältnisse* (Munich).
———. 1917. *Das mitteleuropaische Wirtschaftsproblem* (Vienna).
———. 1919. *Donaukonföderation oder Grossdeutschland* (Berlin).
STOLPER (KASSOWITZ), TONI. 1960. *Ein Leben in Brennpunkten unserer Zeit: Gustav Stolper* (Tübingen).
STRAUB, OSWALD. 1929. *Austria farà da se! Österreich schafft's allein! Gedanken über das Anschlussproblem* (Vienna).
STRAUSS, EMIL. 1934. *Die Entstehung der tschechoslowakischen Republik* (Prague).
———. 1936. *Tschechoslowakische Aussenpolitik* (Prague).
STREERUWITZ, E. STREER RITTER V. 1937. *Springflut über Österreich* (Vienna).
STRESEMANN, GUSTAV. 1932. *Vermächtnis* (Berlin).
STRÖBEL, HEINRICH. 1922. *Die deutsche Revolution, Ihr Unglück und ihre Rettung* (Berlin).
STRONG, D. F. 1939. *Austria (October 1918-March 1919). Transition from Empire to Republic* (New York).
SZEPS, BERTHA (Frau Szeps-Zuckerkandl). 1939. *My Life and History.* Transl. by J. Sonnenfield (New York).
TABOUIS, GENEVIEVE. 1938. *Jules Cambon* (Paris).
TARDIEU, ANDRÉ. 1921. *La Paix* (Paris). (For the English version, see *The Truth about the Treaty*, Indianapolis, 1921).
TAYLOR, A. J. P. 1956. "The war aims of the Allies in the First World War." In: Taylor, A. J. P. and B. Pares, eds. *Essays presented to Sir Lewis Namier* (London).
———. 1941. *The Habsburg Monarchy 1915-1918* (London).
TEMPERLEY, H. W. V., ed. 1920-1924. *A History of the Peace Conference in Paris* (6 v., London).
TERSANNES, J. 1921. *Le problème autrichien et la menace du rattachement à l'Allemagne* (Paris).
THOMPSON, CHARLES T. 1920. *The Peace Conference Day by Day* (New York).
THOMPSON, J. M. 1966. *Russia, Bolshevism, and the Versailles Peace* (Princeton).

TILLMAN, SETH. 1961. *Anglo-American Relations at the Paris Peace Conference of 1919* (Princeton).

TORRE, AUGUSTO. 1940. *Versailles: Storia della conferenza della pace* (Milan).

TOSCANO, M. 1934. *Il patto di Londra* (2nd ed., Bologna).

———. 1963. *Pagina di storia diplomatica contemporanea* (2 v., Milan).

TOYNBEE, ARNOLD. 1925. *The World after the Peace Conference* (New York).

TRAININ, I. P. 1947. *Natsionalye protivorechiia v Avstro-Vengrii i ee raspod* (National struggles in Austria-Hungary and their development) (Moscow-Leningrad).

TRAMPLER, DR. K. 1935. *Deutsch-Österreich 1918-1919. Ein Kampf um Selbstbestimmung* (Berlin).

TREITSCHKE, H. VON. 1897. *Zehn Jahre deutscher Kämpfe* (Berlin).

TURNER, HENRY ASHBY. 1963. *Stresemann and the Politics of the Weimar Republic* (Princeton).

TYROK, V. M. 1955. *Ocherki istorii Avstrii 1918-1929* (Historic Outline of Austria 1918-1929) (Moscow).

ULLMAN, H. 1919. *Was jeder Deutsche über Deutschböhmen wissen muss?* (Teplitz).

VANSITTART, LORD ROBERT G. 1958. *The Mist Procession* (London).

VERDIER, A. 1924. *La constitution fédérale et la République d'Autriche* (Paris).

VERDROSS, A. 1919. *Deutsch-Österreich in Grossdeutschland* (Stuttgart).

VERMEIL, E. n.d. *L'Allemagne Contemporaine, social, politique, culturelle., 1890-1950*, 1 (English version: *The German scene 1890-Present*, London, 1956).

VEROSTA, STEPHEN, ed. 1947. *Die Internationale Stellung Österreich's. Eine Sammlung von Erklärungen und Vorträgen aus den Jahren 1938 bis 1947* (Vienna).

VIETSCH, EBERHARD VON. 1961. *Wilhelm Solf. Botschafter zwischen den Zeiten* (Tübingen).

VOGELSANG, THILO. n.d. *Die Aussenpolitik der Weimarer Republik 1918-1933*, Schriftenreihe der Niedersächsischen Landeszentrale für Heimatdienst **4.**

VOLZ, HANS. 1938. *Grossdeutschland. Dokumente der deutschen Politik.* Reihe: Das Reich A. Hitler's, **6,** 1-2 (Berlin).

VONDRACEK, F. J. 1937. *The Foreign Policy of Czechoslovakia 1918-1935* (New York).

WARUM. 1926. *Warum fordern wir den Anschluss?* Österreichisch-Deutscher Volksbund (Wien).

WATHERS, MARY A., SISTER. 1954. *The Policy of England and France toward the Anschluss of 1938* (Washington, D.C.).

WEIL, GEORGES. 1904. *Le Pangermanisme en Autriche.* Avec Préface de M. Anatole Leroy-Beaulieu (Paris).

WERKMANN, K. M. VON. 1931. *Deutschland als Verbündeter* (Berlin).

WERNER, LOTHAR. 1935. *Der Alldeutsche Verband 1890-1918*, Histor. Studien, **278** (Berlin).

WERTHEIMER, MILDRED S. 1924. *The Pan-German League* (New York).

WHEELER-BENNETT, J. W. 1939. *The Forgotten Peace: Brest-Litovsk* (London and New York).

———. 1954. *The Nemesis of Power: The German Army in Politics: 1918-1945* (New York).

WHITESIDE, A. G. 1962. *Austrian National Socialism before 1918* (The Hague).

WIERER, RUDOLF. 1960. *Der Föderalismus im Donauraum* (Graz-Cologne).

WIESER, FRIEDRICH. 1919. *Österreich's Ende* (Berlin).

WILSON, WOODROW. 1927. *Public Papers of W. Wilson. War and Peace. Public Papers (1917-),* eds. R. Stannard Baker and W. E. Dodd (2 v., New York).

WINDISCHGRÄTZ, PRINCE L. 1921. *My Memoirs* (Boston).

WINKLER, FRANZ. 1935. *Die Diktatur in Österreich* (Zürich).

WINKLER, WILHELM. 1919. *Die zukünftige Bevölkerungsentwicklung Deutsch-Österreichs und der Anschluss an Deutschland.* Flugblätter f. Deutschösterreich's Recht. **31,** ed. Dr. A. R. von Wotawa (Vienna).

———. 1919. *Die Tschechen in Wien*, **39,** Flugblätter, ed. Dr. Wotawa (Vienna).

WINTER, ERNST KARL. 1966. *Ignaz Seipel als dialektisches Problem* (Vienna).

WOLFF, THEODOR. 1936. *Der Marsch durch zwei Jahrzehnte* (Amsterdam).
WOLKAN, R. 1920. *Der österreichische Staatsgedanken* (Innsbruck).
ZEMAN, Z. A. 1961. *The Breakup of the Habsburg Empire*, 1914-1918 (London).
ZERNATTO, GUIDO. 1938. *Die Wahrheit über Österreich* (New York).
ZIMMERMANN, LUDWIG. 1958. *Deutsche Aussenpolitik in der Ära der Weimarer Republik* (Berlin).
ZÖLLNER, ERICH. 1961. *Geschichte Österreichs: Von den Anfängen bis zur Gegenwart* (2nd ed., Vienna).

Dissertations and other unpublished studies:

HAAS, HANS. 1968. "Österreich-Ungarn als Friedensproblem" (Salzburg). Dissertation.
RÖGLSPERGER, HELGA. N. D. "Die französische Politik und die Anschlussfrage 1918-1919" Hausarbeit 5, Institut für Zeitgeschichte (Vienna).
SCHÄFER, THEO. 1970. "Die Genesis der Anschlussbewegung und die Anschlussdiplomatie 1918-1919" (Vienna). Dissertation.

III. ARTICLES

(Articles in dailies are not listed)

AUSTERLITZ, FRIEDRICH. 1919. "Wohin gehen wir?" *Der Kampf* (Vienna), Jan. **1919:** pp. 1-11.
———. 1919. "Otto Bauer's auswärtige Politik." *Ibid.*, Oct. 18, **1919:** pp. 677-682.
BAUER, OTTO. 1938. "Nach der Annexion." *Der sozialistische Kampf* (Paris) No. 1, June 2, 1938.
———. 1927. "Wandlungen und Probleme der Anschlusspolitik." *Der Kampf*, 20. Jahrgg., July.
———. "Kritisch, aber nicht reaktionaer." Rede am S. D. Parteitag, 3 Okt. 1933, in *Archiv*, Mitteilungen des Vereins für Geschichte der Arbeiterbewegung, 3. Jahrgg, Heft 1963, pp. 45-67.
———. 1938. "Das Sebstbestimmungsrecht der Sudetendeutschen?" *Der sozialist. Kampf.*
BELOW, G. VON. 1925. "Zur Erinnerung an L. M. Hartmann." *Vierteljahrsschrift für Sozial-und Wirtschaftsgeschichte* (Stuttgart) **18:** pp. 312-339.
BROCKDORFF-RANTZAU, U. VON. 1929. "In Memoriam. Graf Brockdorff-Rantzau." *Europäische Gespräche* (Berlin) **7:** pp. 1-47.
CRAIG, GORDON A. 1965. "The World War I Alliance of the Central Powers in Retrospect; The Military Cohesion of the Alliance." *Journal of Modern History*, **37:** pp. 336-344.
DUDAN, A. 1918. "Il problema dell'Austria." *Politica* 1.
EPSTEIN, KLAUS. 1957. "The Development of German-Austrian War Aims in the Spring of 1917." *Journal of Central European Affairs*, **17.**
FRAUENDIENST, W. 1944. "Deutschösterreich und das Reich. Das Berliner Protokoll vom 2.3.1919." *Berliner Monatshefte* **22:** p. 43f.
FOERSTER, F. W. 1920. "The Austrian Problem." *Atlantic Monthly*, Sept.
———. 1931. "Germany, Austria, and the European Crisis." *Foreign Affairs*, July.
GASIOROWSKI, ZYGMONT J. 1957. "Czechoslovakia and the Austrian Question 1918-28." *Südostforschungen* (Munich).
GOULD, S. W. 1950. "Austrian Attitudes toward Anschluss, October 1918-September 1919." *Journal of Modern History*, **12:** pp. 220-231.
GRUBER, KARL. 1947. "Austria Infelix," *Foreign Affairs*, Jan. 1947.

HARTMANN, LUDO M. 1907. "Die Nationalitätenfrage und die Sozialdemokratie," *Neue Gesellschaft* **6** (Berlin).

HEADLAM, MORLEY J. W. 1929. "L'Autriche et la question de l'Anschluss." *L'Esprit International* (Paris) **1929**: p. 203.

HERKNER, HEINRICH. 1919. "Professor Foerster gegen den Anschluss Deutsch-österreichs." *Preussische Jahrbücher,* Jan.-March, pp. 261-263.

HILFERDING, RUDOLF. 1915. "Über Mitteleuropa." *Der Kampf* March.

KAINDL, R. F. 1920. "Bismarck und der Anschluss Österreichs an Deutschland." *Deutsche Revue* (Stuttgart) **45**, v. 4: p. 97f.

KAUTSKY, KARL. 1916. "Mitteleuropa." *Neue Zeit* **34**, v. 1, Nr. 14-18.

————. 1922. "Germany since the War," *Foreign Affairs*, Dec.

KLEIN, FRANZ. 1934. "Les Variations psychologiques de l'Idée de l'Anschluss." *L'Europe Nouvelle* (Paris), Feb.

KOGAN, A. C. H. 1960. "Germany and the Germans of the Habsburg Monarchy on the Eve of the Armistice of 1918: Genesis of the Anschluss Problem," *Journal of Central European Affairs,* pp. 25f.

LICHTENBERGER, HENRI. 1921. "Le problème autrichien." *Revue politique et parlementaire* (Paris) **107**: pp. 22-35.

LOW, ALFRED D. 1960. "The First Austrian Republic and Soviet Hungary." *Journal of Central European Affairs,* July, pp. 174-203.

————. 1970. "Austria Between East and West: Budapest and Berlin, 1918-1919." *The Austrian History Yearbook, 1968-69* (Houston) 1970, 4-5: pp. 44-62.

MAMATEY, V. 1950. "The United States and the Dissolution of Austria-Hungary." *Journal of Central European Affairs.*

NATIONALITÄTENPROGRAM. 1918. "Ein Nationalitätenprogramm der Linken." *Der Kampf,* Apr. 18, 1918, pp. 269-274.

NEUMANN, SIEGMUND. 1938. "The Austrian Republic. An Obituary." *Virginia Quarterly,* summer.

PASVOLSKY, LEO. 1929-1930. "Obstacles to the Union of Austria with Germany." *Current History.*

PERGLER, CHARLES. 1918. "Austria faces the Future," *Yale Review,* Jan.

PINON, RENÉ. 1919. "La réconstruction de l'Europe danubienne." *Revue des Deux Mondes,* June 1, p. 581f.

PIRKER, M. 1919. "Die Zukunft der österreichischen Alpenländer." *Preussische Jahrbücher.*

REDLICH, JOS. 1921. "Austria, a World Problem." *New Republic,* Feb. 9.

————. 1922. "Reconstruction in the Danubian Countries." *Foreign Affairs,* Sept. 19.

————. 1923. "Austria and Central Europe." *Yale Review,* Jan.

RENNER, KARL. 1918. "Erstaunliche Geschichtsklitterung," *Der Kampf,* pp. 294-308.

SCHMITT, B. E. 1960. "The Peace Treaties of 1919-1920." *Proc. Amer. Phil. Soc.* **104**: pp. 101-110.

SETON-WATSON, R. W. 1919. "The Treaty with Austria," *The New Europe,* Sept. 18.

SELIGER, JOSEPH. 1918. "Das selbständige Deutschböhmen," *Der Kampf,* Nov. 1918: pp. 719-723.

SIEGER, DR. JOSEPH. 1919. "Die Auflösung Deutschösterreichs und Mitteleuropa," *Die Grenzboten* (Berlin) **1919**: p. 40f.

————. 1919. "Deutschösterreich nach den Landtagswahlen," *Die Grenzboten,* pp. 264-269.

SNELL, JOHN L. 1954. "Wilson and Germany and the Fourteen Points," *Journal of Modern History,* Dec. 1954.

STODDARD, T. LOTHROP. 1918. "Austria faces the Future," *Review of Reviews,* Jan. **1918.**

————. 1919. "France's Fears of German Austria," *Literary Digest* (New York) March 29, 1919.

————. 1918. "The passing of an Empire," *New Statesman* Dec. 28, 1918.

————. 1918. "What shall be done with Austria and the Balkan Nations?", *Outlook* (New York) Oct. 2, **1918.**

STRAUSS, EMIL. 1919. "Der Kampf um das Selbstbestimmungsrecht Deutschböhmens," *Der Kampf,* Jan. **1919:** pp. 23-31.

SWEET, P. R. 1947. "Seipel's views on the Anschluss in 1928: An unpublished exchange of letters," *The Journal of Modern History,* 19, March-Dec. 1947: pp. 320-323.

VARGA, E. 1916, "Ungarische Sozialisten und Radikale über Mitteleuropa," *Neue Zeit,* p. 661f.

WARD, BARBARA. 1938. "Ignaz Seipel and the Anschluss." *Dublin Review,* July, p. 331f.

INDEX

9570

32/